Development of Learning and Teaching-Learning Process

Psychology of Learning and Development

J. C. Aggarwal

SHIPRA

(First Published 2006)

Rs. 1295; US$ 64.75

ISBN: 978-93-86262-00-4

2017 Impression

Psychology of Learning and Development

Published by:
SHIPRA PUBLICATIONS
H.O.: LG 18-19, Pankaj Central Market,
I.P. Ext., Patparganj, Delhi 110092, India
Ph. +91 11 2223 5152/6152
New Delhi 110002; Ph.9650028065
Email: info@shiprapublication.com
Website: www.shiprapublication.com

Preface to the Revised Edition

The author extends his thanks to the teachers and students for their reasonably positive response to this book.

Following chapters are added in the edition:

1. Mental Hygiene and Delinquency
2. Memory and Forgetting
3. Assessment of Personality
4. Statistics: Meaning and Uses: Tabulation of Data Central Concepts
5. Central Tendency: Mean, Median and Modes
6. Measurement of Variability: Standard and Mean Deviation
7. Correlation: Rank Difference, Normal Curve

The book is now divided into six units containing thirty-two chapters.
The Units are as under:

Unit I	Nature of Psychology and Learners (Psychology and Educational Psychology)
Unit II	Learning and Motivation
Unit III	Intelligence
Unit IV	Personality
Unit V	Exceptional Children
Unit VI	Educational Statistics

It is hoped that the revised edition would be more useful to the readers. The author thanks to all the authors and publishers whose publications he has made use of in preparing this book.

J.C. Aggarwal

Preface

The book is divided into five units containing twenty-five chapters.

Unit I	Psychology and Educational Psychology (Nature of Psychology and Learners)
Unit II	Understanding the Learner: Stages of Human Development
Unit III	Learning and Modification
Unit IV	Intelligence
Unit V	Personality

The most important feature of the book is that it is both examination-oriented and student-oriented. Nevertheless it also aims at developing insight and motivating the readers to make a deeper study of the issues relating to adolescent behaviour.

Every possible effort is made in this publication to give suitable example in the Indian context.

Interspersed with diagrams, illustrations and tables the text is presented in a lucid and simple language.

The book should serve the needs of a wide range of potential readers, especially those interested in the development and education of the adolescents. It should also respond adequately to the in service education programmes of teachers.

The author extends his thanks to all the authors and publishers whose publications he has made use of in preparing this book.

J.C. Aggarwal

Contents

UNIT I: Nature of Psychology and Learners (Psychology and Educational Psychology)

1

Psychology : Meaning, Nature, Methods and Scope

1.1 MEANING OF PSYCHOLOGY

While discussing the meaning of psychology, two vital points may be kept in mind. First, formerly psychology was studied as a sub-branch of philosophy and very recently it acquired the status of an independent discipline. Second, broadly speaking psychology has passed through three stages before acquiring the present meaning.

The evolution of the meaning of psychology may be illustrated as under:-

Phases of the Evolution of the Meaning of Psychology

First Phase : Psychology as the Study of Soul

↓

Second Phase : Psychology as the Study of Mind

↓

Third Phase : Psychology as the Study of Consciousness

↓

Present Phase : Psychology as the Study of Behaviour

Fig. 1.1: Evolution of the Present Meaning of Psychology

Psychology as the Study of Soul. The word psychology is derived from two Greek words: '*Psyche*' meaning soul and '*Logos*' meaning science. Thus psychology is considered as the Science of Soul. Democritus (about 400 B.C.), Plato (427-347 B.C.) and Aristotle (384-322 B.C.)—three great philosophers interpreted psychology as the science of mind. They believed that the soul was an entity and it controlled all mental activities. Soul was not separable from body. Its abode was in the human heart. Since soul could not be defined properly, this concept of psychology was rejected.

Psychology as the Science of Mind. Scholars like Descartes (1596-1650 A.D.), Kant (1724-1804 A.D.) considered psychology as the Science of Mind. However, the concept of mind had different connotations. Accordingly, this meaning of psychology was also rejected.

Psychology as the Science of Consciousness. The psychologists like William Wundt (1832-1920 A.D.) and William James (1892-1910), defined psychology as the Science of Consciousness. They held that the mind constituted only conscious experience. Freud (1856-1939) criticised the emphasis on consciousness and stressed that unconscious aspect consists of 9/10th of one's mind. This definition was rejected on account of the following:

1. It has a very narrow vision.
2. It does not include the subconscious and unconscious aspects.
3. It is subjective and unscientific.
4. It does not help in the detailed study of children, old people and insane people.

Psychology as the Science of Behaviour. J.B. Watson (1878-1958) defined psychology as "The Science of Behaviour". This definition found wide acceptability as is evident from the views of the following psychologists:

According to Crow and Crow, "Psychology is the study of human behaviour and human relationships".

Koffika, Kurnt observes, "Psychology is the scientific study of behaviour of living creatures in their contact with the outside world".

McDougall, William states, "Psychology is the science which aims to give us better understanding and control of behaviour of the organism as a whole".

Woodworth, R.S. (1869-1962) puts it, "Psychology undertakes to make a scientific study of the individual considered as a unit as he really is in his dealings with other individuals and with the world". He further observes, "Any manifestation of life is activity and behaviour is a collective name for all such manifestation". Woodworth concludes the discussion with these remarks, "First psychology lost its soul. Then it lost its mind. Then it lost its consciousness. It still has behaviour of a sort".

Skinner explains behaviour as, "By response or behaviour is meant all forms of processes, adjustments, activities and experience of the organism". James Drever thinks that "behaviour is the total response which man or animal makes. Behaviour is both mental as well as physical".

Behaviour includes 'cognitive' activities like thinking, reasoning and imaging, 'affective' activities like feeling happy, angry and sad and also 'motor' activities like dancing, swimming and walking.

1.2 NATURE OF PSYCHOLOGY

There has been a good deal of controversy as to whether psychology is a science or an art. Arguments have been advanced on both the sides. However, an overwhelming opinion of psychologists is that it is a positive and developing science. The American Psychological Association (AP) calls psychology a science and a profession.

Before drawing any conclusion, we may briefly mention the characteristics of science.

As propounded by Aristotle, science consists of a body of general truths.

Galbraith states, "By science we mean a body of knowledge that seeks to tell the truth the whole truth and nothing but truth".

According to Huxley, "By science, I understand all knowledge that rests upon evidence and reasoning".

Thus scientists are interested in finding out the truths as exemplified in principles which have the following important characteristics.

1. Principles are arrived at as a result of the pursuit of methodical ways and means based on certain principles.

2. In science, the fundamental points are not random bits of information but are systematically related.
3. The principles repeat in the real sense of the word.
4. Principles are uniform.
5. They have a great practical value.
6. Scientific statements and principles are objective and free from personal prejudices.
7. There is a well-equipped laboratory to carry out scientific investigations.

By applying scientific criterion, we shall find whether psychology is a science or not.

1. Like natural and physical sciences (physics, chemistry etc.), psychology is also an empirical field of study.
2. It employs several methods of inquiry such as observation and experimentation.
3. It frames hypotheses and analyses evidence before interpreting the collected data.
4. Psychological experiments are also conducted in laboratories.
5. Like science, psychology emphasises the search for truth.
6. Psychology establishes principles governing behaviour.
7. Psychology has its pure and applied aspects.

From the above-mentioned characteristics, we can say that psychology is a science but at the same time, it must be admitted that it is not an exact science. Its important limitations are as under. On account of these limitations, some scholars are of the view that it is not a science.

1. Psychology deals with human beings and no individuals are alike. Every human being has something unique in body, mind and spirit.
2. Psychology deals with behaviour. The behaviour of human beings is not constant.
3. The subject matter of psychology is very complicated.
4. The principles of psychology do not often repeat in view of the plastic nature of human behaviour.
5. Psychological data are the product of human behaviour, experiences and environment which are constantly changing. The data, therefore, cannot provide dependable evidence for the formulation of appropriate general laws and principles.

Broadly speaking there are two types of sciences—physical and social. Psychology is not a physical science but it is certainly a social science.

Following are the main characteristics of the nature of psychology.

First. Psychology is the scientific study of behaviour.

Second. Psychology is concerned with factors, principles and techniques which relate to behaviour.

Third. Psychology uses different methods for the collection of data.

Fourth. It depends upon experiments also.

Fifth. A psychologist has a hunch that 'this might be true'. He does not say 'It is true'. Thus the nature of psychology is not fixed.

Sixth. Psychology is a developing science.

Psychology is a Positive and Developing Science

Psychology studies facts and describes 'what is'. It does not concern with 'what ought to be' as stressed by normative sciences like ethics, logic and philosophy etc. However, some scholars are of the view that the study of psychology becomes redundant and useless if it is not concerned with 'what ought to be'. After all there are several psychologists engaged in providing guidance and counselling. Psychological experiments are not conducted for the sake of theoretical knowledge alone.

It is true that psychology is a developing science and is not as developed as the natural sciences. We may, therefore, say that psychology is a developing, pure and applied science. It is normative as well as positive.

1.3 PSYCHOLOGY AS AN INDEPENDENT DISCIPLINE

Usually 1879, the year in which William Wundt (1832-1920), a German psychologist established the first psychological laboratory at Leipzing in Germany, is considered the year associated with the attainment of independent status by psychology. Wundt also took the first step in making psychology as a science. Others associated with the growth and development of psychology as a science are:

(1) Hermann Von Helrmholtz (1821-1894), (2) Gustav Fechner (1801-1887), (3) G. Stanley Hall (1846-1929), (4) W.B. Cannon (1871-1945), (5) John B. Watson (1878-1958), (6) I.P. Pavlov (1849-1936), (7) Max Wertleimae (1880-1943), (8) Wolfgang Kohler (1887-1967), (9) Kant Koffurka (1866-1941), (10) Sigmund Freud (1856-1939), (11) Alfred Binnet (1870-1937), (12) Carl Gustan Jung (1875-1961) and (13) Jean Piaget (1896-1980).

1.4 HISTORICAL DEVELOPMENT OF PSYCHOLOGY

Robert L. Isaacson and Max L. Hutt in their publication "*Psychology, the Science of Behaviour*" (1971) describe the evolution of the subject of psychology in these words, "The present day activities of psychologists are derived historically from at least four different streams of influence: philosophy, clinical studies, physiology and mental testing".

Sources of Psychology

(1) *Philosophy*

1. Greak philosophers namely Plato and Aristotle.
2. Hindu, Jain and Buddhist philosophy.
3. Chinese philosophers noteably Confucious.
4. Kant of Germany.
5. William James of the USA

(2) *Clinical Studies*

1. Sigmund Freud
2. Jung
3. Adler

(3) *Physiology*

1. Gustav Fechner.
2. Hermann Von Helrmholtz.
3. Wilhelm Wundt.
4. Pavlov.

(4) *Mental testing*

1. Alfred Binnet

1.5 METHODS OF PSYCHOLOGY

Important methods that psychology use are given below:

1. Case study.
2. Experimentation.
3. Interview.
4. Introspection.
5. Observation.
6. Projective methods.
7. Sociometry.

(These methods are discussed in the next chapter)

1.6 SCOPE OF PSYCHOLOGY

Through psychology we study behavioural activities of the individuals. All individuals make efforts to make the optimum adjustment to their environments. They get lot of stimulation from the environment. Psychology is considered with all the activities relating to behaviour which the individuals make. Thus the scope of psychology becomes very vast.

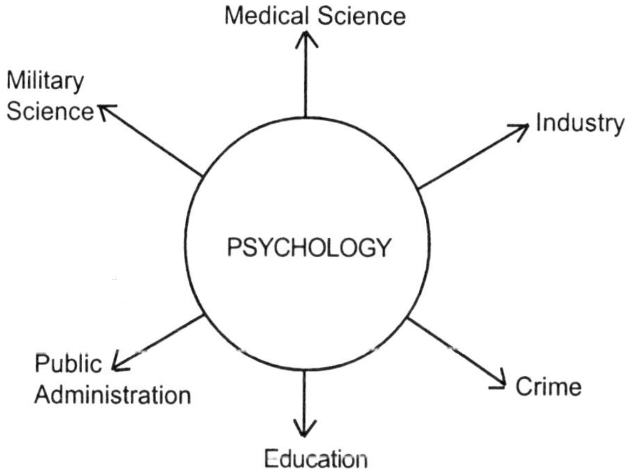

Fig. 1.2: Application of Psychology: Broad Fields

The vastness of its scope may be seen from the number of its branches which are given below; each branch with its theme.

1. Abnormal Psychology—Study of abnormal behaviour of individuals.
2. Adult Psychology—Study of behaviour of the adults.
3. Adolescent Psychology—Study of behaviour of the adolescents (usually in the age group of 12-19)
4. Animal Psychology—Study of behaviour of animals.
5. Applied Psychology—Study of application of general principles of psychology to the problems of behaviour in various fields.
6. Comparative Psychology or Animal Psychology—Study of behaviours of different animals.

7. Child Psychology—Study of behaviour, development and growth of children.
8. Clinical Psychology—Study of behaviour of problem children and their treatment.
9. Criminal Psychology—Study of behaviour of criminals.
10. Development Psychology (Genetic Psychology)—Appeared as a discipline in 1953 dealing with the development of human beings from conception to death.
11. Differential Psychology (Individual Psychology)—Study of variations in the behaviour of human beings.
12. Educational Psychology—Study of behaviour in educational settings.
13. Experimental Psychology—Study of carrying out experiments on behaviour in controlled situations.
14. General Psychology (Pure Psychology)—Study of fundamental principles of behaviour.
15. Human Psychology—Study of behaviour of human beings only.
16. Military Psychology—Study of behaviour in war.
17. Para Psychology—Study of extra sensory perception, telepathy and allied problems.
18. Physiological Psychology—Study of functions of nervous system and physical structure as related to behaviour.
19. Social Psychology (Group Psychology)—Study of behaviour of an individual in the group and study of group behaviour.

2

Methods of Psychology and Educational Psychology

2.1 NEED FOR METHODS OF PSYCHOLOGY

Educators and psychologists employ several methods to study how different aspects of the behaviour and personality of the individual develop from infancy to old age, the characteristics of each stage of development and the measures for achieving the optimum development. They are also interested in finding out the most useful methods of teaching-learning. They want to find out the individual differences of children and are in search of techniques, strategies and maxims, for catering to their specific needs. This search for new methods and in their modification becomes an on-going process which is visible as well as invisible.

As educational psychology is an applied branch of psychology, the educators make use of different methods of psychology in the light of the specific environment in which they work.

2.2 CLASSIFICATION OF THE METHODS OF PSYCHOLOGY

There are several ways of classification of methods of educational psychology.

Classification I—By Wlliam and others

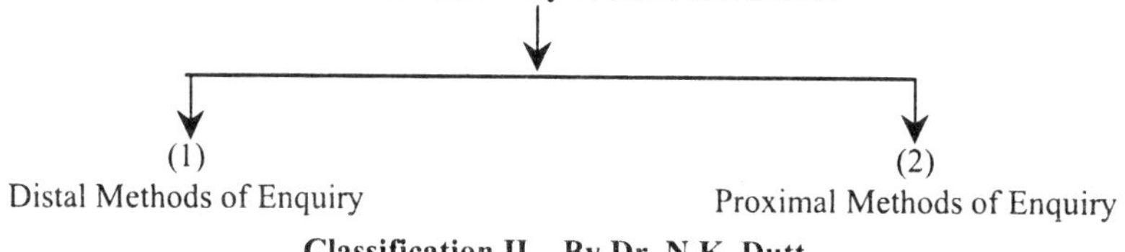

Classification II—By Dr. N.K. Dutt

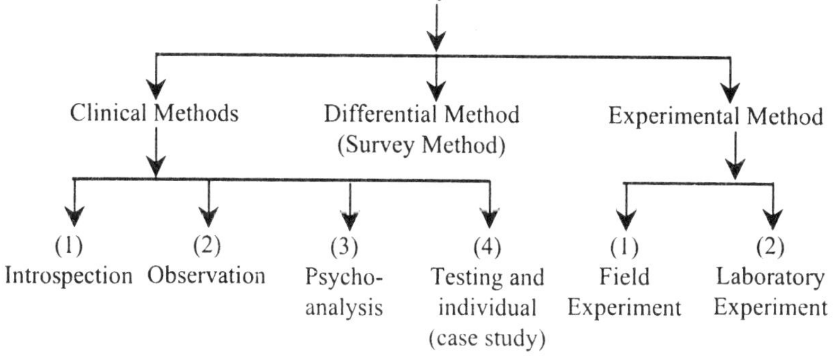

2.3 THE CLINICAL METHOD

In clinical method, a detailed information is collected on the behavioural problems of maladjusted and deviant cases. The maladjustment may be in the area of learning and backwardness in school subjects. In the clinical method, the case history of an individual or group is prepared to detect and diagnose specific problems. Case history may be of an individual or groups. After the analysis of case history remedial measures are suggested. Techniques used are: (1) Physical examination, (2) Tests, (3) Interview.

Two approaches are generally followed in this method. These are (1) The clinical study or case history, (2) Developmental case study or genetic study relating to groups.

2.4 DIFFERENTIAL OR SURVEY METHOD OR STATISTICAL METHOD

The differential or survey method which is sometimes called the statistical method is used to study individual differences among the students. It is based on sampling. This method makes use of techniques like interview, observation, questionnaire and tests, etc.

The differential or survey method differs from the experimental method in the sense that here the researcher cannot intentionally manipulate the variable. Each is studied as an independent variable. It is also not used for the treatment of an individual as is the case in the clinical method.

The major purpose of survey is to find out 'what is the existing situation'?

There are three basic elements in survey—(i) Of what exists, (2) Of what we want, and (3) Of how to get them.

Examples of the Use of Differential Methods in Educational Psychology. (1) Study of the intelligence, (2) Study of attitudes and value regarding behaviour.

Techniques used. (i) Tests, (ii) Questionnaires, (iii) Interviews, (iv) Rating scales, (v) Score cards.

Types of Survey Studies/Descriptive Studies

1. Case study.
2. Casual comparative studies.
3. Community study.
4. Content or document analysis.
5. The follow-up studies.
6. Educational surveys including school surveys.
7. Market surveys.
8. Public opinion surveys.
9. Motivation research surveys.
10. Social surveys.
11. Time and motion study.
12. Trend studies.

Most Important Elements of a Survey

These are:

1. *Of what exists* by studying and analysing important aspects of present educational situation.

2. *Of what we want* by clarifying educational goals and objectives.
3. *Of how to get them* through discovering the possible means of achieving the educational goals.

Characteristics of the Survey Method

1. The survey method gathers data from a relatively large number of cases at a particular time.
2. It is essentially cross-sectional.
3. It is not concerned with the characteristics of individuals but with generalised statistics of the whole population or a representative sample.
4. It involves a clearly defined problem.
5. It involves definite objectives.
6. It requires expert and imaginative planning.
7. It requires careful analysis and interpretation of the data gathered.
8. It requires logical and skilful reporting of the finding.
9. Surveys vary greatly in complexity. Some are concerned only with the frequency of events, while others seek to establish relationship with events.
10. The survey method does not seek to develop an organised body of scientific principles.
11. It provides information useful to the solution of local problems.
12. Surveys are both quantitative and qualitative. They may involve finding out the number of students taking up vocational courses or they may aim at finding out the characteristics essential for taking up vocational courses.
13. Results arising out of surveys may be either verbal or expressed in mathematical symbols.
14. Surveys are more realistic than the experiments as they investigate phenomena in their natural setting.

2.5 PSYCHO-ANALYSIS OR PSYCHO-ANALYTIC METHOD

Dr. Sigmund Freud (1856-1929) is the discoverer and originator of the method of psycho-analysis. He postulated that 9/10th of our mental activities are unconscious and sub-conscious. The psycho-analysis method is designed to study the unconscious and sub-conscious behaviour.

According to Freud, our repressed ambitions, wishes, thoughts and problems are deposited into our unconscious mind. This repression results in restlessness and maladjustment. The psycho-analysis helps us in digging out the root causes and bringing them at the conscious level. The individual gets relief from tension and uneasiness and this helps in his readjustment.

Steps Involved in the Psycho-Analytic Method

1. Establishing rapport with the individual to get adequate information.

2. Using techniques like free association and dreams etc. for getting information. Projective techniques come under this category (Discussed separately).
3. Synthesising the findings.

2.6 CROSS SECTIONAL VS. LONGITUDINAL METHOD

In the cross sectional method, changes in the behaviour pattern of children that take place from one age period to another occur are observed to get an idea of the development of a trait or a characteristic. For instance, the problem of emotional development is observed during infancy, childhood and adolescence. In the longitudinal method, the behaviour of the same children is observed over an expanded time span.

2.7 CASE STUDY METHOD

Meaning of Case Study: A case study is in-depth study of a child. It is usually used to study the various aspects of a learner to bring about desirable changes in him. Usually it is employed in the case of those learners who do not respond to normal teaching-learning process. A case study provides detailed information regarding the family background of the learner, his development in his infancy and childhood, information regarding his schooling etc.

Following are the important definitions of a case study.

In the words of Yang Hsin Pao, "Case study method may be defined as an intensive study of an individual in which the investigator brings to bear all his skills in gathering of enough information about a person to permit one to understand how he or she functions as a unit of society.

Biesanz and Biesanz observe: "The Case Study is a form of qualitative analysis involving the very careful and complete observation of a person".

P.V. Young defines a Case Study as "The Case Study is a method of exploring and analysing the life of a person".

Purposes of Case Study: Following are the purposes of Case Study:

1. Diagnosing the problem of the learner.
2. Providing treatment to the learner.
3. Providing guidance and counselling to the learner.

Characteristics of a Case Study

1. Case Study should be based on adequate and complete data.
2. It should be based on valid data.
3. Its data should be continuous.
4. Its data should be systematic.
5. Its data should present synthesis.
6. The synthesis of data should be as much prognostic as diagnostic.
7. Data should be kept confidential.
8. Analysis should be objective.
9. Follow-up must find an important place.

Various Steps in Case Studies

1. Determination of the status of the phenomenon under investigation through direct observation or measurement.

2. Determination of the most probable antecedents of the case.
3. Formulation of a definite hypothesis or a set of hypotheses through a knowledge of similar cases.
4. Verification of the hypothesis.
5. Remedial steps for removing the causes for maladjustment.
6. Follow-up of the case.

Treatment of the Problem of the Case

Some of the important treatment techniques of the subject (learner) are as follows:

(i) Simple advice, supplying information, giving suggestions and counselling.
(ii) Direct treatment or psychotherapy.
(iii) Play therapy in the case of children. Play therapy also includes doll playing and drawing.
(iv) Psychodramatic techniques and role playing.
(v) Group therapy.
(vi) Occupation therapy by engaging the subject in productive work.
(vii) Attitude therapy by changing the attitude of parents and others.
(viii) Change of environment of the individual.
(ix) Juvenile homes, orphanages, residential schools.

Merits of Case Study Approach

1. It permits an in-depth study of the problem of a learner.
2. It brings to light some vital but unknown facts about learner's growth and development.
3. It is helpful in diagnosing a problem.
4. It is helpful in finding an appropriate solution of the problem.
5. It is helpful in providing treatment of the problem.
6. It is helpful in the overall guidance and counselling of the learner.

Demerits and Limitations of Case Study

1. It involves a lot of time.
2. It needs an enormous data to be collected.
3. The learners and their parents may not be forthcoming to provide necessary information.
4. It needs the cooperation of several groups/individuals.
5. It is expansive.
6. It needs expertise.

Types of Learners to be Taken up for Case Study

According to Rothney and Roens, case studies may be prepared in the following type of learners:

1. Learners who constantly present behavioural problems in class.
2. Learners who do not seem to be able to do the work of the grade.
3. Learners whose behaviour makes them appear to be 'model'.
4. Learners of exceptionally high achievement.

5. Learners who show exceptionally high ability in Arts.
6. Learners who show exceptional skill in practical arts or painting.
7. Learners who are very persistent in striking for success.
8. Learners who are trying very hard against great obstacles.
9. Learners who show exceptionally high ability in music.

Case History Outline

I. Identifying Data

Name of the learner, date of birth, class, sex, parents, occupations etc.

II. Types of Problems

1. Scholastic, 2. Conduct, 3. Health, 4. Emotional, 5. Recreational, 6. Delinquency

III. Nature of Case Study Data

1. Academic history,
2. Family history,
3. Psychological data,
4. Mental,
5. Medical,
6. Temperamental,
7. Physical history,
8. Social history.

IV. Plan of Action

When the required data about the learner has been collected, the case history should be written up. A tentative diagnosis and plan for treatment should be formulated before the treatment starts.

Guidelines for Planning the Case History and Providing Treatment

1. If possible, select a learner from your class who needs your help and more attention.
2. To start with, try to plan the case in a small way. As you proceed, if you feel that you should elaborate the case, plan it on a large scale.
3. While collecting data, the learner should not be put on the defensive. He should not feel that he is guilty or he is one who is very much deviated from other learners. Try to discuss the problems at friendly and normal level. The teacher should be like a friend to whom the learner tells about all his worries and difficulties.
4. While writing the case, use plain and simple language and the points should be direct and matter of fact. This does not mean that you should avoid interpretations and recommendations. That can be added after discussing the factual data as it is.
5. While preparing the case report, use both general and specific illustrations.
6. You should not attempt to apply treatment which is beyond your experience. Normally, a teacher can handle such problems arising out of learning difficulties, lack of interest or minor behaviour problems.

7. After the case has been released from treatment it should be followed up so that the subject (learner) does not have a relapse. This is specially important in cases involving skills, such as, reading, spelling and arithmetic. Some learners who have improved tremendously during the period of treatment will tend to return to the old habits later unless they are carefully supervised.

2.8 EXPERIMENTATION

Meaning of Experimentation

1. According to W.S. Monroe and M.D. Englehart, "Experimentation is the name given to the type of educational research in which the investigator controls the educative factors to which a child or group of children is subjected during the period of enquiry and observes the resulting achievement".

2. In the words of Festinger, "The essence of an experiment may be described as observing the effect on a dependent variable of the manipulation of an independent variable".

3. Ruch describes an experiment as, "It defines the experimental problem, states under which the observations are to be made, describes the instruments and apparatus to be used in making accurate observations and outlines the procedure to be followed in interpreting the results".

4. J.W. Best described it as "Experimental research is the description and analysis of what will be, or what will occur, under carefully controlled conditions". Thus the keywords in an experimental research are:

(a) What will be.

(b) What will occur.

(c) Carefully controlled conditions.

5. Jahoda and others regard social experiment as a method of testing hypothesis.

6. Greenwood suggests that an experiment is the proof of a hypothesis which seeks to take up two factors into a casual relationship through the study of contrasting situations which have been controlled excepting the one.

Types of Experiments

1. Trial and Error Experiment.
2. Controlled Observational Experiment.
3. Natural Experiment.
4. *Expost Facto* Experiment.
5. Laboratory Experiment.

Characteristics of an Experiment

An experiment calls for the satisfaction of three basic interrelated conditions, *i.e.*, Control, Randomization and Replication.

1. *Control*: Control is the basic element in experimentation. In it the influence of extraneous factors that are not included in the hypothesis are prevented from operating and confusing the outcome which is to be appraised.

Following types of controls are exercised in an experiment.

(*a*) Physical control.
(*b*) Selective control.
(*c*) Statistical control.

2. *Randomization*: As it is very difficult to exercise complete control, efforts are made to assign cases in the experimental and control groups randomly.

3. *Replication*: This implies conducting a number of sub-experiments within the framework of an overall experimental design.

Use of Experimentation in Education

Among the main uses of experimentation in education are:

1. Determining and evaluating the adequacy and effectiveness of educational aims and objectives through the measurement of outcomes.
2. Serving as basis for the formulation, execution and modification of educational policies and programmes.
3. Ascertaining the effects of any change in the normal educational programmes and practices.

Major Steps in the Experimental Method in Education

1. Selecting and delimiting the problem.
2. Reviewing the literature on the problem.
3. Defining the problem.
4. Planning the experiment.
5. Conducting the experiment.
6. Measuring the outcomes of the experiment.
7. Analysing and interpreting the outcomes.
8. Drawing up conclusions.
9. Follow-up work.

General Description of an Experimental Approach

Control Factor: Control is the basic element of an experiment. Here efforts are made to minimise the influence of extraneous factors.

Experimental Factor: This is the new arrangement to develop pupil growth in skills and knowledge in new setting.

Comparison: A comparison is made between the result of the two situations.

Various Steps in Following a Simple Experiment

Steps	*Experimental Group*	*Control Group*
Step 1	Pre-Test	Pre-Test
Step 2	Application of experimental factor	Application of control factor
Step 3	Final test	Final test
Step 4	Measuring learner mean gain (Final test scores minus pre-test scores)	Measuring learner mean gain (Final test scores minus pre-test scores.)
Step 5	Calculating the difference between the control pupil mean and experimental learner mean to find out the relative effectiveness of the control and experimental approach.	

Merits of the Experimental Method

1. Experimental method is the most systematic method of getting reliable data.
2. In the experimental method, research is conducted under rigorously controlled conditions. The experimenter can control the application and withdrawal of independent variables.
3. The findings of the experimental method are verifiable by other experimenters under identical conditions.
4. Experimental method provides adequate information about the problem.
5. Experimental method provides objective information about the problem.
6. It tests the traditional beliefs and throws new light on them and opens avenues for future progress.
7. It helps to protect from subjective opinions.
8. It increases our knowledge of cause-effect relations in the behaviour of the learners and provides guidelines for making teaching-learning effective, interesting and inspirational.
9. It provides innovative ideas for further experimentation.

Limitations of the Experimental Method

1. Psychologists like Thorndike and Skinner conducted experiments on animals like cats and dogs and deduced principles, on the basis of these experiments. This raises the issue, how far is it justifiable to generalise those principles and laws on human beings?
2. Human nature is changing. One may not act exactly in the same manner even in identical situations.
3. Experiments are conducted in artificially determined pattern of behaviour. In real life situation is quite different.
4. Each child is unique. He differs from other children in several aspects. This fact hinders objective generalisations.
5. Experimental data does not provide insight into the total behaviour of the learner. For all practical purposes behaviour is an interaction between the learner and the environments. The experimentalists often omit important factors by their tendency to eliminate and isolate experimental variables or to keep them constant.
6. Various types of actions of children do not fit into a laboratory setting.
7. Experimental method is time-consuming.
8. Experimental method is costly.
9. Experimental method needs specialised knowledge and therefore every teacher cannot be expected to conduct an experiment.
10. Experiments in social sciences are not possible in the same sense as they are in physical sciences.
11. Some religious leaders and other thinkers have raised ethical issues regarding administration of some experiments and tests especially which encroach upon the privacy of the subjects (individuals). For instance, few would like to raise infants in extreme deprivation for

conducting experiments. Some religious leaders condemn tests on frogs etc.

12. It is not always possible to construct tools that will make accurate measurements of individual differences.
13. In several experiments, it is not possible to manipulate human beings according to the research designs that are theoretically possible.
14. It is not possible to reach certainty in matters of social sciences including Educational Psychology.

Practical Hints

1. It must be ensured that the nature of training to the two groups constitutes an important factor.
2. During the course of the experiment, changes taking place in the control group should be carefully observed.
3. Measurement should be complete and comprehensive.
4. Results should be interpreted carefully.

2.9 INTERVIEW METHOD

Meaning of an Interview

In a simple language, an interview may be defined as a face to face verbal communication in which one person, *i.e.*, the interviewer (Teacher or the counsellor or the research worker) attempts to elicit information on a variety of topics from the interviewee (learner). It is a two way approach which permits an exchange of ideas and information. Goode, Barr and Scates observe: "In the interview for investigational purposes, the research worker (teacher) is gathering data directly from others (learners) in face to face contacts".

Importance of Interview Approach

In the words of Goode, Barr and Scates, "Perhaps no such research technique is as close to the teacher's problems as the interview".

Types of Interviews

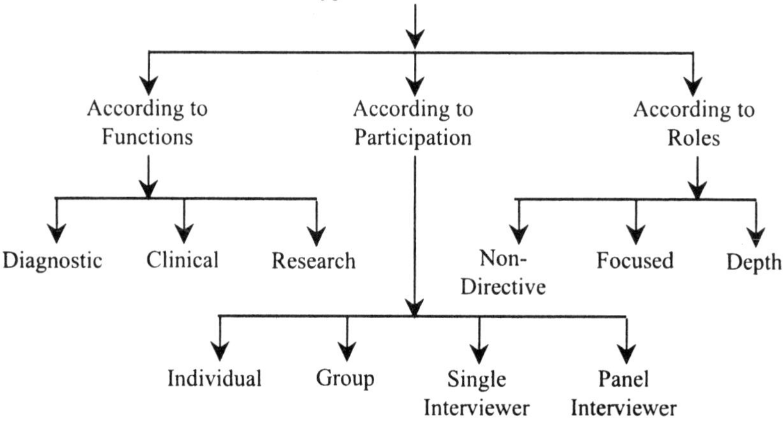

Lofton W. Hartmann is of the view that this technique is indispensable in diagnosis.

William A. Bownell is of the opinion that this technique usually reveals conditions that the average teacher would never have dreamed of.

Diagnostic Interview: Its purpose is to locate the possible causes of the learner's problems, getting information about his past history, family relation and personal adjustment problem.

Clinical Interview: It is followed after the diagnostic interview.

Purposes of Interviews

1. To determine the fitness of a person for admission, for a job or for scholarship, etc.—Assessment interview.
2. To assess personality assessment interview of a student for finding out the status of development of his personality.—Personality assessment interview.
3. To diagnose the problem for getting some information about the home, environmental and school situations of the student or the client—Diagnostic interview.
4. To prepare for further interviews—Preliminary interview.
5. To give some information to the students on subjects or careers, etc.
6. To collect data about a problem—Research interview.
7. To find out the causes of indiscipline and take further action—Disciplinary interview.
8. To help the counselee or the student in gaining insight into the problem and assisting him in solving the same—Counselling interview.

It is to be remembered that in educational institutions, the primary purpose of personality assessment is to find out the existing status of the development of the various facets of personality and to take further measures for bringing about improvement in the child.

'Who', 'Whom', 'How', 'Why', 'Where', 'When' and 'What' of Interview

1. *Who is to interview*? The interviewer (teacher) must be clear in his mind of his strengths and weakness, so that prejudices or bias could be minimised.
2. *Whom*—He should understand his client (learner) thoroughly.
3. *How*—He should know the technique of interviewing.
4. *Why*—He should be very clear in his mind for the purpose of interview.
5. *Where*—Suitable place should be selected for this purpose.
6. *When*—Proper motivation should be developed in the learner.
7. *What to Ask*—He should prepare his questions thoughtfully.

Preparation for the Interview

1. A quiet and orderly place should be selected for interview purposes.
2. The teacher or the psychologist should prepare for the interview by gathering all the data concerning the student.
3. The teacher or the psychologist or the counsellor should prepare clear objective for the interview.

4. The teacher or the counsellor should keep an open mind regarding the child.
5. Each interview should be considered as a step in the process of guiding the pupil.

Techniques of Interviewing

Rapport: Rapport is a technical term used to denote the feelings of friendliness, security and mutual confidence between the teacher and the child. Rapport should be established.

Sympathy: The teacher-counsellor expresses sympathy for the child.

Assurance: The teacher or the counsellor tries to ease the child's fear by encouraging him that this is a step for his personality development.

Approval: The teacher or the counsellor expresses his approval with something that the counselee or the student has said or done.

Humour: The teacher or the counsellor attempts to ease tension in the mind of the counselee with humorous remarks.

Personal Reference: The teacher or the counsellor tells about some of his own experience to illustrate his point by saying. 'I would do this'.

Non-personal Reference: The teacher or the counsellor cites an example of the experience of another person.

Question Form: The teacher or the counsellor asks questions to stimulate the counselee to think further about his problem.

Threat: The teacher or the counsellor sometimes threatens the counselee that unpleasant results may occur if the counselee does not follow a certain specified course of action.

Merits of an Interview

1. It is the most dynamic way of understanding the individual.
2. It is natural-like conversation.
3. It can be made flexible so as to suit many situations.
4. It is relatively easy to conduct.
5. It is possible to get some of the most confidential information from the child, which otherwise he may hesitate to reveal through writing.

Limitations of an Interview

1. It needs a trained and competent interviewer.
2. It is like natural in terms of labour, money and time.
3. It suffers from the subjective bias of the interviewer.
4. The interviewee may not unfold himself.
5. The interviewee may have a language handicap to express his feeling freely.

2.10 INTROSPECTION METHOD

Meaning of Introspection

Introspection is composed of two words—'intro' and 'spection'. 'Intro' means 'within' and 'spection' means 'looking'. Thus introspection—looking within. Introspection means self-observation—looking within oneself to experience one's own mental state. It is a process of examining one's own mental process of thought, feelings and motives. An individual observes, analyses and reports about his own feelings. Let us explain the process with the help of an example. Suppose you are sad and in this state of sadness you introspect your own mental feelings and examine what is going on in the mental process in the state of sadness.

Angell regards introspection as looking inward or looking within.

According to Stout, introspection is concerned with the nature of experience itself and with the laws of mental process.

William James considers introspection as looking into our own minds and reporting what we there discover. To Wordsworth, introspection means self-observation.

'Whom', 'What', 'Why' and 'How' of Introspection

'Whom' implies oneself. 'What' means 'mental state'. 'Why' implies finding out the mental state and reporting to the counsellor if needed. 'How' denotes observing oneself.

History of Introspection Method

Introspection is one of the earliest methods used by philosophers. Earlier psychologists used only this method. However, it was given the status of a scientific method by Wundt and Titchener, one of the outstanding pupils of Wundt.

Merits of the Introspection Method

1. *Firsthand information*: An individual gets first hand information through his own efforts about himself.
2. *Privacy*: Information revealed through introspection is confined to the individual. It is for him to disclose any of its aspects.
3. *Simple Method*: Every individual with some practice can use this method.
4. *Economical*: No apparatus is required in the use of this method.
5. *No Binding*: This method can be used by the individual at any time and at every place.
6. *Flexibility*: There are no set or specific rates for the use of this method.
7. *Readily available*: This method is readily available to the individual.
8. *Knowledge about one's feelings, perception and thoughts*: It is the only method at the disposal of the individual to know about one's own behaviour.
9. *Supplementary information*: It can be used with other methods also. Results obtained from other methods can be compared.
10. *Development of objective methods*: Introspection generated research which helped in the development of more objective methods.

Limitations of Introspection Method

1. *Subjective results*: Results obtained by introspection are more subjective. As observed by Ross, "The observer and the observed are the same, the mind is both the field and the instrument of observation.

2. *Non-verifiable nature*: It is not possible to verify the observation of the individual.
3. *No uniform principles*: One's introspection is personal. From it, it is not possible to generalise.
4. *Variable state of mind*: The same individual, if he introspects in different states of mind, would find different results. A man who is angry and introspects, may not be able to get actual picture about himself.
5. *Limited application*: It is not possible to use introspection method for children, abnormal individuals and animals.
6. *Unconscious and past experiences*: Method of introspection is not helpful in revealing unconscious and past experiences.

Suggestions for Making the Optimum Use of Introspection

1. *Attentive and Serious introspection*: Introspection should be carried out when mind is attentive and an individual is serious.
2. *Repeated introspection*: For ensuring accuracy and precision, introspection should be done repeatedly.
3. *Training in introspection*: Training for introspection may be obtained from a trained psychologist.
4. *Objective attitude*: The attitude of the introspectionist should be objective and impartial.

Summing up

Information obtained from introspection should be supplemented by other methods.

2.11 OBSERVATION METHOD

Meaning of Observation

Following definitions of observation help to understand the meaning of observation. In the words of Good, "Observation deals with the overt behaviour of persons in appropriate situations".

Goode and Hate state: "Observation includes the most casual uncontrolled experiences as well as most exact film records of laboratory experimentation".

"Observation may be defined as "measurement without instruments". In education, observation is the most commonly employed of all measurement techniques. In the present as well as in the past, students have been labelled as good, fair or poor in achievement and lazy or diligent in study etc. on the basis of observation. Similarly, teachers have listened to speeches and ranked students 1, 2, 3 and so on.

Observation as One of the Oldest Techniques: Observation is one of the oldest techniques that man has made use of. Even today, it is our common experience to notice farmers feel the breeze, watch the sky, sun, moon and stars—all to determine what the weather is likely to be and what season is approaching.

The physicians and the psychologists depend heavily on what they observe of the patient's talk, gestures and facial expressions.

Rousseau wrote, "Watch nature long and observe your pupil carefully before you say a word to him".

Types of Observation: Participant and Non-participant Observation

In participant observation, the observer or the investigator works his own way into the group he is observing and becomes a member of the group. In non-participant observation, the observer remains aloof from the group and simply observes.

Characteristics of Good Observation

1. Observation must be specific.
2. Behaviour must be observed scientifically.
3. Observed facts should be recorded immediately.
4. Observation should be quantitative as well as qualitative, i.e., certain specific behaviours should be noted.
5. Observation should be done by someone who is trained to do such work.

Qualities of the Observer

1. He should observe without any bias.
2. His eyesight should be normal.
3. He should be alert.
4. He should have the ability to estimate.
5. He should have the ability to discriminate.
6. He should observe in normal situation.
7. He should keep immediate record of each specific event observed.
8. He should have clear perception.
9. He should be emotionally balanced.

'What', 'Why', 'Whom', 'Who', 'How' and 'When' of Observation

1. *What to Observe*: Specific activities or units of behaviour to be observed must be clearly defined.
2. *Why to Observe*: The aim of observation should be very clear.
3. *Whom to Observe*: An appropriate group of learners should be selected in case it is a research work not related to classroom. In the case of normal teaching, the teacher must have the necessary knowledge about his students.
4. *Who is to Observe*: The teacher or the counsellor must prepare himself for the observation to be conducted effectively. He must free himself from any bias.
5. *How to Observe*: Instruments and forms of observation should be prepared carefully and kept handy.
6. *When to Observe*: Specific conditions under which observations are to be made should be determined scientifically.

Merits of Direct Observation

1. Observation being a record of the actual behaviour of the child, is more reliable.
2. It is a study of an individual in a natural situation and is therefore more useful than the restricted study in a test situation.
3. It can be used with children of all ages; of course, the younger the child, the easier to observe him. This method has been found very useful with shy children.
4. It can be used in every situation.
5. It is adaptable both to individuals and groups.
6. It can be used with a little training and almost all teachers can use it. It does not require any special tools or equipment.

Limitations and Demerits

1. It reveals the overt behaviour only—behaviour that is expressed and not that is within.
2. The observer may get only a small sample of student behaviour. It is very difficult to observe everything that a student does or says.
3. Records may not be written with hundred per cent accuracy as the observation is recorded after the actions of the observed. There is some time-lag.
4. There is a great scope for personal prejudices and bias of the observer.
5. An observer may not be adequately trained.
6. Some private experiences like sex cannot be observed.

Principles to be Followed in Making Observation More Objective

1. Observe situation as a whole.
2. Select one student to observe at a time.
3. Students should be observed in their regular activities, such as in classroom, on the play ground or in going from class to class.
4. Observation should be made over a period of days.

Requisites of Good Observation

As a research tool good observation is based on:

I. Proper planning.
II. Proper execution or proper observation.
III. Proper recording.
IV. Proper analysis and interpretation.

I. Proper Planning of Observation

1. Specific activities or units of behaviour to be observed must be clearly defined.
2. An appropriate group of subjects should be selected for observation
3. Scope of observation—whether individual or group—should be decided.
4. The length of each observation period, number of periods and interval between periods should be detailed.

5. The form of recording should be determined.
6. The instruments to be used should be selected carefully.
7. Physical position of the observer should be demarcated.
8. Proper tools for recording observation should be kept handy.

II. Proper Execution of Observation

A scientific execution demands skill and resourcefulness on the part of the investigator. This depends upon:

(*i*) Proper seating and other arrangement for the subjects.
(*ii*) Assuming proper physical position for observing.
(*iii*) Focussing attention on the units of behaviour on the specific activities under observation.
(*iv*) Observing discretely the length and number of periods and intervals decided upon.
(*v*) Proper handling of the recording instrument being used.
(*vi*) Utilising suitably the training received in terms of expertness.

III. Recording of Observation

Generally, two methods are employed for recording observation. Which of the two methods to use depends upon the nature of the activities or behaviour of the group to be observed. The skill of the observer also plays an important role in deciding upon the method.

The first method is to record the observation immediately, *i.e.*, during observation itself.

The second method is to record soon after the observation is over.

IV. Proper Analysis and Interpretation

Results should be interpreted very cautiously and without any bias. Various limitations of planning and recording should be taken note of.

Devices Used in Observation

(*i*) Check-lists;
(*ii*) Rating scale;
(*iii*) Score cards;
(*iv*) Blank form for tallying frequencies; and
(*v*) Electronic media can also be used where possible.

2.12 SOCIOMETRY METHOD

Origin of the Sociometry

USA—A Pioneer in Sociometry

J.L. Moreno writes in the preface of '*Sociometry Reader*' that each of the three S's—Socialism, Sociometry and Sociology—is related to a particular country—Socialism to Russia, Sociology to France and Sociometry to the USA. USA is considered to be a pioneer in Sociometry. Of course, seeds of social measurement existed in other countries also.

Meaning of the Concept Sociometry: This has been described by Jennings thus: "Stated briefly, sociometry may be described as a means of presenting simply and graphically the entire structure of relations existing at a given time among members of a given group. The major lines of communication or the pattern of attraction and rejection in its full scope, are made readily comprehensive at a glance".

William J. Goode and others state, "These and other variants of sociometric techniques offer rather simple methods of ranking individuals on a continuum of 'acceptability' or 'outgoingness' on the part of group members. When their use is justified they may be powerful research tools since they meet the general problems of scaling very well".

According to Bronfen Brenner, "Sociometry is a method of discovering, describing and evaluating social status, structure and development through measuring the extent of acceptance or rejection between individuals in groups".

F.N. Kerlinger defines sociometry as "Sociometry is a broad term indicating a number of methods of gathering and analysing data on the choice, communication and interaction pattern of groups".

Thus in a simple language, sociometry may be defined as an approach which is used to study the social status of the learner(s) in the group.

Importance of Sociometry

Sociometry is considered to be the most systematic trend towards group measurement in social sciences.

Sociometric studies have been made of many types of social groups including classroom groups. Being peer rating rather than rating by superiors, sociometry adds another dimension to the understanding of social relationships.

Advantages of Sociometry

1. This technique helps us to have an idea of the social structure of the group at a glance.
2. This enables us to form appropriate groups of students for carrying out various activities and projects.
3. This enables us to find out the changes taking place in the group structure.
4. It is useful in enabling us to understand the characteristics of an individual who is liked or disliked by the group.
5. It gives an insight into the qualities of leadership as appreciated by a particular group and helps us to compare one group with the other.
6. It is very helpful for the guidance worker who studies the pupil relationship.
7. It helps us to compare one group with the other.

Limitations of Sociometry

1. It involves expertise.
2. It is very time consuming.
3. It needs utmost secrecy.
4. It is a complicated approach.
5. It is rather expensive.

Simplest Form of Sociometric Matrix

For finding out the social structure of a group of 10 students, one line questionnaire is given to the students asking '*Whom would you like to be the secretary of your club?*'

Students would be asked to mark against one of the roll numbers. Thereafter tabulation of the responses would be made.

Choosers Chosen	1	2	3	4	5	6	7	8	9	10	11
1	—	—	—	—	—	—	—	—	—	—	0
2	—	—	✓	—	✓	—	—	—	—	✓	3
3	—	—	—	✓	—		—	—	—	—	1
4	—	—	✓	—	—	—	—	—	—	—	1
5	✓	✓	✓	✓	—	✓	—	—	✓	—	6
6	—	—	—	—	—	—	✓	—	—	—	1
7	—	—	—	—	—	—	—	—	—	—	0
8	✓	—	—	—	—	—	—	—	✓	—	2
9	—	—	—	—	—	—	—	—	—	—	0
10	—	✓	—	—	—	—	—	—	—	—	1

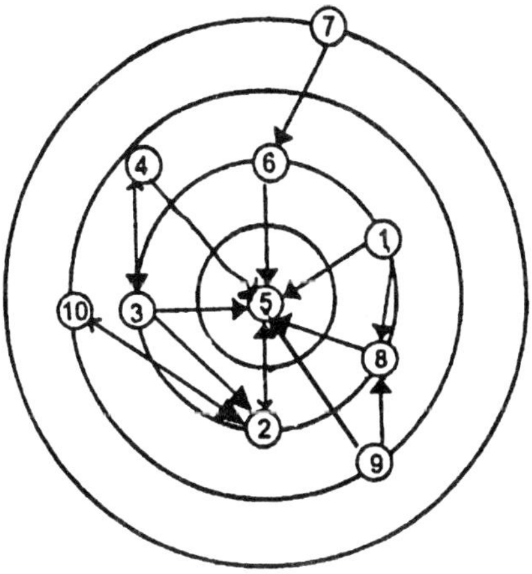

Fig. 1: Sociogram

Interpretation

1. Roll No. 5 is the 'star' as he has been chosen by the maximum number of students (6).
2. Roll Nos. 1, 7 and 9 did not get any choice. This indicates that they tended to be introvert, *i.e.*, not being social. However this should not be concluded that they were hated by the group.
3. Roll No. 5, *i.e.*, the star preferred Roll No. 2. This indicates mutual closeness between 2 and 5.
4. Other mutual choices were: 3 and 4; and 2 and 10.

Example in which Three Choices are Made

Example. Each member of a group consisting of ten students is asked to write his first, second and sometimes third choices about some significant and pertinent type of social setting. He may be asked questions like this:

1. Whom would you like to be the secretary of your debating society?
2. Whom would you like to sit next to you in the class or in the bus while going for a picnic?
3. With whom do you enjoy most.
4. With whom would you like to work in the science laboratory?
5. With whom would you like to walk home?

All these questions are positive questions and hence show social acceptances.

Negative questions may also be given to show social rejections.

In the above example, the individual has to name three persons in order of preference.

Data may be tabulated as under:

(i) Let the members of the group be numbered from A to J.

(ii) Write "Choosers" in the vertical column and "Chosen" in the horizontal column.

(iii) Total choices received by each member are shown at the bottom.

(iv) In the cells, check marks may be shown.

(v) Let *f* stand for first, *s* for second and *t* for third choices respectively.

(vi) Add the number of each choice.

A similar table can be prepared for social rejections. In the vertical column will be listed the 'rejectors' and in the horizontal column rejectees'.

Sociometric Matrix Showing Who Chooses Whom

Q. Whom would you like to be the Secretary of your Club?

Chosen	A	B	C	D	E	F	G	H	I	J
Chooser	A		F		S	T				
B				F	S	T				
C	S	F			T					
D			T		S		F			
E			F						S	T
F							F	S		
G	F			S	T					
H		F			S					T
I					T			S		F
J		F			S			T		
First Choice	1	3	2	1	—	—	2	—	—	1
Second Choice	1	—	—	1	5	—	—	2	1	—
Third Choice	—	—	1	—	3	2	—	1	—	2
Total	2	3	3	2	8	2	2	3	1	3

Guidelines for Using the Technique of Sociometry and Interpretation of Sociomatrix

1. One person should be concentrated at a time.
2. A detailed study of the choices made and received should be undertaken.
3. The 'isolates' and the 'stars' may be looked for. An 'isolate' is one whom nobody chooses. Of course he is not rejected. A 'star' is a member of the group who receives most of the choices. Here E is the 'star' with maximum choices in his favour. I is an 'isolate' with one choice only.
4. Attempts should made to discover the causes for such selections. An individual may be isolated because:
   (i) He is a new member of the group.
   (ii) He is of a shy and withdrawing nature.
   (iii) He does not try to form friendship with others.
   (iv) He may belong to a lower or upper socio-economic level and therefore he is not acceptable to the group.
5. Look for individuals who select each other. This might be due to factors like—
   (i) Close relations.
   (ii) Neighbours.
   (iii) Common interests and the like.
6. A triangle shows three persons selecting each other. This may be an evidence of cliques, or sharp divisions in the group.

Role of the Research Worker/Teacher

In general, he can work on three points:

1. Providing opportunities for developing friendly relations.
2. Improving social skills.
3. Building up competency for accomplishing something.

Reliable results can be achieved only when all the members constituting a group are fully acquainted with each other. The worker or the counsellor must establish friendly relations with the members of the group so that they may give their frank opinion about an individual or individuals.

Summing up

Several methods of psychology have emerged during the course of its development. In educational psychology, these methods are increasingly being used keeping in view specific environment affecting education. The use of these methods have been very useful in understanding and modifying the behaviour of the students. However, different methods should be used to correlate the findings. We should not depend on any particular method.

3

Meaning, Scope, Functions/Significance of Educational Psychology

3.1 MEANING OF EDUCATIONAL PSYCHOLOGY

Educational psychology is the applied branch of psychology in educational setting. It applies the application of principles and practices in the various dimensions of education primarily with a view to modify the behaviour of the learners in an education environment so that they amicably adjust themselves with the society with the optimum satisfaction and security.

Here some significant definitions are given which throw light on the meaning of educational psychology in its various facets.

1. According to '*The Encyclopaedia of Educational Research*'. "Educational psychology is the study of the learner and the learning-teaching process in its various branches directed towards helping the child come to terms with society with a maximum of security and satisfaction".

2. Anderson has observed, "While general psychology is a pure science, educational psychology is its application in the field of education with the aim of socialising an individual and modifying his behaviour".

3. Prof. E.D. Peel regards educational psychology as the "Science of Education".

Judd considers educational psychology as "the science which explains the changes that take place in the individuals as they pass through the various stages of development".

4. Skinner explains the meaning of educational psychology as, "Educational psychology is that branch of psychology which deals with teaching and learning". He further observes, "Educational psychology covers the entire range and behaviour of the personality related to education".

5. In the views of Crow and Crow, "Educational psychology describes and explains the learning experiences of an individual from birth through old age".

6. Stephen regards educational psychology as "the systematic study of the educational growth and development of a child".

7. In the words of Trow, "Educational psychology is the study of psychological aspects of educational situation".

8. Water B. Kolesnik writes, "Educational psychology is the study of those facts and principles of psychology which help to explain and improve the process of education".

9. David P. Anasuble defines educational psychology in these words, "Educational psychology is the special branch of psychology concerned with the nature, conditions, outcomes and evaluation of school learning and retention".

A perusal of the above definitions would indicate that the definition given by '*The Encyclopaedia of Educational Research*' provides the true meaning of educational psychology. Other definitions, by and large, put emphasis on the study of the learner but do not emphatically state the ultimate aim of studying. A mere study of the behaviour of the learner is not enough unless it is related to the modification of the behaviour towards desired ends.

From above it is concluded that educational psychology is that applied branch of psychology which studies the experiences and behaviours of the learners in relation to educational environment which is mainly provided by the teacher for the purpose of bringing about desired changes. Therefore, educational psychology becomes a psychology of teaching and learning. Teaching and learning are the main processes of education and the learner is a key figure in the process.

3.2 NATURE AND LIMITATIONS OF EDUCATIONAL PSYCHOLOGY

Nature of Educational Psychology

Following points bring out the nature of educational psychology. Some of the points overlap.

1. Educational psychology is an applied science.
2. Educational psychology is a social science.
3. Educational psychology is a positive science.
4. Educational psychology is a specific science.
5. Educational psychology is a developing and growing science.
6. Educational psychology is an academic discipline.
7. Educational psychology is not as exact as natural and physical sciences.

Limitations of Educational Psychology

Educational psychology suffers from the following limitations:

First, it supplied ideas and knowledge about behaviour and its use depends upon the efficiency and foresight of the teacher.

Second, laws of educational psychology are not as exact as the laws of physical and natural sciences as human nature is not the same.

Third, educational environment is always in flux. It changes from place to place and moment to moment.

3.3 SCOPE OF EDUCATIONAL PSYCHOLOGY: SEVERAL WAYS OF CLASSIFICATION

Scope of educational psychology is as vast as the scope of education itself. Gates and others have very aptly remarked, "The boundaries of educational psychology are uncertain and changing". The explosion of 'Information

Technology' (IT) has been exercising a far-reaching influence on the scope of educational psychology. New and novel situations need new and novel approaches to educational matters. Nevertheless, we mention here the most significant areas of the scope of educational psychology.

Classification I

Scope of Educational Psychology According to the Educational Psychology Division of the American Association Delimited in 1947.

1. Human growth and development.
2. Learning.
3. Personality and adjustment.
4. Measurement, evaluation and statistics.
5. Techniques and methods of educational psychologies.

Classification II

Broad Areas of Educational Psychology

1. *Learner: Growth and Development*

(a) Heredity and environment affecting the learner.
(b) General growth and development of the learner at different stages of education.
(c) Emotional, intellectual motor, moral, physical and social development of the learner.
(d) Individual differences of the learners.
(e) Learner's aptitudes, interests and intelligence.

2. *Learning*

(a) Concept of learning.
(b) Process of learning.
(c) Primary and concomitant learning.
(d) Domains of learning: Cognitive, Affective and Psychomotor.
(e) Learning process and theories.
(f) Factors affecting learning.
(g) Transfer of training.
(h) Learning situations.

3. *Personality and Adjustment*

(a) Emotions.
(b) Mental health of the learner.
(c) Mental health of the teacher.
(d) Character development.
(e) Social interaction.

4. *Evaluation and Measurement*

(a) Meaning of the concepts of evaluation and measurement.
(b) Basic principles of evaluation and measurement.
(c) Measurement of aptitudes, attitudes and intelligence.
(d) Measurement of learning.
(e) Measures of adjustment.

(f) Applications of the results of measurement and evaluation.

5. *Techniques and Methods in Educational Psychology*

(a) Scientific study of educational problems.

(b) Statistical techniques

(c) Implications of research for the classroom teacher.

Classification III

In Terms of Learner and Learning

1. The Learner (Pupil).
2. The Learning Experiences.
3. The Learning Environment or Situation.
4. The Learning Process.
5. The Teaching Situation.
6. Evaluation of Learning Experience.

1. *The Learner.* This includes the study of growth and development of the individual and the concept of maturity in various aspects of personality—physical, mental, social and emotional. Study of the learner also deals with the influences of his family, social class and peer groups on his personality and behaviour. Social behaviour and social norms of his peer group; emotional health and problem behaviour of the learner are also studied in detail from the mental hygiene point of view. This also includes the study of the abilities, needs and motivational forces, like self-concept, life-goals, values, anxiety of the individual learner as well as the differences that exist among different individuals.

2. *Learning Experiences*: This includes providing activities and subjects according to the maturity level of the students.

3. *The Learning Situation*: In the learning situation, educational psychology studies such factors as classroom management and discipline, techniques and aids which facilitate learning, methods of teaching, motivational techniques and practices, guidance and counselling.

4. *The Learning Process*: In the learning process, educational psychology deals with the nature of learning and how it takes place. It considers the various theoretical view points as well as experimental evidences to explain the role and nature of reinforcement, forgetting, problem solving, transfer of training and the learning of concepts, skills and attitudes.

5. *The Teaching Situation*: Effectiveness of educational psychology becomes relevant only when its methods and findings become a part of educational practices in the teaching-learning situation.

6. *Evaluation of Learning Experiences*: In recent years, evaluation of learning experiences has assumed great significance in the subject-matter of psychology.

Scope of Educational Psychology of B.Ed. Course as Determined by the University Grants Commission (UGC)

Development of Learner and Teaching-Learning Process
Course Objectives

To enable trainee teachers to

1. acquire knowledge and understanding of stages of human development and development tasks with special reference to adolescent learners.
2. develop understanding of process of children learning in the context of various theories of learning.
3. understand intelligence, motivation and various types of exceptional children.
4. develop skills for effective teaching-learning process and use of psychological tests.

Unit I

Nature of psychology and learners

(a) Psychology: Its meaning, nature, methods and scope; functions of educational psychology.
(b) Stages of human development; stage, specific characteristics and developmental tasks.
(c) Adolescence in Indian context—characteristics and problems of adolescents; their needs and aspirations.
(d) Guiding and counselling adolescents.

Unit II

Learning and motivation

(a) Nature of learning; learning theories—Behaviourists (Skinner's), Information Processing, (Roger's) and Humanistic (Maslow's).
(b) Factors influencing learning and teaching process; learner related; teacher related; process related and content related.
(c) Motivation—nature, types; techniques of enhancing learner's motivation.

Unit III

Intelligence

(a) Nature and characteristics of intelligence and its development.
(b) Theories of intelligence; two factor theory—Multifactor Theory (PMA) and SI Model.
(c) Measuring Intelligence—Verbal, Non-verbal and Performance tests (one representative of group test and individual test of each).

Unit IV

Exceptional children

(a) Concept of exceptional children—types and characteristics of each type including children with learning disabilities.
(b) Individual differences—nature; accommodating individual differences in the classroom.
(c) Learner centred techniques for teaching exceptional children.

Unit V

- Personality—Definition, meaning and nature; development of personality; type and trait theories of personality.

Practicum

- Observing the behaviour of an early, mid–adolescent and describing her/his characteristics and problems.
- Administering and interpreting the results of two tests of intelligence—verbal, non-verbal or performance.
- A case study of an exceptional child and suggesting how to provide for this particular child education.

3.4 'WHEN TO TEACH', 'WHAT TO TEACH', AND 'HOW TO TEACH' QUESTIONS OF EDUCATIONAL PSYCHOLOGY

Educational psychologists are more concerned with the answer of these questions. The first question refers to the developmental processes that gradually mature as the child grows up. Similarly the problem of what to teach is important because of its close relationship with the process of maturation. Certain types of learning can be useful to the child only when he has matured sufficiently in certain faculties. We cannot think of teaching mathematics to a three year child, though he may be taught to count simple things. The problem of how to teach is equally important because there are ways and means of teaching which can make the education of a child more effective, meaningful and useful.

3.5 IMPORTANCE OF EDUCATIONAL PSYCHOLOGY

Educational psychology, being functional in its character is very helpful to all sections of society engaged in pursuing different dimensions of education at all levels of education, *i.e.*, formal, non-formal and informal.

Educational psychology is of great importance to parents, teachers, guidance workers, career masters, and psychoanalysts etc.

According to W.A. Kelly (1941), educational psychology is helpful in the following ways:

1. It provides a knowledge of the nature of the child.
2. It gives understanding of the nature, aims and purposes of education.
3. It gives understanding of the scientific methods and procedures which have been used in arriving at the facts and principles of educational psychology.
4. It presents the principles and techniques of learning and teaching.
5. It gives training in methods of measuring abilities and achievement in school subjects.
6. It provides a knowledge of the growth and development of children.
7. It assists in the better adjustment of children and helps to prevent maladjustment.
8. It helps to understand the significance and control of emotions.
9. It gives an understanding of the principles and techniques of correct training.

3.6 FUNCTIONS AND SIGNIFICANCE OF EDUCATIONAL PSYCHOLOGY TO TEACHERS

The work of the teacher is like that of a gardener to a great extent. The gardener needs the knowledge of the plant life. The teacher also needs the knowledge of the learner. It is the duty of the gardener to ensure that all the plants grow and yield good flowers and fruits and he can do so when he is well-acquainted with all the details about them. The objective of the teacher is to ensure that all the learners under his care and charge develop into happy and healthy personalities and he can do so only when he knows how the learners develop and behave. This knowledge is provided to the teacher by educational psychology.

The work of the teacher may also be compared to that of an artist who must know his material thoroughly if he wants to produce a fine piece of art. What will happen to the artist if he starts his work without fully understanding the kind of material he has to work with. The teacher as an artist, is not only required to know the subject-matter but also to know the child's nature and the techniques of moulding his behaviour in accordance with the objectives.

The work of the teacher assume all the more significance and needs more delicacy and expertness than that of the gardener and the artist as here, human beings are involved.

R.A. Davis in '*Applicability and Applications of Psychology with Particular Reference to Classroom Learning*' (1943) has pointed out the significance of educational psychology as, "Psychology has made a distinct contribution to education through its analysis of pupil potentialities and differences as revealed by means of various types of psychological tests. It has also contributed directly to the knowledge of pupil growth and maturation during the school years".

G.M. Blair in '*The Psychological Interpretation of Teaching*' (1947) has stated the importance of educational psychology to the teacher in these words, "Modern teacher, if he is to succeed with his work should be a specialist who understands children, how they grow, develop, learn and adjust. He should be diagnostician, who can discover special difficulties of children and at the same time possesses the requisite skill for carrying forward the necessary remedial work. He should also be performing important educational and vocational guidance functions. No person untrained in the methods of psychology can possibly fulfill the obligations and tasks which are the responsibilities of the teacher."

Educational psychology performs the following functions:

1. *Providing knowledge of John and Latin (Knowledge of the learner and the subject matter)*: Sir John Adams has put it thus in his book '*New Teaching*'. The verbs of teaching govern two accusatives, one of the person and another of the thing as, 'the master taught John Latin'." He says that there are two definite subjects—John, the student and Latin the subject which are governed by the verb taught". Now the teacher must understand both John as well as Latin if he wants to make 'teaching' effective. Educational psychology helps him in understanding 'John'. He may be a great scholar of Latin but he will not succeed in teaching Latin to John if he has no knowledge of the mental

set up of John. Acquisition of knowledge is now no more the main object of education but it is still very significant in the process of education. Acquisition of knowledge is also a sort of modification in the behaviour of the child. For this purpose the educator will have to consider the mental process of the child and not only the quality of knowledge which he is going to put into the living mind.

2. *Acquainting with the knowledge and significance of individual differences*: No two persons are exactly alike. There is individual difference. Pupils always differ in their level of intelligence, aptitudes, likes and dislikes and in other propensities and potentialities. Different minds are to be trained by the teacher. There are gifted, backward, retarded, talented and handicapped children. All of them should not be treated in the same manner. Knowledge of educational psychology helps the teacher to cater to individual differences of children.

3. *Providing knowledge of the process of learning*: Teaching and learning go side by side. All education depends upon the learning of new responses and the capacity of a human child to learn new responses. Educational psychology discusses the nature of learning theories and types of learning for different age levels and situations. Therefore, knowledge of educational psychology becomes essential to a teacher to study all these problems.

4. *Inculcating a scientific attitude among the teachers*: The knowledge of psychology can make the teacher more scientific in his educational practices and consequently he will be more objective and methodical in his work.

5. *Helping in knowing, evolving and using methods of teaching*: Educational psychology has discovered many secrets about mental forces. Recent researches made in the field of educational psychology give us valuable suggestions for better methods of teaching and memorising, for making desirable habits and eradicating anti-social tendencies. Educational psychology tells us how significant play and recreation are for the children and how play-way and project methods turn the work of learning into an interesting play.

6. *Bringing out a dynamic and progressive change in the outlook and attitude of the teacher towards his pupils*: The knowledge of psychology can change the outlook and attitude of the teacher towards children by understanding them adequately.

7. *Helping the teacher in his own personal development*: The study of educational psychology can help the teacher to understand himself. He will realise his own merits and weaknesses and make attempts to overcome his weaknesses.

8. *Helping to know nervous system*: The entire education depends on the function of the brain and nervous system. It becomes essential for a teacher to study the nervous system which controls human behaviour. He must have the knowledge of sensory organs which are the gateways of knowledge.

9. *Realising the significance of play*: Play is a natural tendency having great educational potentials. Knowledge of educational psychology helps the teacher to provide for a variety of activities for children.

10. *Enabling the teacher to understand the significance of measurement*: Educational psychology has made many strides in this respect quite recently. It has produced many reliable tests and instruments of mental measurement. These are proving to be extremely useful in the field of education. We can quite easily measure mental capacities, basic intelligence, temperamental attitudes and special inclinations of children and base educational programmes on these findings. These measurements show that all the children differ and that every child is a unique being. The teacher can know that children with I.Q. below 90 cannot do well in medical, engineering, administrative or other similar vocations. But he knows that such young ones are not doomed if they cannot do well in intellectual callings. He can easily explore some other fields where such children can also flourish.

11. *Assisting the teacher in the character development of the learner*: Educational psychology helps a lot to the formation and development of character. The teacher comes to know the methods he should adopt in inculcating suitable character traits, and moral principles among the children.

12. *Enabling the teacher to understand the need for productive activities*: A great stress is being laid these days on work experience and socially useful productive work. Educational psychology helps the teacher to know how various activities in these fields can be used for the fulfilment of the basic needs of children.

13. *Helping the teacher in guidance and counselling*: Students need various types of guidance and counselling. A teacher with the knowledge of educational psychology can render very useful service.

14. *Undertaking research in education*: Educational psychology enables the educators and the classroom teachers in conducting research on subjects with which they are primarily concerned.

15. *Understanding the specific needs of the learners*: A knowledge of educational psychology enables the teacher to prepare programmes for the gifted as well as the backward students.

16. *Developing human relations*: A knowledge of educational psychology is helpful in understanding the nature of different sections with whom the teachers come to know.

17. *Providing guidance to parents*: An elementary knowledge of educational psychology to parents goes a long way in making them understand the need for providing suitable environment to their children.

18. *Increasing career guidance competency*: Educational psychology is helpful to the teachers in giving career guidance to students.

19. *Preparing suitable curriculum*: Curriculum preparation for different age groups is a very complicated process and educational psychology provides guidelines.

20. *Preparing good textbooks and other instructional material*: The knowledge of psychology provides guidance to the textbook writers to prepare textbooks. Keeping in view the needs of various categories of students.

21. *Guiding the teacher in the realisation of the aims of education*: The main aim of education is the harmonious and all-round development of the educand. Development comes from within and the inner potentialities must

be understood and approached for the desired modification in the development of the child. The knowledge of educational psychology helps the teacher to understand the inner potentialities which underlie the behaviour of the child.

3.7 SUMMING UP

The basic functions of the educational psychology are concerned with the following elements:

Who is to learn? The child is to learn and educational psychology helps us to understand the child.

Why to learn? The child is to learn to adjust himself amicably with the environment/society so as to derive maximum satisfaction.

From whom to learn? Primarily the child is to learn from the teacher. The teachers, therefore, in the first instance learn how to make them effective. They must develop their own personality as it has a great bearing on the personality of the child.

Where to learn? Among the most important places of learning is the school. Accordingly the school should provide maximum facilities to the learner.

How to learn? This calls for child-centred learning. The teachers should adopt such methods which lead to optimum learning.

When to learn? This raises the issue of creating motivation.

How to measure the learning outcomes. This is concerned with the use of appropriate tools of measurement.

4

Stages of Human Development : Specific Stage Characteristics and Developmental Tasks

4.1 MEANING OF HUMAN DEVELOPMENT

The primary aim of education is the development of the whole child which implies well-balanced personalities; aesthetically sound, culturally refined, emotionally stable, mentally alert, morally upright, physically strong, socially efficient, spiritually enlightened, vocationally self-sufficient and internationally liberal. It is, therefore, very important to understand the meaning of development, its very dimensions, factors influencing development and the role of the teacher and the school in this task.

In the words of A. Angyal, "Development cannot be considered in terms of the mind alone but rather in terms of the individual as a whole in relationship with his experience with others". Thus J.E. Anderson explains development as, "Development does not consist merely of adding inches to one's height or improving one's ability. Instead development is a complex process of integrating many structures and functions".

In the words of E.B. Hurlock, "Development means a progressive series of change that occur in an orderly predictable pattern as a result of maturation and experience".

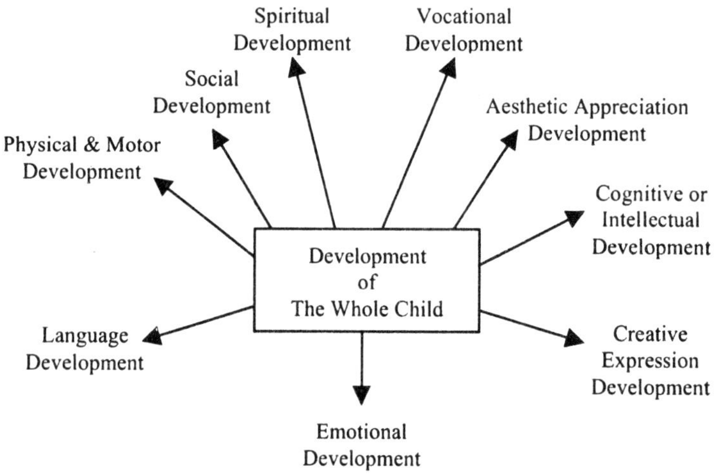

Fig. 4.1: The figure illustrates the various aspects/patterns of the development of the learner

4.2 CHARACTERISTICS AND PRINCIPLES OF DEVELOPMENT

Following are the general principles of growth and development of individuals:

1. *The Principle of Individual Differences*: There are individual differences in the development of children. The difference is mostly in the intellectual capacity of all human beings. Difference in special aptitudes is most marked among children. This is caused by differences in heredity, endowments and environment.

2. *Principle of Continuous Growth and Development Process*: The growth and development starts from the moment of conception of the individual in the mother's womb and continues till he reaches his grave. It is a continuous stream of development. Development proceeds by stages but it is a continuous process. Changes in the patterns of body and behaviour take place throughout life. Emergence of each type of behaviour is dependent on the development that has gone before.

3. *Principle of Uneven Tempo of Growth and Development*: Growth and development though is continuous, yet its rate of development is in fits and starts and not uniform at all times. In the earlier stages it is quick, but slows down in later years of infancy. Again at the state of puberty, there is a sudden rise in the growth and development.

4. *Principle of Uniformity of Development Pattern*: Although development has individual differences, yet it follows a definite sequence common to the off-springs of human beings. The outstanding example is that off-springs develop their head first and other parts of the body later on. Motor and language development in human off-springs has a definite sequence.

5. *Principle of Development from General to Specific Responses*: If we examine the different developmental aspects of the child we will find that general activity precedes specific activity in all his/her actions. The movements of the child are of general nature in the beginning but later on they become specific.

6. *Principle of Interrelation*: It has been observed that the growth and development in various aspects like physical, mental, social, etc. are inter-related and interdependent. Growth and development of the child in one aspect leads to the development in other aspects as well. It has also been observed that children who are highly intelligent, generally have a robust health, whereas children with lower intelligence have weak health and regress in their emotional and social development.

7. *Principle of Developmental Direction*: There are two important principles of development: (a) Cephalo-cadal, and (b) Proximo-distal.

By cephalo-cadal development we mean that it has a longitudinal axis, *i.e.*, that human development is from head to foot. This implies that control of the body as well as improvement in the structure itself, develops first in the head and progresses later to parts further from head. Another example of this aspect of development is that a child can lift his head by his neck before he can do so by lifting his chest.

The proximo-distal tendency means that child develops from the centre of the body, *i.e.*, the spinal chord to the periphery of the body, *i.e.*, fingers. In the beginning, the child is able to control his large fundamental muscles and smaller muscles later on. The outstanding example is that the control over fingers comes after control over the arm and the hand.

8. *Principle of Integration*: This principle implies that the development of the child is both from general to specific and specific to general The child while busy in his specific activities arrives at a general rule. Again he gives a tryout of his general rule on certain specific activities. Thus, the development of the child integrates both general and specific activities.

9. *Principle of Predictability of Development*: We know that every child develops in his own way and develops nearly constantly. It is with this presumption that we can also predict his future range of development. This prediction is only possible in the case of children of average or normal development. We shall not be able to predict in the case of abnormal or highly intelligent children.

10. *Principle of Spiral and Non-Linear Development*: This principle implies that the development of the child is not in a straight line (linear) but it is in the form of a cork-screw (spiral). He advances in his development in one period but takes rest in the following period. This enables him to consolidate his development.

11. *The Principle of Struggle*: While the child is developing up towards maturity there are conflicting impulses and demands. The child struggles against these in his striving for maturity.

12. *The Principle of Indigenous Motivation*: As the child matures in his capacities of doing, thinking and feeling, he has an impulse to put them to use and he does it wholeheartedly. This has been described by Jersild as 'Indigenous Motivation'.

13. *The Principle of Anticipation*: The child in his/her process of development also uses his capacity of self-repair. He modifies his behaviour and even habits keeping in view what he is going 'to become' in future. Thus, he consciously anticipates his future direction of development.

14. *The Principle of Interaction of Heredity and Environment*: The development of the child is a product of both. This is true at all times and stages of his development.

4.3 EDUCATIONAL IMPLICATIONS OF THE PRINCIPLES OF DEVELOPMENT

A knowledge of principles of growth and development will enlighten the parents and teachers on the potentialities of their children. They should, therefore, provide suitable opportunities for the maximum development of their children. For planning and implementing suitable programmes for the all-round development of children, following guidelines may be taken into consideration:

1. *Need for Paying Attention to Individual Differences of the Learners*: The parents and teachers should keep in view that there are individual variations in the rates of growth and every child develops in a unique way. Hence they should pay individual attention to every child. It stipulates the provision of diversified courses and provision of all activities according to

needs and interests of various stages of growth.

2. *Need for Developing Motivation*: Teachers should organise teaching-learning programmes, procedures and practices according to the maturational levels of children.

3. *Need for a Pragmatic Outlook*: Every stage of growth has its possibilities and limitations. Teachers and parents should not place undue demands on the child. Such demands lead to mental tension for the child.

4. *Need for Correlation*: Teachers should keep in mind that children develop on the principle of interrelatedness of development growth. It is, therefore, necessary for them to search for the principle of correlation.

5. *Influence of Heredity and Environment*: Parents and teachers should keep in view that it is difficult to change the heredity of the child but environment can be modified.

6. *Emphasis on Doing*: 'Doing' helps in the development of mental, physical and social skills.

7. *Creativity Aspect*: Children are creative and they need assistance and guidance to develop their creativity.

8. *Individual Attention*: Each child needs attention and a neglected child in the home or in the class loses interest in work and play.

9. *Different Modes of Teaching-Learning*: Singing songs and learning rhymes, drawing pictures and reading stories help the child's mind to grow at the pre-primary, primary and middle stages.

10. *Recognition Aspect*: For proper development, all children need adequate praise and recognition for their work.

11. *Satisfaction of Curiosity*: Children are curious to learn and respond with interest to new things.

12. *Reasonable Repetition*: Children learn through repetition; of course excessive repetition tends to kill interest.

13. *Need-Satisfaction at Each Stage*: Each stage in the development of an individual has developmental needs peculiar to it and these must be taken note of.

14. *Observation*: Observation of children leads to better understanding on the part of parents and teachers.

15. *Clarity*: When parents and teachers speak clearly, use appropriate words and adopt a proper style and manner, children are likely to do the same.

16. *Healthy Environment*: Children need an environment which promotes initiative and trust.

17. *Consistency and Firmness*: Consistency, firmness, love and patience on the part of parents and teachers will go a long way in the wholesome development of children.

18. *Human Relations*: Children need close, loving and sensitive relationships with the adults who are charged with the responsibility of looking after them. The feeling of being wanted and loved in the children is vital to their inner development. Children need a sense of security which should be provided by parents and teachers. Anger and violence are damaging to the inner development of the children. Healthy relationships established in the earlier stages of life help to set the pattern of future development.

4.4 INTERRELATIONSHIPS AND INTERDEPENDENCE OF VARIOUS PATTERNS OF DEVELOPMENT

It has been observed that the growth and development in various aspects like cognitive, emotional, language, motor, physical and social is inter-related and interdependent. Development in one aspect of the child leads to the development in other aspects as well. As observed by Pestalozzi, "Education is the natural, harmonious and progressive development of man's innate powers". Gandhiji wrote: "By education, I mean an all-round drawing out of the best in child and man—body, mind and spirit". Education, therefore, has to develop all these in such a way that the development is balanced and harmonious. While taking measures for the all-round development, it must be remembered that all the aspects of development are inter-related and interdependent.

An individual is one 'whole'. He cannot be compartmentalised. All parts of the individual need equal attention. It is very difficult to decide whether it is the hand or the head or any other part which needs more attention at the cost of the other.

Interrelationships of Physical Development and Other Aspects of Development

Healthy mind in a healthy body is an old adage and it is true to the core. Appropriate physical development makes valuable contribution to other aspects of development. When a child is physically weak, he cannot devote necessary attention to the cognitive aspect. A physically weak individual may remain emotionally disturbed. Likewise he may not be able to participate in social interactions. His language and motor development may also suffer. A physically unhealthy person, other things being equal, is unable to perform effectively his duties to himself, to the community and to the God. He cannot offer his prayer properly.

Interrelationship of Emotional Development and Physical Development and Other Aspects of Development

A child under emotional strain is likely to be physically unhealthy and socially inefficient. An emotionally unstable individual is not able to acquire cognitive abilities. His motor development may remain stunted.

Interrelationship and Interdependence of Motor Development and Other Aspects of Development

Motor development is closely related to physical development, creative and productive activities. As observed by A.I. Gates, "The acquisition of motor skills is of value not only from the point of view of the personal satisfactions that accrue from competence in self-help and independence of adult aid, but also from the point of view of good social relations with others".

Interrelationship of Social Development with other Aspects of Development

Social development is dependent upon language development, physical development, cognitive development and motor development. Social development leads to development of other aspects. Likewise if an individual does not mix up with others, he may feel lonely. Loneliness may lead to emotional disturbance which may create difficulties in cognitive and language development.

Interrelationship of Cognitive Development with Other Aspects of Development

Without cognitive development, an individual may remain ignorant and indifferent to other aspects of development. He may be termed as a 'snob'. He may not be able to appreciate and understand social relationships. Undue emphasis on cognitive development may ignore emotional side of an individual's personality. His health may also be adversely affected.

To sum up, for the harmonious and total development of an individual, it is absolutely necessary to pay due attention to each aspect of the development as all aspects are interrelated and interdependent.

Fig. 4.2 illustrates the interrelation of various aspects of development.

Fig. 4.3 illustrates the interrelationship of cognitive development with other aspects of development.

Likewise are the interrelations of other aspects of development.

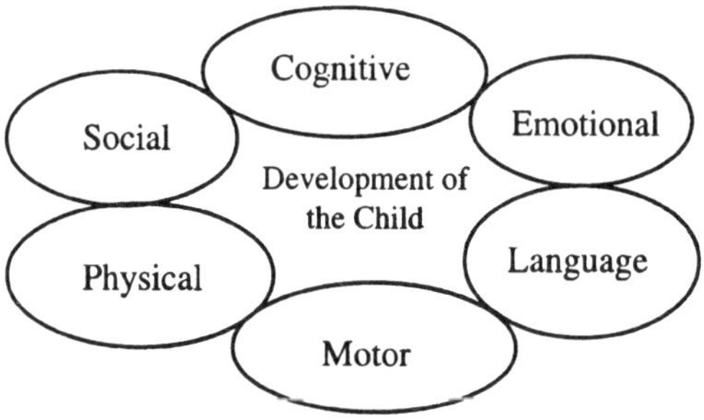

Fig. 4.2: Interdependence of Various Aspects of Development

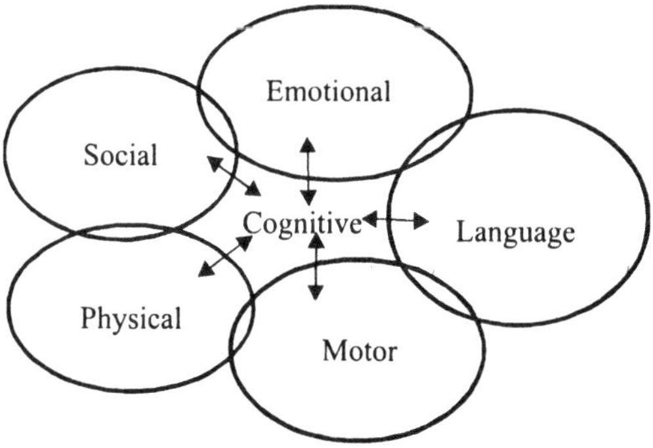

Fig. 4.3: Interrelationship of Cognitive Development with other Aspects of Developments

4.5 STAGES OF DEVELOPMENT

Psychologists and educators differ on the stages and ages of development of an individual. A brief account of development of specification of each stage is given here.

Rousseau's Classification of Stages of Development

Rousseau has divided the individual's development into four stages as given below:

Table 4.1: Rousseau's Classification of Stages of Development

Stage	*Period and Approximate Age*	*Characteristics*
1. Infancy	1 to 5 years	1. Free wandering stage 2. Simple play things 3. Physical development
2. Childhood	Between 5 to 12 years	1. Development of senses 2. Non-verbal lessons 3. Activity and experience
3. Pre-adolescence	12 to 15 years	1. Period of developing intellect 2. Study of natural sciences 3. Manual work and industrial arts
4. Adolescence	15 to 20 years	1. Sex instruction 2. Moral education through activities and occupations 3. Understanding of complex social relationships

Jean Piaget's (1896-1980) Classification of Development Stages

Piaget, a Swiss educator, observed children for about 50 years and wrote more than 20 books on the various aspects of development. He pointed out four stages of development as shown below:

Table 4.2: Piaget's Classification of Stages of Development

Stage	*Age/Periods*	*Characteristics*
1. Sensory Motor Stage	Birth to 2 years	Manipulation of objects in the environment
2. Pre-Operational Stage	Between 2 to 6 years	Child begins to acquire vocabulary
3. Concrete Operational Stage	Between age of 6 and 11 or 12	Child learns to add, subtract, multiply and divide
4. Formal Operational Stage	Between 11 or 12 to 14 or 15	The child begins to think logically

Dr. Ernest Jones' Classification of Stages of Development

Table 4.3 gives the classification of stages of development as suggested by Jones:

Table 4.3: Jone's Classification

1.	Infancy	—	up to the ages of 5 years.
2.	Later childhood	—	from 5 years to 12 years.
3.	Adolescence	—	from 12 years to 18 years.
4.	Maturity	—	from 18 years onwards.

Table 4.4: Generally Acceptable Stages of Development

Age Groups	*Stage of Development*	*Schooling Stage*
Birth to 2 years	Infancy	
2 years to 6 years	Early childhood	Pre-primary (Nursery/Kindergarten etc.)
6 years to 12 years	Later childhood	Primary/Elementary
13 years to 18 years	Adolescence	Secondary and senior secondary
18 years to 40 years	Young adulthood	
40 years to 65 years	Mature adulthood	
over 65 years	Aged adulthood	

Note: Scholars and thinkers differ as regards the age at various stages of development.

Each stage of development is characterised by a set of somewhat coherent, distinguishing and unique features. Each stage in life has its own problems of adjustment.

The entire development is influenced by these factors: (i) Heredity, and (ii) Environment.

4.6 CHARACTERISTICS OF EACH STAGE OF HUMAN GROWTH AND DEVELOPMENT AND EDUCATIONAL IMPLICATIONS (see also next chapter)

Strictly speaking, there is no sharp line of demarcation between the duration of one stage of growth and development and another stage. Nevertheless, each stage has certain specific characteristics which must be kept in view while teaching or bringing up children.

I. Infancy (from Birth to 2 years)

Characteristics: The period is marked by rapid physical growth.

Importance: Modern researches have established that the period of infancy is the foundation on which the future development of the child depends.

Highlighting the importance of the period of infancy of the child, Ruth Strang of Columbia University remarked "*During the first two years of his life he lays the foundation for his future*". Dr. F. Goodenough, a prominent child psychologist is of the view, that "*One-half of an individual's mental structure has been attained by the age of three years*".

Educational Implications

1. The environment in the family should be of affection and love. The child should have the feeling that everybody in the family loves him.
2. Freedom should be given to the child in his movements.

II. Early Childhood (from 2 to 6 years)

Characteristics: This is the most important and impressionistic period of child's life. He learns his first lesson of citizenship in the home and the school. He develops the instinct of curiosity. He loves make-believe plays.

Educational Implications

This period of a child's life is of great educational significance. It has been correctly held by Watson that "*the scope and intensity of learning during this period exceeds that of any other period of development*". The following points should be kept in view both by parents and teachers while planning the education of the child at this stage.

1. Provision of Healthy Environment.
2. Rational Treatment.
3. Satisfaction of Curiosity.
4. Learning by Doing.
5. Dynamic Methods of Teaching.

Education may be imparted to children with the use of the Montessori Method and the Kindergarten Method which are based on sound psychological principles required for this stage.

These methods provide opportunities for the child to develop his five senses as well.

Play-way spirit should permeate all learning activities.

III. Later Childhood (from 6 to 12 years)

Characteristics: Bodily proportions change. Generally boys are considered superior in games requiring physical strength while girls are considered superior to boys on the use of fine muscles and in acquiring skills like drawing, painting, sewing etc. According to Watson, "A derivative of anger, annoyance becomes more prominent in later childhood. There is rapid intellectual advancement".

Educational Implications

This stage is known as the formative age of the child. He develops his basic outlook, values and ideas. We, as parents, teachers and social workers have an important role to play.

The school authorities have a special responsibility towards the development of the child.

Following points should be kept in view while dealing with children:

1. Child's individuality should be respected.
2. It should be kept in mind that each child is unique.
3. Co-curricular activities should be organised.
4. Group competitions may be arranged.
5. Games should be regularly organised.
6. Creative talent should be developed.

Adolescence (from 13 to 18 years)

Chief Characteristics: (i) There is an outburst of various aspects of development; (ii) It is the period of opposite pattern; (iii) It is the period of preparation for living well in society; (iv) The period is marked by far-reaching sex changes.

Educational Implications: (i) Compulsory physical exercises and games; (ii) Monthly health check-up; (iii) Provision of good library; (iv) Organisation of clubs; (v) Guidance services; (vi) Rational approach by the teacher; (vii) Meeting fears of inadequacy; (viii) No discrimination; (ix) Excursions and educational tours; (x) Sex education.

(Discussed in detail separately)

4.7 SIGNIFICANCE OF THE KNOWLEDGE OF THE GROWTH AND DEVELOPMENT PROCESS TO THE TEACHERS

A knowledge of development patterns at each stage is essential for psychological, practical and scientific reasons. Proper acquaintance with the pattern of human development would enable the teacher to know to a considerable extent at what age what behavioural changes occur and when these patterns are usually replaced by more mature patterns. This is important as too much is expected from students and if they do not show such results, they develop a feeling of inadequacy. A knowledge of development pattern enables the teachers to adjust the teaching-learning process according to the needs and interests of the students. The teachers come to know when students need special guidance.

Deviation from normal behaviour becomes a cause of anxiety for the teachers.

4.8 DEVELOPMENTAL TASKS AT VARIOUS STAGES

Meaning of Developmental Tasks

Developmental tasks are those essential skills and appropriate behaviour patterns at various stages during the life span which the society expects its members to master.

R.H. Havighurst (1953) has defined a development task in these words: "A development task is a task which arises at or about a certain period in the life of the individual, successful achievement of which leads to his happiness and to success with later tasks, while failure leads to unhappiness and difficulty with later tasks". Development tasks are based on the aspiration and needs of the society. B.L. Neugarten (1969) has explained that "Every society is age-graded and every society has a system of social expectations regarding age-appropriate behaviour. The individual passes through a socially regulated cycle from birth to death as inexorably as he passes through the biological cycle; and there exists a socially prescribed time-table for the rendering of major life events. Although the norms vary somewhat from one socio-economic, ethnic or religious group to another, for any social group it can easily be demonstrated that norms and actual occurrences are closely related".

Characteristics of Developmental Tasks

(i) Every society or culture has certain norms.
(ii) Every society or culture expects its members to follow these norms.
(iii) These norms are in terms of certain essential skills.
(iv) Mastery over these skills leads to happiness and failure leads to unhappiness.
(v) Skills are related to age groups.
(vi) Norms vary somewhat from one socio-economic group to another.

Purposes of Developmental Tasks

According to Elizabeth B. Hurlock, developmental tasks serve the following three purposes.

First, they are guidelines to enable the individual to know what society expects from him at a given age.

Second, developmental tasks motivate the individual to do certain things what the social group expects him to do, during his life.

Third, developmental tasks serve to show the individual what lies ahead and what he will be expected to do when he reaches the next stage of development in the life span.

Hazards Related to Developmental Tasks. These are as under:

1. Inappropriate expectation—physical or psychological limitations of the individual.
2. Bypassing a developmental stage. Each stage must be lived through.
3. Lack of opportunity to learn the developmental task.
4. Lack of guidance.
5. Lack of motivation.
6. Poor health.
7. A low intellectual level.

Factors Promoting Developmental Tasks

1. Provision of opportunities to learn to develop the developmental tasks.
2. Adequate guidance in acquiring the developmental tasks.
3. Developing motivation.
4. Good health.
5. Appropriate level of intelligence.
6. Creativity.

Developmental Tasks at Various Stages

I. Birth to 6 years

1. Learning to walk.
2. Learning to take solid food.
3. Learning to talk.
4. Learning to control the elimination of body wastes.
5. Learning sex difference.
6. Achieving physiological stability.

7. Forming simple concepts of social and physical reality.
8. Learning to relate oneself emotionally to parents, siblings and other people.
9. Learning to distinguish right and wrong and developing a conscience.

II. 6 to 12 years

1. Learning physical skills, ordinary games.
2. Building wholesome attitudes towards oneself as a growing organism.
3. Learning to get along with age-mates.
4. Learning appropriate sex role, *i.e.*, masculine or feminine role.
5. Developing fundamental skills in reading, writing and calculating.
6. Developing concepts necessary for everyday living.
7. Developing conscience, morality and values.
8. Achieving personal independence.
9. Developing attitudes towards social groups and institutions.

III. Adolescence (12 to 20 years)

1. Accepting one's physique.
2. Accepting a masculine or feminine role.
3. Gaining emotional independence from parents and other adults.
4. Establishing new relations with age-mates of both sexes.
5. Achieving assurance of economic independence.
6. Selecting and preparing for a vocation.
7. Developing necessary concepts for civic competence.
8. Developing intellectual skills.
9. Developing socially acceptable behaviour.
10. Preparing for marriage and family life.
11. Developing harmonious moral and scientific values.

4.9 GUIDELINES FOR PARENTS AND TEACHERS RELATING TO DEVELOPMENTAL TASKS

For planning and implementing suitable programmes for the all-round development of children, following guidelines may be taken into consideration:

1. Each stage in the development of an individual has developmental tasks peculiar to it and these must be taken note of.
2. No two children are alike in all respects. Hence individual needs must be attended to.
3. Observation of children leads to better understanding on the part of parents and teachers.
4. Children need an environment which promotes initiative and trust.
5. When parents and teachers speak clearly, use appropriate words and adopt a proper style and manners, children are likely to do the same.
6. Consistency, firmness, love and patience on the part of parents and teachers will go a long way in the whole development of children.
7. Children learn through doing and playing. Various types of activities should be provided to them.

8. Children learn through concrete objects in the beginning.
9. Children need encouragement to develop at their own pace.
10. Children need a close, loving and sensitive relationships with the adults who are charged with the responsibility of looking after them.
11. The feeling of being wanted and loved in the children is vital to the inner development of the child.
12. Children need a sense of security which should be provided by parents and teachers.
13. Anger and violence are damaging to the inner development of the child.
14. Healthy relationships established in the earlier stages of life help to set the pattern of future development.
15. Each child needs attention and a neglected child in the home or in the class loses interest in work and play.
16. 'Doing' helps in the development of mental, physical and social skills.
17. Children are creative and they need assistance and guidance to develop their creativity.
18. Singing songs and learning rhymes, drawing pictures and reading stories help the child's mind to grow at the pre-primary, primary and middle stages.
19. For proper development, all children need adequate praise and recognition for their work.
20. Children are curious to learn and respond with interest to new things.
21. Children learn through repetition; of course excessive repetition tends to kill interest.

5

Human Physical Development Pattern

5.1 SIGNIFICANCE OF PHYSICAL DEVELOPMENT OF HUMANBEINGS

"Healthy mind in a healthy body", an old adage is true to the core.

Hall has very emphatically observed: "A ton of knowledge, bought at the expense of an ounce of health which is the most ancient and precious form of wealth and worth costs more than its value". Similar views have been expressed by Carlyle when he writes: "We manufacture clever devils by the thousand because health is not the object of party politics". Great seer Swami Vivekananda has also stressed the importance of well-built bodies when he remarks, "What India needs today is not the *Bhagwad Gita* but the football field". W.M. Ryburn remarks: "We need in Indian education a general philosophy of physical education; we need a conception of education in which physical education takes its rightful place and in which its vital importance is recognised".

The physical development of the child is very important for a number of reasons. Appropriate physical development makes valuable contribution to the all-round development of an individual. When a child is busy in some physical activity, he is emotionally as well as mentally involved in it. Physical development of the individual is important both for the individual and social development. It is also important for ethical, moral and spiritual development. A physically unhealthy person, other things being equal, is unable to perform his duties to himself, to the community and the God. He cannot offer his prayers effectively.

By not giving proper attention and care to the physical development of the child, we may be guilty of causing serious handicaps to the total development of the child, including his emotional, intellectual and social, even ethical and spiritual. A knowledge of the process of the physical development pattern of the child will enable the teacher to equip him for setting his programmes according to the needs of the children.

5.2 MEANING AND DIMENSIONS OF PHYSICAL DEVELOPMENT PATTERN

Physical development refers to a process which brings about bodily and physiological changes—internal as well as external—in an organism from the conception till his death. Generally these changes take place In the following dimensions:

(i) *Gross Physical Structure or Physique*: It involves changes in height, weight, body proportions and general physical appearance.
(ii) *Internal Organs*: It involves changes in the functioning of glands, nervous systems and other body systems—circulatory, respiratory, digestive, muscular, lymphatic and reproductive.

5.3 GENERAL PATTERN OF PHYSICAL DEVELOPMENT

George G. Thompson (1979) has described the physical development in childhood in these words: "Neither shoulder breadth nor pelvic breadth increases as rapidly as trunk length, but the pelvic broadens, more rapidly than the shoulders. The total configurational change is a longer-legged, longer-bodied and more rectilinear and flatter-bodied child".

G. Stanley hall has given the following description of children from 8 to 12 years of age in his book *Adolescence*: "The years from 8 to 12 years constitute the unique period of human life ... the brain has acquired nearly its adult size and weight, health is almost at its best, activity is greater and more varied than ever before or than it will ever be again and there is peculiar endurance, vitality and resistance to fatigue. The child develops a life of his own outside the home circle and its natural interests are never so independent of adult influence".

In the words of R.M. Liebbert, Rita Wicks Poulos and Gloria Strauss Marmor: "Viewed in its larger perspective, bodily growth occurs through approximately the first twenty years of life in humans. It is generally felt to be fruitful to divide this overall growth period into three major sub-divisions—infancy and early childhood (up to about the fifth year of life), middle and late childhood (up to about age twelve), and adolescence (up to about age twenty). Growth is more rapid and more likely to show spurts during both the infancy—early childhood period and the adolescent period than during middle childhood".

Although there are wide individual differences among children, yet physical growth and development seems to follow to some extent a general pattern. This general pattern of development and growth may be summarised as under.

1. *Changes in Height and Weight:* The Table 5.1 illustrates increase in height and weight at different ages.

On an average, at birth a baby is about 56 cm. in height and between 4 and 5 kg. in weight, boys being slightly taller and heavier. During the first two years, there is rapid increase in both height and weight. There is a steady and slower growth from the third year till the onset of puberty. By five years the height of the child, approximately increases by 80 per cent and he acquires almost 3½ times his birth weight. During the period of adolescence we again find a sudden increase in both height and weight. Girls reach puberty about a year or two earlier than boys do. Therefore, at the age of 12, they are found slightly taller and heavier than boys. But they are again surpassed by the boys at about the age of 14. By the end of adolescence, the young men are generally higher and heavier than the young women. Generally both men and women get their maximum height and weight up to the end of adolescence.

But there is much variation in weight as it is more susceptible to environmental influences. Therefore, it is no surprise to note the sudden increase or decrease in weight in later years after attaining maturity.

Weight of the brain increases rapidly in the early years of life. By the time the child completes the age of four his brain gains almost 80 per cent of its final weight, another 10 per cent being added by the time he completes his eight years. By the 20th year, the brain gains almost all its weight.

2. *Changes in Body Proportions*: There are changes not only in the size of the body of the child but also marked changes in the proportion of the different parts of the body. For instance, the head constitutes about one-fourth of the height of the body at birth. The size of the head is relatively much larger than the arms and legs. As the child grows older, the proportion of the head decreases. By the end of adolescence, head becomes one-eighth of the body. The other parts of the body, legs, arms, etc. also change in proportion.

Table 5.1: Mean Height and Weight of Male and Female Children (All-India)

Age Group	*Mean Height (cm.)*		*Mean Weight (kg.)*	
	Male	*Female*	*Male*	*Female*
3 months	56.2	55.0	4.5	4.2
4-6 months	62.7	60.9	6.7	5.6
7-9 months	64.9	64.4	6.9	6.2
10-12 months	69.5	66.7	7.4	6.6
1 year	73.9	72.5	8.4	7.8
2 years	81.6	80.1	10.1	9.6
3 years	88.8	87.2	11.8	11.2
4 years	96.0	94.5	13.5	12.9
5 years	102.1	101.4	14.8	14.5
6 years	108.5	107.4	16.3	16.0
7 years	113.9	112.8	18.0	17.6
8 years	119.3	118.2	19.7	19.4
9 years	123.7	122.9	21.5	21.3
10 years	128.4	128.4	23.5	23.6
11 years	133.4	133.6	25.9	26.4
12 years	138.3	139.2	28.5	29.8
13 years	144.6	143.9	32.1	33.3
14 years	150.1	147.5	35.7	36.8
15 years	155.5	149.6	39.6	36.8
16 years	159.5	151.0	43.2	41.1
17 years	161.4	151.5	45.7	42.4
18 years	163.1	151.7	47.4	42.4
19 years	163.5	151.7	48.1	42.4
20 years	164.1	151.7	49.2	43.5

Source: Growth and Physical Development of Children. All India—Indian Council of Medical Research, New Delhi, 1968.

3. *Bones*: Most of the bones at birth are soft. The child's bones contain relatively a great amount of water and smaller quantity of mineral matter than those of an adult. More blood flows through their bones than through the bones of adults. They are, therefore, more pliable.

4. *Teeth*: Teeth begin to appear in a systematic order after the age of six months. On an average, around seven months of age, the first two front teeth in the lower jaw erupt and are followed by four molars, one on both sides of the front teeth on both jaws. By the time the baby is 2 to 2½ years old, it will have twenty teeth. Girls show more advanced teeth growth than the boys, except in the case of wisdom teeth, where boys are usually ahead of the girls.

5. *Nervous System*: There is a marked growth of nervous system during the pre-natal period and the first four years after birth. Before birth, the development primarily consists of increase in the number and size of nerves. After the age of four years, the growth of the nervous system proceeds at a relatively slow rate.

6. *Muscular System*: Muscles at the time of birth are more delicate and less firmly attached to the bones than those of adult muscles. The movements of the muscles are random and uncoordinated. Gradually muscles get changed in shape, size and composition and become firmer and stronger.

7. *Circulatory and Respiratory System*: In early childhood, lungs as well as heart are very small but gradually they grow in volume and height. The veins and arteries do not follow the same growth pattern as that of the heart and lungs. They grow rapidly prior to adolescence but show little growth during adolescence.

8. *Digestive System*: The young child has a small tubular-shaped stomach as compared with the bag like shape stomach of the adult. A young child needs more feeding in the earlier years.

9. *Lymphatic System*: It is concerned with the elimination of waste and destruction of bacteria in the body. From birth onward this system shows the sign of rapid development until it reaches its maximum between the age of eleven and twelve years. After 12 years of age, it decreases rapidly.

10. *Reproductive System*: The development of sex organs is very slow during early childhood but picks up speed as the child advances towards adolescence.

5.4 CHARACTERISTICS OF PHYSICAL DEVELOPMENT PATTERN AND NEEDS OF CHILDREN

A. From 5 to 8 years

S.No.	*Physical Characteristics*	*Needs*
1.	Average increase in height of about 5 cms.	Adequate sleep for 10 to 12 hours.
2.	Girls mature faster than boys.	Frequent periods of rest and recreation.
3.	Legs lengthen rapidly.	Active play and large space for play.
4.	Nose and throat difficulties are frequent.	Guidance in eating and health protection.
5.	Tend to take more food than their stomach can hold.	Preventive measures against child-hood diseases like measles.
6.	Show resistance taking a bath.	Proper dress according to weather.
7.	Average gain in health.	Care of teeth, etc.
8.	Gradual improvement in speed, stea-diness of movement and accuracy.	Varied play activities.

B. From 9 to 12 years

S.No.	Physical Characteristics	Needs
1.	Children are extremely active.	Careful eye examination.
2.	Relatively free from disease.	Correction of postures.
3.	Relatively healthy and sturdy.	Frequent change of physical activity.
4.	Choosy about food but eat a great deal.	Independence in caring for physical needs.
5.	Girls increase steadily in physical skills.	Adequate nutrition.
6.	Girls usually have less stamina than boys.	Supervision of strenuous physical activities.
7.	Interested in competitive games which require skill.	do
8.	More easily fatigued after physical activity.	do

C. Physical Development at the Adolescent Stage (Discussed Separately)

5.5 GROWTH AND DEVELOPMENT RATE, GROWTH AND DEVELOPMENT CURVE: CHARACTERISTICS AND STAGES

Growth and development rate is rhythmic and regular. It comes in cycle of waves, "periods" or "phases" of growth. This growth rate is not haphazard and random. According to W.H. Krogman, "The child outgrows in obedience to certain biological laws".

According to studies, there are four distinct periods or phases or rates of growth and development. Two periods are characterised by slow growth and development and two by rapid growth and development.

Growth and Development Rate at Different Stages in Different Parts and Organs of the Body: From birth to two years growth rate is rapid. This is followed by a period of slow growth up to the time of puberty or sexual maturity which usually takes place between the eighth and eleven years. Onwards till fifteen or sixteen years, rate of growth is rapid and it is followed by a period of fairly abrupt tapering of the growth up to the time of maturity.

(i) The '*body size*' category which includes the skeleton, muscles and internal organs shows more rapid growth during the infancy—early childhood period, and the adolescent period than during middle childhood.

(ii) The '*lymphatic system*' (thymus, lymph nodes, and intestinal lymphoid mass) reaches an adult level by seven years of age and is even larger during pre-adolescence before it declines.

(iii) Similarly, the '*neural system*' (head, brain and spinal cord) is almost fully developed by the age of six. In contrast, the '*reproductive organs*' grow very slowly until adolescence at which point they undergo rapid growth.

Table 5.2: Rhythmetic sequence in the Physical Development Pattern

Age	1-2 years	2-11 years	12 to 16 years	17-18 years
Rate	Rapid	Slow	Rapid	Slow

The Physical Growth and Development Curve: For weight and height curve reflects a steady increase during childhood. The rate is rapid at first and it slows down.

Physical growth follows a cephalocaudal direction, i.e., the rate of growth is faster at the head in initial stages until this area is well developed. Growth rate then becomes more rapid towards the lower parts of the body. (see Fig. 5.1)

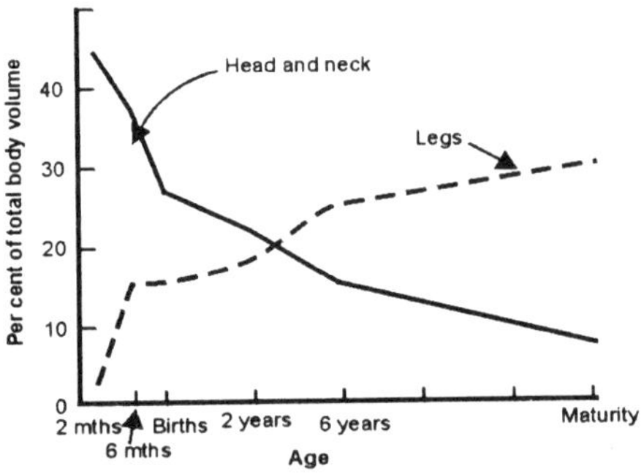

Fig. 5.1: Growth in Relative Volume of the Cephalo and Caudal Parts of the Human Body. (Data from Arey, L.B., "*Development Anatomy*", 1934)

The growth rate of heart beat declines rather sharply during the first two years of postnatal life and then continues a less precipitous decline with further development. (Fig. 5.2)

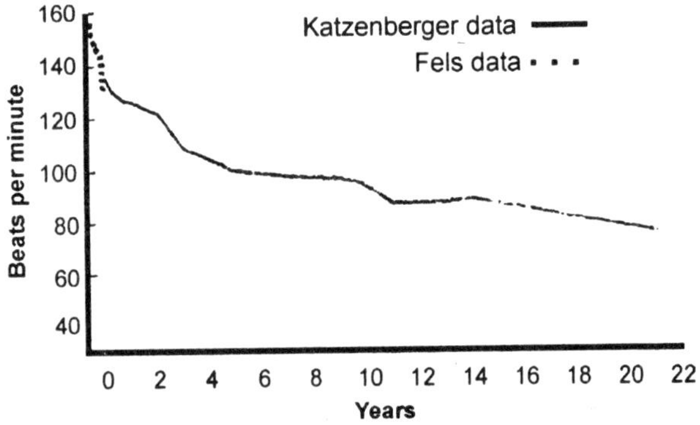

Fig. 5.2: Heart rate at Various Developmental Levels

The general development of motor behaviour is reflected in Fig. 5.3.

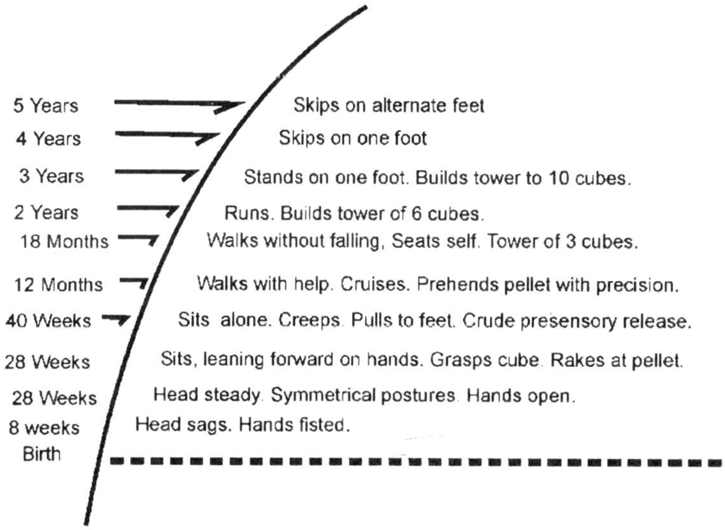

Fig. 5.3: Levels of Maturity

5.6 COMMON CAUSES OF DELAYED MOTOR AND PHYSICAL DEVELOPMENT

1. Poor physical conditions caused by illness, malnutrition, etc.
2. Lack of opportunities to develop manual skills.
3. Nagging, scolding and ridiculing of the child by parents and teachers when he does not succeed in an activity.

5.7 FACTORS AFFECTING THE PATTERN OF PHYSICAL GROWTH AND DEVELOPMENT

1. The traits and characteristics inherited at the time of conception.
2. The physical as well as mental health of the mother during pregnancy.
3. Nutrition received by the embryo within the womb of the mother.
4. Conditions and care at the time of delivery.
5. Normal or abnormal delivery.
6. Single birth or multiple births.
7. Care of the baby and its mother.
8. Presence or absence of physical defects.
9. Presence or absence of illness and disease.
10. Proper or improper medical care.
11. Nutrition received by the child after birth.
12. The living conditions—physical, social and cultural.
13. The opportunities for recreation, self-expression, play and exercise.
14. Adequate or inadequate rest and sleep.
15. Emotional and social adjustment of the child.

5.8 EDUCATIONAL IMPLICATIONS OF THE PHYSICAL DEVELOPMENT PATTERN OF THE CHILDREN FOR THE TEACHER

A knowledge of the process of physical development of the children would serve the teacher in the following ways:

1. The teacher comes to know about the specific needs of children. Consequently he can plan his programmes and help them in their emotional and social adjustments also.
2. Physical welfare of the children is an integral part of the development of the whole child. It is, therefore, very important for the teacher to know the details in this regard.
3. Physical growth and development exercise a great influence on the development of other aspects like intellectual and social development, etc.
4. Knowledge of the pattern of physical growth and development helps the teacher to arrange school programmes like co-curricular activities.

5.9 ORGANISATION OF PHYSICAL DEVELOPMENT PROGRAMME

A programme of physical growth and development is not confined to the playground but should pervade the classroom and in fact the entire school programme. Physical development in the classroom may take the following forms:

1. Direct instruction emphasising the necessity of having a good physique.
2. Suggestions regarding the maintenance of good health.
3. Emphasis on right postures.
4. Provision of good seating and lighting arrangements in the classroom.
5. Provision of nutritious diet.
6. Regular medical check-up and follow-up.
7. Free and guided play activities.
8. Activities involving handling of tools and materials.
9. Exercise and morning walk.
10. Yogic exercises.
11. Preparing charts and models.
12. Proper postures.
13. Games and sports.
14. Opportunities of skipping, hopping, jumping, throwing, grasping, etc.
15. Excursions.
16. Community cleanliness programmes.

5.10 SUMMARY: IMPORTANT CHARACTERISTICS OF PHYSICAL DEVELOPMENT PATTERN

Important General Characteristics of Child's Development

1. It is rapid during infancy (from birth to three years).
2. Period of pre-childhood is the period of fixation, *i.e.*, what is acquired in infancy is fixed or stabilised.
3. Period of early childhood (7 to 9 years) shows again a period of growth

and development but the speed is slow in comparison to infancy.

4. Later childhood (10 to 12 years) is again a period of fixation.
5. The first three years of adolescence are marked as the years of rapid growth and development. This is followed by a period of slow growth.
6. All the sensory and motor organs of the child's body are in the process of growth.
7. The urge for motor activities like walking, running, jumping, catching, throwing, etc., is at its peak.
8. Muscular development takes place rapidly.
9. In the middle and late childhood, coordination of hands and fingers becomes possible.
10. Children take delight in strenuous physical activities.
11. Children enjoy movement.
12. There is an urge among children to participate in activities which involve speaking, seeing and manipulating.

6

Human Social Development Pattern

6.1 MEANING OF HUMAN SOCIAL DEVELOPMENT PATTERN

Human social development pattern implies the qualities which bring about desirable changes in the social behaviour of the human beings. It is also referred to as socialisation of the human being. Usually we simply use the term social development to denote social human development pattern.

Social development pattern means the development of an individual in such a way that he becomes an efficient and useful member of the society to which he belongs. He conforms to the culture of the society of which he is a member. An individual, by nature, is a human being who cannot live in isolation. He is compelled by biological, psychological and social needs to live in a group or society. The process of the development of such qualities which bring desirable changes in the social behaviour of an individual is referred to as social development or socialisation of the child.

Important definitions of social development throwing light on its various dimensions are given below:

1. E.B. Hurlock notes: "Social development means the attaining of maturity in social setting".
2. Freeman and Showel write: "Social development is the process of learning to conform to group *standards*".
3. H.E. Garret is of the view that "Socialisation or social development is the process whereby the biological individual is converted into a human person".
4. Herbart Sorenson thinks that, "By social growth and development we mean increasing ability to get along well with oneself and others".
5. James Drever states: "Socialisation (social development) is a process by which the individual is adapted to his social environment (by attaining social conformity), and becomes a recognised, cooperating and efficient member of it".
6. L.D. Crow and A. Crow write: "Social development means acquisition or the ability to behave in accordance with social expectations".
7. Freeman and Showel: "Social development is the process by which a person acquires the necessary knowledge, skills and disposition that make him an acceptable member of his own group".

6.2 CHARACTERISTICS OF SOCIAL DEVELOPMENT PATTERN

1. Social development begins with the infant's first contact with other people.

2. Social development continues throughout life.
3. Social development is the net result of the child's constant interaction with his social environment.
4. Social development helps in learning and acquiring social qualities of character.
5. Social development enables the child to adjust himself to his social environment and to maintain social relationships.

6.3 SOCIAL DEVELOPMENT PATTERN OF THE CHILD AT DIFFERENT STAGES

A. Social Development Pattern or Behaviour of the Pre-School Child

The child at this stage is ready to expand his social contacts. By the age of two years, he can obey certain commands given to him. He calls attention of other persons to objects he feels interested in. He is more or less self-centred. The pre-school child is active. A pre-school child has usually one or two friends. He plays with them only for short intervals. Race, caste, colour or sex or social and economic status have no effect in the selection of friends at this stage. Nursery school experiences contribute in acquiring acceptable social habits.

B. Social Development Pattern or Behaviour of the Primary School Child (6 to 10 years)

By the time a child enters school, he wants to have many friends. At this stage he is not satisfied just by the company of his parents. He is interested in the play activities of his group, of the same age and sex. However, quarrels are also common among friends. Boys of this stage tend to be more aggressive. Girls more frequently engage in bickering. Bullying and teasing are more common. Children are interested in group activities and team work. Team games become more interesting than individual work. Social behaviour of the child is greatly influenced by the social environment in which he lives.

C. Social Development Pattern or Behaviour of the Child During the Middle School Stage (10 to 12 years)

1. The period is marked by a greater degree of social awareness.
2. There is a great expansion of child's social world.
3. A child tries to be independent of his parents and other elders.
4. A child becomes an active member of a 'peer group'.
5. There is a sort of segregation among boys and girls of the same age.
6. The child enters the peak of 'gang age'. There is increasing loyalty towards his own gang and conflict with other gangs. The gang life develops many good as well as bad social qualities in the child.

D. Social Development Pattern or Behaviour During Adolescence

(Discussed Separately)

Note: It is not possible to divide the social behaviour pattern at clear-cut stages or ages. Patterns overlap.

Social Development Pattern at Different Ages

Age/Ages	*Social Development Pattern*
First month	Cannot differentiate between human voices and other voices.
Second month	Begins to recognise the sounds of human being and to give smiles to others.
Third month	Recognises the mother and begins to feel unhappy on separation.
Fourth month	Shows selective attention to the human face and feels happy in company.
Fifth month	Reacts to smiling and scolding. Differentiates between friendly and angry voices.
Sixth month	Recognises familiar faces with a smile and shows definite expression of fear of strangers.
Eighth and ninth month	Attempts to imitate the speech, simple acts and gestures of others.
Tenth to twelfth month	Plays with his image and even kisses it as if it were another person.
At twelfth month	Can refrain from doing things in response to 'no-no' or some other form of request.
One year	Emotional aspects like fear, shyness are seen and social behaviour is linked with these.
1½ years—2 years	Likes to play with toys alone (Solitary social behaviour)
3 to 6 years	Likes to play with others (Social play behaviour), three to six friends. Friends are generally changed.
6 to 8 years	Plays with small groups.
8 to 10 years	Begins to identify the sex difference.
10 to 12 years	Begins to participate in competitive games. Membership of friends increases.
Adolescence period	Discussed separately.

6.4 FACTORS AFFECTING THE SOCIAL DEVELOPMENT OF THE CHILD

1. *Influence of Culture on Social Development*: A child's social behaviour is regulated by the culture of the society in which he lives. The behaviour patters of one generation, pass on from generation to generation. Our *Sanskaras* shape our outlook and finally personality. There are two ways in which the behaviour patterns of culture are transmitted to the next generation. (a) Directly and formally as in educational programmes at various stages of education, and (b) Informally through interactions between parents and their children which occur in the course of bringing up children. These interactions include the parent's expression of attitudes, beliefs, interests and values, etc. Some of the informal social development takes place through interactions with relatives, neighbours, peer groups and teachers and other groups of the society.

2. *The Family*: Among the various social groups, the family makes the first and the most significant influence on the social development of the child. It provides the hereditary transmission of basic potential for his development. It also provides environmental conditions and personal relationship. Parent-child relations have various dimensions of interaction. As such, they remain

basic for social development of the child. Parent-child relationships determine behavioural adjustment of the child in the family.

Religion: Like home, religion has long been regarded as a primary social institution. Earlier religion played a dominant role in the social development of the child.

3. *Peer Groups*: The child is introduced to the social world outside his family, through per groups. The peer groups satisfy various needs of the children like acceptance, achievement, affection, approval, belongingness, fame, recognition, expression of thought and opinion etc. According to A.T. Jershid (1947), peer association is a meaningful process through which the child changes with his age group into youth and adulthood.

4. *School*: The school life plays an important role in the social development of the child. Its curriculum, co-curricular activities and teacher's influence have a great bearing on the social development of the child.

5. *Community and Neighbourhood*: The environment prevailing in the community has a great influence on the social development of the child.

6. *Mass Media*: Agencies like cinema, newspapers, radio and television, etc., also play a vital role in bringing about social changes in children.

7. *Bodily Structure and Health*: A healthy child has more ability and strength to make himself adjusted in the challenging social setting. A child with poor health or any physical deformity or defect develops feelings of inferiority as well as insecurity in social settings.

8. *Intelligence*: The more intelligent a child is, the more chances of his social adjustment.

9. *Emotional Development*: Emotional development of the child bears a positive correlation with his social development. Emotional adjustability is one of the very important elements of social adjustment.

10. *Physical Health of the Individual*: A healthy child with normal physique is likely to develop more self-confidence than the unhealthy child with not normal physique.

6.5 HINDRANCES IN THE SOCIAL DEVELOPMENT OF THE CHILD

1. Social evils like untouchability and caste prejudices, etc.
2. Co-education according to conservative view.
3. Language barriers.
4. Miscellaneous factors like income, occupation and religion of the family.

6.6 ROLE OF THE SCHOOL IN THE SOCIAL DEVELOPMENT OF THE CHILD

The role of the school has considerably changed in the rapidly changing civilizations. The traditional role of imparting the basic skills of the three R's is now no longer considered to be adequate to meet the present challenge. The present day school has also to perform some of the functions of the family. It must develop certain desirable moral attitudes and good social habits among students. It is through co-curricular and extra-curricular activities that the task of socialisation can be achieved more successfully. In India today we find that the number of first generation learners in schools and colleges is swelling up. They come from varied backgrounds. Some of them come from deprived homes. It is only the sympathetic understanding and sincere desire of the teacher to act positively in an unprejudicial manner that can help in these situations.

Class in the Process of Social Development

Class provides innumerable opportunities to the children to move and mix with students belonging to different strata of society. This is the beginning of the socialisation of the child for his future life. Here children get many chances to mix without any distinction of caste, colour or creed. The children who are selfish or self-centred learn to adjust their behaviour in terms of class norms. The teachers are expected to be vigilant to ensure that the students do not think in terms of untouchability, caste distinctions and other prejudices.

6.7 TEACHER'S ROLE IN THE SOCIAL DEVELOPMENT OF THE CHILD

A teacher's role is very vital in the social development of the child. In recent years, the role of the teacher in functional terms has been gradually decreasing on account of the influence of the electronic and print media. At the pre-school stage and at the elementary stage, teacher's influence on the development of character and personality is of great significance. There is o doubt that, the role of the teachers in the social development of the child is still of great significance.

Following are the important suggestions for the social development of the child which the teacher's should always keep in mind:

1. The teachers should demonstrate democratic outlook.
2. Teachers and parents may encourage the children to mix with inter-caste rather than intra-caste and inter-regional rather intra-regional groups.
3. The teachers should respect the personality of children.
4. The mechanism of praise and blame, reward and punishment should be carefully used to socialise the children.
5. The teacher should not show any discrimination. He must ensure a safe and healthy social environment in which the children may imbibe desirable values of freedom, equality, integrity, honesty, patriotism, etc.
6. Community activities like camps, common meals, social service, etc., should be frequently organised.
7. There should be close cooperation between the teachers and parents on matters relating to proper socialisation of the children.
8. Adequate stress may be laid on group activities.
9. Exhibitions on "Know Our Country" may be organised from time to time.
10. Stories depicting self-sacrifice made by great men for the cause of general good may be told to children so that they are motivated to rise above petty gains and work for the betterment of the humanity.

11. With proper guidance and responsibilities, the students' council can build up a sense of shared responsibility among children.
12. Proper socialisation of children necessitates that the ideology of the common school system functions in letter and spirit in India.
13. Children may be taken from time to time to public places like museums, courts, places of historical importance, etc.
14. People engaged in different economic activities or vocations may be invited to school for giving a faithful and pragmatic description of what they do and how useful their work is to the nation. This will enable the children to acquaint themselves with those around them in the society. This will also develop vocational socialisation in children.
15. Work experience should be introduced in schools. This will enable the children to have first hand experiences of the activities pursued in farms and factories.
16. Children should be encouraged to participate in the social events like the celebration of the birthdays of great personalities.
17. The school or college programme should be full of numerous co-curricular and curricular activities in which children meet, cooperate and learn from each other.
18. Children should be told about the socially accepted institutions in their society.
19. The introduction of common school dress, common lunch, etc., in the schools and colleges will prevent children of poor and lower middle classes from facing humiliation due to the inflated ego of the children of the well-to-do families who take pleasure in showing off their wealth and status through costly clothes.

6.8 CONCLUDING OBSERVATIONS

The task of social development of the child is not an easy one. The educational thinkers point out very emphatically that appropriate conditions in the learning-teaching situation must be created and made available in the school so that it may become an effective instrument of social development. These conditions are: (i) A democratic social climate in the school; (ii) Effective interpersonal relationships; (iii) Motivated learning situations; (iv) Group methods of teaching; (v) Social discipline, (vi) School-community inter-relationships; (vii) Student participation and involvement in the school management; (viii) A rich programme of co-curricular activities; (ix) Equal treatment to children irrespective of caste or status etc. considerations; (x) Emphasis on egalitarian ideals and values.

7

Human Emotional Development Pattern

7.1 SIGNIFICANCE OF EMOTIONAL DEVELOPMENT PATTERN

Emotional development pattern plays an important role in the personal and social development of an individual. An individual with stable emotional pattern leads a happy, healthy and peaceful life. He is at ease with himself and his surroundings. On the other hand an individual who is emotionally disturbed becomes a problem for himself as well as for others. Continuous emotional disturbance affects the individual's growth and development. Therefore, the development of emotions is extremely important for the harmonious development of the personality of an individual. Emotions influence all the aspects of an individual's personality. Proper training and education will go a long way to enable the young people to control their emotions and obtain mental balance and stability. Emotions are the prime motive forces of thought and conduct and their control is very important. It has been rightly said, "To keep one's emotions under control and be able to conceal them is considered a mark of strong character".

7.2 MEANING OF EMOTIONS

With a view to understand the meaning of emotional development it is necessary to know the meaning of emotions as they are the prime movers of emotional development.

Etymology: The word emotion is derived from the Latin word '*Emovere*' which means to 'stir up', 'to agitate' or 'to excite'.

Kimbel Young notes: "Emotion is the all-round state of the organism marked by increased bodily activity and strong feelings directed to some subject".

According to Crow and Crow (1973), an emotion "is an affective experience that accompanies generalised inner adjustment and mental and psychological stirred up states in the individual, and that shows itself in his own behaviour. By making use of this explanation R.S. Woodworth (1945) has defined emotion in this way. "Emotion is a *moved or stirred up* state of feeling that is the way it appears to the individual himself. It is a disturbed muscular and glandular activity—that is the way it appears to an external observer".

William McDougall (1949) says: "An instinct is an inherited or innate psycho-physical disposition which determines its possessor to perceive and to pay attention to objects of a certain class, to experience an emotional excitement of a particular quality upon perceiving such an object, and to act in regard to it in a particular manner, or, at least, to experience an impulse to such an action". This statement gives us the nature of emotions as well. According to McDougall, an instinctive behaviour has three aspects:

(i) Cognitive or knowing or perceptual aspect.
(ii) Affection or feeling or emotional effect.
(iii) Cognitive or doing or striving or executive, active or behaviour aspect.

Let us take an example. A child sees a bull coming towards him. He experiences an instinctive fear and undergoes the above three processes. Firstly, he perceives the bull, secondly he experiences an emotion of fear and thirdly he tries to run away. It is, therefore, concluded that an emotion is an affective experience that one undergoes during an instinctive excitement.

McDougall discovered 14 basic instincts and pointed out that each and every emotion, whatever it may be, is the product of some instinctive behaviour.

The instincts in their alphabetical order with their associated emotions are listed as under:

Sl. No.	*Instinct*	*Emotion Accompanying an Instinct*
1.	Acquisition	Feeling of ownership
2.	Appeal	Distress
3.	Construction	Feeling of creativeness
4.	Curiosity	Wonder
5.	Flight or Escape	Fear
6.	Food seeking	Appetite
7.	Gregariousness	Feeling of loneliness
8.	Laughter	Amusement
9.	Parental	Tenderness, Love
10.	Pugnacity or Combat	Anger
11.	Repulsion	Disgust
12.	Sex mating	Lust
13.	Submission	Negative feeling

7.3 CHIEF CHARACTERISTICS OF EMOTIONS

1. The emotional experiences are associated with some instincts or biological drives.
2. Emotions, in general, are the product of perception.
3. The core of an emotion is feeling which is essentially linked with some sort of urge or impulsive act to do. There is only a difference of degree between feeling and emotion.
4. Every emotional experience involves several physical and psychological changes in the organism. Some of these changes like the bulge

of the eyes, the flush of the face, the flow of tears, the pulse rate, etc., are easily observable. There are also internal physiological changes like circulation of blood, the impact on the digestive system and the changes in the functioning of some glands, etc.

5. Emotions are frequent.
6. Emotions are expressed in relation to the concrete objects or situations.
7. Emotions are temporary.
8. Emotional expressions in early childhood are intense irrespective of the intensity of the stimulus.
9. Small children fail to hide their emotions and express them indirectly through different activities like crying, nail-biting, thumb-sucking and speech difficulties.
10. Emotions are prevalent in every living organism.
11. Emotions are present at all stages of development and can be aroused in young as well as in old.
12. Emotions differ from person to person.
13. Same emotion can be aroused by a number of different stimuli—objects or situations.
14. Emotions rise abruptly but die slowly.
15. Emotions are subject to displacement. The anger aroused on account of one stimuli gets transferred to other situations. The anger caused by the rebuking of the officer to his subordinate may be transferred in beating the children at home.
16. One emotion may give rise to a number of likewise emotions.

7.4 POSITIVE AND NEGATIVE EFFECTS OF EMOTIONS

Positive Effects of Emotions

1. Emotions provide energy to an individual to face a particular situation.
2. Emotions work as motivators of our behaviour.
3. Emotions influence our adjustment in the society.

Negative Effects of Emotions

1. Highly emotional conditions disturb the mental equilibrium of an individual.
2. Highly emotional conditions disturb the reasoning and thinking of an individual.

7.5 UNDERSTANDING EMOTIONS OF ANGER, FEAR, LOVE AND JEALOUSY

Emotion	*Signs*	*Contributory Factors*	*Values*	*Methods of Dealing*
1. Anger	(i) Extreme rage	1. Unnecessary interference in the child's daily affairs	1. Sometimes performance of brave tasks	1. Understanding the causes of anger
	(ii) Resentment			
	(iii) Irritation	2. Assignment of tasks beyond his capacity	2. Development of insight	2. Minimising provocations
	(iv) Feeling of fear, grief, jealousy	3. Imagined or real favouritism shown by parents and teachers	3. Change in the attitude of parents	3. Restraints on the part of elders
				4. Changing the programme
2. Fear	(i) Trembling	1. Sight of an abnormal object and animal	1. Safe-guards against harm	1. Narration of examples set by others
	(ii) Crying			
	(iii) Running away	2. Loud sound or flash of light etc.	2. Developing cautious approach	2. Encouraging children to face situations boldly
		3. Strict discipline	3. Hard work	3. Showing love
		4. Unfamiliar persons or things	4. Punctuality	4. Sympathetic approach
		5. Fear of darkness	5. Change in the outlook of elders	5. Appropriate discipline
		6. Fear of being alone		
		7. Fear of ghosts		
		8. Failure in examination or in some important task		

Emotion	*Signs*	*Contributory*	*Values*	*Methods of Dealing*
3. Love	1. Happiness	1. Caring	1. Mutual love	1. Feeling of acceptance. Giving suitable tasks
	2. Belonging	2. Protecting	2. Admiration	
	3. Feeling of creativeness	3. Feeling	3. Change in the attitude	
		4. Fondling	4. Enthusiasm	
		5. Smiling		
4. Jealousy	(i) Kicking	1. Feeling of getting less attention	May lead to hard work	1. Showing affection
	(ii) Biting			
	(iii) Pinching	2. Comparison with the performance of others.		2. Fair treatment
	(iv) Scratching			3. Avoiding undue competition
	(v) Bed-wetting			
	(vi) Thumb sucking			
	(vii) Refusal to eat			

7.6 EMOTIONAL BEHAVIOUR PATTERN AT DIFFERENT STAGES

A. Emotional Behaviour Pattern of the New Born Infant

According to J.B. Watson (1919), the new born infant, displays three primary 'emotions': '*love*' in response to strolling, '*fear*' in response to loud noises and loss of support and '*anger*' in response to physical restraint. Watson believed that all other emotional responses were built upon these primary emotions through the conditioning process.

B. Emotional Development Pattern During Infancy

In the words of Hurlock, "At birth and shortly afterwards, the first sign of emotional behaviour is general excitement to strong stimulation. There are no indications of clearly definite emotional patterns that can be recognised and identified as specific emotional states".

C. Common Emotional Pattern in Babyhood

	Emotion	*Stimuli that give rise*	*Response*
1.	Affection	Playing with the baby. Taking care of the baby. Providing toys.	Expresses by hugging and kissing
2.	Anger	(i) Interference with the movements of the baby (ii) Thwarting of some wish (iii) Not being able to do what he sets out to do	1. Screaming 2: Kicking 3. Waving the arms
3.	Curiosity	Anything new or unusual	Expression of curiosity through facial expression, *i.e.*, opening the mouth
4.	Fear	1. Loud noises 2. Strange persons 3. Objects 4. Dark rooms 5. Animals	1. Attempting to with-draw 2. Crying 3. Temporary holding of breath 4. Stopping the activity
5.	Joy	Physical well-being	(i) Smiling (ii) Laughing (iii) Moving arms and legs

D. Common Emotional Pattern During Early Childhood

	Emotion	*Stimuli that give rise to*	*Response*
1.	Anger	Conflict over play things,. Thwarting of wishes. Attack from another child.	Temper tantrums. Crying. Screaming. Stamping. Kicking. Jumping up and down. Striking
2.	Attention	Loves people, things, pets or objects that give him pleasure	Expresses his affection physically or verbally
3.	Curiosity	New things or persons	Sensorimotor exploration. Asking questions

(*Contd.*)

	Emotion	*Stimuli that give rise to*	*Response*
4.	Fear	Unpleasant experiences. Frightening scenes on T.V. etc.	Panic, running away, hiding, crying
5.	Grief	Loss of something that the child loves	Crying, losing interest in normal activities including eating
6.	Jealousy	Parental attitude towards different children, usually new sibling	Open expression, bed-wetting, pretending to be ill showing naughtiness
7.	Joy	Physical well-being. Acquiring new objects. Playing pranks with others.	Expression of smile. Clapping hands. Jumping. Hugging the person or object.

E. Emotional Pattern during Late Childhood

According to E.B. Hurlock, following are the chief characteristics of the emotional pattern:

1. Emotional expressions are pleasant ones.
2. The child laughs uproariously.
3. The child displays a release of pent-up animal spirits.
4. Emotional expressions are immature by adult standards.
5. Children who are popular tend to be less anxious and jealous than those who are less popular.
6. In order to win social approval, the child tries to curb the forms of expression that are socially unacceptable.
7. As he grows older, he begins to express his anger through moodiness and sulkiness.
8. Girls are likely to express more fears, worries and feelings of affection than boys.
9. Girls often dissolve expressions of anxiety and fears into tears.

Nevertheless all emotions are not of a pleasant sort. Several outbursts of temper occur.

F. Emotional Pattern During Adolescence (Discussed Separately)

7.7 CLASSIFICATION OF EMOTIONAL PATTERN

1. Aggressive *vs.* Submissive emotional pattern.
2. Normal *vs.* Abnormal emotional pattern.
3. Pleasant *vs.* Unpleasant emotional pattern.
4. Stable *vs.* Unstable emotional pattern.

7.8 COMPARISON BETWEEN THE EMOTIONAL PATTERN OF CHILDHOOD AND ADULTHOOD

	Childhood	*Adulthood*
1.	Too much intensity.	Comparatively less intensity.
2.	Short duration of emotions.	Long duration of emotions.
3.	Emotions transitory in nature.	Emotions marked by greater degree of stability.
4.	Easy detection of emotions.	Difficult to detect emotions.
5.	Intensity of feelings rules over reasoning.	Emotional response relatively guided by reason.

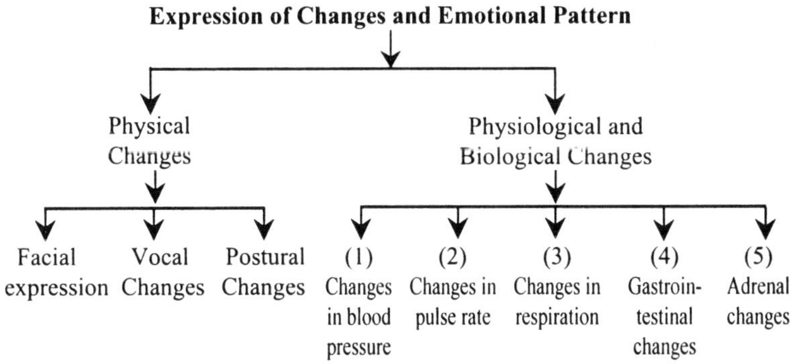

7.9 FACTORS AT HOME AND AT SCHOOL WHICH DISTURB THE EMOTIONAL DEVELOPMENT OF CHILDREN

Some of the important factors which disturb the emotions of children in school and at home are:

1. Lack of security.
2. Economic disparities.
3. Faulty methods of teaching.
4. Fearful atmosphere in school.
5. Emotionally unbalanced teacher.
6. Traditional concept of discipline.
7. Poor physical conditions in schools.
8. Disregard of individual differences.
9. Lack of co-curricular activities.
10. Lack of sex education.
11. Faulty examination system.
12. Faulty curriculum.

7.10 TRAINING, SUBLIMATING AND MODIFYING EMOTIONS

1. *Redirection*: An emotion is dynamic in nature and cannot be suppressed totally. It cannot be destroyed. It is just like a tumultuous stream which cannot be obstructed permanently without giving some outlet. But as we can harness a wild stream by building a dam against it and giving new channels to the powerful waters, quite in the same way, emotional waves can also be re-channelled for the advantage of the organism itself and for the whole society to which he belongs. Let us take the example of 'anger'. It is a furious emotion. It exists in its wild form in every organism. We have simply to tame and redirect it to broad and beneficial channels for the benefit of the person and the society.

2. *Sublimation*: Sublimating is also a sort of redirection with this difference only that in the former case the emotion does not lose its original form while in the latter case it is so much elevated that it changes its form. It assumes nobler and higher form. Lust is transformed into *love* for fine arts or social services or devotion to some deity. *Anger* turns to be *zeal and enthusiasm*. *Fear* takes the form of *anxiety for the betterment* of mankind.

3. *Catharsis*: Intensity of emotions is dangerous for health especially when they do not find expression. Even their expression in original form is very costly for the mind and the body. Therefore, catharsis of pent-up emotions is necessary for the well-being of the organism. Play and extra-curricular activities are very useful devices for this purpose.

4. *Inhibition*: Human life is very complex in the present civilisation. We need to control our emotions at every step. Redirection, sublimation and catharsis are not always possible and at every moment. Often we have to suppress our emotions for a short time or for a long time. It can be done with the help of strong will. But we should know that inhibition should not be permanent and we should give some outlet to the pent-up emotions in some form as soon as possible.

7.11 ROLE OF THE SCHOOL AND THE TEACHER IN THE EMOTIONAL DEVELOPMENT OF THE CHILD

School is expected to provide a purified, constructive and creative environment to children and teachers can play an important role in this. A teacher should not merely preach the significance of the emotional control, but he should also teach emotional control by personal example. The teacher should be patient and sympathetic towards the expression of the children's emotions. He should not be harsh, otherwise repression and inhibition would emerge and consequently conflicts would arise which may lead to neurotic and psychotic disorders in the children. He should rather sublimate the emotions of children by presenting suitable opportunities and situations for their healthy expression. Scientific methods of teaching and organisation of co-curricular activities would promote the emotional development of the child in the right direction. Undue reliance on codes of ethics, standards and ideals of society, etc. leads to emotional disturbances in children in the long run, particularly when they find their superior themselves transgressing them. "Example is better than precept" is a famous saying.

Important Ways for the Emotional Development of Children

1. *Providing Emotional Security*: When the child enters the school for the first time, he finds quite a new world for him over there. He was just like a prince in the domain of his home. His likes and dislikes had great significance. He felt himself secure physically as well as emotionally. He had a sense of belongingness and his feeling of self-assertion was also satisfied adequately. But everything is changed in the school. He has little significance and voice in the matters over there to start with. All the other children appear to him well-knit and well adjusted in their own groups while he stands aloof. Sometimes he is ridiculed by the fellow students. All these things make him very uneasy emotionally. If the teacher is also indifferent to him or he proves to be a bit harsh for him, he loses his emotional balance. The teacher should be very careful of this situation. He should try to make the shift from home to school very agreeable for the newcomers. He should see that the newcomer may not feel the change adversely. There may be a welcome committee comprising some pupils under the guidance of a teacher to help the newcomers in desirable adjustment.

2. *Equal Treatment Irrespective of Income*: Poverty is not a bad thing in itself but sometimes it happens to be the cause of emotional disturbance for some pupils in certain situations. At home the poor child was quite contended and happy in his limited world. But when poor children come across rich ones in the school, they find colossal differences between themselves and their rich classmates as regards their clothes, their modes of life, their meals and pocket allowances etc. Some of them may develop jealousy, worry and inferiority complex if they cannot make proper adjustment with hard realities. Sometimes the teachers aggravate the situation when they happen to be quite partial and do not treat the poor children at par with the rich ones. Heavy financial demands may also disturb the poor children emotionally as they are often unable to meet the same easily.

The school is responsible to the poor students as much as to the rich ones. Resources of poor students should be studied individually and effort should be made to meet their monetary needs in connection with their education. Simple living should be a guiding principle in all the educational institutions.

3. *Dynamic Methods of Teaching*: Faulty methods of teaching do not develop motivation in the children. They make lessons a drudgery. The children begin to hate the very process of education. There is always tension in their minds. Learning is no more a joyful activity for them.

The improvement in the methods of teaching can go a long way in bringing back emotional security for many children. Educational work can easily be turned into play and then it will be interesting, joyful and at the same time more instructive.

4. *Role of Love in Schools*: In most of the traditional schools teaching is based on fear. Children know that they will be caned if they are not successful in studies. They get heavy home task which is often impossible to complete without help and guidance which is not always available at home. They sleep at night with the 'dreams of canes'. They wake up in the morning with fear and constant worry. Under such circumstances emotional tranquillity is hardly possible.

There is a famous saying, "Love the child and the child will love you. Hate the child and he will hate you". Love should be the basis of all work.

5. *Balanced Emotional Behaviour of the Teacher*: Some teachers themselves need emotional stability. Emotionally unbalanced teachers prove contagious for the innocent children. They themselves become a prey to inferiority complex, persistent worries or over-excited emotions. They are generally irritable and provocative. For the balanced emotional development of children, teachers themselves should be emotionally developed.

6. *Due Regard to Individual Differences*: All children differ mentally, emotionally and physically. But we provide little individual attention to the children in schools. Some of them are backward in studies, while some of them are very superior. But they are dragged on the same lines. The backward lag behind still more. This leads to emotional disturbance.

7. *Creative and Democratic Concept of Discipline*: Traditional methods of discipline are faulty. Sometimes schools bnecome just like jails and some teachers like jailors. Discipline in such a situation is based on fear. It may

serve the purpose superficially but in reality the things are far from being satisfactory. There should be positive devices of discipline. Discipline should be creative and constructive. Children should be made responsible for handling their own affairs as far as it is possible.

8. *Provision of Co-curricular Activities*: All the children and especially adolescents need provision for the expression of their pent-up emotions and for redirection of their emotional behaviour. In the absence of such provision, emotional stability is not possible. Various co-curricular activities organised properly can solve this problem quite satisfactorily.

9. *Provision of Sex Education*: During adolescent period, lack of information about sex causes emotional disturbance. Teacher should provide necessary information about the sex matters and problems. There should be no shyness and this work should be done seriously.

10. *Continuous Evaluation*: The present system of examination is faulty. Chance factor counts much in this system. It does not measure the all round development of the child and causes disturbance. Evaluation should be made continuous and objective.

11. *Healthy Physical Conditions in the Schools*: Poor physical conditions in the school bring fatigue and boredom to the children. They are very soon fed up with the school and its activities. Lack of creational activities is also responsible for emotional disturbance. The school authorities should be careful in this respect also.

12. *Rich and Varied Curriculum*: The curriculum in schools should relate to the real life of children. Learning in schools should be related to the modern needs of children.

Summing up

Whenever, a slight deviation from normal emotional behaviour pattern in children is noticed, steps must be taken to find out the reasons and corrective measures adopted. It must be kept in view that a lot of patience is needed on the part of the teachers in this regard.

8

Human Cognitive Development Pattern

8.1 MEANING OF HUMAN COGNITIVE DEVELOPMENT PATTERN

With a view to understand the human cognitive development pattern, it is necessary to understand the meaning of the word 'cognitive'. There are three aspects of human behaviour—cognitive, psychomotor and affective. Cognitive relates to knowledge aspect or mental or intellectual development, psychomotor to physical and health development and affective to emotional as well as ideal development. A teacher to be effective must understand the significance of all the three aspects.

Cognitive development pattern implies the development of the mental abilities and capacities which help the learner to adjust his behaviour to the ever changing environmental conditions. According to J.S. Bruner (1964), "Intellectual development is the capacity to deal with several choices at the same time".

Cognitive development is not merely acquiring knowledge and adding to it. Knowledge must be accompanied by understanding and wisdom otherwise it is barren.

Cognitive development is inherent in the development of those basic skills which help us in getting to know the environment. The formulation of all awareness of the environment rests on the proper development of the five senses *i.e.*, touch, taste, smell, hearing and sight. While the senses are the 'gateways' to all experiences in the environment, the child learns from these experiences and develops an understanding of the world around him with the assistance of certain skills which are 'observation', 'memory', 'classification', 'sequential thinking', 'reasoning' and 'problem solving'. Thus all these elements help in the development of cognitive behaviour.

8.2 PROCESS OF COGNITIVE DEVELOPMENT PATTERN

The process of cognitive development implies the progressive changes in the mental process which go on from birth to death. Mental process is an activity on the part of the organism which is of a psychological nature or involved in the mind. There are mental tests to evaluate a specific ability or performance. Cognitive development includes various aspects, such as, development of concepts, perception, language, memory, reasoning, thinking, imagination and intelligence.

8.3 VARIOUS AREAS OR ASPECTS OF COGNITIVE OR MENTAL DEVELOPMENT PATTERN

1. *Intelligence and Mental Development*: The results of intelligence tests show that mental or intellectual growth is rapid in infancy, moderate in childhood and slow in youth.

2. *Sensation and Perception Pattern During Various Stages*: Both sensation and perception are considered important aspects of mental development. The elementary impressions are gathered by sense organs. Impression take the form of perception when they are interpreted and some definite meanings are attached to them.

Through experience, child's sensations become perceptions and he is able to give meaning to it. Child's sensory equipment becomes mature at the age of five. He shows great interest in seeing, hearing, touching, smelling and tasting. However, child's sensations do not automatically assume meaning. During his early childhood, the child is more likely to misrepresent things and objects because of lack of experience. For example, when viewed from a distance, a train may appear to a child as a toy train. But gradually child's perceptions become more and more accurate through right kinds of experiences. By the time a child enters the school, he has gained enough experience. Yet he needs assistance and guidance to improve his ability to perceive by having first hand experiences and observations of objects, persons and situations around him. Gradually he develops a proper perception of space, time, form, movement and distance.

Perception patterns become more organised and refined when an individual passes through the years to his adolescence. Now they tend to become more definite, detailed and rich. At this stage they need not be associated necessarily with objects. They are beginning to be influenced by his beliefs, ideals, opinions, etc.

3. *Concept Formation*: Another important aspect of the child's mental development is the formation of concept. A concept is the generalised meaning that is attached to an object or idea. It is the result of one's perceptual experiences. It involves both discrimination and generalisation. Discrimination begins sometimes after the child tries to generalise his perceptual experiences and he begins to acquire concepts. Experience is an important factor in concept formulation. In the early childhood, a child tries to develop various concepts from the concrete experiences in the form of actual objects.

Normally, concept formation proceeds from concrete to abstract, from vague to clear and from inexact to exact, depending on the type of experiences a child receives. The child has a very poor concept of time. As stated by Crow and Crow, "Time as such means little to the young child. He cannot distinguish among 'to-day', 'tomorrow', and 'next week' except as they represent words rather than actual duration of time".

In later years, various experiences provided by reading, lecturing and movies, etc., help in concept formation.

Generally, concepts may be broadened, and developed. They may even take a new shape. Wrong concepts can be altogether abandoned.

Gradually as a result of learning and maturation, child's concepts become clear, definite and specific.

4. *Development of Language*: The development of language contributes to the mental growth and development of the child. Important aspects of language development are speech, vocabulary and length of responses, etc.

5. *Development of Memory*: Memory is also an important element of mental development. There is little memory at birth but it gradually increases with maturation and experience. This has been explained by Hurlock and Schwartz in these words: "Memory of an impressionistic kind appears in the first half of the year and instances of the true remembrance appear by the end of first year. During the first year memory is only aroused by sensory stimuli. With the learning of speech the child is able to remember ideationally by the end of the second year. During the first and second years the memory is stronger for persons and objects than for situation. In pre-childhood from 3 to 6 years, situations become significant factors in the child memory. By 3 years the child can recount the story heard a few days ago and he can also give information about past experiences".

A child has a good memory in the earlier stages but this memory is generally a rote memory. His memorisation is without reasoning. He seldom uses logic and insight in memorisation. A child can cram and reproduce the matter easily. The memory tends to function more logically during later childhood and adolescence. A selection process of remembering and forgetting begins to operate. After that memory tends to decrease.

Memory depends upon person to person. It is generally affected by health and situation of the child. The stimuli which are associated with a kind of memory significantly influence, its remembrances or forgetting.

6. *Creativity*: It may be stressed that creativity is the most single ability which is at the root of human progress. Like many other activities, it can be developed at a young age.

In a general sense, creativity is the ability to think in novel ways which result in some new and original solution.

7. *Problem Solving*: All thinking and reasoning involve meeting difficulties, facing complex situations and finding out solutions. An individual is beset with all these since childhood. Thinking and reasoning powers are used in problem solving and these begin to grow as early as two and a half or three years of age. Gradually the ability to reason grows.

8.3 FACTORS AFFECTING COGNITIVE DEVELOPMENT PATTERN

1. *Heredity*: Cognitive development of an individual is greatly affected by the interaction between inherited intelligence and the individual's experience.

2. *Physical Growth*: There is a strong relation between physical growth and cognitive development. A healthy person is likely to have a better intelligence than a person who has a poor physique.

3. *Physical Environment*: Physical environment like fresh air, sufficient light and ample space has a great bearing on cognitive development.

4. *Family Environment*: The kind of discussions held in the family, type of reading material like books and magazines read by the family affect the cognitive development.

5. *Socio-economic Status of the Family*: Parents of high socio-economic group have better access to send their children to good schools.

6. *School Environment*: The methods of teaching, availability of good reading material in the library, attitudes of teachers and school discipline, etc. affect cognitive development.

It is concluded that cognitive development is the result of a large number of factors. It is not an automatic process. It is a gradual and painstaking process.

8.4 COGNITIVE DEVELOPMENT CURVE

Learning Curve: It is observed that children are able to learn more difficult things as they grow older (see Fig. 8.1).

Steepness of the cognitive ability curve during middle childhood and adolescence is illustrated in Figures 8.2 and 8.3.

Cognitive Development is indicated by growth in vocabulary (see Fig. 8.4).

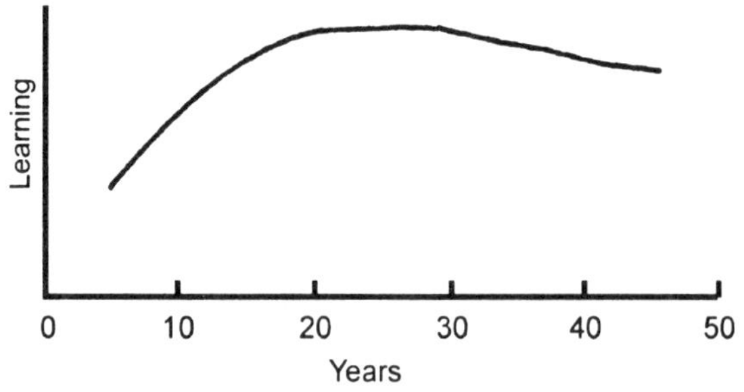

Fig. 8.1: Cognitive Growth Curve (Learning Growth Curve)

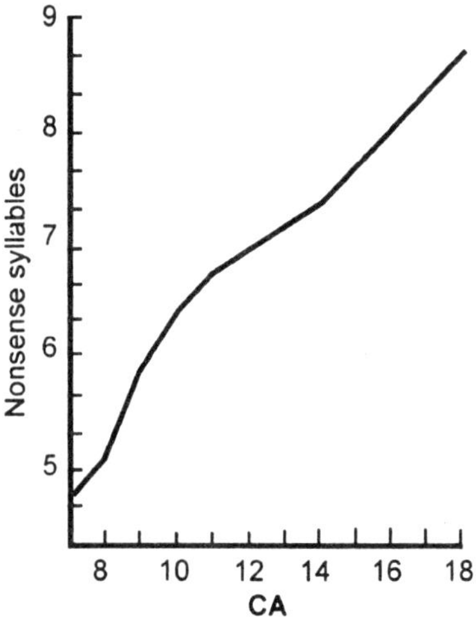

Fig. 8.2: Learning Ability Curve During Middle Childhood

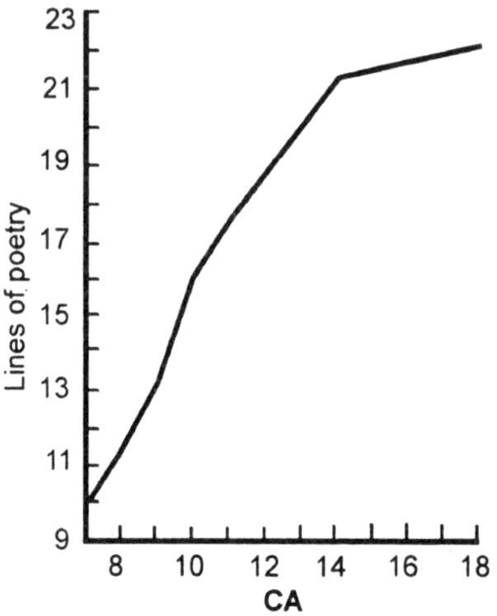

Fig. 8.3: Learning Ability Curve During Adolescence

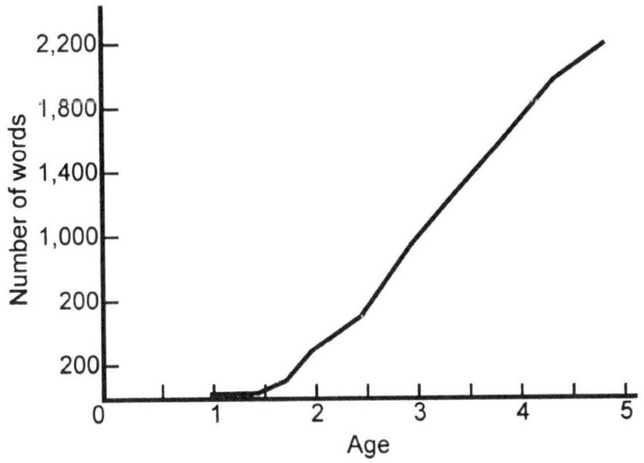

Fig. 8.4: Vocabulary Development Curve During Early Childhood

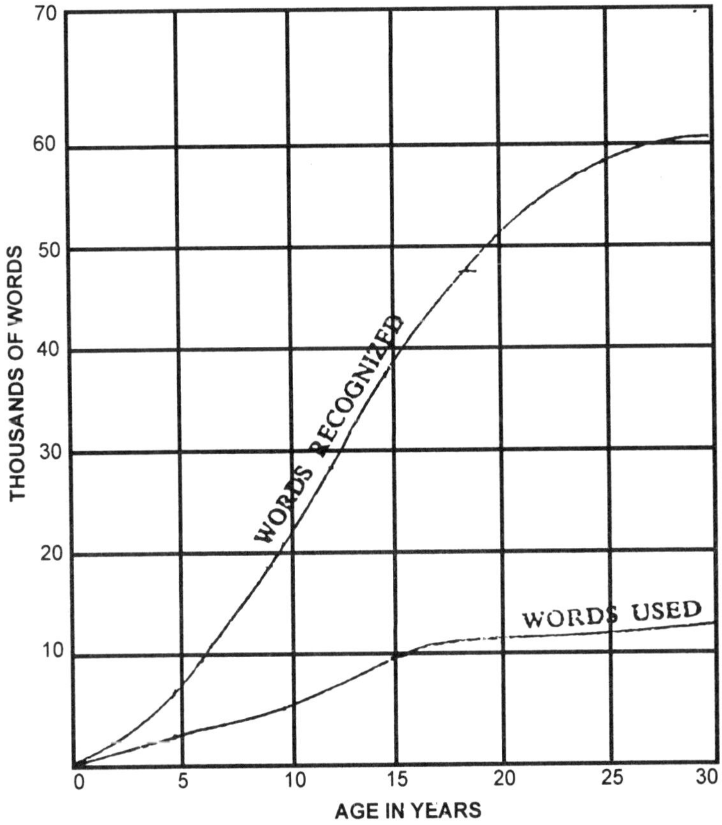

Fig. 8.5: Cognitive Development

8.5 JEAN PIAGET'S THEORY OF COGNITIVE DEVELOPMENT PATTERN (MENTAL OR INTELLECTUAL DEVELOPMENT)

Brief Life Sketch of Jean Piaget (1896-1980)

Piaget is regarded as one of the pioneers in psychological investigation of children although he neither undertook formal study nor passed any examination in psychology. He was a biologist by training. At an early age of 22, he obtained his Doctorate Degree in Zoology on Mollusks of Valias. He worked on child development for more than 50 years and produced enormous literature on Development Psychology. He read Philosophy, Psychology and Sociology etc. He pursued clinical research at the Alfred Binnet Laboratory at Paris. By observing, dissecting and experimenting with children, he developed his educational theory regarding cognitive development or learning by children. His work as a Professor of Child Psychology at the University of Geneva (Switzerland) made him famous throughout the world.

Piaget began his study of child development with the observation of his own three children. From this beginning, his investigations were gradually extended to other children. These investigations resulted in the publication of a large number of papers and books which are often quoted by eminent psychologist and other thinkers on education.

Cognitive Development Pattern at Various Stages

The most detailed description of the development of cognition has been provided by Jean Piaget. Piaget divides cognitive process development into 4 stages or 4 major periods:

(i) Sensorimotor,
(ii) Pre-operational,
(iii) Concrete Operational, and
(iv) Formal Operational.

Piaget asserts that all children progress through all these stages in a fixed order. According to his theory, human intellect is constructed over time as the individual experiences progressively more complex interactions with the environment.

Two Processes: In Piaget's system, two processes—*Organisation* and *Adaptation*—actively operate during each of the four stages.

Organisation is the process by which different elements within a system maintain communication, e.g., we have a tendency to organise basic sensory information (such as, images and other experiences) in order to form more complex ideas and thought.

Adaptation consists of complementary processes of *assimilation* and *accommodation*. These two processes are the basis for Cognitive Growth.

Assimilation: 'Assimilation' implies incorporation of something from the environment. New ideas, concepts and stimuli are taken in and incorporated into one's 'existing set of schemes'. A scheme is the organised pattern of behaviour which the child develops when he is engaged in any activity. For example, when a child is engaged in sucking, there is a certain pattern of movements of the cheeks, lips and hands. When a child is confronted with a new object, he will try to understand the new object by applying his old scheme to it. He grasps it and adapts himself to a new object by assimilating it. His old scheme does not change in the process.

Accommodation: 'Accommodation' involves modification or change of some elements of an old scheme or learning a new scheme which is more appropriate for the new object. A baby who has already got a scheme of sucking mother's breast accommodates to the object placed in the mouth—finger, nipple, pencil, a toy—depending on its shape, form and the size. The baby develops a new scheme or a modified scheme. This is called 'accommodation'.

Thus a baby assimilates when he understands and perceives the new in the light of his old perceptions. A baby forms a new scheme when he modifies or changes his old perception to suit the new. This implies adjusting or accommodating. In this way a baby forms new structures or new schemes and consequently develops cognivity.

A. Cognitive Development at the Sensorimotor Stage (Birth to Two Years)

There are six steps at this stage.

Step I: During the first month of life, the babies are unaware of themselves and of the object around them, e.g., they do not realise that the bottle they suck and the bottle they grasp are one and the same thing. The infant has a lack of what Piaget calls *object permanence.*

Step II: During first four months, babies motor activities become more coordinated. They begin to look at the thing which is being grasped.

Step III: Between 4 to 8 months, the infants attempt to control and manipulate the objects which arc often conical. They may hear an interesting noise but since they do not know what caused it, they try to make the noise recur by repeating whatever they were doing when they heard the noise. The baby at this stage also realises that objects exist when they are out of sight.

Step IV: During 8 to 12 months, thinking gives way to more instrumental activity. The child has achieved object permanence. He has developed some internal image of the object to help him recall it and its location—he displays sense of space and time—but the child is limited intellectually.

Step V: 12 to 14 months: The child is able to locate the hidden toys. Piaget sees much of the cognitive growth as the formulation of increasingly complex hypotheses in the light of the experiences.

Step VI: 18 to 24 months: During this period the child can infer what the moving hand holds. This last stage is important because it represents the beginning of the child's ability to represent mentally objects that are no longer physically present. In essence, it is the start of abstract thought.

B. Cognitive Development Patterns at the Pre-Operational Stage (2-7 Years)

1. The major advance made during this period is the ability to represent the external world mentally by means of arbitrary symbols that stand for objects.
2. This is the period in which language develops and begins to reflect the child's cognitive abilities and limitations.

3. The pre-operational period is transitional period.
4. The perspective of the child on the world is expanding rapidly, but the child is still confused in the use of physical concepts and in evaluation of cause and effect.
5. During this phase, the child makes appropriate generalisations and attributes his feelings to inanimate objects—assuming, for example, that clouds 'cry' to make rain.
6. Alternate perspectives are not imaged by the child. This is also known as stage of proportional thought.
7. The child cannot do abstract thinking.
8. The child does not think of operations. He is thus a static thinker.
9. The child's thinking is for a very short duration.

C. Cognitive Development Pattern at the Concrete Operational Stage (7-11 Years)

This period (Concrete operational stage) is characterised by the emergence of operations, such as, conservation. *Conservation* is Piaget's term for the idea that a property or attribute of an object remains the same despite some transformation that changes the appearance of the object. Piaget found that when a child at pre-operational stage is shown two identical balls of clay and then sees one rolled into a saucer he may claim that the saucer contains less clay because it is thinner than the ball. The child is taking only one aspect (shape) into account. The child does not know that this saucer has taken shape from the same ball.

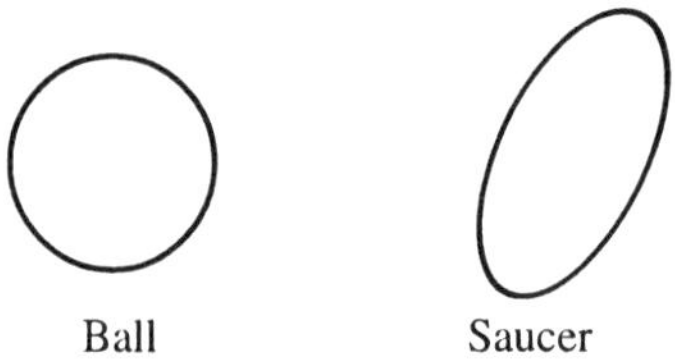

At about age 7, the child grasps the solution to conservation problems by developing three concepts that characterise concrete operations. The first is *compensation*—sausage is thinner but that change is balanced by its increase in length. The second is *reversibility*—if you role sausage back, you get the same ball you started with. The third is *identity*—nothing has been added to or subtracted from the clay, so the sausage and the ball contain same amount of clay.

Children at the level of concrete operations are able to consider two aspects of a problem simultaneously. In their social interpretations, they consider not only what they are saying but also listen to others.

The child performs operations: combining, separating, multiplying, repeating, dividing and substituting etc.

He begins to analyse. He is aware of variables. He classifies.

D. Cognitive Development at Formal Operations Stage (11-15 Years or Adulthood)

Here the youth begins and the nature of thought undergoes a change. The complex abstract and mature logic of adult begins to manifest itself during adolescence with the systematic analysis, exploration and solution of problems.

During this period, thinking is purely abstract and hypothetical. Piaget has been most concerned with the capacity to reason with respect to problems, concepts of geometry, language, space, time, number, order etc.

During the teenage years young people realise that thoughts are private and that no one else knows what they are thinking. They value friendship and sincerity and spend much time trying to discern real motives. The adult is more sensitive to the discrepancy between reality and ideals. Teenager has knowledge of the rules and his knowledge is different from that of small children.

Lastly, during this period (Formal operations), the crystallisation of personality development takes place. Forming of social and ideational position is closely linked with the acquisition of moral values.

At this stage, the individual has reached his intellectual maturity.

Problems Related to Cognitive Development

1. Poor environmental stimulation.
2. Poor hereditary environment.
3. Lack of proper attention, assimilation etc. on the part of the learners.
4. Defective teaching-learning material.
5. Low level of learner's intelligence.

8.5 EDUCATIONAL IMPLICATIONS OF PIAGET'S THEORY OF COGNITIVE DEVELOPMENT AND THE ROLE OF THE SCHOOL AND TEACHER

1. The child is learning *by himself*, the teacher occupies a secondary position. The child *discovers* things actively. Infants explore the world. Knowledge should not be imposed.

2. It is the duty of the school, teachers and parents to provide materials to children to sharpen their interests. Let the child explore and solve the problems. The classroom in early grades might be arranged in a series of counters stocked with intriguing materials to arouse children's curiosity. Children should be allowed to manipulate things and see results.

3. Instruction should be geared to the *level* of the child. As the level of the child changes at each stage, the level of instruction or exploratory activities should also change.

4. The knowledge of cognitive stages of growth of a child does help the teacher in more than one way. The teacher should be sensitive to understand the child's actions and be guided by his spontaneous interests.

5. Social interactions have a great educational value for Piaget. Positive social actions, therefore, should be encouraged.

6. Cognitive behaviour skills of the teacher have the following dimensions.

(a) *Knowledge*: Imparting information.

(b) *Comprehension*: Making the content clear.
(c) *Application*: Enabling the learners understand the use of theoretical statements in real situations.
(d) *Analysis*: Enabling the students to breakdown material into its constituent parts for comparison etc.
(e) *Synthesis*: Enabling the students to combine elements in components to form new structured wholes.
(f) *Evaluation*: Enabling the learners to make judgements (quantitative and qualitative) about the extent to which material satisfies criteria.

Following activities should prove useful in developing proper cognitive development pattern:

(i) Story making, telling, writing and listening.
(ii) Picture competition.
(iii) Essay writing involving imagination.
(iv) Assembling of parts of some dismantled object.
(v) Modelling.
(vi) Quiz questions.
(vii) Debates and elocution contests.
(viii) Problem-solving opportunities.

9

Characteristics, Needs and Problems of Adolescents

9.1 MEANING AND DEFINITION OF ADOLESCENCE

The term adolescence is derived from a Latin word '*adolescence*' meaning 'to grow', 'to mature'. Now this term primarily implies to emerge or to 'achieve identity'. It is very difficult to define exactly the period of life which constitutes adolescence. No sharp chronological boundaries may be fixed to this period. Generally speaking, it covers a period of seven or eight years, normally from 12 to 18 or 20 with large variations in many cases. Some children may manifest traits of its advent as early as the 10th year while others may manifest it till the fifteenth or sixteenth year. Twelve or thirteen may be considered as the normal period for boys in India and even for girls when adolescence begins.

Adolescence is best defined in relation to puberty. This is the period which begins with puberty and ends with the general cessation of physical growth; it emerges from the later childhood stage and merges into adulthood.

Following are the important definitions of adolescence:

1. According to G.R. Medinnus and R.C. Johnson, "Adolescence begins when signs of sexual maturity begin to occur in both physical and social development and ends when the individual has assumed adult roles and is concerned in most ways as an adult by his reference group".
2. A.T. Jersild observes, "Adolescence is that span of years during which boys and girls move from childhood to adulthood mentally, emotionally, socially and physically".
3. According to Dorthy Rogers, adolescence is "a process rather than a period, a process of achieving the attitudes and beliefs needed for effective participation in society".
4. The Hadow Report in England has described this stage as, "There is a tide which begins to rise in the veins of youth at the age of eleven or twelve. It is called by the name of adolescence. If the tide can be taken as flood, and a new voyage began in the stream and along the flow of its current, we think it will move on to fortune".
5. WHO defines adolescence both in terms of age (spanning the ages between 10 and 19 years) and in terms of a phase of life marked by special attributes. These attributes include:
   - Rapid physical growth and development
   - Physical, social and psychological maturity, but not all at the same time

- Sexual maturity and the onset of sexual activity
- Experimentation
- Development of adult mental processes and adult identity
- Transition from total socio-economic dependence to relative independence

To distinguish adolescents from other similar (and sometimes overlapping) age groupings, which however differ in these special characteristics, WHO has also defined youth and young people.

- Youth—persons between 15 and 24 years
- Young people—persons between 10 and 24 years.

9.2 GENERAL CHARACTERISTICS OF THE PERIOD OF ADOLESCENCE

1. *Combination of Opposites.* The adolescent is a combination of opposites. Sometimes he is an altruist and sometimes a miser. On the one hand, he behaves like a child in many ways and on the other hand he likes to be treated as an adult. He wants to have the privileges of adulthood but does not want to undertake its obligations and responsibilities.
2. *Know-it-All Attitude.* The adolescent lacks experience though he may exhibit a 'know-it-all' attitude.
3. *Feeling of More Grown-Up.* He regards himself as more suited than the adults and grown-ups to frame rules, laws, codes and morals which will be just and true.
4. *Intensely Emotional.* He is intensely emotional. He fluctuates between two extremes. He may be active and happy at one time and moody and dull at another.
5. *Self-Seeker.* He is seeking his own place in the life around him.
6. *Self-Assertive.* There is a strong tendency of self-assertion which is prominent owing to the new orientation which sets in life.
7. *Revolting Tendency.* The adolescent wants to free himself from bondage. There is a tendency to revolt against authority.
8. *Maximum Growth of Intelligence.* The growth of intelligence reaches its maximum during this period.
9. *Intensively Passionate.* The adolescent is extremely passionate for expressing his own opinions and appreciation.
10. *Group Work.* A group of adolescents set to practical work with great zeal and works patiently.
11. *Relative Influence of Teachers.* He responds more readily to the influence of the teacher than of the parents.
12. *Hero-Worship.* There is unlimited admiration for some adult whom he considers to be outstanding. An adolescent is essentially a hero-worshipper.
13. *Physical Attractiveness.* There is lot of interest in and need on physical attractions and good grooming.
14. *Sex Attraction.* Girls are more interested in boys than boys are in girls; of course both are interested in the opposite sex.
15. *Homosexuality.* In extreme cases, homosexuality (associated with the same sex) develops.

16. *Day-Dreams*. An adolescent exhibits exuberant imagination. This period is characterised as a period of day-dreams.
17. *Gangs/Groups*. Adolescents are keen to form small groups or gangs.

The views of William H. Burton and E.A. Peel deserve special attention regarding characteristics of adolescents.

According to Burton, "The adolescent is awkward, graceful, respectful, selfish, altruistic, narrow-minded, sympathetic, cruel individual".

In the words of Peel, "He (the adolescent) thus appears excessively aggressive and occasionally shy, excessively affectionate and then quite suddenly detached and cool".

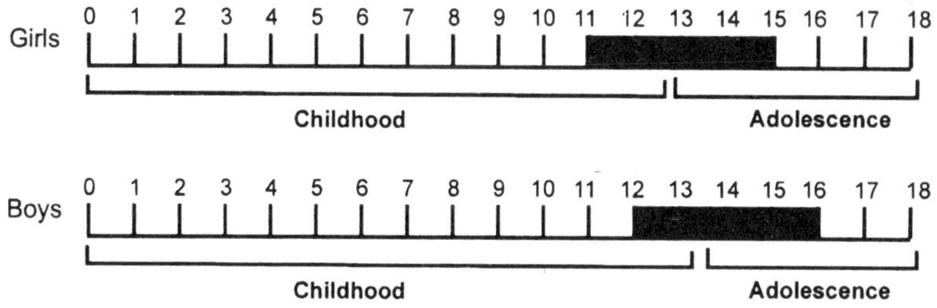

Fig. 9.1: Puberty Overlaps the End of Childhood and the Beginning of Adolescence

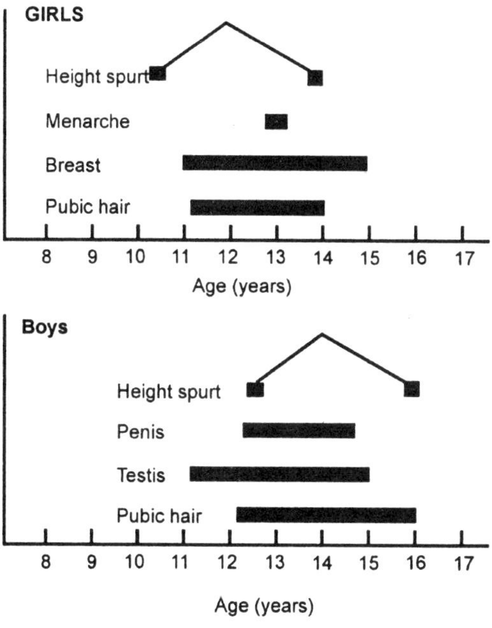

Fig. 9.2: Pattern of Development of Secondary Sex Characteristics in Girls and Boys

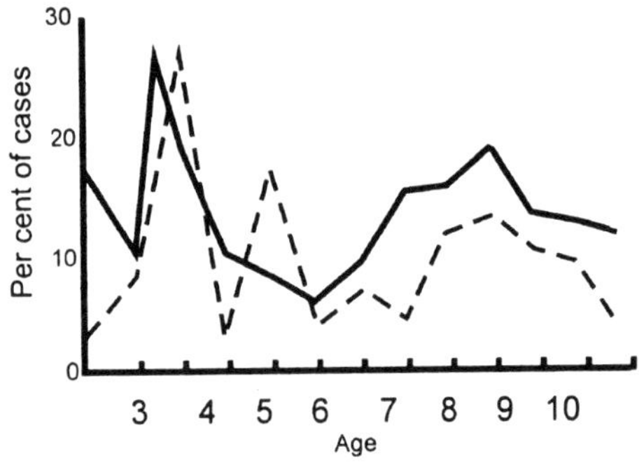

Fig. 9.3: Irritability Tends to Increase Early in Puberty and then to Decline

9.3 SPECIFIC NEEDS OF ADOLESCENCE WITH SPECIAL REFERENCE TO INDIAN ADOLESCENTS

Although in many respects, several needs of adolescent stage are similar to the needs of the other stages but they are quite different in the matter of intensity and forcefulness. These needs are interrelated. The following chart illustrates the specific needs of the adolescence.

Significant Specific Needs of the Adolescence

(1)
Physical Needs

1. Need for enough nutrition for physical development.
2. Need for oulets for the utilisation of abundant energy.
3. Need for acquaintance with body development aspects.
4. Need for sex.
5. Need for security.
6. Need for adventurers life.

(2)
Emotional and Psychological Needs

1. Need for satisfaction of heightened emotions.
2. Need for recognition of self identification.
3. Need for the satisfaction of arousal of sexual emotions.
4. Need for development of confidence.

(5)
Social Needs

1. Need for acceptance in the society.
2. Need for suitable peers.
3. Need for adjustment in the group and society.
4. Need for equal treatment.

(3)
Intellectual Needs

1. Need for the satisfaction of heightened curiosity.
2. Need for independent thinking.

(4)
Moral Needs

1. Need for search for values.
2. Need for equality.
3. Need for sound

(6)
Vocational Needs

1. Need for practical experience.
2. Need for appropriate vocational guidance.

9.4 PHYSICAL NEEDS OF THE ADOLESCENTS AND THEIR SATISFACTION

Hall has very emphatically observed, "A ton of knowledge, bought at the expense of an ounce of health which is the most ancient and precious form of wealth and worth costs more than its value". Similar views have been expressed by Carlyle when he writes, "We manufacture clever devils by the thousand because health is not the object of party politics". Great seer Swami Vivekananda has also stressed the importance of well-built bodies when he remarks, "What India needs today is not the *Bhagwad Gita* but the football field". Our schools must give due importance to this aspect of education. W.M. Ryburn remarked: "We need in Indian Education—a general philosophy of physical education—we need a conception of education in which physical education takes its rightful place and in which its vital importance is recognised".

A properly directed physical development programme should result in health, happiness, efficiency and character.

Physical Development at the Adolescent Stage

At the adolescent stage, marked changes take place in the following domains:

(i) Height and weight.
(ii) Bodily proportions.
(iii) Change in voice.
(iv) Increase in motor performance.
(v) Sexual changes. (Discussed separately)

Educational Implications of Physical Growth and Development

A programme of physical growth and development is not confined to the playground but should pervade the classroom and in fact the entire school programme. Physical development in the classroom may take the following forms:

1. Direct instruction emphasising the necessity of having a good physique may be given.
2. Suggestions regarding the maintenance of good health are very helpful.
3. Emphasis on right postures should be laid.
4. Provision of good seating and lighting arrangements in the classroom, thereby impressing upon them the importance of studying under healthy surroundings should be made.
5. Providing ample opportunities to the children for physical activity should be given its due importance.
6. Medical examination of school children by the school doctor should be made at suitable intervals.
7. Physical exercise for every child should be compulsory in the school.
8. Various activities promoting physical development should be well planned and children should be encouraged to take part in these activities.
9. Activities like woodwork, spinning and weaving, book binding,

gardening etc. may be introduced in the school as a group project. Such activities will lead to motor development as well as promote cooperation, and emotional adjustment among students.

10. At this stage students also have sexual development. It is necessary for us to impart them sex education.
11. Teachers should be conversant with norms of motor development of the child.
12. A variety of co-curricular activities should be introduced to provide outlets for the development of emotions and instincts which have a close link with physical growth and development.

Montaigne has very aptly remarked, "Physical education does neither train up the soul nor body, but the whole man". Froebel rightly stated, "Early education must deal directly with the physical development and influence the spiritual development through the exercise of senses".

9.5 EMOTIONAL AND PSYCHOLOGICAL DEVELOPMENT NEEDS AND THEIR SATISFACTION

Meaning and Need for Emotional Development

Emotional development is one of the major aspects of adolescence growth and development. Not only adolescent's physical growth and development is linked with his emotional make-up but his aesthetic, intellectual, moral and social development is also controlled by his emotional development. To keep one's emotions under control and be able to conceal them is considered a mark of strong and balanced personality. Therefore, adolescents must be trained to control their emotions and achieve a mental balance and stability which will lead to individual happiness and social efficiency.

How Emotions Work

All of us observe a large number of persons and objects in the world. We have some feelings for them in our mental make-up. Sometimes our feelings become strong either in favour or against the object of individual or an occasion. This disturbs our mental balance. This disturbance is known as *Emotion*. It not only disturbs our mind, but the entire organism. It is expressed in various movements and expressions of body and it tries to adjust to face the situation.

Educational Implications of Satisfying the Emotional and Psychological Needs of the Adolescents

A suitable educational programme needs to be developed to enable the adolescents to control their emotions and obtain a mental balance and stability which will mark for individual happiness and social efficiency.

Emotions can be suitably modified by the following mechanisms:

(i) Redirection
(ii) Sublimation
(iii) Catharsis
(iv) Inhibition

Factors in School Environment Which Disturb the Emotional Development of the Adolescents

Some of the important factors which disturb the emotions of adolescents in school are:

1. Lack of security.
2. Economic disparities.
3. Faulty methods of teaching.
4. Fearful atmosphere in school.
5. Emotionally unbalanced teacher.
6. Traditionally concept of discipline.
7. Poor physical conditions in schools.
8. Disregard of individual differences.
9. Lack of co-curricular activities.
10. Lack of sex education.
11. Faulty examination system.
12. Faulty curriculum.

Role of the School and the Teacher in Satisfying the Needs of the Emotional Development of the Adolescent

Following are the ways for meeting the needs of the adolescents:

1. Providing equal treatment irrespective of considerations of wealth, status or gender of the adolescents.
2. Using dynamic and progressive methods of teaching-learning.
3. Love and affection on the part of the teacher to be made the basis of work.
4. Balanced emotional behaviour of the teacher himself.
5. Creative and democratic classroom and school discipline.
6. Healthy physical conditions in the school.
7. Due regard to individual differences of the adolescents.
8. Due regard to the individuality of the adolescents.
9. Adequate provision for a variety of co-curricular activities.
10. Provision of scx cducation.
11. Rich and varied curriculum.

9.6 INTELLECTUAL/MENTAL NEEDS OF THE ADOLESCENTS AND THEIR SATISFACTION

Meaning of Intellectual Development

Mental or intellectual development implies the growth and development of those abilities and capacities of the adolescents that enable them to accomplish a task that needs complex cognitive abilities and enable them to adjust their behaviour to the ever changing environmental conditions. Cognitive abilities include abilities like sensation, perception, imagination, memory, reasoning, understanding, generalisation, interpretation, problem-solving and decision-making etc. In fact most parts of the school programmes relate to mental developments.

Main Characteristics of the Mental Development of the Adolescents

The adolescents learn to reason and seek answer to 'how' and 'why' of every thing rationally and scientifically. Power of critical thinking and observation is much developed. They are more creative and inquisitive. They are almost critical of everything. They develop a lot of imagination. This becomes the beginning of the artist, inventor, philosopher, poet and writer etc. in the adolescent. An adolescent tends to become a day-dreamer.

Factors Affecting Intellectual Development

Intellectual development of the adolescent in the school is affected by curricular and co-curricular programme, teaching-learning environment, and the role of the teachers.

Measures for the Satisfaction of Intellectual Needs or Intellectual Development of the Adolescents

Among the important factors are:

(a) Provision of rich curriculum.
(b) Provision of streaming.
(c) Provision of varied activities like debates and discussions.
(d) Provision of socialised teaching.
(e) Project work related to subjects.
(f) Subject related educational tours.
(g) Library and reading room facilities.
(h) Problem solving teaching-learning.
(i) Challenging questions.
(j) Exploratory activities.

9.7 MORAL DEVELOPMENT OR SATISFACTION OF THE MORAL NEEDS OF THE ADOLESCENTS

Meaning of Moral Development: By morality we mean conformity to the moral code of the social group. The term comes from the Latin word '*mores*', meaning manners, customs or folkways. To act in a moral way means to act in conformity to group standards of conduct. Morality also includes a sense of right or wrong—a behaviour which has to do with the conscience of the individual. Moral behaviour is *learnt*. Moral standards vary from group to group depending upon what has been accepted by the group as the socially approved behaviour. True morality comes *from within* the individual. It is internal in nature and not imposed by external *authority*. Immoral behaviour is that behaviour which is unfavourable to the group.

Bowley and others are of the view that a person of moral character has the following qualities: (i) Self-control, (ii) Reliability, (iii) Persistence in action, (iv) Industrious, (v) Feeling of responsibility, (vi) Consciousness.

Several thinkers equate morality with character.

B.N. Jha has stated that character is "a mental factor of the individual, which determines his social behaviour. It is a mental organisation which lies at the back of all his connotations".

A person of character has the following characteristics in his behaviour:

(a) He is firm and not impulsive in his behaviour.
(b) He is not dominated by others in his actions.
(c) He has a strong sense of self-respect and is governed by his self-regarding sentiment.
(d) He is intelligent and cheerful in his behaviour.
(e) He is hard working and faces difficulties with courage and optimism.
(f) He is idealistic in his approach. His inner and outer self is dominated by some ideals.

Role of the School Environment. Behaviours and norms adopted in the immediate environment influence the adolescent in shaping his moral behaviour. It is very unfortunate that generally elders observe double standards of morality. We hardly practise what we preach. These double standards are observed by adolescents. It is, therefore, very essential that elders set high standards of morality.

Role of the Teacher. It has been stressed again and again that nothing can be more helpful in moulding the adolescent's moral behaviour than the teacher's own conduct. A teacher has to set a high standard of moral behaviour before the adolescent.

Activities for Facilitating Moral Development

The school plays a very important role in the moral development of the adolescent. Through the organisation of various curricular and co-curricular activities, teachers can foster among children various moral qualities. In the teaching of different subjects like languages and social studies etc., teacher may stress moral qualities like love, sacrifice, self-control, truthfulness and uprightness, etc. Social service programmes should be undertaken on a large scale.

Self-government may be organised.

A comprehensive programme of guidance and counselling needs to be organised.

9.8 SOCIAL DEVELOPMENT NEEDS OF THE ADOLESCENTS AND THEIR SATISFACTION

Meaning of Social Development

Educators have defined social development in a number of ways.

Freeman and Showel observe, "Social development is the process of learning and conforming to group standards, morals and traditions and becoming imbued with a sense of oneness, inter-communication and co-operation".

H.E. Garret states, "Socialisation or social development is the process whereby the biological individual is converted into a human person".

E.B. Hurlock thinks, "Social development means the attaining of maturity in social relationships".

Herbert Sorenson writes, "By social growth and development we mean increasing ability to get along well with oneself and others".

Thus social development refers to the process of development by which a child acquires the necessary attitudes, skills and values that make him an acceptable member of the group to which he belongs.

Characteristics of Social Development During Adolescence

Following are the important characteristics of social development during adolescence:

1. Adolescence is marked with too much sex consciousness resulting in sexual social relationships.
2. During adolescence loyalty becomes very much pronounced and adolescents are in a mood to sacrifice their selfish interests for the greater cause of the group, society and nation.
3. Adolescence stage is often marked with increased friendly relationships.
4. Emotional behaviour of the adolescent dominates his social characteristics and qualities.
5. There is too much diversity in the adolescents regarding their social interests.

To sum up, we may say that the adolescence is a period of maximum social awareness, increasing and intimate social relationships.

Factors Affecting Social Development of the Adolescents

Important factors are given below:

1. *Personal Factors*: These include: (i) Physical strength and health, (ii) Level of intelligence, (iii) Emotional set up.
2. *Environmental Factors*: These comprise: (1) Family environment, (2) Social and physical environment of the school, (3) Peer group relationships and gang influence, (4) Community environment, (5) Social clubs, (6) Mass media.

According to T.P. Joseph, an adolescent wants a friend 'someone to be trusted', 'someone to talk', 'someone who is dependable'.

Harrocks and Benimoff observe regarding the peer influence on the adolescence as, "The peer group is the adolescent's real world, providing him a stage upon which to try himself and others'.

Role of the School in the Social Development or Satisfaction of the Social Needs of the Adolescence

The function of the school has considerably changed in the rapidly changing civilisations. The traditional function of imparting the basic skills of the three R's is now no longer considered to be adequate to meet the present challenge. The present day school has also to perform some of the functions of the family. It must develop certain desirable social habits. It is through co-curricular and extra-curricular activities that the task of social development can be achieved more successfully. It is only the sympathetic understanding and sincere desire of the teacher to act positively in an unprejudicial manner that can help.

Class in the Process of Socialisation. Class provides innumerable opportunities to the adolescents to move and mix with other groups. This is the beginning of the social development of the child. Here children get many chances to mix without any distinction of caste, colour or creed. The teachers are expected to be vigilant to ensure that the students do not think in terms of untouchability, caste distinction and other prejudices.

Role of the Teacher in Social Development of the Adolescent. A teacher can play a vital role in the social development of adolescent under his change. He exerts a great influence upon the development of the personality of the adolescent.

Following are the important suggestions for the social development of the adolescent.

1. Adolescents may be taken from time to time to public places like museums, courts and places of historical importance etc. to observe social interaction.
2. People engaged in different economic activities or vocations may be invited to school for giving a description of what they do and how useful their work is to the nation. This will enable the adolescents to be acquainted with those around them in the society.
3. Work experience will enable the adolescents to have first hand experiences of the activities pursued in farms and factories.
4. Adolescents should be acquainted with the social events like the celebration of the birthdays of leaders.
5. The school programme should be full of numerous co-curricular and curricular activities in which adolescents meet, cooperate and learn from each other's personality.
6. The introduction of common school dress, common lunch, etc., in the schools will present adolescents of poor and lower middle classes from facing inferiority complex due to the ego of the children of the well-to-do families.
7. Teachers and parents may encourage the adolescent to mix in intercaste and regional groups.
8. The teachers and the parents should respect the personality of adolescents.
9. The mechanism of praise and blame, reward and punishment should be carefully used for the social development of the adolescents.
10. Appropriate social education may be provided to the parents so that they understand the significance of the social development of the adolescents.
11. The teachers should demonstrate democratic outlook.
12. Community activities like camps, common meals, social services etc., should be frequently organised.
13. There should be a close cooperation between the teachers and parents on matters relating to the proper social development of the adolescents.
14. Adequate stress may be laid on group activities.
15. Stories depicting self-sacrifices made by great men for the cause of general good may be told to adolescents so that they are motivated to rise above petty gains and work for the betterment of the humanity.
16. The teachers should not show any discrimination. They must ensure a

safe and healthy social development in which the adolescents may imbibe desirable values of freedom, equality, integrity, honesty, patriotism etc.

Concluding Remarks. The task of social development of the adolescent is not an easy one. The educational thinkers point out very emphatically that certain conditions in the learning-teaching situation must be created and made available in the school so that it may become an effective instrument of social development. These conditions are: (i) A democratic social climate in the school; (ii) Effective interpersonal relationships; (iii) Motivated learning situations; (iv) Group methods of teaching; (v) Social discipline; (vi) School-community inter-relationships; (vii) Student participation and involvement in the school management; (viii) A rich programme of co-curricular activities

10

Adolescents, Sex Education

Problems, Worries, Fears and Development Tasks

10.1 INTERRELATEDNESS OF NEEDS AND VARIOUS ASPECTS OF DEVELOPMENT OF ADOLESCENTS

While discussing various needs and problems of development of the adolescents, it is important to keep in view the following important points.

1. *Needs give birth to problems.* Problems create worries and anxieties which in turn result in fears. Satisfaction or dissatisfaction of the needs thus have a great bearing on the development of the personality of the adolescent.

Needs → Problems → Worries → Anxieties → Fears

2. The interrelatedness of the various aspects of the development of the personality of the adolescent may be illustrated as under:

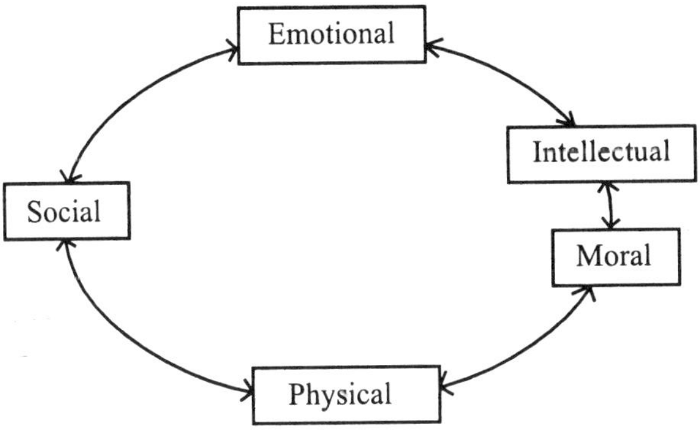

Fig. 10.1: Interrelatedness of the Various Aspects of the Developement of the Adolescent

3. A proper balance has to be struck between traditional values and modern values.

4. Ethical, moral and spiritual values on the one hand and scientific and technological values on the other hand have to be taken note of while considering adolescence needs and problems.

10.2 CLASSIFICATION OF PROBLEMS OF ADOLESCENTS

- Problems of adjustment relating to physical growth and development
- Problem of adjustment relating to mental development
- Problems of adjustment relating to emotional development
- Problems of adjustment relating to environment
- Adjustment problems relating to miscellinous factors

Problems of Adjustment relating to Physical Growth and Development

1. Abnormal physical development like facial expression, fatness, shortness, tallness, thinness, etc. resulting in inferiority complex and sometime indirect or direct unkind remarks of others.
2. Lack of normal physical strength.
3. Problems relating to gait and voice.
4. Problems resulting from some physical handicap.
5. Problems relating to sex.

Problems of Adjustment relating to Mental Development

1. Problems relating to development of intelligence.
2. Problems relating to learning of subjects.
3. Problems relating to competition in evaluation.
4. Problems relating to independent thinking.
5. Problems relating to participation in debates, discussions, etc.

Problems of Adjustment relating to Emotional Development

1. Excessive involvement in fantasy.
2. Rapid changes in moods.
3. Excessive depression or over enthusiasm.
4. Excessive sensitiveness or excessive stubbornness.
5. Lack of appreciation of others' feelings.
6. Lack of decision making ability.
7. Lack of humour.
8. Lack of tolerance.

Problems of Adjustment relating to Environment in the School

1. Change of class or section.
2. Methodology of teaching-learning.
3. Nature of curriculum.
4. Nature of discipline.
5. Availability of co-curricular activities.

Problems Relating to Miscellaneous Factors

1. Economic background of the family.
2. Social background of the family which includes:

(i) Caste factor,
(ii) Regional factor,
(iii) Language factor,
(iv) Religious factor.

10.3 SPECIFIC PROBLEMS AND WORRIES OF ADOLESCENCE

Adolescence is marked by specific attitudes and behaviour patterns. Among the most important of these according to E.B. Hurlock are: (i) Feeling of vague status during transitional period, (ii) Heightened emotionally (iii) Rapid sexual maturing (iv) Marked physical changes (v) Major changes in adolescents interests and behaviour patterns, (vi) A dreaded attitude, (vii) Unrealism, (viii) Threshold of adulthood.

Adolescence has been called a period of '*Challenge and Potential*'. The adolescent has enormous potential—physical, ideational and intellectual. At the same time he is faced with great challenges on account of his rapid physical growth, soaring as well as falling ideals, his search for identity as he is neither considered as a child nor an adult, his growing sexual desires, heightened emotions and lack of appropriate energies for channelising his enormous energy. All these issues and problems make the adolescence period as the period of '*Stress and Storm*'. An adolescent is faced with several alternatives on account of his '*conflicts and dilemmas*'. '*To do or not to do*' attitude creates several problems the solution of which needs guidance and counselling. Since an adolescent, in general, has the notion of 'knowing all things', several difficulties confront him.

Some of the important specific characteristics of adolescence problems and worries as given by various thinkers are briefly described here.

1. *Becoming Independent*: J.A. Hadfield (1962) is of the view, "When we speak of adolescent as growing up we mean that the youth is leaving behind the phase of protective childhood and is becoming independent".

2. *Age of Ideals*: Jean Piaget defines adolescence as, "the age of great ideals and the beginning of theories as well as the time of simple adaptation to life".

3. *Rapid Physical Growth and Development*: Rate of growth is so rapid in some cases as it seems almost 'as they go to bed one night as children and wake-up the next morning as adults'.

4. *Health and Adolescence*: It has been stated, "A growing youth has a wolf in his stomach". At this period, appetite for food is often enormous. There is a widespread notion that "this is physically a critical period". Various ailments that often manifest themselves are anaemia, nosebleed, nervousness, growing pains, palpitation of the heart and especially among girls, headache, etc.

5. *Sex and Adolescence*: One writer has remarked, "Sex power permeates the whole body and the entire life of feeling, thought and will".

6. *Emotions and Adolescence*: In the words of Richmond, "Adolescence is the heyday of the emotional life, the blossom time of all those feelings and emotions which depend at bottom upon sex". Masterson has observed, "Emotional disorders frequently arise during adolescence. Such disorders

range from simple depression to being over anxious about health to suicidal thoughts or attempts". Many adolescents who engage in delinquent, bizarre, or self-abusive behaviour do so as a call for help during a difficult period. Some adolescents use drugs, alcohol, or sex as a response to emotional disorders. The emotions of the adolescents drive them from one extreme to the other. At one time a boy or a girl may be shiftless, lazy or at another full of enthusiasm and energy.

7. *Self Assertion, Daring Exploits*: Frederick Tracy writes in *The Psychology of Adolescence*, "History abounds with records of the boldness and self-assertions of young men in their teens, and of their reckless and daring exploits, some of which have resulted in great good, and others in great evil, but it also finishes the chronicle of many acts of self-abasement, of self-immolation, and of sacrifice, on which the same double comments may be made".

8. *Day-Dreams*: Some psychological associate day-dreams with 'great buzzing, blooming confusion of the complete life that youth is coming more keenly to realise'. According to Hollingworth, "Adolescent day-dreams centre chiefly around love, achievement, and security" and in many cases in self-pity and death. The day dreamer sees himself in the role which he would like to play in life.

9. *Adolescence and Crime*: Hollingworth is of the opinion that adolescence is a period of marked criminality. It has been shown by research studies that most criminals begin their careers during adolescence.

10. *Mensturation (Girls)*: Mensturation causes deep-rooted worry and anxiety arising from ignorance, superstitious talk and the fear of an incurable disease.

11. *Breast Development/Dress (Girls)*: Generally a girl tends to worry about size of her breasts. The need to be attractive and to dress like others of her age-group is dominant at this stage.

12. *Masturbation (Boys)*: Masturbation leads fear among boys that it may result in loss of virility.

13. *Nocturnal Emission (Boys)*: Spontaneous erection and the first involuntary discharge of semen in boys (popularly known as 'wet dreams') may lead to fear.

14. *Acne*: Girls and boys worry about pimples that are caused by hormone imbalances which are characteristics of this age.

15. *Pre-marital Sex*: Quite a large number of those who indulge in pre-marital sex are unaware of its consequences.

16. *Teenage Pregnancy*: Teenage pregnancy poses serious health and emotional hazards.

17. *Smoking*: Students take to smoking unaware of its harmful consequences.

18. *Sexuality Transmitted Diseases* (*STD*): Young people need to have scientific knowledge of such diseases.

19. *Use of Drugs, Alcohol, etc.*: A large number of adolescents experiment with the use of drugs and alcohol etc. at this stage.

20. *Myths and Misconception*: Adolescents are confronted with several types of myths and misconcepts which exercise harmful physio-socio and emotional effects.

10.4 DEVELOPMENTAL TASKS FOR ADOLESCENTS AND THEIR IMPLICATIONS

Purposes of Developmental Tasks

In an earlier chapter, the meanings of developmental tasks, their nature and significance for stages other than adolescence are dealt with. There are specific purposes of developmental tasks. Here we are concerned with the developmental tasks of adolescents and these are given below:

(i) Developmental tasks are guidelines which enable the adolescent to know what society expects of him.

(ii) Developmental tasks motivate the adolescent to do what the social group expects him to do.

(iii) Developmental tasks indicate the adolescent what lies ahead and what he will be expected to do when he reaches the next stage of development in his life span.

Developmental Tasks During Adolescence

Developmental tasks during adolescence are as under:

1. Accepting one's role according to one's physique.
2. Gaining emotional and other types of independence from parents and other adults.
3. Establishing new relations with peers of both sexes.
4. Achieving assurance of economic independence.
5. Selecting and preparing for a vocation or profession.
6. Developing attitudes and skills necessary for civic competence.
7. Developing knowledge attitudes and skills to participate in a democracy.
8. Desiring and achieving socially desirable behaviour.
9. Preparing for a happy married and family life.
10. Building rational and scientific values in harmony with global scenario.

Hazards Related to Developmental Tasks

There are three main hazards or problems in normal development of developing tasks. These are:

(a) Inappropriate expectations of the adolescent himself or the social group to which be belongs.

(b) By passing the stage of development on account of failure to acquire the development tasks for that stage.

(c) Hazards arising out of the previous stage.

10.5 PEDAGOGIC PRACTICES FOR DEVELOPMENTAL TASKS OF ADOLESCENTS

Some of the important pedagogic practices for meeting the developmental tasks are given below:

1. Rich and varied curriculum.
2. Individualised as well as group methods of instruction.
3. Continuous evaluation of the developmental tasks of the adolescents.
4. Provision of co-curricular activities.
5. Introduction of vocational courses and socially useful productive work.
6. Provision for guidance and counselling.

10.6 DEVELOPMENTAL TASKS AND CLASS AND SCHOOL ORGANISATION

Significance of Understanding the Developmental Tasks/Needs and Characteristics of the Adolescence Period

For facilitating the growth and development of the adolescent, it is necessary to understand him properly. This is the most critical period of a student's development with which the teacher has to deal. It is a period of day-dreams, of adventures, of intense affections and stirring of the 'heart'. Some educationists think this period to be a period of great 'stress and strain', 'storm and strife'.

According to Rabindranath Tagore, "In the world of human affairs there is no worse nuisance than a boy at the age of fourteen. He is neither ornamental nor useful. It is impossible to shower affection on him as a little boy; and he is always getting in the way".

According to William H. Burton, "The adolescent is an odd, awkward, graceful, respectful, selfish, altruistic, idealistic, narrow-minded, sympathetic, cruel individual".

E.A. Peel (1956) is of the view, "The adolescent is beset by problems of divided loyalties, accentuated by the lack of adult privileges and responsibilities. He thus appears excessively aggressive and then excessively shy, excessively affectionate and then quite suddenly detached and cool. These are all problems of the stress and strains of transition".

10.7 NEEDS AND DEVELOPMENTAL TASKS OF INDIAN ADOLESCENT

1. A balance between security and freedom is needed.
2. Adolescents need noble causes in the promulgation of which they may utilise their excess emotion and energy.
3. Separate physical education programmes for adolescent boys and girls need to be planned.
4. Social mixing is considered important at this stage.
5. Different types of co-curricular activities are needed for providing new experiences and utilising energy.
6. Sex education on a scientific basis is needed.
7. Unobtrusive adult guidance is needed.

Some Problems of Adolescence in India

These may be listed as under:

1. Lack of interest in school work.
2. Lack of proper facilities.
3. Adjustment to emotional problems.

4. Lack of adequate sex guidance.
5. Adjustment with school discipline.
6. Vocational adjustment.

10.8 SCHOOL PROGRAMME AND ADJUSTMENT OF ADOLESCENTS : DEVELOPMENTAL TASKS AND NEEDS. ROLE OF TEACHERS

Innumerable opportunities can be provided by the schools to adolescents for making necessary adjustments.

1. *Due Regard to Individual Differences*: Adolescents differ as much mentally and emotionally as physically. But we provide little individual attention to tham in schools. Some of them are backward in studies, while some of them are very superior. But they are dragged on the same lines. The backward lag behind still more and this results in emotional disturbance. We must study their specific needs and take suitable steps to meet these needs.

2. *Rich and Varied Curriculum*: The curriculum in schools often does not relate to the real life of adolescents. Learning in schools is unrelated to their modern needs. It is not according to the requirements of society and that of the students and hence emotional disturbance is created among the students This means providing a diversified curriculum.

3. *Provision for Vocational Education*: Apprenticeship system provided vocational education in ancient and medieval times. In ancient India, vocation was on family basis and the son learnt the vocation by working with the father. It has, therefore, become necessary now for the schools to impart vocational education to students. Moreover far reaching changes have taken place in the economic, commercial, industrial and other areas which need vocational pursuits and accordingly vocational guidance.

4. *Use of Dynamic Methods of Teaching*: Faulty methods of teaching do not develop motivation in the adolescents. Therefore, lessons become a drudgery. The adolescents begin to hate the very process of education. There is always tension in their minds. Learning is no more a joyful activity for them.

Improvement in the methods of teaching can go a long way in providing emotional security to adolescents. Instructional work can easily be turned into play and then it will be interesting, joyful and at the same time more instructive.

5. *Freedom for Self-development*: For the development of a creative mind, freedom for self-development and freedom for activity must be given in a school. "This freedom will not be the licence it is sometimes supposed to be. It will be the controlled freedom of an individual living in a community of which he is one part, and his fellow pupils and teachers are other parts. It will be a freedom from an exaggerated force or undue influence on the part of a teacher, a freedom for the particular pupil to use his particular talents and capabilities and to develop his personality along his own line, under the guidance of the teacher", writes Ryburn.

6. *Creative and Democratic Concept of Discipline*: Traditional methods of discipline are faulty. Sometimes schools are considered just like jails and some teachers like jailors. Such discipline is negative. It may serve the purpose superficially but in reality the things are far from being satisfactory.

There should be positive devices of discipline. Discipline should be creative. Children should be made responsible for handling their own affairs as far as it is feasible.

7. *Provision of Co-curricular Activities*: All the children and especially adolescents need provision for the expression of their pent-up emotions and for redirection of their emotional behaviour. In the absence of such provision, emotional stability is not possible. Varied co-curricular activities can solve this problem quite satisfactorily.

8. *Provision of Sex Education*: Teachers should provide necessary information about the sex matters and problems. During adolescent period lack of information about sex causes emotional disturbance.

9. *Continuous Evaluation*: The present system of examination is faulty. Chance factor counts much in this system. It does not measure the all-round development of the adolescent and causes disturbance. Evaluation should be made continuous and objective.

10. *Satisfaction of the Urge for Practical Activity*: Dr. Zakir Hussain observes, "The future Indian school will not perpetuate the stupid tyranny of requiring its boys and girls, bursting with active energy, to sit silent and sombre, brooding over books and swallow irrelevant, unwanted, unassimilated information getting passively educated by others. The prevalence of a certain peculiarity, namely, urge for practical activity, makes this stage comparatively easy for the organiser of education and a fairly uniform type of school based on hand work can serve the needs of the vast majority of children".

11. *Healthy Physical Conditions in the Schools*: Poor physical conditions in the school bring fatigue and boredom to the adolescents. They are very soon fed up with the school and its activities. Lack of recreational activities is also responsible for emotional disturbance. The school authorities should be careful in this respect also.

12. *Emotional Stability of the Teacher*: The role of the teacher in this respect is very important. It is a great factor in the wholesome emotional development of the adolescent. He should control his own emotional expression and manifestations in the presence of adolescents, otherwise he would prove himself contagious.

Summing up

The teachers can and should play an important role in providing suitable programmes for the adolescents so that they utilise their energy in worthwhile tasks. They should treat all adolescents irrespective of their social status. Love, sympathy, firmness and patience are the important elements which go a long way in providing congenial environment for the optimum display of the adolescents. They should be quite sensitive to the specific needs and problems of the adolescents. "Example is better than precepts" is a famous saying and is very essentially applicable to the teachers.

10.9 ADOLESCENT AND SEX EDUCATION

Importance of Sex Development

Healthy attitudes towards sex related issues contribute substantially to adjustment. There is no doubt that ignorance about sex related problems is one of the main causes of unhappiness and maladjustment in life. Moreover a large number of anti-social acts are committed by the adolescents on account of proper and timely information not being made available to them. Therefore, there is an urgent need of imparting sex education to the youngsters and the adolescents.

There still is good deal of prejudice and misconceptions regarding giving sex education to boys and girls. The parents often believe that such information will spoil their morals, as it would deal with male-female sex relationship. It is necessary to remove such misconceptions from the minds of the parents and to convince them that this subject will inculcate in the minds of the youngsters a healthy attitude towards the opposite sex, based on a sense of social responsibility and equality.

Youngsters who are kept ignorant of their own body changes are naturally unable to adjust themselves physically and psychologically at the time of onset of changes of adolescence, and develop an unrestrained behaviour. This ignorance may lead to family disharmony and marital conflict. The adolescents nurse several misconceptions about sexual changes and development.

Sexual changes are very prominent during the period of adolescence.

(A) Primary Sex Features

1. Boys develop their sex organs.
2. Sex glands—the gonads—start producing sperms. Boys may suffer from night dreams.
3. The growth of sex glands among girls is not visible. The first menstrual flow is indicative of their sexual growth.

(B) Secondary Sex Features

These features are not related to sex organs but are indicative of sexual maturation which is a part of adolescence. These are different in the case of males and females. Among the males the features are:

(a) Growth of pubic hair around the sex organ,
(b) hair in the arm pit, legs, arms and the chest,
(c) The growth of beard, and
(d) The tone of voice deepens.

Among the girls the growth of sex organs is not visible. Other changes are:

(a) The development of breasts.
(b) Increase in the width of hips.
(c) A rounded appearance of body and limbs.
(d) Growth of pubic hair, and
(e) A shrill voice.

Sexual identity includes the expression of sexual needs and feelings and the acceptance or rejection of sex.

Adolescence period is the onset of puberty. Puberty implies a series of physical changes that make the organism capable of reproduction.

Puberty leads to sexual activity, erotic fantasy, experimentation and masturbation.

Specific Problems of Adolescents Regarding Sex which Need Sex Education

These are as under:

1. Mensturation related problems among girls.
2. Breast related problems among girls.
3. Nocturnal emission related problems among boys.
4. Masturbation related problems among boys.
5. Pre-marital sex related problems.
6. Teenage pregnancy related problems.
7. Sexually transmitted diseases (STD) related problems.
8. Family planning related problems.
9. Selection of partner-related problems.
10. Homosexuality and heterosexuality related problems.

Healthy Attitude Towards Sex Education

Sex Education should not be considered as something secretive. Talking about sex is ordinarily considered something secretive, sinful or not worthy of mention in a conservative society, and people feel very much inhibited in talking about sex. Now it is increasingly being realised that without sex education people cannot live a happy and well-adjusted life because it has been noted that many marital, emotional and mental problems among human beings occur as a result of the misdirection and wrong understanding of the sex urge. Alva Myrdal has observed: "In general more wholesome attitudes towards sex questions will not be created until they are discussed openly and as a matter of fact phenomena". Children ask questions about sex as the subject fascinates them and it is our answer and the way we give them that plays an important part in forming their future attitudes towards sex. Frank and honest response can help them to develop a healthy outlook.

Scope of Sex Education

Sex education includes in its scope not only physical and biological aspects of the growth of an individual including reproduction, but also, what is very important, matters pertaining to ethics, morality and development of a responsible, wholesome and correct attitude towards the other sex.

Prof. Uday Shanker is of the firm opinion, "Education without sex education is ridiculous as the 'how' of population control cannot be answered without sex education. Sex education is no imposition, it concerns a vital matter in which children are interested. Interest in sex is instinctive and starts from early infancy. In pre-adolescent boys and girls, the sex drives intensifies. Enlightenment on sexual aspects is to be given intelligently and pleasantly but gradually and methodically. There need not be 'sex teacher' or 'sex classes' like history or geography classes. There cannot be any general rules as to the time and place or manner of imparting sex education. Through the teaching of general science, biology, physiology or hygiene, a good deal of physiological knowledge about sex differences and about animal and human reproduction, involving all the process of mating, fertilisation, pregnancy or birth can be imparted.

A publication entitled '*Sex Education: How and Why*' (1976) authored by Dr. W. Mathur, gives the following outline of the topics to be taken up by the teachers and others with a view to provide guidance to adolescents on sex related matters.

Programme of Sex Education for Adolescents : 14-18 Years Age Group

	Objectives	*Context*	*Approach*
1.	To help adolescents develop into a responsible adult.	Knowledge of the phenomenon of ovulation, foetal development and birth of a baby. Marriage for reproduction, need of assistance at birth.	a) Talks with the aid of audio-visual aids. b) Emphasis on leading highly moral and ethical life in the interest of family happiness and community peace.
2.	To make adolescents understand venereal diseases	Different venereal diseases. This mode of infection and their damaging effect on the patients.	Causes of these diseases, their symptoms and the conditions of the patients should be illustrated by means of films, film strips and pictures.
3.	To make adults aware of promiscuity and prostitution.	Danger's of promiscuous sex relations. Its adverse influence on the family life and its being a great social evil. Prostitutes as chief sources of the spread of venereal diseases.	Frank discussion. Students to be told emphatically that all extramarital sex relations must be avoided in the interest of personal health and family happiness.
4.	To make student careful of homosexuality.	Homosexual an unethical and unnatural practice. An offence under law punishable by imprisonment. Can convey venereal diseases.	Adolescents must not be permitted to go out with strangers. They should be motivated to utilise their surplus energy and spare time in sports, cultural programmes, community welfare service and nation building activities. Such programmes should be systematically organised.

Role of Parents in Sex Education

To make sex education effective, it must commence from the earliest stages of child's life. It is the family where foundation is laid of a child's personality and where, by stages, his outlook on life and character are moulded.

Parents have thus to play a central role in the scheme at all stages. It is in fact, a part of family life education that goes on from infancy to maturity.

Sex education is therefore essentially a preventive measure to help children to become emotionally stable and develop character. This knowledge should be given to make them aware of the pitfalls of early life and should create in their minds sound moral values and proper attitudes.

Role of the Teachers

During the school stages, the teachers must play a very important role in giving requisite knowledge to the students and guide them to acquire a sense of regard and helpfulness towards the other sex. The instruction should be given according to the age of the student and his state of physical, mental and psychological development. Such information should be integrated with other subjects such as Civics, Nature Study, Biology and Physiology. Sex education should thus permeate the entire school curriculum. It should never be taught as a separate subject, but incidentally in the context of other subjects and in response to children's questions.

It is possible that some teachers may themselves not be quite familiar with the subject. The education authorities should organise in-service training course for teachers.

It would be beneficial if the parents are kept informed of this as a character building activity, and if parents and teachers meet regularly to sort out their mutual problems to determine a common course of action so that there may not be conflicts in the advice to young people.

General Guidelines for Teachers in Imparting Sex Education to Adolescents

1. A friendly, open-mindedness classroom climate, free of embarrassment to students should pervade.
2. Students should be free to ask questions which trouble them.
3. Answers given by the teachers should be honest and sensible.
4. Sex should be talked in an objective and a matter-of-fact way like any other subject.
5. A question box may be used in which adolescents may put questions anonymously if they do not feel free to ask questions in the class.
6. Films and other aids may be used to clarify concepts.
7. An adequate number of books on sex education should be kept in the open shelf school library.

11

Indian Adolescents: Needs, Aspirations, Interests, Attitudes and Self-Concepts

11.1 SITUATIONAL ANALYSIS OF ADOLESCENTS IN INDIA

In India, this age group forms 21.4 per cent of the total population (National Youth Policy 2000). Characterised by distinct physical and social changes, the separate health, education, economic and employment needs of adolescents cannot be ignored. Adolescents are also entitled to enjoy all basic human rights—economic, social, political and cultural—but their inability to exercise these rights places the onus on policy makers and adults to implement separate measures to ensure their rights. Moreover, it is necessary to invest in adolescents as the future leaders and guardians of the nation's development.

The significance of India's adolescence population in achieving its development goals must be recognised. It is, therefore, very necessary to cater to the needs, interests, goals and values of the adolescents.

As observed in *Adolescence in India*, "A pre-requisite for policy planning and focus is a comprehensive situational analysis of adolescence". The lack of reliable data on the adolescent age group is a major impediment in discussing interests, goals and values of Indian adolescence.

Adolescence Stages

Three main stages of adolescence can be discerned:

1. *Early adolescence* (12-13 years)—Characterised by a spurt of growth and the development of secondary sexual characteristics.
2. *Mid adolescence* (14-15 years)—This stage is distinguished by the development of a separate identity from parents, of new relationships with peer groups and the opposite sex, and of experimentation.
3. *Late adolescence* (16-19 years)—At this stage, adolescents have fully developed physical characteristics (similar to adults), and have formed a distinct identity and have well-formed opinions and ideas.

Adolescence Groups

Adolescents are generally perceived as a homogeneous group, yet they can be stratified on the basis of gender, caste, class, geographical location (urban/rural) and religion. Adolescents also include a whole gamut of categories: School and non-school going, drop-outs, sexually exploited children, working adolescents—both paid and unpaid, unmarried adolescents as also married males and females with experience of fatherhood and motherhood.

Most Crucial Areas of Concern

An overview, based on the secondary data available, confirms the need for a separate focus on the health, education, employment and protection of human rights of adolescents. Reproductive health, in particular, represents the most critical area where an emphasis on the special needs and concerns of adolescents is required. In India, given its predominantly patriarchal set up, ideology of son preference, incidence of early marriage and high rates of maternal mortality, a strong focus on the needs of adolescent girls is warranted. However, both sexes are vulnerable to problems such as those of drug abuse, HIV/AIDS and other infections and sexual abuse.

11.2 CHANGES IN THE SOCIETY AFFECTING ADOLESCENCE DEVELOPMENT

Far reaching changes have been taking place in recent years in all societies. Schools, as social institutions have to rethink the way they are structured. At present, by and large, they tend to be based on the 20th century. Other models for schools need to be considered if students' development, especially of adolescents is to be enhanced.

Following are the developments which affects adolescence growth and development and create new problems:

1. New developments in information technology including computer aided learning, inter-active video and television offer important opportunities to improve the quality of many adolescents. At the same time they exercise an adverse influence also. Developments in this area, however, require a large investment of effort and finance. In many developing countries, the reality is that only a few elite schools would have such technology, thus aggravating the equity problem.
2. The current trends towards democratisation in the societies will hopefully promote better understanding. In order to support such a change, we will need an education for the adolescents which enables them to live harmoniously in the plural society of today.
3. The global problems we face with the environment will acquire a new responsibility on the adolescents.
4. Human rights and dignity will still be an issue at the forefront of our concern.
5. The ecological developments taking place are producing changes in the people's work and living conditions. The adolescents need to be acquainted with these concerns.
6. The gap between the rich and the poor societies is increasing. This also reflects on the status of adolescents in educational institutions.
7. The emergence of self-concept, egoism and sex instinct during adolescence have to be considered in the light of new information technology.
8. Schools alone cannot influence the adolescents in the fast changing societies. In a world where mutual respect and cooperation is essential, it will be important to develop environment at school, at home and in wider society in which adolescent's self-esteem is enhanced.

11.3 MAJOR NEEDS, INTERESTS AND ATTITUDES OF INDIAN ADOLESCENTS

As already observed, there is a lack of reliable and scientific data on this issue. However, it must be accepted that on account of the influence of electronic media, Indian adolescent cannot remain unaffected by globalisation. Nevertheless, following interests, aspirations and attitudes of Indian adolescent are discernible although it is very difficult to generalise as there are several sub-groups on account of the vastness of the country and its plural culture.

1. Needs (See Chapter 9.3)

2. Interests

1. *Recreation Interests*: (i) Interest in folk dance, (ii) Television watching (iii) Celebrating birthdays and attending parties, (iv) Folk dance and music, (v) Pop dance and singing, (vi) Watching movies, (vii) Reading comics and sensational literature, (viii) Travelling, (ix) Interest in pen-friendship, (x) Interest in television games, (xi) Watching and listening cricket commentaries, (xii) Playing cards, (xii) Trends towards fun gambling, (xiv) Interest in smoking as a fashion symbol, (xv) Trends towards use of drug and pills, (xvi) Interest in fine arts, (xvii) Exchanging jokes, (xviii) Interest in drinking, it being status symbol.

2. *Religious Interests*: (i) Usually sceptical of religious beliefs, (ii) Disinterest in the observance of religious rites and ceremonies, (iii) Indifference to formal religion.

3. *Social Interest*: (i) Attending group parties, (ii) Mixing with the opposite sex, (iii) Interest in global matters, (iv) Demonstrating self identity in the group, (v) Group loyalty.

4. *Vocational Interests*: (a) Interest in professions related to Commerce, (b) Interest in information technology and especially computers, (iii) Declining.

5. *Miscellaneous Interests*: (i) Interest in conversation in groups, (ii) Interest in the beautification of the body, (iii) Interest in new things, (iv) Interest in foreign travels, (v) Interest in foreign studies, (vi) Heightened sex interest, (vii) Interest in collections.

3. Aspirations and Goals

(i) Becoming rich overnight, (ii) Getting foreign degrees, (iii) Getting foreign assignments, (iv) Settling in foreign lands, (v) Joining multinational companies, (vi) Capturing political power, (vii) Occupying high civil posts, (viii) Becoming leaders, (ix) Becoming independent of joint family and having nuclear family, (x) Choosing one's life partner, (xi) Aspiration to excel in studies, (xii) Aspiration to do something novel or invent something.

Measurement of Interest

There are several interest inventories to measure interests.

Attitudes

Meaning of an Attitude

Following definitions throw light on the meaning, characteristics and dimensions of attitude.

In the words of Anastasi, "An attitude is often defined as a tendency to react favourably or unfavourably towards a designated class of stimuli, such as, national or a racial group, a custom or an institution".

Thurstone states, "Attitude denotes the sum total of man's inclinations and feelings, prejudice or bias, perceived notions, ideas, fears, threats and conceived about any specific topic. Thus a man's attitude about pacifism means here all that he feels and thinks about peace and war. It is admittedly a subjective and personal affair.

According to G.W. Allport, "Attitude is a mental state of readiness, organised through experience, exerting a directive and dynamic influence upon an individual's response to the objects and situations with which it is related".

Frank Freeman defines an attitude in these words, "An attitude is a dispositional readiness to respond to certain institutions, persons or objects in a consistent manner which has been learned and has become one's typical mode of response. An attitude has a well-defined object of reference. For example, one's views regarding class of food or drink (such as, fish and liquors), sports, maths or democrats are attitudes.

Characteristics of an Attitude

1. It is a point of view, or a frame of reference substantiated or otherwise, true or false which one holds towards an idea, object or person.
2. It includes certain aspects of personality as interests, appreciations and social conduct.
3. An attitude is learnt.
4. An attitude is adopted.
5. An attitude has several aspects, such as, direction, intensity, generality or specificity.
6. The attitudes of a student are formed on the basis of his experience and interaction with real situations.
7. An attitude can be measured.

Components of an Attitude : According to Harrison, an attitude has three components:

1. Beliefs, 2. Emotions, 3. Behaviour.

Types of Attitudes and their Characteristics

(1)	(2)
Positive Characteristics	*Negative Characteristics*
(i) Assisting others	(i) Prejudice
(ii) To be caring	(ii) Entering into arguments and conflicts
(iii) To be unselfish	(iii) Tension
(iv) To be at peace with the world	

Factors Leading to Individual Differences: These are:

1. Physical surroundings.
2. Cultural background.
3. Home environment.
4. School environment.
5. Neighbourhood environment.
6. Social environment.
7. Political environment.
8. Maturity level.
9. Religious environment.

Development of Positive Attitude and the Role of the Teacher

1. Personal example of positive attitude
2. Friendly, sympathetic but attitude of firmness on the part of the teacher.
3. Understanding the background and needs of the students.
4. Appreciation of individual differences and accordingly adopting disciplinary measures.
5. Making teaching-learning effective.

Measurement of Attitude: The two most frequently used methods for the measurement of social attitude are "The Methods of Equal Appearing Intervals" developed by Thurstone and "The Method of Summated Ratings" developed by Likert.

11.4 IMPORTANT PROBLEMS AND ISSUES INVOLVED IN THE PROPER DEVELOPMENT OF INDIAN ADOLESCENTS

1. *Serious Problem of 10-14 Year Group*: Since adolescents comprise a major part of the reproductive age group, addressing their needs will be critical in determining India's population. An analysis within the age group itself indicates that proportion of 10-14 year olds is greater than the 15-19 year group.

2. *Problem of Gender Discrimination*: Any programme for adolescents must recognise the problem of gender discrimination of the adolescents.

3. *Problem of Under Nutrition*: If India wishes to achieve the goals of 'Health for All' and adequate 'Nutrition for All', it must attend to the problem of under nutrition among adolescent girls. A sizeable number of adolescents girls are actually malnourished. This will increase the risk of difficulty to child birth.

4. *Problem of Poor Understanding of Reproductive Health*: A poor understanding of reproductive health and sexual issues creates several problems in this area.

5. *Problems of High Level of Pre-marital Sexual Activity, Mainly among Young Adolescent Males*: In this regard, following trends are noticed:

(i) The magnitude of adolescent sexual activity is significant, and is higher in boys than girls. There is also under-reporting of non-marital relationships by adolescent girls due to fear of social disapproval.

(ii) Men are more likely to be sexually active and at an earlier age than girls, and attitudes on premarital sexual activity remain conservative. Furthermore, the acceptance of premarital sexual activity is greater among boys than girls.

(iii) Parents and teachers play a minor role in giving information, and are usually reluctant to impart such information. The majority of information on sexual and reproductive issues is obtained from peers (which can sometimes be misleading and inaccurate).

(iv) Commercial sex workers usually serve as partners for first-time sexual encounters.

(v) Contraceptive use is low and rarely used in first-time sexual encounters, including commercial sex workers. Contraceptive awareness is usually about sterilisation, which is unsuitable for most adolescents. Knowledge of HIV/AIDS, safe sex and preventive behaviour (like use of condoms) is low, across all ages and education levels.

(vi) Knowledge of sexual and reproductive issues is extremely poor. In some studies, 50 per cent of female adolescents did not know about mensturation, and the limited knowledge was based on social factors (such as, not being permitted to cook) than the actual physiological changes.

(vii) There is considerable interest among adolescent boys for information on reproductive health.

(viii) Education did not increase knowledge of sex and reproduction.

(ix) The educational system does not adequately meet the needs for imparting sex education.

(x) Sexual and reproductive decision-making by adolescents is constrained by age and gender factors. Adolescent women have little choice on whom and when to marry, and are usually not in a position to negotiate contraceptive use. This varies slightly with age, with an older wife more likely to make such decisions.

(xi) There is a huge demand for adolescent health facilities, information and counselling services.

6. *Unwanted Pregnancies and Abortions*: There is a lack of knowledge of appropriate use of contraceptives. Son preference is another reason.

7. *Maternal Mortality*: This is on account of the fact that the body has not yet reached full maturity. Marriage age is very low.

8. *Sexually Transmitted Diseases (STDs), including HIV/AIDS*: Young people between the ages of 10 and 25 years make up 50 per cent of all new infections.

9. *Drug Abuse*: In India, it is estimated that a substantial number of drug users are in the age group of 12 to 18.

10. *Violence against Women, Sexual Abuse and Trafficking of Girls*: Available data indicate that a high incidence of rape occurs in the 10-16 year age group.

11. *Gender Difference in Literacy and Education*: The gross enrolment ratio (GER) for girls including adolescent girls lags behind boys. Likewise drop-out rates in the case of adolescent girls are higher than boys.

12. *High Incidence of Unemployment among Adolescents*: Overall, the unemployment rates are almost three times as high for adolescents as that among aged 15 and above.

(*Source*: Adapted from '*Adolescents in India : A Profile*'. UNFPA 2000).

Dr. Tapisha G. Kumar, in a write-up in '*The Hindustan Times*' (Nov. 27, 2000) under the caption 'Wonder Years' detailed the following facts regarding Indian adolescents.

13. *Depression Leading to Suicide*: Every year, suicide is one of the most leading causes of death among them. Each year, 15 to 25 per cent of high school students seriously consider taking this course with depression being the prime motive.

14. *Alcohol and Tobacco Abuse*: Alcohol and tobacco abuse is very common among 2.5 to 3 per cent of children between 15 to 20 years of age.

15. *Sex Encounter*: In Delhi alone, 15 per cent of children in the age group 15 to 20 have already had their first sexual encounter.

16. *HIV Infections*: Sex encounter combined with the lack of awareness at this stage has also increased the possibility of HIV (Human Immunodeficiency Virus) infections. India has currently an HIV infection rate of 1.7 per 1000 of which more than 40 per cent is concentrated around teenagers.

17. *Emotional Stress*: Family pressures to study and perform better indirectly result in emotional stress for a teenager.

18. *Improper Company*: Hanging around with improper friends may also lead to drug abuse, HIV and early pregnancy.

19. *Miscellaneous Issues*: Teenagers face numerous issues ranging from pubertal changes, pimples, obesity, short height and changes in body structure, to medical problems like asthma, diabetes, thyroid disorders, eating disorders (anorexia) and bed wetting.

11.5 DIRECTIONS HELPFUL TO FIND SUITABLE SOLUTIONS TO ADOLESCENT'S PROBLEMS

1. Support by society for the career development of adolescents and counselling.
2. School's responsibility for career development as well as moral development of adolescents.
3. Constructive and cooperative educational environment.
4. Creation of a 'pedagogy of democratic fellowship in which adolescents collaborate and support each other in their learning.
5. Classrooms to be mini-social realities in which adolescents assume different roles including those of leadership.
6. Teachers to play the role of facilitators, organisers and managers of learning.
7. Science courses to give students the opportunity to consider the social, economic and ecological impact of scientific and technological innovations.

8. Environmental Science to play an important role in helping the adolescents appreciate the interdependence of living things and the fragile balance in the biosphere.

9. Providing equality of opportunity.

10. Technology courses to be designed in such a way as they address students' needs in their own environment.

11. Along with mother tongue, foreign language to be given greater attention in the case of adolescents whenever needed.

12. Providing suitable television programmes to adolescents.

13. Encouraging the involvement of adolescents in the mass media programmes meant for them.

14. Introducing a variety of vocational courses for the adolescents.

15. Developing skills of thinking, planning, communicating, organising, problem solving, monitoring and assessing.

16. Developing educational systems to reinforce rural development programmes.

17. Introducing non-military national service for adolescents.

18. Greater-learning opportunities at work places.

19. Programmes for balanced personal opportunities.

20. Programmes for developing in the adolescents a sense of service and the advancement of public good.

21. Developing in the adolescents skills how to learn.

22. Laying emphasis on the development in the adolescents values of self-awareness and esteem and confidence in order to deal with a rapidly changing world.

23. Developing in the adolescents a positive outlook for the future.

24. Developing in the adolescents a commitment to promote interpersonal development.

25. Promoting in the adolescents values of tolerance and respect for different perspectives and views, cultures, religions and races and towards opposite sex and to disabled people.

11.6 SELF-CONCEPT AND EDUCATIONAL IMPLICATIONS

Meaning of Self-Concept

Self-concept implies a person's perception or view of himself. Self-concept is what the individual thinks of his actual self. It is *me.* Some psychologists refer to it as *personal field, behavioural field, life-space,* or *psychological field.* Self-concept plays an important role in the development of personality of an individual. The positive self-concept is likely to enable an individual to lead a happy, contended,and well-managed life. His development is optimum. It is, therefore, important that children are trained to learn from the very beginning to develop a positive self-concept which is socially desirable. The idea of self starts growing from the period of infancy and grows during childhood, adolescence and maturity. As the child grows up, he starts feeling that he is separate from others. He slowly begins to learn that certain things belong to him. The part of the environment in which he lives is known as his *phenomenal self* and the rest of the environment of which he is aware or to which he responds is called *phenomenal environment or perceived environment* and not *self.* Following figure adapted from A. Ward Combs and D. Snygg's book, *Individual Behaviour : A Perception Approach to Behaviour* explains these concepts.

As the child starts advancing, he starts feeling that he has a personality and an identity of his own which is different from others. He may be a part of the total environment but it is not his own. Hence there is a line of demarcation between *phenomenal self* and phenomenal environment as indicated in Fig. 11.1. It indicates what the individual thinks about himself. Self-concept is the '*me*' part of the individual.

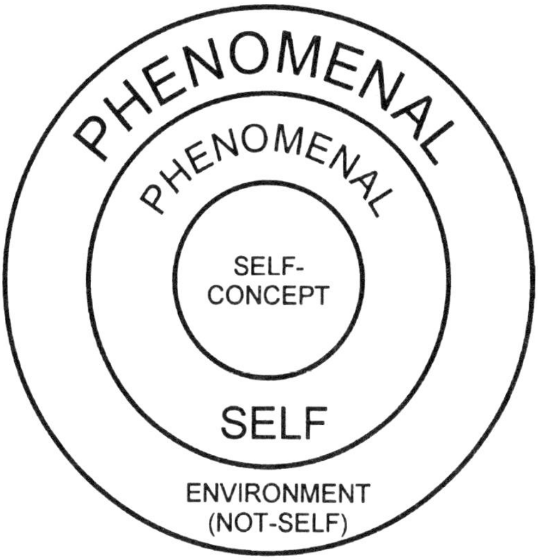

Fig. 11.1: Diagrammatic representation of the concept of self-concept

The *phenomenal self* includes all the aspects of the environment with which the individual identifies himself, *i.e.*, the family, the school etc.

Components of Self-Concept

Components of self-concept are: beliefs, ideas or perception an individual has about oneself—one's physical, emotional, psychological and social achievements and characteristics.

Characteristics of Self-Concept

1. Self-concept is organised. An individual organises a lot of information about himself.
2. Self-concept has several dimensions.
3. Self-concept is hierarchical.
4. Self-concept becomes increasingly differentiated with the increase in age.

5. Self-concept is stable.
6. Self-concept is negative as well as positive.

Table 11.1: Comparative Study of Individual with Positive/Strong and with Negative/Weak Self-Concept

	Dimension or Parameter of Self-Concept	*Individual with Positive/Strong Self-Concept*	*Individual with Negative/Weak Self-Concept*
1.	Personal status	Friendly. Acceptable. Self-confident. Flexible. Open-minded. Assertive. Ambitious. Dominating	Unfriendly. Unacceptable. Shaky. Rigid. Intolerant. Suspicious. Irresponsible. Nervous. Meek. Coward
2.	Ability to cope with challenging and problematic situations	Enormous. Dashing. Imaginative. Constructive. Analytic. Competitive	Very little. Non-enterprising. Floundering. Non-analytic. Directionless
3.	Ability to communicate with others	Talks easily, coherently and effectively	Feels difficulty to communicate. Superfluous in talk.
4.	Ability to cope with school work	Enormous. Gets on well with classmates	Very little. Unsocial.
5.	Ability to make choices	Makes wise choices	Makes wrong choices.

Self-concept and Student's Performance: A student with a positive or high self-concept has high self-esteem. High self-concept develops self-confidence and poor self-concept hinders initial school adjustment and academic progress also. Students with high concept tend to accept their failure as well as limitations. They are better achievers. They are more determined to achieve their goals. They do not suffer from inferiority complex. They are free from mental sickness and work vigorously and express their ideas and beliefs to others with confidence and conviction. They have the ability to impress others. They are rational in their approach.

Development of Self-Concept: Self-concept is based on what children believe their teachers, peers and parents think of them. Positive self-concept is developed through love, encouragement, positive comments and understanding attitude of the teachers and parents. Teachers should adopt suitable strategies and provide opportunities to children to develop their self-concept.

(See also 11.5)

12

Guidance and Counselling for Adolescents

Meaning and Need for Educational Vocational Guidance and Counselling

In this chapter, the meaning, need, aims and characteristics of guidance, educational guidance, vocational guidance and counselling are discussed so as to acquaint the students to understand the background of providing guidance and counselling to the adolescents. In a way it is an introductory matter for the main theme 'Guidance and Counselling for the Adolescents'.

12.1 MEANING OF GUIDANCE

The general meaning of guidance denotes some form of assistance given to an individual for the purpose of making wise choices and attaining optimum development of his abilities, aptitudes and interests. But this is not adequate for a detailed and comprehensive treatment of the subject-matter. It is, therefore, essential to give the views of experts in this regard.

Following are the important definitions of guidance:

Chisholm states "Guidance seeks to help the individual discover his own talents in comparison to the opportunities of the world and help him prepare himself so that he can find or develop a place in which he can live a well-balanced life and contribute his part to the welfare of his fellow men".

In the words of Ruth Strang, "Guidance is a process of helping every individual, through his own efforts, to discover and develop his potentialities for his personal happiness and social usefulness".

Dr. J.A. Humphreys and Dr. A.E. Traxler, define guidance as: "At any level, guidance implies that the individual attains self-direction just as fast as far as his mental, social and emotional abilities permit. Guidance of the younger or less mature individual, of course, calls for closer direction than does guidance of the older or more mature individual. The term guidance, moreover, aptly applies to working with an individual all along the lines from early childhood into adulthood".

According to Jones, "Guidance involves personal help given by someone; it is designed to assist a person in deciding where he wants to go, what he wants to do, or how he can best accomplish his purposes; it assists him in solving problems that arise in his life. It does not solve problems for the individual, but helps him to solve them. The focus of guidance is the individual, not the problem, its purpose is to promote the growth of the individual in self-direction".

According to the Secondary Education Commission, "Guidance involves the difficult art of helping boys and girls to plan their own future wisely in the full light of all the factors that can be mastered about themselves and about the world in which they are to live and work. Naturally, therefore, it is not the work of a few specialists, but rather a service in which the entire school staff must cooperate under the guidance of some persons with special knowledge and skill in this particular field. Guidance in this sense is not confined to the vocational field only. It covers the whole gamut of youth problems and should be provided in an appropriate form at all stages of education through the cooperative endeavour of understanding parents, teachers, headmasters, principals and guidance officers".

12.2 NATURE AND CHARACTERISTICS OF GUIDANCE

From above mentioned definitions, we conclude:

1. Guidance is assisting the individual to find his own place.
2. Guidance is assisting the individual to know his assets and liabilities.
3. Guidance is assisting the individual to find his path through his own efforts.
4. Guidance is assisting the individual to help himself for promoting his self-direction.
5. Guidance is assisting the individual to adjust himself.
6. Guidance is a point of view that reflects a positive towards oneself and others.
7. Guiaance is assisting an individual to develop his potentialities and talents to the optimum level.
8. Guidance is helping the individual to make appropriate educational, personal, recreational and vocational choices.
9. Guidance is assisting the individual to establish harmonious relations with his parents, neighbours, peers etc.
10. Guidance programme is organised.
11. Guidance programme has a structure, system and personal.
12. Guidance consists of specialised services—testing, counselling, educational and vocational information, placement and follow-up.
13. Guidance programme is an integral part of the school programme.

All these characteristics of guidance apply to school guidance programme.

12.3 AIMS, FUNCTIONS AND KINDS OF GUIDANCE

The aims and functions of guidance are:

1. Optimum development of the potentialities of an individual.
2. Orientation of the individual to educational, and vocational opportunities and requirements.
3. Assisting individual to adjust himself to various situations.
4. Assisting the individual to assess himself what he is.
5. Assisting the individual to appreciate where he was.
6. Assisting the individual to become aware of his assets and limitations.
7. Assisting the individual to find his own path in accordance with his assets and limitations.

8. Assisting the individual to follow his chosen path.
9. Assisting the individual to promote his career.

12.4 BRIEF HISTORY OF GUIDANCE

During the late 1920s and early 1930s, in the U.S.A., education and guidance were considered almost synonymous. During the same period, psychologists like Binnet, Cattell, Terman and Thorndike introduced psychological testing in the field of guidance. About the middle of 1930s, the emphasis shifted and more attention was given to economic problems, placement or employment and occupational trends. More and more of assistance was given to the employer in order to make him more effective in his work. This trend was described by some writers as 'personal movement'.

Modern meaning of guidance concept, however, does not restrict itself to any one discipline. It is being influenced by sociology, psychology, economy and education etc.

12.5 EDUCATIONAL GUIDANCE: MEANING AND NEED

Meaning of Educational Guidance

Following definitions of educational guidance bring out the meaning of educational guidance.

1. In the words of G.E. Myers, "Educational guidance is a process concerned with bringing about between an individual pupil with his distinctive characteristics on the one hand, and differing groups of opportunities and requirements on the other, a favourable setting for the individual's development or education. If there is a single group, of opportunities and requirements, as is the case with a fixed curriculum, the problem is simply one of the education by the best methods possible in a meeting already determined and not one of educational guidance".

2. Jones defines educational guidance as the assistance given to the pupils in their choices and adjustments with relation to schools, curriculum's, courses and school life.

3. Ruth Strang observes that educational guidance is positive. It is a developmental programme concerned with the questions. What is this boy or girl good for? What kind of education will reveal his capacities and help him to develop them? According to the same author, educational guidance is intended to aid the individual in choosing an appropriate programme and in making progress in it. This involves (1) knowledge of the abilities and interests of the individuals, (2) awareness of a wide range of educational opportunities, and (3) programmes and counselling which help the individual to choose wisely on the basis of these two kinds of knowledge.

4. Brewer defines it as "Educational guidance is a conscious effort to assist in the intellectual growth of an individual—anything that has to do with instruction or with learning may come under the term of guidance".

5. Dunsmoor and Miller observe, "Guidance as a form systematic assistance whereby students are aided in achieving satisfactory adjustment to school and life".

6. In the words of Dr. K.G. Rama Rao, "Guidance in the wider context of a total curriculum and embracing education of everyone of the basic activity pattern—intellectual as well as social, economic as well as artistic, moral as well as spiritual, domestic as well as physical—becomes all inclusive as well as competes with instructional and testing or examining functions of the school in preparing the school-leavers for work and life in general".

7. Shirely, Hamrin and Clifforde Erickson write, "Guidance in the secondary school refers to that aspect of the education programme which is concerned especially with helping the pupil to become adjusted to his present situation and to plan his future in line with his interests, abilities and social needs. Guidance or personal work represents an organised effort on the part of the school, equipped with both a knowledge of the pupil and information as to opportunities, of an educational, a social and a vocational character to help the individual pupil become adjusted to his present situation in such a way as to provide the greatest development for him and to aid him in planning for his future. It is rightly said that this programme helps John see through himself and then to assist him in seeing himself through".

Need for Educational Guidance

Educational guidance is needed to make the best use of the potential of children.

Lack of educational guidance has created what is known as the problem of 'educated unemployment'.

Lack of educational and vocational guidance has led to a dearth of suitable hands for many occupations needing a specialised training.

It has been rightly said, "Nothing but a well-organised network of guidance services throughout the country will save us from the impending tragedy".

Almost every system of education is based on two assumptions. The first is that every student should strive for maximum self-development and the other is that every student should take his place in the society as its useful member. These two assumptions imply that the school and community activities of a child should be based on some definite pattern. Educational guidance services must assist the child to achieve this end.

For achieving above purposes of guidance, several kinds of services are organised in the school.

12.6 VOCATIONAL GUIDANCE : MEANING AND NEED

Meaning of Vocational Guidance

The General Conference of International Labour Organisation in its vocational guidance recommendations described "Vocational Guidance" as "assistance given to an individual in solving problems related to occupational choice and progress with due regard for the individual's characteristics and their relation to occupational opportunity". In the definition adopted by the National Vocational Guidance Association, U.S.A., in 1973, "Vocational Guidance is the process of assisting the individual to choose an occupation, prepare for it, enter upon and progress in it".

To quote Prof. G.E. Myers, "Vocational guidance is fundamentally an effort to conserve the priceless native capacities of youth and the costly training provided for youth in the schools. It seeks to conserve these richest of all human resources by aiding the individuals to invest and use them where they will bring greatest satisfaction and success to himself and greatest benefit to society".

According to Super, "Vocational guidance is the process of helping a person to develop and accept an integrated and adequate picture of himself, and of his role in the world of work to test this concept against reality and to convert it into a reality with satisfaction to himself and benefit to society".

It may be stressed again that it is impossible to separate sharply the vocational aspects of guidance from other aspects of guidance such as educational, social, health, etc.

Need for an Organised Programme of Vocational Guidance

I. *Individual Differences*: The fundamental reason why guidance is needed is that there are two sets of differences—differences among individuals and differences among courses of action open to them.

II. *Vocational Guidance from the Financial Point of View of an Individual*: Very often we notice many young people entering occupations by chance and not in accordance with their suitability. The result is that there is an economic loss to the young workers. A lot of money is being spent unnecessarily in the preparation of two vocations rather than one. Take the case of a boy who works for two years as an apprentice in a particular trade and then changes to some other. What is its effect? The individual takes a longer time to adjust himself to the proper occupation and loses money that he might have earned if he would have continued working in his previous occupation.

III. *Vocational Guidance from the Financial Point of View of the Employers*: Often industry and business incur heavy losses because of change in labour. When an electrician's apprentice decides to leave his job and becomes an automobile mechanic, the new worker takes time to gain proficiency to the point attained by one who has left. The quality and the quantity of work suffers. Besides, the time spent on the selection and appointment of the previous work is also wasted.

Changes in occupations are much more common with younger than with old workers and are also much more expensive than mere changes in the places of employment, both to the employers and the workers themselves.

IV. *Vocational Guidance from the Financial Point of View of the Society*: Ultimately it is the society that suffers all the costs of these wasteful methods of entering occupations. Inferior goods at a higher cost are made available to the society. D.D. Eisenhower has observed, "The wealth of the world is created by the work of skilled hands on raw materials".

V. *Vocational Guidance from the Health Point of View*: Wrong choice of occupations affects adversely the health of the workers. A delicate eye-sight is injured by work which greatly affects the eye-sight. Sometimes nervous system is shattered by making efforts to maintain a speed of production beyond one's capacity and so on.

VI. *Vocational Guidance from the Point of View of Personal and Social Values*: In the choice of an occupation are involved the happiness of the worker, satisfaction in his work, his personal growth and his contribution to human welfare. A frustrated and dissatisfied worker is a curse to himself as well as to the society. Failure in one occupation has a great demoralising effect on an individual. "Each failure in the experience of a young worker increases the probability of another", writes G.E. Myers.

Super writes, "Occupation is not merely a means of earning a livelihood but also a way of life, a social role".

VII. *Vocational Guidance for the Purpose of Utilising Human Potentialities*: The society loses much through its failure to discover potential genius. A great deal of genius remains undiscovered in every generation.

VIII. *Vocational Guidance from the Point of View of the Complex Nature of the Society*: It has been discussed already the far-reaching changes that have taken place in economic, political and social structure of the country. We require scientists, engineers, technicians, technologists, etc., to man our industrial and commercial establishments etc. New and altogether new occupations are coming to the forefront. Ours is an expanding economic structure and this fact intensifies the need for help to individuals.

IX. *Vocational Guidance from the Point of View of the Availability of the Growing Amount of Information Concerning Individuals*: The new methods of studying the individuals help us to understand the individual in a more scientific and comprehensive way in a factor which is of great assistance to a guidance worker in guiding an individual in the matter of making a choice.

12.7 COUNSELLING AND ITS TYPES : ROLE OF THE COUNSELLOR

Meaning of Counselling

Webster's Dictionary defines counselling as "Consultation, mutual exchange of opinions, deliberating together".

Wrenn says, "Counselling is personal and dynamic relationship between the two individuals—one of whom is older or more experienced than the younger, who together approach a more or less well-defined problem of the younger or less experienced or less wise, with mutual consideration for each to the end that the problem may be more clearly defined and that the one who has the problem may be helped to a self-determined solution of it".

Counselling is a process in which a pupil is approached by the counsellor on an individual basis and is helped in arriving at a decision or making choice finding a direction.

Types of Counselling

There are three types of counselling:

1. Directive Counselling,
2. Non-Directive Counselling, and
3. Eclectic Counselling.

1. Directive Counselling

E.G. Williamson favours this type of counselling. It is counsellor directed counselling. Counsellor is the leader or it is he who dominates. It is the counsellor who discovers the problem, diagnoses it and provides a solution to it. Majority of the talking is done by the counsellor. In this type of counselling, the emphasis is upon the problem. What caused the problem? How can it best be solved?

According to Andrew and Willy, the basic assumptions of the directive counselling are:

1. A Counsellor has superior training, experience and information and is competent to give advice about how a problem is to be solved.
2. The maladjustment of an individual does not entirely impair the intellectual ability of the client, hence counselling is primarily an intellectual process.
3. Because of such factors as bias, the client is not always capable of solving his problems.
4. The objectives of counselling are achieved primarily through a problem solving situation.

Role of the Counsellor in Directive Counselling

The role can be portrayed by presenting the various steps the counsellor uses:

(a) *Analysis*: The collection of pertinent data by a variety of tools and techniques.

(b) *Synthesis*: The mechanical and graphical organisation of the data.

(c) *Diagnosis*: Drawing a conclusion about the causes of disturbance.

(d) *Prognosis*: A prediction of the future development of the student's problem.

(e) *Counselling and Treatment*

(f) *Follow-up and Evaluation*

Merits

(1) It takes less time and is economical with respect to time.

(2) The counsellor comes to the solution soon. This gives him happiness.

(3) Directive counselling gives more significance to the intellectual rather than to the emotional aspect of individual's personality.

Demerits of Directive Counselling

(1) It kills the initiative of the child and as such it makes him somewhat helpless.

(2) It does not guide the counsellee to be efficient and he cannot express himself freely.

(3) There is lot of regimentation in it because of the dominant role played by the counsellor. It is undemocratic.

(4) Lastly, the counsellee is made dependent upon the counsellor.

2. Non Directive Counselling

Non-Directive Counselling is also known by other names such as permissive counselling or counsellee or client-oriented counselling. Carl Rogers is the leading exponent of this type of counselling.

This type of counselling is totally opposite to directive type of counselling. In non-directive counselling, the counsellor remains silent to the maximum extent and allows the counsellee to speak freely about the problem. The counsellor passes an occasional remark as to keep his client on the track. The counsellor asks a few questions. In this way the counsellor helps the pupil to think out the solution of the problem himself. Complete responsibility is placed on the individual and the counsellee plays the primary role.

Steps and the Role of the Counsellor in Non-Directive Counselling

Carl Rogers has outlined the role of the counsellor by listing down the following steps in non-directive counselling:

The individual or the counsellee comes for help.

The helping situation is usually defined.

The counsellor encourages the counsellee to express his feelings freely.

The counsellor accepts and clarifies negative feelings.

Negative feelings or impulses are followed by tentative expressions of the positive impulses.

Counsellor accepts and recognises positive feelings of the counsellee.

This provides a basis on which the counsellee can go ahead to the new level of integration.

Counsellor clarifies possible course of action.

Counsellee develops further insight, a more complete and accurate understanding of the problem.

Merits of Non-Directive Counselling

1. In the present day personnel work, the non-directive counselling movement may be linked to the progressive movement in education. Both stress the freedom of the individual.
2. As a therapy, it has indisputable values.
3. Non-directive counselling can be compared to confessions made in the church and as such when one is allowed to talk, one brings one's repressed thoughts to the surface and relieves one's tensions.
4. This facilitates integrated positive action.
5. This develops a feeling of increased independence on the part of the counsellee.

Demerits of Non-Directive Counselling

1. It is a time consuming process. The counsellee may begin a never ending dialogue.
2. In view of above, it may deprive many other counsellee to seek necessary counselling.
3. The resources, judgement and wisdom of the client cannot be relied upon.
4. How most problems be solved by simply talking out things in the interview situation is a big limitation.

3. Eclectic Counselling (Best Type)

Eclectic counselling is a combination and synthesis of directive and non-directive types of the counselling or viewpoints. As stated earlier, the two extremes forms of (Directive and Non-Directive) are combined. Here both the counsellor and the counsellee are active and cooperative. Both do the talking turn by turn. The problem is solved jointly.

This also raises one problem—how much freedom should the counsellee be allowed? Answer is simple—fifty per cent. But the factors of the personality of the counsellee and the situation should also be taken into consideration.

To Conclude: In the absence of any clear-cut indication of the superiority of one counselling method over another, the eclectic approach seems justified provided it is coupled with the positive concept that counselling is essentially a learning process for both the counsellor and the counsellee.

Characteristics of Counselling Process

So whatever be the type, it has been found out that counselling process has the following five characteristics:

1. Counselling is a professional service.
2. Counselling is centred upon the problems of the client.
3. Good counselling results in client-made decisions.
4. Counselling is one to one process.
5. Counselling must be based on the accuracy of the counsellor's prediction.

Guidance and Counselling

It is sometimes said that guidance is the heart of education and counselling as the heart of counselling.

Guidance is relatively a broader term and counselling is one of the services under the guidance programme.

Need for guidance arises when an individual is confronted with some problems. Problem may be solved by providing information. This is the initial phase of guidance. The individual having the problem may be charged with emotion. He may be unable to adjust himself with the environment on account of emotional tension. In such a situation he needs counselling to overcome tension.

13

Organisation of Guidance and Counselling Services for Adolescents in Schools

13.1 NEED FOR GUIDANCE SERVICES

Jones has very rightly observed that everyone needs guidance at sometime in his life; some need it constantly and throughout their lives while others need it only at rare intervals at times of some crisis. The need for guidance is all the more needed in the case of adolescents who, as observed by William Burton are "odd, awkward, graceful, respectful, selfish, altruistic, idealistic, narrow-minded, sympathetic, cruel individuals". Likewise E.A. Peel has observed, "The adolescent is beset with problems of divided loyalties, accentuated by the lack of adult privileges and responsibilities. He thus appears excessively aggressive and then excessively shy, excessively affectionate and then quite suddenly detached and cool. These are all problems of the stresses and strains of transition".

The need for a comprehensive programme of guidance has become imperative in view of the following considerations:

1. Complex nature of society.
2. Individual differences.
3. Changed agricultural, commercial, industrial and technical patterns of the country.
4. Changed occupational pattern of the country.
5. Changed occupational structures.
6. Changed educational pattern of the country.
7. Need for conservation of human energy.
8. Vocationalisation of education.
9. New researches in educational psychology.
10. More leisure and the need for its proper utilisation.
11. Impact of electronic mass media.
12. Impact of press media.
13. Juvenile delinquency.
14. Urbanisation and congested cities.
15. Growing tension on account of increased stress.
16. Changed family structure and lack of guidance and counselling at home.
17. Employment of women in large numbers.

18. Need for correct understanding of religious matters.
19. Political exploitation.
20. Population explosion.
21. Industrial psychology and its requirements.
22. Search for identity of the youth.
23. Need for making educational choices.
24. Need for effective learning.
25. Need for proper involvement in co-curricular work.
26. Need for wholesome relations.
27. Increasing use of drugs etc.
28. New diseases like HIV/AID.
29. Complex sexual environment behaviour.
30. Increasing openness in society.
31. Impact of globalisation.

13.2 SCOPE OF EDUCATIONAL, VOCATIONAL GUIDANCE AND COUNSELLING FOR ADOLESCENTS

There is no facet of life of an adolescent which is not covered in the scope of guidance and counselling. Following are the major areas in this respect:

1. Career Guidance
2. Civic Guidance
3. Community Guidance
4. Cultural Guidance
5. Educational Guidance
6. Emotional Guidance
7. Family Relations Guidance
8. Health Guidance
9. Human Relations Guidance
10. Leisure Time Utilisation Guidance
11. Moral Guidance
12. Personal Guidance
13. Physical Guidance
14. Professional Guidance
15. Psychiatric Guidance
16. Recreational Guidance
17. Religious Guidance
18. Sex Guidance
19. Social Guidance
20. Spiritual Guidance
21. Vocational Guidance

13.3 AIMS, PURPOSES AND FUNCTIONS OF EDUCATIONAL GUIDANCE AT THE SECONDARY AND SENIOR SECONDARY STAGE OF SCHOOLING (ADOLESCENCE STAGE)

1. To assist the adolescent secure information regarding the possibility and desirability of further schooling.
2. To assist the adolescent to know the purpose and functions of different categories of senior secondary schools and other institutions.
3. To assist the adolescent to know in detail the offerings and facilities of the school he might attend.
4. To assist adolescent to know the requirements for entrance into the school of his choice.
5. To assist the adolescent to adjust himself to the curriculum, the school and the social life connected with it.
6. To help the adolescent in the selection of the subjects at the senior secondary stage.

7. To help adolescent in the selection of textbooks and other instructional material.
8. To help the adolescent in developing study habits.
9. To help the adolescent in making satisfactory progress in various subjects.
10. To help the adolescent in the selection of hobbies.
11. To help the adolescent in the selection of co-curricular activities.
12. To help the adolescent in knowing the availability of scholarships, loans, etc.
13. To help the adolescent to find out his aptitudes, interests etc.
14. To assist the adolescent to follow his chosen career and path.

Close Relationship between Educational and Vocational Guidance and Counselling

All aspects are closely related. The distinguishing mark is the nature of the dominating purpose. The student's career plan and selection of courses are functionally related. In special circumstances counselling is also needed to supplement the other two programmes.

13.4 AIMS, PURPOSE AND OBJECTIVES OF VOCATIONAL GUIDANCE FOR THE ADOLESCENTS

Jones has stated the following aims of vocational guidance:

1. To assist the students to acquire such knowledge of the characteristics and functions, the duties and rewards of the group of occupations within his choice.
2. To enable him to find what general and specific abilities, skills, etc. are required for the group of occupations under consideration and what are the qualifications of age, preparations, sex, etc. for entering them.
3. To give opportunity for experience in school (try-out courses) and out of school (after-school and vocation jobs) that will give such information about conditions for work as will assist the individual to discover his own abilities and help in the development of wider interests.
4. To help the individual develop the point of view that all honest labour is worth and that the most important bases for choice of an occupation are: (a) the peculiar service that the individual can render to society, (b) personal satisfaction in the occupation, and (c) aptitude for the work required.
5. To assist the individual to acquire a technique of analysis of occupational information and to develop the habit of analysing such information before making a final choice.
6. To assist him to secure such information about himself, his abilities, general and specific, his interests and his powers as he may need for wise choice.
7. To assist economically handicapped children who are above the

compulsory attendance age to secure, through public or private funds scholarships or other financial assistance so that they may have opportunities for further education in accordance with their vocational plans.

8. To assist the student to secure a knowledge of the facilities offered by various educational institutions for vocational training and the requirement for admission to them, the length of training offered and the cost of attendance.
9. To help the worker to adjust himself to the occupation in which he is engaged; to assist him to understand his relationships to workers in his own related occupations and to society as a whole.
10. To enable the student to secure reliable information about the danger of alluring short-cuts to fortune.

13.5 WHY SPECIAL EMPHASIS ON GUIDANCE AT THE HIGHER/SENIOR SECONDARY STAGE

There are three important reasons which give rise to the necessity of a specialised guidance service at this stage. The first is that there is a marked difference in the curriculum of an elementary and secondary school and that of a higher secondary school. Curriculum of a Higher Secondary school is a diversified one which involves the problem of selecting subjects in class XI.

The second reason is that much emphasis is placed upon the vocational point of view. Important decisions are to be made in class XI and class XII. In class XI the selection of subjects is largely influenced by vocational requirements. Important decisions are taken and help is needed when the students are about to leave the school, either to secure jobs or to go to college or to some other type of further training.

The third reason is that the students are passing through a very critical stage in their lives where vital decisions for future are involved.

13.6 GUIDANCE PROGRAMME IN SCHOOL : SCOPE

Scope of Guidance in the School

The following figures explain the scope of guidance programme and services in school.

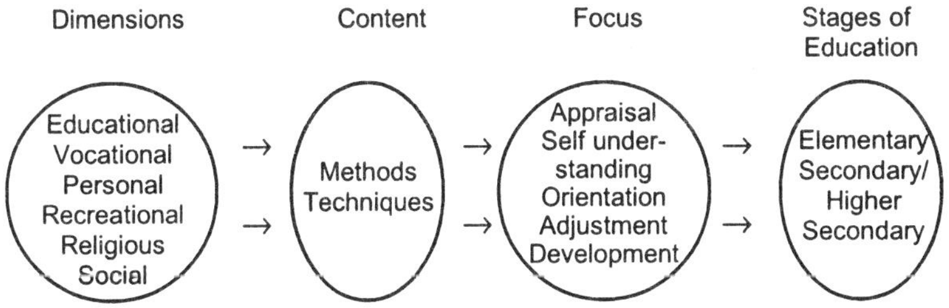

Fig. 13.1: Scope of Guidance and Guidance Process

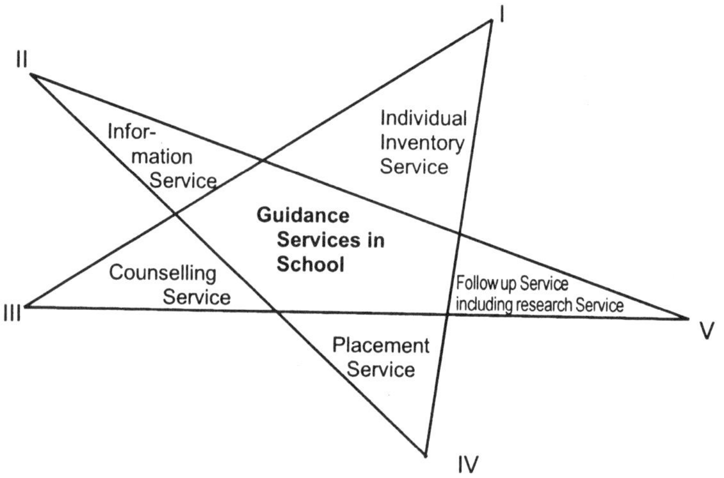

Fig. 13.2: Showing Broad Categories of Guidance Services in the Secondary and Senior Secondary Schools

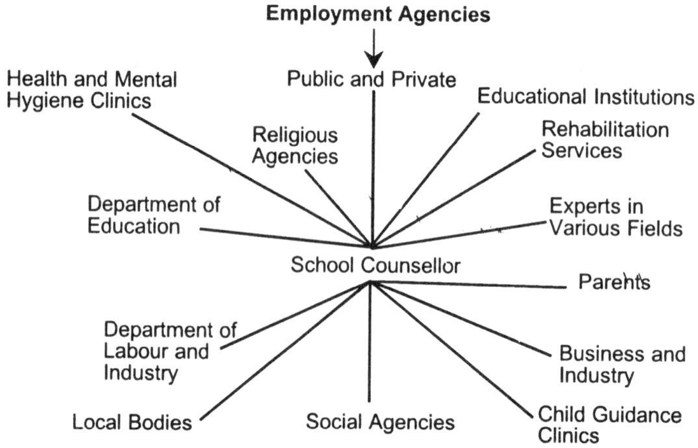

Fig. 13.3: Guidance Services in the School and Community Resources

Classification of Guidance and Counselling Service for Adolescents

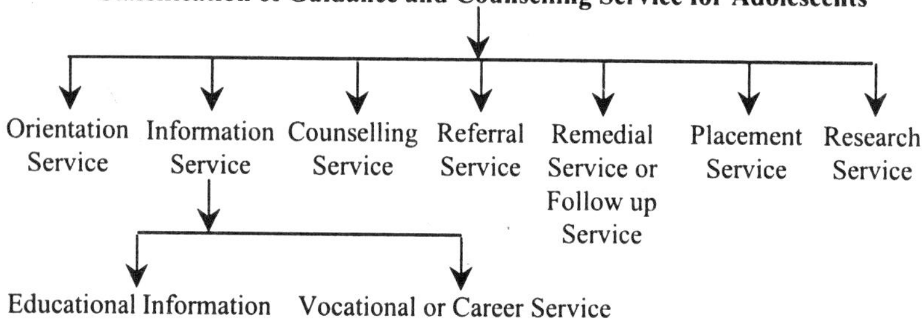

1. *Individual Inventory Service.* Compilation of individual inventory giving detailed information about each student concerning his abilities and achievements in different areas is the first essential requisite of every guidance programme in the school. This information should be kept up-to-date and must be used for the all—round development of the adolescent. It may be compiled in the form of a cumulative record.

2. *Information Service.* Students of higher secondary schools generally need three types of information which is very helpful to them in making decisions about various courses, occupations and institutions such as: (a) Information about colleges and training opportunities, (b) Information about available occupations, and (c) Information about scholarships and other financial help available during the training period. Information may be collected from papers and magazines, government notifications and bulletin's and information centers of the Employment Exchanges, etc. The usefulness of this information will be lost if the information is not kept up-to-date. This information may be supplemented by talks of people from different occupations.

3. *Counselling Service.* Counselling service is regarded as the 'heart' of the guidance programme. This service must assist an individual in identifying, understanding and solving problems that confront him. Counselling can be done by a well-trained counsellor. A detailed discussion on the role of the counsellor is available elsewhere in this book.

4. *Placement Service.* This service implies help to the individual in obtaining employment. There are three stages of this service:

(a) Assessing the abilities, aptitudes and interests of the individual student.
(b) Analysing several occupations, particularly the ones in which the student expresses his interest.
(c) Relating occupations and abilities.

5. *Follow-up Service.* This implies continuation of the programme to check the effectiveness of the programme.

13.7 EDUCATIONAL VOCATIONAL GUIDANCE PROCESS AND COUNSELLING

1.	Appraisal of the student by means of	(a)	Tests and rating scales		
		(b)	Parents ratings		
		(c)	Diagnostic records		
		(d)	Individual inventories		
		(e)	Sociometric analysis		
		(f)	Observations		
		(g)	Anecdotes		
		(h)	Case studies		
		(i)	Cumulative records		
2.	Adjustment by means of	(a)	Change in the environment through	1.	Socialised curriculum
				2.	Co-curricular activities
				3	Physical surroundings
				4.	Community resources
				5.	Educational and vocational opportunities
				6.	Group contacts

(b)	Changes in the individual through	1. Interviews 2. Developmental exercises 3. Instruction 4. Guidance 5. Group process

13.8 ORGANISATION OF GUIDANCE SERVICES IN A SENIOR SECONDARY SCHOOL : SPECIAL CONSIDERATIONS

The Principal is responsible for all the activities of the school. A qualified teacher who is well-versed and interested in guidance should be made the incharge of the guidance unit of the school. The teacher may then become, in effect, the part-time school counsellor. The special subject teachers can render a useful help in the guidance programme.

A separate room should be provided for the counsellor with a view to enabling him to put his relevant materials concerning the records of the students, information materials concerning educational and vocational choices and to conduct interviews without any disturbance by taking the students into confidence. A small library containing books giving information regarding hobbies and different vocations may be set up in the counsellor's room. Books should be issued by the counsellor to the students in accordance with their capabilities and aptitudes.

A Guidance Committee may be formed in the school with the counsellor as its secretary. The Guidance Committee, composed largely of teachers, is in a better position to study the needs, purposes and procedures essential to the development of guidance service and to set necessary guidance policy. The Guidance Committee is also expected to play an important role in impressing upon all-round growth of an individual.

13.9 GUIDANCE PERSONNEL

Guidance personnel consists of the Counsellor, Teachers, Area Counsellors, Psychologist and Health Specialist.

13.10 FUNCTIONS OF THE COUNSELLOR AND GUIDANCE PROGRAMME

1. To administer psychological tests
2. To interpret the results of the psychological tests.
3. To collect and give information about different types of courses at school and in technical training institutes.
4. To give information about different occupations.
5. To give individual counselling to students who have difficulty in choosing courses or in taking up employment on leaving school.
6. To stimulate students to put forth maximum efforts.
7. To assist teachers with pupil problems which the teachers find difficult.
8. To assist youth employment services in the placement of pupils in various jobs.

9. To take up follow-up work with a view to assessing the outcome of guidance services in regard to students who have received guidance.
10. To assist in familiarising new classroom teachers and other school personnel with guidance services available.
11. To explain school records with which the students are not familiar.
12. To obtain as much of an objective measurement of a pupil's abilities, interests, aptitudes and physical characteristics as possible.
13. To give assistance and counselling through interviews with each pupil to enable him to understand himself and his problems.
14. To maintain close contact with the school doctor in all health problems of students.
15. To obtain a knowledge of the relevant aspects of a student's home environment, economic status and personality.
16. To confer with parents and arrange group meetings of parents as needs arise.
17. To be constantly alert to signs of emotional difficulties.
18. To refer difficulties to available specialists.
19. To provide counselling for a pupil relating to educational or personal problems or plans.
20. To arrange excursions for pupils with a view to providing them with realistic educational and occupational information.
21. To arrange career conferences when considered appropriate.
22. To assist students in making vocational choices commensurate with their ability and skill.
23. To arrange case conferences about an individual student who is experiencing some type of difficulty.
24. To assist pupils to develop initiative and independence so that they may progress in self-direction.
25. To aid potential drop-out to make the school experience as profitable as possible.
26. To arrange for group guidance through class meetings, sessions with guest speakers, films and activities to promote social adjustment.

(*Note* : Normally full time counsellor is appointed only in a big school. A cluster of schools usually have a counsellor.)

13.11 METHODS OF EDUCATIONAL AND VOCATIONAL GUIDANCE

There are two methods of guidance: (i) Individual guidance, (ii) Group guidance.

Group guidance includes the following techniques:

1. Talks by teachers, school counsellor and experts on educational matters.
2. Use of audio-visual aids, including electronic media to disseminate career information.
3. Career conferences and exhibitions.
4. Group discussions.
5. Orientation courses.
6. Parent-teacher meets.

7. Commercial and industrial visits.
8. T.V. talks and panel discussions.
9. Counselling.

13.12 FACILITIES REQUIRED FOR GUIDANCE

1. Physical Facilities

A separate room with necessary furniture may be provided for guidance activities.

2. Financial Facilities

(i) A non-recurring expenditure of Rs. 20,000 may be incurred for the purchase of test materials and information material needed for the guidance programme every 5th year.

(ii) A recurring expenditure on the following items:

(a) Audio-visual material.

(b) Occupational information materials.

(c) Organising field trips (Guidance).

(d) Career conferences and exhibitions.

(e) Films and film strips.

(f) Answer sheets for tests.

13.13 CAREER GUIDANCE : NEED AND SIGNIFICANCE OF CAREER PLANNING

A publication entitled *Working Together for a Better Future* (1987) of the Department of Education and Science and the Department of Employment (U.K.) has explained the significance of career planning and need for guidance as under:

1. If they are to look forward to a better future, our young people need to be better educated and trained for adult life. They must have a wide range of opportunities in education and training. And they must have information and guidance to allow them to make sound choices as they go through school and beyond.

2. The process starts in the home : families and friends have crucial role to play in shaping people's expectations and aspirations. This role need to be properly recognised in schools. Parents to be involved to the fullest extent in what their children are doing and the choices they are making.

3. Schools themselves play a vital part in developing expectations and capabilities from the earliest age. Good schools today encourage self-awareness, the ability to work with others, and a sense of initiative and enterprise—qualities which are very bit as valuable in adult life as examination certificates. A broad and balanced curriculum which makes the most of each pupil's potential in every area—regardless of sex, ethnic origin or disability—should render school leavers versatile and adaptable unconstrained by early specialisation.

4. Much can be done from the primary years onwards to give children insights into the world of work and a preparation for the decisions ahead

which will affect the future directions of their lives. If these decisions are to be properly informed, full and reliable information and sensitive guidance must be available at the right time for all.

5. It is essential that when choices of options for further study first have to be made—around 13+—that the right decisions are taken in each case—the crucial stage for which pupils must be fully prepared.

6. At 16+ and 17+, important choices have to be made between staying on at school or going on to college, vocational training or employment. These choices must be properly informed.

7. Those children on the point of leaving school or college equally need a realistic appreciation of all the choices open to them. And at subsequent stages too, people must have access to relevant, reliable and complete information and skilled guidance about options.

Issues Involved in Career Planning

Five questions are generally being faced in planning a career:

1. How to plan a career?
2. How to manage it?
3. How to maintain it?
4. How to retain it?
5. How to make progress in it?

Appropriate solutions to all these questions should be feasible through a well-designed educational and vocational guidance programme.

Specific Duties and Responsibilities of Career Master

1. Forming and organising the school Guidance Committee.

2. Setting up an educational and occupational Information Centre in the school.

3. Giving orientation talks to students regarding guidance services available in the school.

4. Orienting class X students and their parents with regard to the electives available in the senior secondary school.

5. Orienting students of classes X and XII with regard to university and non-university courses, apprenticeship schemes, etc.

6. Collecting and displaying educational and occupational information.

7. Disseminating occupational and educational information through talks, group discussions, film shows etc.

8. Preparing news albums.

9. Arranging career talks by experts from different fields.

10 Organising Career Days, Career Weeks, Career Conferences, etc.

11. Arranging visits to places of work, like industries, business establishments, offices, higher educational institutions, etc.

12. Organising Parents' Days.

13. Organising a 'Guidance News' Section in the school magazine.

14. Giving orientation talks to students of class VIII in the feeder schools; prior to their joining the secondary or senior secondary school or orientation

talks to new pupils as soon as they have joined class IX of the secondary school.

15. Acquainting students with and assisting them to adopt proper methods of study.

16. Arranging individual discussion with pupils and parents for giving them educational and occupational information.

17. Notifying employment opportunities available to secondary and senior secondary school students.

Career Information Service

The career information service in the school should provide information on the following:

1. Information on occupational opportunities after the completion of class X and class XII.
2. Information on courses available after the completion of class X and class XII.
3. Information on scholarships and stipends etc.
4. Information on competitive examinations.
5. Information on occupations suitable for girls.
6. Information on occupations for the handicapped.
7. Information on occupations based on intelligence and interest.
8. Information on apprenticeship facilities available.
9. Information on training facilities.

Career Talks : An Outline for A Career Talk

I. Introduction

1. A brief history of the occupation
2. Scope and Information of the occupation in modern life.

II. Nature of Work and Working Conditions

1. The general nature of the work involved.
2. The work done mainly outdoor or indoors, or both.
3. The place of work noisy, crowded, humid, dusty, etc.
4. The work done mainly with others or alone.
5. The work done on a shift system.
6. The employment steady or seasonal.
7. Employment in this occupation found mainly in urban areas, rural areas, or both.
8. The related occupations to which a worker may be transferred, jobs to which may he may be promoted.
9. Rate of accident involved in the occupation.
10. Diseases related to the occupation.

III. Requirement for Entry into the Occupation

1. The categories of personnel employed.
2. The entry jobs.

3. The level of education that is required for entry into this occupation.
4. School subjects or school activities useful for entry into this occupation.
5. Institutions providing training facilities for entry into this occupation.
6. The entrance qualifications required for entry to the training course. The duration of the course, cost of training etc.
7. The physical and personal qualifications required for entry into the occupation.
8. Any special abilities or interests required.
9. Any age limit.
10. Any special licence or membership in any organisation required or any special examination required for entry into the job.
11. Apprenticeship or on-the-job training required in the occupation.

IV Methods of Recruitment

1. Job to be secured through an employment exchange or not.
2. Application for the job to be made in response to a 'wanted advertisement' in the newspapers.
3. Direct application or not.
4. Application to be sent through the Public Service Commission.
5. Recruitment made periodically or otherwise.
6. Vacancies reserved for Scheduled Castes/Tribes, backward classes etc.

V. Wages and Other Benefits

1. The starting salary and allowances.
2. The avenues of promotion.

Career Conference

Meaning of a Career Conference: A career conference is a conference in which information regarding various aspects of different occupations is disseminated to the students. Career conference technique has been found to be very valuable as a means of supplementing the information given to a group by the counsellor or the class teacher. A number of successful persons explain the vocations in which they work and answer questions about their jobs.

14

Concept of Learning: Meaning, Nature and Process

14.1 MEANING AND DEFINITIONS OF THE TERM LEARNING

Learning is a term used in the modification of the behaviour of the learner which occurs as a result of training or experience. With the modification in behaviour, the learner now can do what he could not do earlier. The outcomes of learning from learning activities or experiences may result in the modification of attitudes, skills, social competence and abstract and creating thinking. Learning is an enrichment of experience.

A school is the most important place of learning for the learners.

Following definitions of learning would help to understand the meaning of learning, its nature and broad dimensions.

1. According to Wordsworth, R.S., "Any activity can be called learning so far as it develops the individual (in any respect, good or bad) and makes his behaviour and experience different from what that would otherwise have been."
2. Skinner views are: "Learning as acquisition and retention."
3. For Boaz, "Learning is a process by which the individual acquires various habits, knowledge and attitudes that are necessary to meet the demand of life in general."
4. Commins and Fagin define learning in these words, "Learning as a sequence of mental events or conditions leading to changes in the learner?"
5. In the words of Crow and Crow, "Learning involves the acquisition of habits, knowledge and attitudes."
6. *Encyclopaedia of Educational Research* reads, "Learning refers to the growth of interests, knowledge and skills and to transfer of these to new situations."
7. Gates defines learning in these words, "Learning is the modification of behaviour through experience and training."
8. In the words of Hilgard, "Learning is the process by which an activity originates or is changed through reacting to an encountered situation, provided that the characteristics of the change in activity cannot be explained on the basis of native tendencies, maturation or temporary states of organism."
9. In the views of Gooch, "Learning as we measure it is more or less a permanent change in behaviour which occurs under the motivational conditions of practice."

10. According to Munn, "To learn is to modify behaviour and experience."
11. Peal, E.A. states, "Learning is a change in the individual following upon changes in the environment".
12. According to Hunder and Hilgard, "Learning is the process by which behaviour (in the broader sense) is originated or changed through training procedures (whether in the natural environment or in the laboratory)".
13. Travers J.F. writes, "Learning is a process that results in the modification of behaviour."

14.2 NATURE AND CHARACTERISTICS OF LEARNING

1. *Learning is Purposeful*: All true learning is based on purpose. Purpose plays a big role in learning. According to Ryburn, "This purpose is always connected with the use of some instinctive power, with the use of energy with which we are endowed with at birth." We do not learn anything and everything that comes in our way in a haphazard manner. All school activities should be purposeful so that the child should feel real urge for learning.

2. *Learning is Intelligent*: Meaningless efforts do not produce permanent result. Any work done mechanically is without any soul. When a child learns something unintelligently, he is likely to forget it very soon. He does not assimilate but simply commits to memory. Only efforts made intelligently have lasting effects.

3. *Learning is Active*: Learning does not take place without a purpose and self-activity. In the teaching-learning process, the activity of the learning coontts more than the activity of the teacher. The principle of learning by doing is the main principle which has been recommended by all modern educationalists. It is the basis of all progressive methods of education, such as, the Dalton, the Project, the Montessori and the Basic.

4. *Learning is Both Individual and Social*: Learning is more than an individual activity. It is a social activity also. Individual mind is affected by the group and consciously as well as unconsciously an individual is influenced by his friends, relatives, classmates, parents etc., and tends to acquire their ideas, feelings and notions. Social agencies like the family, church, firm and gangs of playmates have tremendous influence on the child.

5. *Learning is the Product of the Environment*: Environment plays an important part in the growth and development of the individual. Environment should be healthy and rich in educative possibilities.

6. *True Learning Affects the Conduct of the Learner*: There is a change in the mental structure of the learner after experience. Calvin describes learning as the modification of the conduct of an organism through experience.

7. *Learning is Growth*: The word growth is generally associated with the body which is growing, but through the mental growth of the learner. Although it is latent yet we can perceive its growth. Through his daily activities the child grows both mentally and physically. Therefore, we say that learning is growth through experience.

8. *Learning is Adjustment*: Learning helps the individual to adjust himself

adequately to the new situations. Children meet with new situations which demand solutions. Repeated efforts are required to react to them effectively. Life is full of experiences, and each experience leaves behind some effects in the mental structure. These effects modify our behaviour.

9. *Learning is Organizing Experience*: Learning is not mere addition to knowledge. It is not mere acquisition of facts and skills through drill repetition. It is the reorganization of experience.

10. *Learning is Universal*: Both men and animals learn. Human beings have a rational will of their own. They are thus, able to get the maximum benefit from the environment.

11. *Learning is a Life-Long Process*: Learning starts from the time the child takes birth in the world and it continues till death. At every step the individual faces problems and tries to solve them. In this process he modifies and improves his behaviour. One keeps on learning so long as one breathes.

12. *Learning and Intelligence*: An intelligent child can learn quickly because he has a basic mental drive to do things. It is this drive which helps him to learn quickly.

The same cannot be said about a child who lacks intelligence. Hence his learning is slow and casual.

13. *Learning by Doing*: Children learn quickly when they participate in some learning activity. They do things with their own hands and thus learn speedily. There is better co-ordination of hands, eyes and the brain during the period of activity. All modern methods of learning emphasise learning by doing.

14. *Learning is Related to Maturation*: Both learning and maturation have positive relation.

14.3 BROAD AIMS, OBJECTIVES AND OUTCOMES OF LEARNING

1. Helping in bringing desirable changes in the behaviour of the learner.
2. Helping in the attainment of teaching-learning objectives in general.
3. Helping in the proper growth and development of the learner.
4. Helping in the balanced and harmonious development of the personality of the learner.
5. Helping the learner how to learn.

14.4 TYPES OF LEARNING

Educators and psychologists have classified learning in several ways. Here mention is made of few important classifications.

Classification of Learning According to Type of Behaviour or Domain: I

(1) Cognitive Learning

(2) Psychomotor or Conative Learning

(3) Affective Learning

Classification of Learning According to Methods of Learning: II

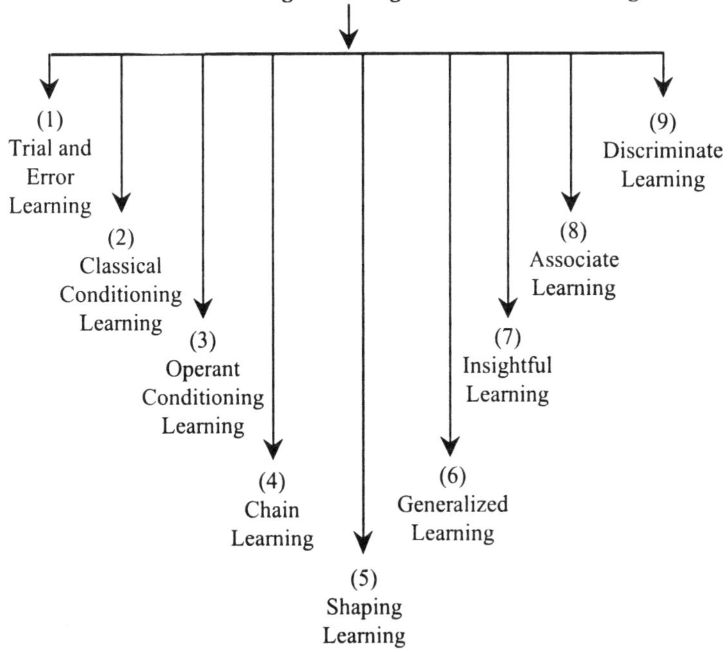

Hierarchical Learning: Classification of Learning an given by Robert Gagne on the Basis of Easy to Difficult Learning: III

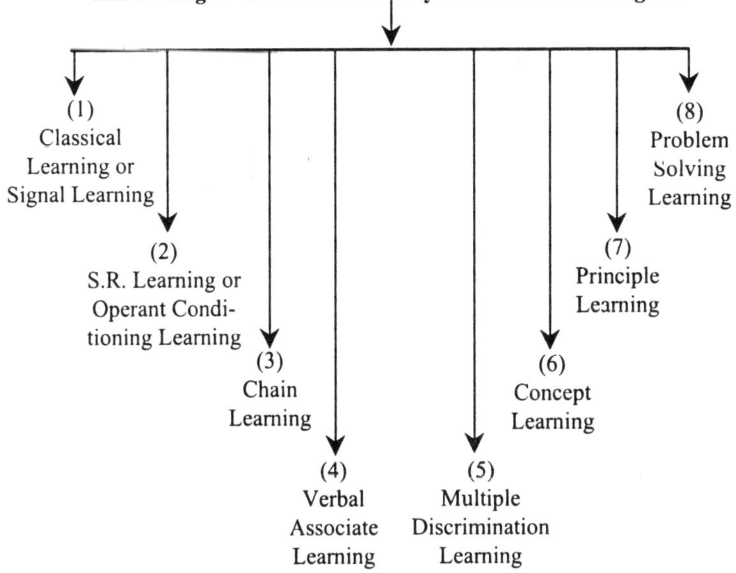

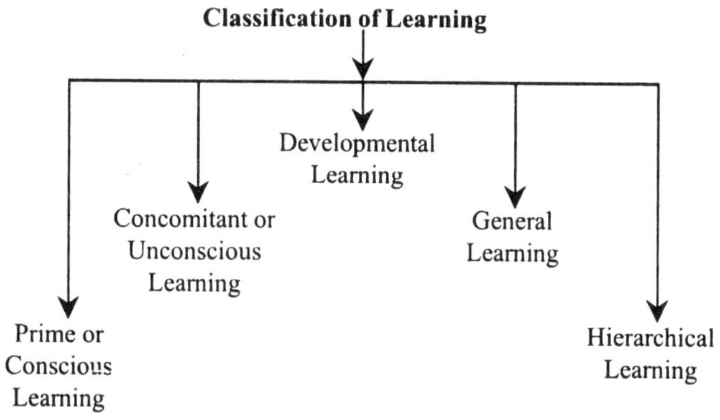

Prime and Concomitant Learning

There are only two broad categories of learning, *i.e.*, Prime learning and Concomitant learning.

Prime learning is deliberate, formal as well as non-formal, purposeful and systematized. It includes all types of learning except concomitant learning. All aspects of the entire instructional programme, *i.e.*, curriculum, textbooks, methods of teaching and evaluation etc. are related to prime learning. Most of the changes in behaviour take place through prime learning.

Concomitant learning is that learning which comes in a casual manner without any direct intention to learn but on some occasions it becomes very powerful. Concomitant learning in a broad sense takes place under the indirect influence of the home, the school and the society. Students learn so many things in the school in a casual manner. It is sometimes called incidental learning. We are reminded of the learning of King Robert Bruce from the efforts of a spider. After making several unsuccessful attempts, ultimately it achieved its objective. The King, who had been unsuccessful in defeating his enemies, picked up courage like the spider again and succeeded. It was not deliberate learning.

It is said that a student gets one-fourth of his learning from his teacher (Prime learning), another fourth from his intellect (Prime learning), another fourth from his fellow students (Prime learning) and the rest (concomitant learning) through his general experience in various situations.

14.5 MAJOR DOMAINS AND MAIN AREAS OF LEARNING

Major Domains of Learning

There are three major domains of learning as given below:

Domain	*Nature of the Domain*
1. Cognitive Domain	It is related to knowing or intellectual ability and is called Cognitive Learning.
2. Affective Domain	It is concerned with emotions, feelings and values and is called Affective Learning.
3. Psychomotor Domain	It relates to learning of skills and is called Conactive or Psychomotor Learning

Main Areas in the Three Domains of Learning

Knowledge Domain	*Affective Domain*	*Psychomotor Domain*
1. Knowledge 2. Comprehension It relates to student's ability to give (a) Meaning to a concept, definition or principle (b) Interpretation, *i.e.* seeing interrelations (c) Extrapolation, *i.e.*, drawing conclusions 3. Application 4. Analysis 5. Synthesis 6. Evaluation The highest form of learning is problem solving. The measurement in the cognitive domain as compared with the affective domain is easy and specific.	(a) Receiving (b) Responding (c) Valuing (d) Organisation (e) Characterisation 1. Learning in the affective domain influences attitudes/feelings and values 2. The measurement of learning in the affective domain as compared with the cognitive domain is less specific and difficult.	(i) Gross body movements (ii) Co-ordianted (iii) Non-verbal communication (iv) Speech behaviour or 1. Initiation 2. Manipulation 3. Precision 4. Articulation 5. Naturalization (mechanisation and internalization). Articulation implies co-ordination of action performed with efficiency in terms of time, speed and case. Naturalization implies performance in skill with natural ease and almost without conscious effort so that it is like a habit.

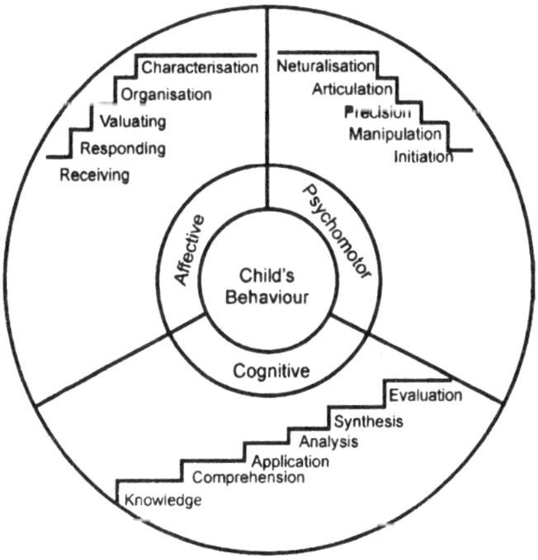

Fig. 14.1: Learning Objectives of Cognitive, Affective and Psychomotor Domains (NCERT)

14.6 EDUCATIONAL IMPLICATIONS OF DOMAINS OF LEARNING

1. Teaching should provide learning experiences for mutual integration of feeling, doing and thinking.
2. Teaching should provide learning experiences in meeting the individual needs of learners.
3. Teaching should provide purposive setting of learning or goal oriented learning. Teaching should provide appropriate guidance to learner to achieve his goal.
4. Teaching situations should provide freedom to develop creative powers.
5. Teaching should provide different learning experiences for satisfying the needs of each and every learner.
6. Teaching should be organized in such a way that the family background and the individuality of the learner are taken into account. A suitable social environment of group work should be provided.
7. Teaching should be based on sympathetic guidance to the learner.
8. The entire range of classroom interactions should be the co-operative group process so as to develop social attitudes in the learners.

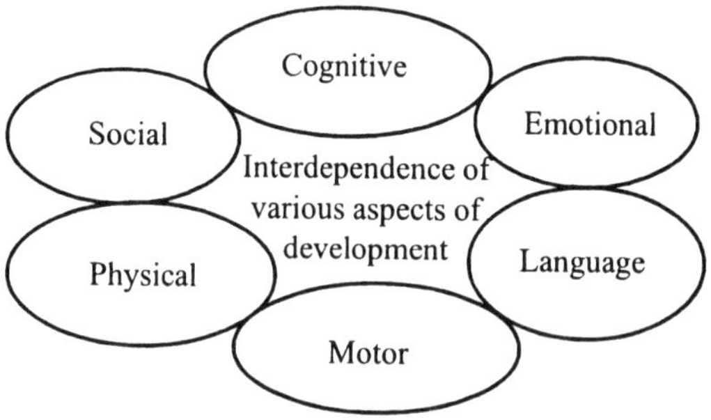

Fig. 14.2: Interdependence of Various Domain of Learning and Educational Implications

14.7 LEARNING PROCESS AND ITS ASPECTS

Learning Process

Fagin (1958) states that learning is a sequence of mental events or conditions leading to changes in the learner. As a sequence of events, the learning process is as under:

1. The individual has needs and is therefore in a state of readiness to respond. These are antecedent conditions within the learner. 2. He meets a learning situation or problem. A new interpretation is required because previously learned responses are not adequate for reaching the goal and satisfying his need. He encounters something new or unexpected, and searches for a different response. 3. He interprets the situation with reference to his goals, and tries a response or responses which seem to satisfy his need. The way he perceives the situation and the response he makes depends both on

his 'readiness' and on external conditions of the situation. 4. If his response leads to desired goals or satisfaction, he will tend to interpret and respond to similar future situations in the same way. If not, he keeps on trying and reinterpreting until satisfying consequences are attained. The learning process is this whole sequence!

Learning process in general includes the following:

(i) Acquisition of new experiences.
(ii) Retention of old experiences in the form of impressions, engrams or skills.
(iii) Development and modification of experience.
(iv) Growth and increase in these experiences.
(v) Creation of new experiences.
(vi) Synthesis and organization of the old and the new experiences, resulting in a novel pattern called learning.

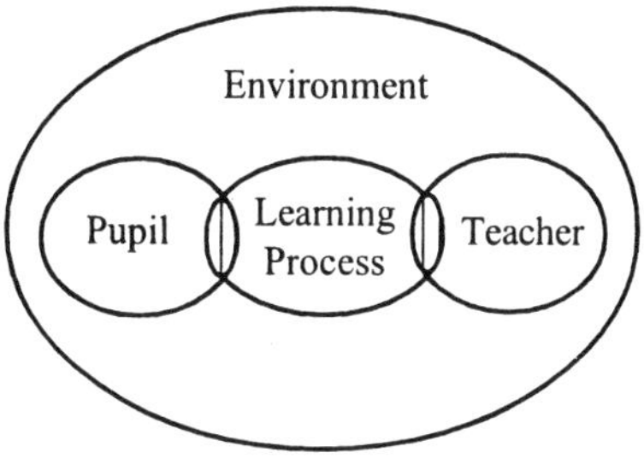

Fig 14.3: Learning Process in the Classroom

Aspects of the Learning Process in the Class

Learning and teaching are interrelated. Learning cannot be visualized without teaching. So is the case with teaching. The teacher creates the learning situation, *i.e.*, the environment. The process is the interaction between pupil and the teacher. The teaching-learning process is explained in the diagram.

1. *The Teacher*: The teacher has to be an inducer of change.
2. *The Environment*: The teacher at the very outlet must set the stage or environment for the effective learning of the pupil.
3. *The Pupil*: The pupil becomes a partner in the teaching–learning process.

15

Factors of Learning: Personal and Environmental

15.1 CLASSIFICATION OF FACTORS OF LEARNING

There are several classifications of Learning. However, here only three ways of classification are detailed.

Factors of Learning: Classification I

Internal Factors Relating to the Child or the Learner (Personal)

1. Learner's physical and mental health
2. Innate capacities and abilities of the learner
3. Aspiration and achievement motivation of the learner
4. Goals of life of the learner
5. Maturation of the learner
6. Readiness of the learner to learn
7. Will and determination of the learner to learn
8. Motivation of the learner

External Factors

1. Nature of the Subject matter/ experience to be learnt
2. Learning techniques and methods
3. Behaviour, personality and ability of the teacher
4. Learning situation
5. Goals or outcomes of learning
6. Class Environment
7. Overall School Environment
8. Home Environment
9. Community Environment
10. Political Environment

Determinants of Learning: Classification II

- Factors relating to the learner
- Factors relating to the teacher
- Factors relating to environment
  - Home environment
  - Subject environment
  - Class physical environment
  - Class psychological environment
  - Community environment

Determinants of Learning: Classification III

- Heredity and learning
- Environment and learning

15.2 THE CHILD AS A LEARNER AND PERSONAL FACTORS AFFECTING LEARNING

Learning by the child depends on the following two factors:

1. The Psychological Factor
2. The Physiological Factor

1. *The Psychological Factor*: The 'psyche' or mental make-up of the child plays a dominant role in the learning process of the child. It motivates the child towards new learning. A child with a strong psyche (mind) reacts to the environment in his own individual way. A child with a weak psyche is not able to react in a proper way and does not get the maximum from the environment.

Some psychologists include conditions of temperature, or ventilation which are internal conditions and affect learning, as the psychological factors.

A related aspect of the psychological factor is the motivational factor. Motivation leads to activity and activity leads to learning.

2. *Physiological Factors*: This factor implies the proper functioning of the physiology of the child. It includes the use of our sensory receptors (visual, auditory, touch, smell, etc.) in the learning process. If our other physiological factors like vision, hearing or glands malfunction, they affect learning process.

A wise teacher takes note of the following:

(i) Individual differences in learning and an individual approach which may however differ from child to child or within the same child when his learning takes place under different situations and conditions.

(ii) Setting up goals or standards not beyond the capacity of the learner.

(iii) Keeping in view that the previous experience of the learner is fundamental in the process of learning.

(iv) Awareness of the fact that knowledge of one's own performance, mistakes and information of successful result helps in learning.

(v) Knowing that the active participation by the learner is essential in learning.

(vi) Realizing that a motivated learner can acquire knowledge and understanding more quickly than one who is not motivated.

(vii) Keeping in view that excessive motivation may sometimes be less effective in some kinds of learning. In some instances it may result in 'pushing' the child too much disregarding his abilities.

(viii) Knowing that learning depends on the mental set or the mood of the learner. The teacher has to find out whether the learner is ready for the task or not. If not, what are the ways and means to make him ready for the purpose.

(ix) Believing that emotion of the learner is a powerful factor in learning and the teacher must learn how to use this to his greatest advantage. In this respect development of good interpersonal relationships in the classroom as well as in the school should not be neglected by the teachers.

(x) Having faith that good study habits of the individual also promote learning.

15.3 SUBJECT MATTER AND ITS PRESENTATIONS AS A FACTOR IN LEARNING

In the course of formal and informal teaching, a resourceful teacher plans and directs pupil experiences in such a way that it leads to effective learning. The study of the process enables the teacher to make the following deductions with the help of which he tries to affect purposeful learning in pupils.

1. By following certain well-tried principles and maxims of teaching to guide the pupil's learning activities.
2. By considering the maturity and the capacity of the learner.
3. By employing fruitful motivational devices.
4. By directing and modifying perception of the learner.
5. By using practice most effectively.
6. By removing emotional disturbances.
7. By directing teaching towards transfer of learning.

15.4 ENVIRONMENT AS A FACTOR IN LEARNING

The teacher at the very outset must set the stage or environment for effective study of the pupils as pointed out below.

(i) A definite place of study.

(ii) Favourable physical conditions for learning such as proper light, adequate space and ventilation, etc.

(iii) A definite time schedule for study—what to study, when to study and how to study.

(iv) A clear idea of the purpose of study.

15.5 TEACHER AS THE INDUCTOR OF CHANGE AND A FACTOR IN LEARNING

The teacher would make learning effective, if he attends to the following elements carefully.

1. *Who is to Learn or Whom to Teach*? The child is to learn and therefore his interests, abilities and aptitudes have to be taken note of. It must be

remembered that he is an active being. Individual differences have to be attended to.

2. *Who is to Teach or from Whom to Learn*? The teacher is to teach. He should, therefore, present a good model of teaching.

3. *Why to Teach or Why to Learn*? Education should not be taken in terms of traditional 3 R's, *i.e.*, reading, writing and arithmetic, but in terms of 7 R's, *i.e.*, reading, writing, arithmetic, recreation, rights, responsibilities and relationships.

4. *What to Teach or What to Learn*? This includes the acquisition of the knowledge, skills and behaviour.

5. *How to Teach*? The teacher must be well versed with the technology of teaching.

6. *How to Learn*? The teacher and the learner must fully understand that learning takes place through mutual cooperation. A learner learns maximum when he is motivated. The teacher, therefore, has to provide motivational situations so that the learner is at his best. He has to be fully conversant with learning theories and teaching strategies.

7. *When to Teach or When to Learn*? This is concerned with creating motivational situations for the learner.

8. *Where to Teach or Where to Learn*? The school should not be taken as the only place of imparting or receiving education. It is one of the agencies of education and of course, the most important one.

15.6 SOME PROBLEMS IN THE FIELD OF LEARNING

1. *Limits of Learning*: The capacity to learn has a limit in every child. One cannot learn more than what is set by physiological capacity.

2. *Role of Practice in Learning*: A judicious use of practice strengthens learning.

3. *Importance of Incentives*: Usually use of rewards leads to better learning. Rewards may be in the form of verbal appreciation or in cash or in certificate, etc.

4. *Place of Insight in Learning*: Insight learning is considered more effective than trial and error.

5. *Transfer of Training in Learning*: Learning is only effective if it can be transferred from one situation to another.

6. *Learning and Maturation*: They are interrelated and interdependent.

7. *Learning and Forgetting*: We learn as well as we forget.

15.7 MAKING LEARNING EFFECTIVE: ROLE OF THE SCHOOL AND THE TEACHERS

Learning is influenced by various conditions of life at home and school. As far as home conditions are considered, *i.e.*, heredity and other influences of the home, very little can be done by the school to modify these. However, schools can ensure that students are given adequate opportunities to develop their hereditary endowment.

The schools should take the following steps to promote learning in the learners to their optimum levels.

1. *Healthy Physical Conditions in the School*: Unsuitable furniture in the class-room (*i.e.*, desks and chairs and blackboards etc.), bad ventilation, over crowding etc. affect the rate of learning and the general response of the learners.

Teachers' health, voice and speech etc. also affect learning.

Therefore, all possible attempts should be made to provide healthy physical environment.

2. *Stimulation and the Role of the Teacher*: Best learning takes place when the teacher is successful in arousing the interest of the student. "The guidance of the teacher is mainly a matter of giving the right kind of stimulus to help him to learn the right things in the right way," writes Ryburn.

3. *Goals Set Before the Pupils*: A definite goal should be set before each child according to the standard expected of him. Immediate goals should be set before small children and distant goals for older ones. It must be remembered that the goals should be very clear and the children must understand these goals.

Complacency in the pupils should be avoided and in no case the pupil should feel that there is nothing more which he should learn and that there is no scope for improvement. R. Strang writes: "A little learning is a dangerous thing insofar as it may make a child content with what he has accomplished. The child's felt need for a skill is decreased once he has obtained enough proficiency to accomplish his immediate purpose. It is important, therefore, that as soon as the child begins to acquire skills, he should set for himself suitable specific standards of accuracy and precision."

4. *Association of Things*: Thorndike points out that things which we want to go together should be put together. Many different things should be brought together as a part of one process. Then it becomes easier to make the students understand their connection. We have discussed at various places that things can be associated in a number of ways.

5. *Guidance and Instruction*: Suitable guidance should be given to the students in selecting the best response to the environment. Demonstration is very helpful to teach various skills.

6. *Emotional Conditions*: Children should be praised when they show good results. This gives them encouragement to show all the more better results and they develop confidence, hope, self-reliance and self-respect. Sympathetic attitude on the part of the teachers gives stimulus and a sense of security to the students. We should discard our habits of fault-finding. This develops fear and feelings of insecurity and of inferiority.

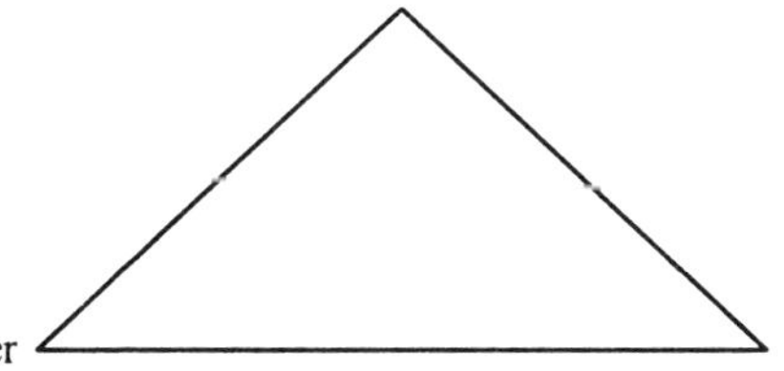

Fig. 15.1: Conditions Related to Content, Teacher and Student

7. *Result of a Total Situation*: Learning is affected by the whole situation. It is not always possible to estimate the result of one individual factor. Learning is fruitful and permanent if the total situation is related to life.

In fact total situation includes all the factors that we have enumerated above. Learning is influenced both by heredity and environment. There is a lot that can be done by the teachers to facilitate learning.

Summing Up

Internal classroom factors which affect learning and improvement are: (1) Goals or Purposes, (2) Motivation, (3) Interest, (4) Attention, (5) Drill or Practice, (6) Boredom or Fatigue, (7) Aptitude, (8) Attitude, (9) Emotional factors—Instincts, (10) Speed, Accuracy and Retention, (11) Age, (12) Learning activities provided by the teacher, (13) Testing, (14) Guidance.

15.8 LEARNING AND MATURATION

Learning and maturation are closely interrelated. Sometimes it becomes difficult to say definitely as to which of the behavioural changes are the result of learning and which are the consequences of maturation.

Maturation, in fact, is a natural process. It is the growth which takes place in the individual. The changes on account of maturation are the results of unfolding and ripening of inherited traits. They are relatively independent of activity, experience and practice. M.L. Biggie and M.P. Hunt have clarified this is these words: "Maturation is a development process within which a person from time to time manifests different traits, the 'blue prints' for which have been carried in his cells from the time of his conception."

This maturation involves changes that are associated with normal growth.

Learning, on the other hand, is a change in the individual which is not on account of genetic inheritance. It is a process which takes place as a result of 'stimuli' from 'without'. Activity, experience and training lead to changes in the behaviour in the process of learning.

The behaviour is said to have matured if a behaviour sequence develops through regular stages, irrespective of intervening practices or training. If training procedures do not modify or speed up the behaviour, such procedures are not casually important and the changes do not classify as learning.

The swimming of tadpoles and the flying of birds can be attributed primarily to maturation. But in the case of human beings it is not easy to decide whether the activities result from maturation or learning. The most simple example is that of a child. The child learns to talk only when he reaches a certain stage or age of maturation. It is also equally true that he does not learn the language just because he attains that age. The language is taught to him. The language which he learns is that which he hears. It is very clear that the two processes—maturation and learning—are closely related to each other. Maturation assists in the process of learning. Learning takes place only if the stage for that type of learning has been achieved through a process of maturation. A teacher would be effective if he understands the complexity of the changes that take place as a result of both processes and the interaction between the two. The reverse would be harmful. For instance, the normal development of speech in the child would be disrupted if a child is forced to learn certain speech patterns before a certain maturation has occurred. On the other hand, failure to provide specific training in speech at the appropriate time may be a great educational error.

15.9 HEREDITY (GENETIC) AND ENVIRONMENT (NURTURE) ON LEARNING

Meaning of Heredity: By the heredity of an individual we mean all those inborn physical and mental traits that he inherits from his parents and ancestors. Every child comes into this world with certain physical and mental features which he got from his parents. He is born with a body and mind which developed from the fertilized ovum he got from his mother and father. His limbs and organs grow from the same. His mental tendencies are also based on the same.

According to Woodworth "Heredity covers all the factors that are present in the individual when he began life not at birth, but at the time of conception about nine months before birth."

Meaning of Environment: By environment we mean all those physical and mental factors that affect and influence the development of the child. The home, the family, the neighbourhood, the companions, the school, the teachers, the political and religion agencies, the society in general, the temperament and other mental traits of parents and other elders, the economic, social and cultural status of the parents—all influence the development of the individual. No individual is the same at maturity as he was born. The environment changed him. Everything that influences the child apart from himself from what he inherited from his parents is his environment.

E.G. Boring, H.S. Longeld and H.P. state "The environment is everything that effects the individual except his genes"

In the words of R.S. Woodworth and D.G. Marques, "Environment covers all the outside factors that have acted on the individual since he began life."

Relative Influence of Environment (Nature) and Environment (Nurture) on the Development of the Child

Many psychologists are of the view that "the inborn nature is the chief factor in development and it solely determines the possibilities to which the child can be educated." They do not find any weight in the influence of environment. They give all importance to nature which determines the development of the young ones.

The other school of thought gives all credit to nurture. The adherents of this school think that a child may be developed to any level. They claim to make Gandhis and Jawahars of any babies put under their charge from their very birth provided such children live in the selected environment for a long time.

Isolated examples in support of both the views are cited. The problem is very important for educators. If heredity is everything, then there is no sense in providing schools with adequate equipment and healthy psychological and physical environment. In the words of Woodworth, "Shall the gardener pin his hope on careful cultivation of the soil or the selection of the best seed?" Answer is very clear. Emphatically both determine the quality of harvest.

Heredity in the Environment

The much-mentioned slogan 'heredity versus environment' is a misconception. We should talk of 'heredity in the environment.' Both heredity and environment are essential for development. Hence any trait of the individual is the 'product' of heredity and environment. The individual does not equal heredity + environment but does equal heredity × environment *i.e.,* O (organism or individual) = H (Heredity) × E (Environment). Heredity sets the probable biological limit, whereas environment determines the level up to which the development is possible. Every development is due to an interaction of heredity and environment.

Personality may be compared to a rectangle. Heredity makes the base while environment the altitude. A rectangle cannot exist without either of the two.

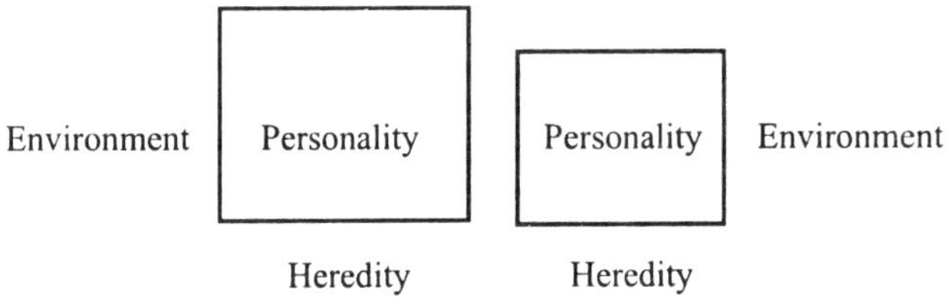

Personality = Heredity × Environment

Sometimes heredity plays a major role in the development of personality and sometimes environment. However, both play their roles. In case both, the base, *i.e.*, the heredity and the altitude, and the environment are inferior, we shall have Jukes and Kalikaks as offsprings (Anti-social and misfit individuals)

15.10 GENERAL PRINCIPLES OF EFFECTIVE LEARNING

1. Different types of learning experiences should be provided to satisfy the needs of each and every learner as notable 'differences' exist between individuals.
2. Learning experiences should be provided for natural integration of feeling, doing and thinking as the learner is a living 'organism', a unitary integrated whole.
3. Rich learning experiences should be provided to meet the needs of the learner as he always seeks to maintain equilibrium or balance by satisfying his needs.
4. The setting of learning should be purposive or goal-oriented as the learner is a goal seeking organism to satisfy his needs.
5. The learning situations should provide freedom to make creative contribution as the learner is an active, behaving and exploring individual.
6. While providing learning experiences for the learner, family background and individuality of the learner should be taken into account as the learner is a social being and needs social environment.
7. The learner needs sympathy and guidance for his personality development as he is quite immature.
8. Learning activities should be based on co-operative group work so as to develop the socialised personality of the learner.
9. Bright students can learn things quickly than the dull ones.
10. A motivated pupil learns more readily than one who is not motivated.
11. Learning through reward or success motivation is more effective than punishment or failure.
12. Learning goals should be neither too high nor too low.
13. The personality of a teacher is a great contributory factor in teaching-learning.
14. Active participation of the learner is more effective than passive reception.
15. Meaningful materials and meaningful tasks are learned more quickly.
16. Moderate practice and repetition is very useful for durable learning.
17. Effective audio-visual aids contribute to make learning effective and inspirational.
18. Transfer of learning will be better if learner himself discovers relationship between new and old tasks.
19. Optimal learning takes place when appropriate teaching strategies are adopted.

15.11 SUMMARY

Factors Influencing Learning and Learning Process							
Personal		*Environmental*					
Health of the Child	*Emotional Psychological and Intellectual*	*Miscellaneous Environmental Factors*	*Relation-ships with*	*Media Influence*	*Methods of Learning*	*Methods of Teaching*	*Maxims of Teaching*
1. Physical development	1. Sensation and perception	1. Natural surroundings	1. Teachers	1. Print Media	1. Whole vs. Part Learning	1. Lecturing	1. From known to unknown
2. Postures	2. Fatigue and Boredom	2. Social surroundings	2. Parents	2. Non-print Media	2. Mediating Method	2. Demonstration	2. Easy to difficult
3. General Health	3. Maturation	3. Cultural surroundings	3. Peers	3. Electronic Media	3. Space vs. Un-spaced Method	3. Individual Practical work	3. Simple to complex
	4. Emotional Conditions	4. Home environment			4. Recitals	4. Individual work in work-shop	4. Concrete to abstract
	5. Needs	5. Class-room environment			5. Memory Systems	5. Field Trips	5. Indefinite to definite
	6. Intelligence	6. School environment			6. Laws of Association	6. Projects	6. Particular to general
	7. Motivation	7. Political environment				7. Discussion	7. Empirical to rational
	8. Attention					8. Conference, Seminar etc.	8. Deductive-inductive
	9. Aptitude					9. Assignments	9. Psychological to logical
	10. Attitude					10. Tutorial (Individual)	
						11. Programmed Instruction	
						12. Teaching Machines	
						13. Electronic Media	
						14. Audio-visual Aids	

16

Nature, Types and Techniques of Enhancing Motivation

16.1 MEANING, DEFINITION AND NATURE OF MOTIVATION

Meaning of Motivation

The word motivation has been derived from the Latin word '*Motum*' which means to 'move', 'motor' and 'motion'. Motivation is an internal force which accelerates a response or behaviour. Some learners learn the same subject matter or task more efficiently than others, some find it more rewarding and interesting than others; and some enjoy it more than others. At any given time learners vary in the extent to which they are willing to direct their energies to the attainment of goals, due to difference in motivation.

The difference in their performance can be due to differences either in their abilities or in their willingness to perform as best as possible. The performance of an individual is considered as a product function of two different variables as follows:

1. A learner's ability/capacity to perform the work;
2. A learner's willingness to use his ability to perform the work.

In algebric terms, if *P* stands for performance in learning, *C* stands for capacity to learn and *M* stands for willingness to use capacity to learn, then *P* may be expressed as follows:

Performance = Capacity to learn × Willingness to use capacity to learn

$$P = C \times M$$

Thus, given the ability, it is the willingness of the learners which determines whether they will be more efficient or less. Similarly, given the willingness, it is the ability of learners which determines whether they will be more efficient or less.

How to make learners performance more or better is an issue that requires an understanding of what motivates learners to do so.

16.2 DEFINITION, SOURCES, TYPES AND NATURE AND CHARACTERISTICS OF MOTIVATION

Definitions of Motivation

The following definitions throw adequate light on the meaning of motivation:

1. *Arun Monappa and Mirza S. Saiyadain*—"Motivation is propensity or the level of desire of an individual to behave in a certain manner at a certain time and in a certain situation."
2. *C.W. Goods*—"Motivation is the process of sustaining and regulating activity."
3. *D.O. Hebb*—"The term motivation refers (i) to existence of an organised phase sequence, (ii) to its direction and content, (iii) to its persistence in given direction or stability of content."
4. *F.G. McDonald*—"Motivation is an energy change within the person characterized by affective arousal and anticipatory goal relations."
5. *T.W. Atkinson*—"The term motivation refers to the arousal of tendency to act to produce one or more effects."

Sources of Motivation: Motivation has four sources:

1. Needs
2. Drives
3. Incentives
4. Motives

Motives: Psychologists do not agree on the meaning of the term 'motives'. These have been defined as follows:

1. *E.C. Murray*: Motive is an internal factor that arouses, directs and integrates a person's behaviour.
2. *Alice Crow*: Motives can be regarded as those internal conditions or forces that tend to impel an individual towards certain goals.
3. *Shoffer and Others*: Motive is a tendency to an activity initiated by a drive and concluded by the adjustment.
4. *M.C. Dougall*: Motive is a condition, physiological and psychological, within the individual that disposes it to act in certain ways.
5. *Allport*: A motive is any internal condition in the person that induces action or thought.
6. *Arun Monappa and Mirza S. Saiyadain*: Motivation is propensity or the level of desire of an individual to behave in a certain manner at a certain time and in a certain situation.
7. *Bernard*: Motivation is the stimulation of actions towards a particular objective where previously there was little or no attraction to that goal.
8. *Goods*: Motivation is the process of arousing, sustaining and regulating activity.
9. *Harold Koontz and Cyril O'Donnell*: Motivation refers to the drive and effort to satisfy a want or goal.
10. *Guilford*: A motive is any particular internal factor or condition that tends to initiate and sustain activity.
11. *Lovell*: Motivation is defined more formally as psycho-physiological or internal process initiated by some need which leads to activity which will satisfy that need.
12. *Skinner*: Motivation in school learning involves arousing, persisting,

sustaining and directing desirable behaviour.

13. *Gates*: Motives are conditions—psychological and physiological with the organism that dispose it to act in a certain way.
14. *Blair*: Arising from our needs motives are the energies which give direction and purpose in behaviour.

Motives are expressions of a person's needs and hence they are personal and internal. Need here means something within an individual that prompts him to action. Motives or needs are 'whys' of behaviour. Motives are the primary energisers of behaviour which prompt people to action. Motives give direction to human behaviour because they are directed towards achievement of certain 'goals'.

Types of Motives

We can divide motives in various ways:

A. Primary Motives and Secondary Motives

Primary Motives are the biological or physiological motives. The examples of such motives are: hunger, thirst, sex, sleep, rest, etc. These motives ensure the preservation of life for the individual and for his race. An important feature of these motives is that they are *inborn* and *innate.*

Secondary Motives are psychological and social motives. Examples of such motives are: need for security, achievement, gaining status and recognition, etc. These motives are acquired like other forms of learning behaviour, when we are trying to satisfy our needs.

B. Innate and Acquired Motives

Innate motives are known as physiological motives and are associated with the birth of the individual. Examples are: hunger, thirst, sleep, sex, etc.

Acquired motives are learnt motives. Examples are: habit, interest, etc.

C. Natural and Artificial Motives

Natural motives are present in the individual by birth. Examples are play, prestige, etc.

Artificial motives are complementary motives to natural motives. Examples are: reward, punishment, etc.

Thus motivation refers to the process by which human needs direct and control the behaviour of a human being. Motivation may also be defined as the process which inspires the people at work to contribute to the best of their capability for the achievement of organisational objectives. In other words, motivation may be defined as the process of stimulating people to action to accomplish desired goals. In simple terms, creation of a will to work or to work more or better is motivation.

Nature and Characteristics of Motivation

The characteristics of motives highlight the nature of motivation.

1. *Personal and Internal*: Motives are personal, internal and invisible because, these are expressions of a person's needs. Motives are the energising forces within us. Motivation is a psychological

phenomenon which arises from the feeling of needs and wants of learners.

2. *Differ from learner to learner*: Motives differ from learner to learner because every learner has his own set of needs at a particular point of time.
3. *Differ from Time to Time*: Motives energising us differ from time to time. Motives come and go. A motive need not have the same energy potential at all points of time.
4. *Different Behaviour from same Motive*: One motive may result in many different behaviours.
5. *Same Behaviour from Different Motives*: The same behaviour may result from different motives. That is why a motive cannot be identified from any specific behaviour.
6. *Continuous Process*: Motivation is a continuous process because human needs are unlimited and fulfillment of one set of needs gives rise to another set of needs.
7. *Pervasive Function*: Motivation is required in all types of organisations (commercial, educational, social, religious, political, small or large) and at all levels. However, its ways, methods, forms and types may differ at different levels.
8. *Behaviour for Estimating Motives*: Repeated behaviour can be used as an estimate of learner motives. It is possible to get repeated observations of one learner's behaviour and then make an estimate of the cause of that behaviour.
9. *Operate in Harmony or in Conflict*: Motives can operate in harmony or in conflict. For example, a learner may want to get high marks in school while also wanting to help his father in the business.
10. *Interact with the Environment*: Motives interact with the environment.
11. *Causes Goal–Directed Behaviour*: Motives cause goal directed behaviour.

16.3 PROCESS AND IMPORTANCE OF MOTIVATION

Process of Motivation

The elements of the process of motivation are:

(1) Motives, (2) Behaviour, (3) Goal, (4) Feedback. The process of motivation has been shown below:

1. *Motive*: Motives prompt learners to action. Motives determine the general direction of learner's behaviour.
2. *Behaviour*: Behaviour is a series of activities of an individual. It is generally motivated by a desire to achieve a goal.
3. *Goal*: Motives are directed towards goals. Goals are the ends which

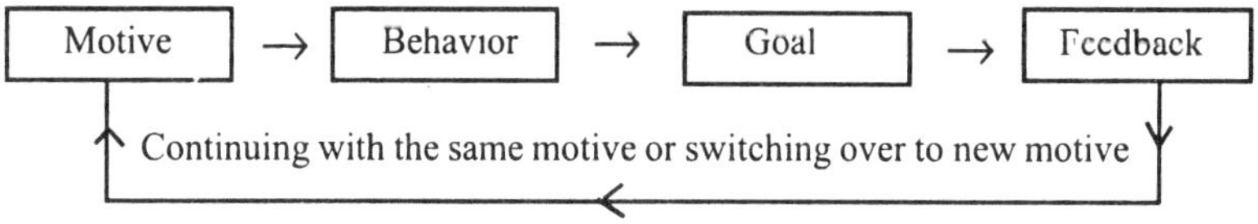

provide satisfaction of human wants.

4. *Feedback*: Feedback may be in the form of reduction or increase in tension.

Importance of Motivation

Motivation is the core of learning. The importance of motivation arises from the benefits which flow from it. These benefits are shown below:

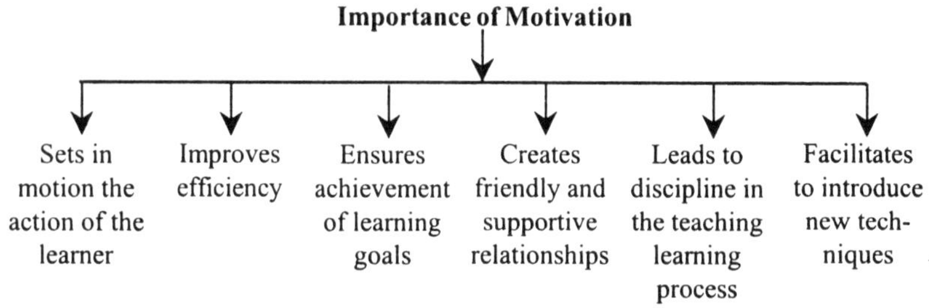

Fig. 16.1: Importance of Motivation

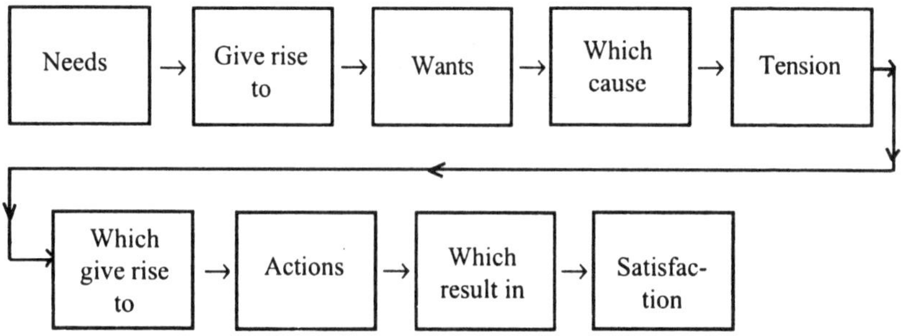

Fig. 16.2: Motivational Cycle: Needs—Satisfaction Chain

16.4 MASLOW'S NEED HIERARCHY

To get work done with the cooperation of learners for the attainment of learning objectives every teacher must study the behaviour of learner. To determine their needs and provide an environment in which appropriate incentives are available for their need satisfaction. Human needs serve as driving force in human behaviour.

Abraham Maslow explained how needs influence human behaviour through his 'Need Hierarchy Theory of Motivation' in 1943.

Table 16.1: Five Types of Human Needs

Need	*Meaning*	*Examples*
1. Physiological needs	These needs relate to the survival and maintenance of human life.	Need for food, clothing, shelter, air, water.
2. Safety needs or Security needs	These needs relate to the economic and physical security.	Security of source of income, personal security, provision for old-age insurance against risks.
3. Social or Affiliation or Acceptance Needs	These needs relate to social interaction. They are the desires to belong and to be socially accepted, to love and be loved, as a social animal. Socialising is one of those reasons why many individuals (especially older people) go to work, and why people generally work better in small groups where they can develop affiliations that are important to them.	Need for love, affection, affiliation, acceptance belongingness.
4. Esteem or Ego Needs	These needs relate to the awareness of self-importance and recognition from others.	Need for self-image, self-confidence, self-respect, status, recognition prestige, attention, and respect from others.
5. Self-Actualisation or Self-fulfillment needs	These needs relate to self-fulfillment, are the desires to realize one's own full creative potential through creativity, self-expression and self-development to become what one is capable of becoming.	Need to grow, sense of fulfillment, maximum self-development, personal achievement.
6. Need to know		
7. Aesthetic need		

Hierarchy of Human Needs

Maslow proposed that human needs can be arranged in a particular order (*i.e.*, hierarchy) of their importance or prepotency) from the lower to the higher level needs. Physiological needs are placed at the lowest level of hierarchy of needs. Then safety needs, social needs and esteem needs are positioned in ascending order. Self-actualisation needs are placed at the highest level of hierarchy of needs. Two new upper class needs are added—Need to know and Aesthetic need.

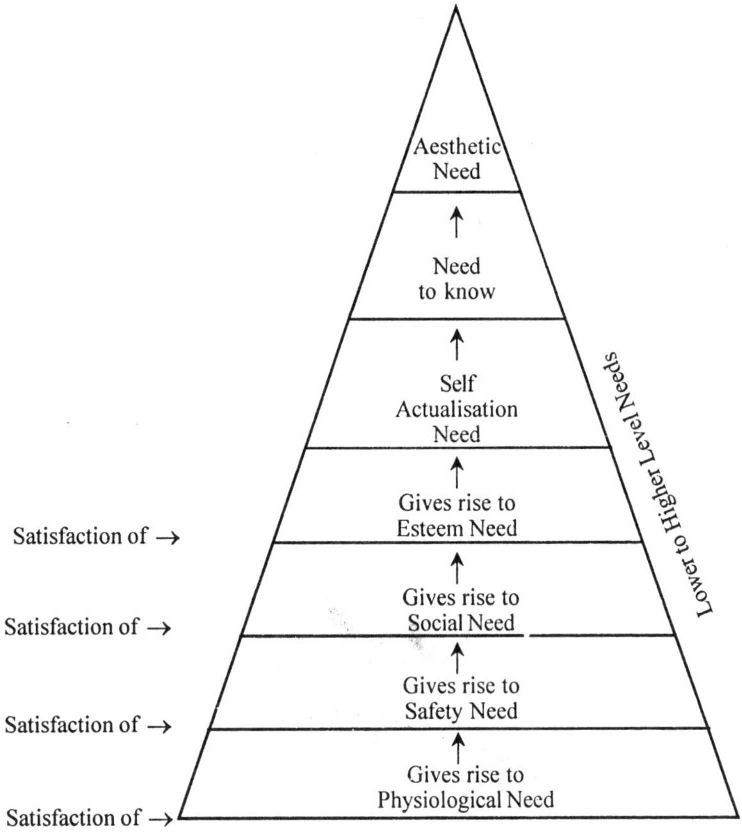

Fig. 16.3: Maslow's Hierarchy of Needs.

16.5 MERITS AND CRITICISM OF MASLOW'S THEORY AS APPLIED TO LEARNING

Merits of Maslow's Need Hierarchy

Following are the merits of Maslow's Need Hierarchy:

1. It is simple to understand and has an intuitive appeal.
2. It recognizes the spectrum of human needs and indicates how humans are motivated in their work behaviour.
3. Its basic proposition that deprivation of a need dominates behaviours, seems to be quite sound..
4. It provides some guidance to teachers and educational administrators.

(a) Identification of unfulfilled needs among the various learner's.
(b) Designing of measures to satisfy unsatisfied needs as a means of motivation.
(c) Designing of measures to arouse new higher level needs.

Criticisms of Maslow's Theory

Maslow's theory is subject to the following criticisms:

1. It is not amenable for empirical validation on account of complexity of developing meaningful measures for various needs.
2. The hierarchy appears to be rigid. The learners need not necessarily follow a step-by-step way of meeting their needs for example—
   (a) Some learners may not be aware of esteem and self-actualisation needs. For example, for majority learning of underdeveloped countries, higher level esteem and self-actualisation needs have no meaning.
   (b) A learner may go in for higher level needs before complete satisfaction of lower level needs.
3. It is doubtful whether Self-actualisation is a need or not. It may be merely a philosophical and ethical aspiration based on wishes and dreams of what one should be than on what one can be or one is.
4. There is a direct link between needs and motivation. Different learners may adopt different practices to fulfill the same type of needs. Different types of needs may be gratified by similar methods.
5. It fails to clarify the complexity of human needs and motivation since the learners differ:
   (a) in awareness of their needs;
   (b) in the extent and depth of their needs;
   (c) in their willingness to fulfill their needs;
   (d) in their ability to fulfill their needs;
   (e) in ordering their needs on a preference scale;
   (f) in choosing ways and means to fulfill their needs;
   (g) in the degree of gratification which they desire from meeting their needs.

For example, for some learners need for self-esteem seems to be more prominent than that of love. There are also creative learners in whom the drive for creativeness seems to be more important. In certain learners the level of motivation may be permanently lower.

6. Need may not necessarily be the only factor which influences a learner's behaviour at a particular point of time. There may be other factors which may affect the behaviour at that time.
7. It is also doubtful—
   (i) Whether deprivation of a need dominates behaviour at all. It may not motivate the learner in a unidirectional positive manner. It may even lead to his depression, diversion, frustration and inaction.
   (ii) Whether relative gratification of needs at a particular level drives the learners to move to next higher level needs.

(iii) Whether a satisfied need motivates a learner. He may remain at that level and continue to seek need fulfillment in a routine manner. Several needs recur in cycles, short or long, and hence satisfaction could not be a permanent or one time affair.

(iv) One need is satisfied at one time. The phenomenon of multiple motivation is of great practical importance in understanding the behaviour of the learner. A learner's behaviour at any time is mostly guided by multiplicity of motives.

Intrinsic and Extrinsic Motivation

Intrinsic Motivation: It comes into display when the resolution of tension is to be found in mastering the learning task itself. The material learned provides its own reward. For example, the student who studies the construction of model dams diligently so that he can make a model, is experiencing a king of intrinsic motivation.

Extrinsic Motivation: It occurs when a student pursues a learning task for reasons which are external. If a student engages in construction of model dams because he thinks it will please his father, who is an ex-engineer, this becomes a case of extrinsic motivation. Motivation is probably a function of an interactive situation where reward for a particular action acts as an incentive. Some of the common forms of extrinsic motivation are:

(a) Purposive goals
(b) Knowledge of results
(c) Punishments and rewards
(d) Praise and blame
(e) Rivalry

16.6 TECHNIQUES OF ENHANCING LEARNER'S MOTIVATION

Ways of Motivating Children in the Class-room

The teaching-learning process aims at maximum learning in a minimum period of time. It is, therefore, necessary that children should be properly motivated and the teacher should be conversant with important ways of motivating children.

1. *Child-Centred Approach*: The child is the focal point in the learning process. The teachers, therefore, should keep in view the needs, interests and aptitudes of children while planning for their education.
2. *New Law of Association*: The child is easily motivated to learn new knowledge if he thinks that he knows all that is required as a base for new learning. This enables him to master new facts and acquire knowledge.
3. *Progressive Methods of Teaching*: The teacher should use new methods like the Montessori Methods, the K.G. Method, the Project Method and the Dalton Plan as methods of teaching. These methods are child-centred and based on important psychological principles.
4. *Use of Teaching-Learning Aids*: The teacher should introduce various aids and devices of teaching, for example, audio-visual aids, radio,

television, etc. to create interest in learning. These will motivate children in grasping and digesting new learning.

5. *Element of Success*: The teacher should divide new learning into smaller and smaller tasks and assign them to the different students of the class. Children will complete them in a short period of time and will have a feeling of success. It is this feeling of success, which will motivate them for future achievement and success.
6. *Learning by Doing*: Children are active by nature. They want to do something with their hands. Let this need of the children be satisfied. A satisfied child is always a well motivated child.
7. *Sense of Achievement in the Child*: The teacher should keep an eye on the progress of every child. He should maintain a proper record of the same. He should inform his pupils about the success achieved by them, after two or three months. This will develop a sense of achievement among the pupils. This will also lead to achievement – motivation.
8. *Group Work*: Children like group life. They may be divided into various groups. Group work leads to quicker, better and easier learning.
9. *Value of Learning*: The teacher should highlight the value of learning among his pupils. They should realize that 'knowledge is power' and can be helpful in life and will make them successful.
10. *Ego-Involvement*: The personality of the child should be given its due recognition.
11. *Healthy Environment*: A healthy class-room environment in itself is a great motivating force.
12. *Constructive and Creative Discipline*: The teacher's attitude towards his children should be sympathetic but firm.
13. *Stimulus Variation and the Teacher*: It has been generally observed that children are not able to attend to one thing for a very long period. The effectiveness of the teaching-learning process in such a situation depends to a great extent on the stimulus variations used by the teacher behaviour. Some of the common teacher behaviours in the class-room which fall under variation are:
    (a) Teacher movement
    (b) Teacher gestures
    (c) Changes in speech pattern
    (d) Changes in sensory focus
    (e) Changes in postures
14. *Reinforcement: Praise and Blame*: These may be classified as:
    (a) *Positive Verbal Reinforcement*: Following a pupil's answer, the teacher verbally indicates pleasures at the pupil's response by the use of words like 'Good', 'Fair', 'Excellent', 'Correct', etc.
    (b) *Positive Non-Verbal Reinforcement*: These include:
    Nods and smiles.
    Teacher's friendly movements towards pupils.
    Teacher's friendly look.

Teacher writing student's response on the blackboard.

(c) *Negative Non-Verbal*: This comprises gestures—sneering, frowning, expression of annoyance, impatience, etc.

(d) *Negative Verbal*: This includes comments like 'No', 'Wrong', 'No good', 'Poor', 'Of course not', etc.

Summing up

Students in the class-room learning need constant motivation from the teachers so that optimum use of their talents may be made for their development. The needs are the basis of motivation. Therefore, techniques that the teachers employ to arouse and maintain motivation will be successful only in so far as they make them perceive that progress is being made towards need-satisfaction.

Principles or Laws of Enhancing Motivation in Learning and Making Learning effective, Efficient and Inspirational

While teaching, the teacher has to keep in view the following principles of learning so that learning becomes effective, efficient and inspirational:

1. *Principle or Law of Self-learning*: It is now universally accepted in a 'learning society' that it is not so important as 'to how much to learn' but it is very important 'to learn how to learn?' The learners must be left free to express themselves, for the only education is self-education. The essential activity in learning is not the adjustment of child to teacher but is to enable him to adjust himself to the environment and also to change the environment to adjust himself. Learning must enable the child to work independently and without the teacher at a later stage. The two important aspects of teaching are, stimulation and inspiration. The teachers must fire the enthusiasm of their pupils. They must encourage them in the development of their natural desire to work and to be active and guide these desires into worthwhile channels. The late President Eliot of Harvard once said: "The supreme value of a teacher lies not in the regular performance of routine duties, but in his power to lead and inspire his students through the influence of his own mental and moral personality and examples". Burton has also said:

"Teaching is the stimulation, guidance, direction and encouragement of learning."

2. *Principle or Law of Association*: Thorndike points out that things which we want to go together should be put together. Many different things should be brought together as a part of one process. Then it becomes easier to make the students understand their relationships.

3. *Principle or Law of Readiness*: The law is indicative of learner's state to participate in the learning process. According to Thorndike, readiness is preparation for action. Readiness does not come automatically with maturation. According to this law, for a conduction unit ready to conduct, to do is satisfying and for it not to do so is annoying. A teacher must be fully alive to this.

4. *Principle or Law of Effect*: It states that a response is strengthened if it is followed by pleasure and weakened if followed by displeasure.

5. *Law or Principle of Exercise or Repetition*: According to it the more a stimulus induced response is repeated, the longer it will be retained. Other things being equal, exercise strengthens the bond between situation and response. Conversely a bond is weakened through failure to exercise it. Thus the law has two sub-parts: (i) law of use, and (ii) law of disuse.

6. *Principle or Law of Multiple Responses*: Confronted with a new situation, the organism responds in a variety of ways before arriving at the correct response.

7. *Principle or Law of Attitude*: The learner performs the task well if he has his attitude set in the task.

8. *Principle of Prepotency or Elements*: The learner reacts to the learning situation in a selective manner. He uses his insight, selects the prepotent elements in a situation and bases his responses upon those elements.

9. *Principle of Motivation*: Learning must be based on various techniques which appeal to the motives of students.

10. *Principle of Stimulation*: Best learning takes place when the teacher is successful in arousing the interest of the student. "The guidance of the teacher is mainly a matter of giving the right kind of stimulus to help him to learn the right things in the right ways," writes Ryburn.

11. *Principle of Goal Setting*: A definite goal should be set before each child according to the standard expected of him. Immediate goals should be set before small children and distant goals for older ones. It must be remembered that the goals should be very clear and the children must understand these goals.

12. *Principle of Individual Differences*: Learning experiences to be provided to the students must take into consideration the individual differences of the learners.

13. *Principle of Emotional Development*: Children should be praised when they show good results. This give them encouragement to show all the more better results and they develop confidence, hope, self-reliance and self respect. Sympathetic attitude on the part of the teachers gives stimulus and a sense of security to the students. We should discard our habit of fault-finding. This develops fear and feelings of insecurity and of inferiority among students.

14. *Principle of Analogy*: The organism responds to a new situation on the basis of the responses made by him in similar situations in the past. He makes responses by comparison or analogy.

15. *Principle of Associative Shifting*: According to it we get any response, from the learner of which he is capable, associated with any situation to which he is sensitive.

16. *Principle of Polarity*: It states that connections act more easily in the direction in which they were first formed than in opposite direction.

17. *Principle or Law of Similarity*: This law states that "other things being equal" the stimuli that are more similar to one another will have greater tendency to be grouped. Thus learning similar things is easier than learning dissimilar things.

18. *Principle or Law of Proximity*: According to this law "perceptual groups are favoured according to the nearness of parts." This means that we perceive all closely situated or located things as groups.

19. *Principle or Law of Closure*: This law states that "closed areas are more stable than unclosed ones and therefore move readily." It is similar to the Thorndike's law of effect. Unless the work is finished the individual does not feel satisfied. He is under tension which is over only when the work is completed.

20. *Principle or Law of Good Continuation*: This law states that "organisation in perception which appears to go in a particular direction appears to be going infinitely in the same direction."

All principles are interlinked.

17

Theories of Learning and their Educational Implications

17.1 MEANING, SIGNIFICANCE AND CLASSIFICATION OF THEORIES OF LEARNING

A learning theory consists of :

1. The observed relationship among independent and dependent variables in learning;
2. The mechanisms or structures presented to underline such relationships; or
3. Inferred relationships underlying mechanisms intended to account for observed data in the absence of any direct empirical manifestation of the relationships.

Classification of Learning Theories: I

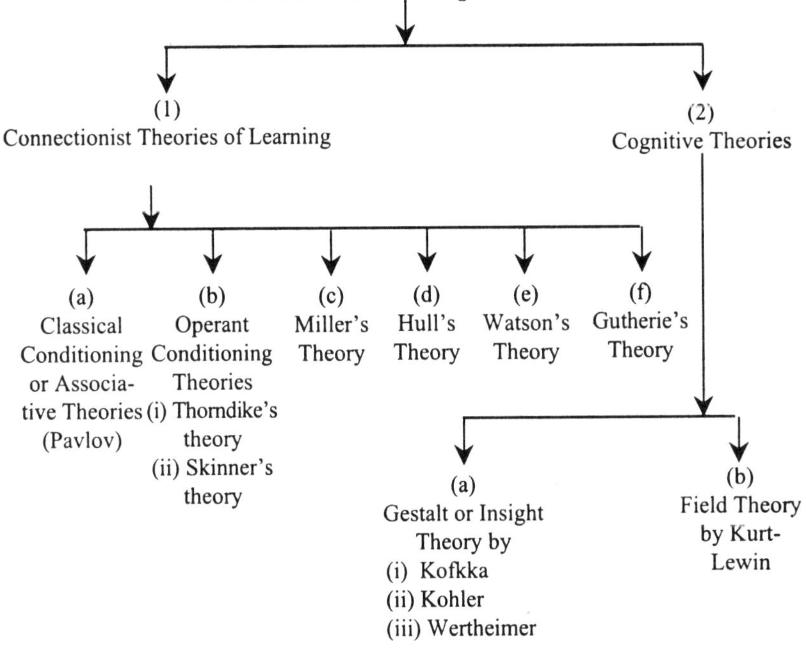

Classification of Learning Theories: II

- Behaviourist Theory
- Information Processing Theory
- Humanistic Theory

A learning theory is envisaged to find answers of the following:

1. Role of drill and practice in learning.
2. Place of trial and error in learning.
3. Role of insight and understanding in learning.
4. Role of transfer of learning in difficult situation.
5. Role of individual differences in learning.

17.2 BEHAVIOURIST THEORIES OF LEARNING

Meaning of Behaviouristic Theory of Learning

With a view to understand this theory of learning, it is important to understand behaviour. By behaviour we mean an activity of an organism that can be observed and measured by another person or organism.

The behaviouristic theory describes learning as a connection between stimulus and response. This theory stresses that learning begins with natural responses (reflexes) and new behaviours result from the acquisition of new bonds of stimulus and response through experiences.

The work of Ivan Pavlov (1849-1936), a Russian thinker and his famous experiment with the salivating dog became the starting point of behaviourism. Watson (1878-1958) and Skinner (1904-1980) have given more stress on objectivity in behaviours. Skinner conducted his experiments on rats and pigeons. His theory is known as operant conditioning. An operant is a set of acts that are performed by an organism while doing something.

Once a desirable response occurs in behaviour, it is reinforced with a suitable reinforcer.

Main Characteristics of Behaviouristic Theory of Learning

1. Learning brings about changes in behaviour.
2. Learning is the result of continual interaction of the individual with the environment.
3. The behaviouristic changes are objectively observable.
4. The chief emphasis of the behaviourists is on environment.
5. The behaviourists attach more importance to environment than heredity.
6. Behaviour is understood by conditioning.
7. Conditioning is composed of stimulus—response links (S-R links).

8. An objective and scientific method can be used successfully to study the phenomenon of conditioning and behaviour.
9. The chief method of learning is conditioning.
10. By virtue of similarity, contrast or contiguity (closeness of occurrence in time or situation), one unit of knowledge gets associated with a new unit of knowledge.

Contribution of Behaviourism to Learning

Following are the chief contributions of behaviourism to education.

1. It points out that all behaviour is learnt in the process of interaction with environment. So the teachers must provide appropriate environment.
2. It emphasises the importance of environment and its impact on human growth.
3. It has indicated the importance of motivation. The teacher can make his teaching effective only when the learners are motivated.
4. Behaviourism has given new methods and techniques of understanding the learners behaviour.
5. It has contributed to the understanding of the emotions of the child. This requires that the teacher himself should present a model of emotionally developed individual.
6. It has given new methodology of teaching known as 'programmed learning' which has been successfully employed in several countries.
7. It has led to the development of new approaches, methods and techniques of dealing with maladjustment in children.
8. It has brought psychology out from the controversy of mentalistic approach to human behaviour.
9. The teacher should define learning objectives very specificaiiy in terms of behaviour.
10. The order of arrangement of objectives should be graded *i.e.* simple to comple: .
11. It states that the role of rewards plays a significant role in learning.
12. According to behaviouristic approach, punishment should be avoided.
13. It has greatly contributed to the psychology of learning.

Limitations of Behaviouristic Approach/Theory of Learning

1. It is criticised on the ground that the results of experiments conducted on animals regarding behaviour are not applicable to human beings who live in a social environment.
2. The approach dehumanises the learning process as it emphasises the mechanisation of the mental process.
3. The approach gives no consideration to the elements of curiosity and spontaneity of human beings.
4. The approach attempts to explain emotions, thoughts and actions solely on the basis of overt behaviour.
5. The approach does not give heredity its due importance in the development of behaviour.

6. The approach is artificial in nature as it does not deal with the depth of mind.
7. The approach considers the human being as a machine.

17.3 THORNDIKE'S THEORY OF LEARNING

Thorndike's Theory of Learning is known by various names *i.e.* S.R. Theory of Learning (Stimulus Response Theory), Theory of connectrivism and Theory of Trial and Error.

Theory of Trial and Error was propounded by E.L. Thorndike. This theory was the outcome of the various experiments conducted by Thorndike on cats, chickens, dogs, fish, monkeys and rats. On the basis of his experiments, Thorndike concluded that an individual makes many random efforts to reach a goal. Most of his efforts go useless in the achievement of this aim. By further trial and error he goes on eliminating useless movements and synthesizing useful ones. At last he reaches the aim. In further trial he need not repeat the useless movements. He will perform the activity quite easily in further attempt as he has learnt to perform the real needed movements after eliminating the useless ones.

Thorndike maintained that the learning is nothing but the stamping in of the correct responses and stamping out of the incorrect responses through trial and error. In trying for the correct solution the cat made so many vain attempts. It committed errors and errors before getting success. On subsequent trials, it tried to avoid the erroneous ways and made correct responses.

Thorndike's Experiments

For illustration, following experiments are narrated.

Experiment No. 1: He put a hungry cat in a puzzle box. There was only one door for exit which could be opened by correctly manipulating a latch. A fish was placed outside the body. The smell of the fish worked as a strong 'motive' for the hungry cat to come out of the box. Consequently, the cat made every possible effort to come out. The situation described by Thorndike himself is as—"It tries to squeeze through every opening; it claws and bites at the bars or wires, it thrusts its paws through any opening and claws at everything it reaches." In this way, it made a number of random movements. In one of the random movements, by 'chance', the latch was manipulated. The cat came out and got its 'reward'.

Experiment No. 2: For another trial, the process was repeated. The cat was kept hungry and placed in the same puzzle box. The fish and its smell again worked as 'motive' for getting out of the box. It again made random movements and frantic efforts. But this time, it took less time in coming out. On subsequent trials such incorrect responses—biting, clawing and dashing were gradually diminished and the cat took less time on every succeeding trial. In due course, it was in a position to manipulate the latch as soon as it was put in the box. In this way, gradually, the cat learned the art of opening the door.

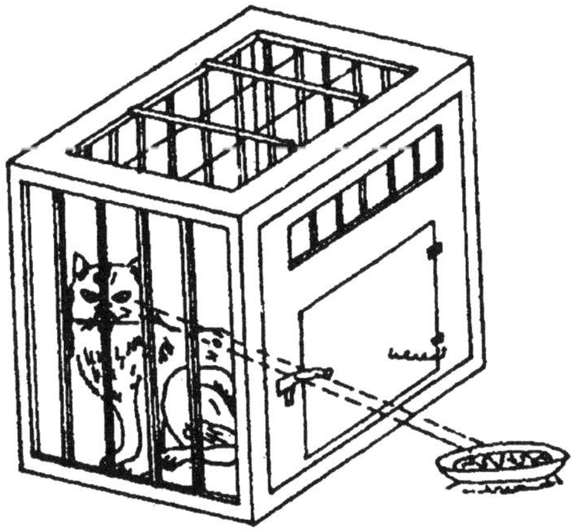

Fig. 17.1: Thorndike's Cat Trying to Come Out

Characteristics of Trial and Error Theory

An analysis of the trial and learning indicates the following characteristics:

1. Where there is drive or motive, there is learning. In the experiment the cat was hungry, so its motive was to get food by learning to come out of the cage.
2. The organism makes a number of varied types of responses. The cat made these responses—clawing, scratching, walking around, pawing, pulling, etc.
3. Some responses lead to the goal and they are known as satisfying responses. The responses of pulling the strings, etc. by the cat was satisfying. Some do not lead to the goal and they are known as annoying responses. The responses of clawing, pawing, scratching, and walking were annoying for the cat.
4. Satisfying responses become better learned as they lead to the attainment of the goal.
5. Annoying responses tend to be eliminated gradually as they do not lead to the goal.

Stages in the Trial and Error Process of Learning

The experiment sums up the following stages in the process of learning:

1. *Drive*: In the present experiment, drive was hunger and it was intensified with the sight of the food.
2. *Goal*: To get the food by getting out of the box.
3. *Block*: The cat was confined in the box with a closed door.
4. *Random Movements*: The cat, persistently tried to get out of the box.
5. *Chance Success*: As a result of this striving and random movement, the cat, by chance, succeeded in opening the door.
6. *Selection of Proper Movement*: Gradually, the cat selected the proper way of manipulating the latch out of its random movements.

7. *Fixation*: At last, the cat learned the proper way of opening the door by eliminating all the incorrect responses and fixing the only right responses. Now it was able to open the door without any error or in other words, it learned the way of opening the door.

Laws of Learning propounded by Thorndike

1. *The Law of Readiness*: According to Thorndike, readiness is preparation for action. Readiness does not come automatically with maturation. It is a law of preparatory adjustment, not a law about growth. Thorndike termed the neurons and synapses involved in establishment of a specific bond or connection, a conduction unit. According to this law, for a conduction unit ready to conduct, to do is satisfying and for it not to do so is annoying.

Educational Implications: The teacher should prepare the minds of the students to be ready to accept the knowledge, skills and aptitudes. For this, he should provide opportunities for those experiences in which students can spontaneously participate. In other words, he should arouse their capacity to link the experiences with their everyday life. 'Simple to complex' is the important maxim. Aptitude tests may be given to the students to find out their readiness to learn.

2. *The Law of Effect*: In simple words, the law of effect means that learning takes place properly when it results in satisfaction and the learner derives pleasure out of it. In the situation when the child meets a failure or gets dissatisfaction, the progress in learning is blocked. All the pleasant experiences have a lasting influence and are remembered for a long time, while the unpleasant ones are soon forgotten. Therefore, the satisfaction or dissatisfaction, pleasure or displeasure obtained as a result of some learning ensures the degree of effectiveness of that learning.

Law of Effect is based on following elements: S.R. Bond

(i) The stimulus (S). It involves an environmental event.
(ii) The Response (R). It indicates a behavioural act.
(iii) Connection or Bond (S-R. Bond). Stimulus and response result in connection or bond.

Table 1: Law of Effect: S-R Connection

Connection between Stimulus and Response	→	Satisfying Connection	→	Resulting in Strengthening the Connection or Bond
Connection between Stimulus and Response	→	Annoying	→	Resulting in weakening the Connection or Bond

Educational Implications: A pleasing environment should be created in the classroom. The teacher should be sympathetic but firm. He himself should enjoy his work. Experiences provided to the students should be satisfying and meaningful. They should be organized in the order of increasing difficulty.

Material should be provided in a number of interesting ways including the use of audio-visual aids.

3. *The Law of Exercise or Repetition*: It states, "Any response to a situation will, other things being equal, be more strongly connected with the situation in proportion to the number of times it has been connected with that situation and to the average vigour and duration of the connection."

According to this law, the more a stimulus-induced response is repeated, the longer it will be retained. The law states, other things being equal, exercise strengthens the bond between situation and response. Conversely a bond is weakened through failure to exercise it. Thus the law has two subparts, (i) law of use, and (ii) law of disuse.

Law of Use: "When a modifiable connection is made between a situation and response that connection's strength is, other things being equal, increased."

Law of Disuse: "When a modifiable connection is not made between a situation and response, during a length of time, that connection's strength is decreased.

Educational Implications of Trial and Error Mode of Learning

Important implications of the theory of Trial and Error are as under:

1. *Importance of Readiness*: According to Thorndike, readiness is preparation for action. It is very essential for learning. If the child is ready to learn, he learns more quickly, effectively and with greater satisfaction than if he is not ready to learn. He warns us not to make the child learn till he is ready to learn and allow not to miss any opportunity of providing learning experiences if the child is already prepared to learn. The right movements concerning the learning situation and the learner's state of mind should be very well recognized and maximum use of this knowledge should be made by the teacher. He should also make an attempt to motivate the students by arousing their attention, interest and curiosity.

2. *Strengthening Bonds*: The main task of the teacher in the teaching-learning process is to see what generalizations, principles and theories etc., he likes to be remembered or forgotten by the students. Consequently he must try to strengthen the bonds or connections between the stimuli and the responses of those things which are to be remembered. This could be done through drill, repetition and reward. For forgetting, he should make attempts to weaken the connections through disuse and annoying elements.

3. *Role of Rewards and Punishments*: The law of effect emphasizes the role of rewards and punishment in the process of learning. Getting reward as a result of some learning motivates and encourages the child to proceed on the same path with more intensity and enthusiasm while the punishment of any sort discourages him and creates distaste and disattraction towards that learning.

4. *Other Implications*

(i) Mere repetition is of no use. Repetition becomes useful when the response is rewarded. In that case, repetition strengthens the connections.

(ii) Understanding grows out of previous experience. The best way to develop understanding is to develop a body of connections appropriate to that understanding.
(iii) Transfer in learning takes place because of identical elements in the two situations.
(iv) Rewards have more strengthening effect than the corresponding weakening effect of punishments.
(v) Forgetting takes place because of the law of disuse.
(vi) The child should be encouraged to do his work independently.

5. *Five Aids to Improve Learning*: Thorndike has given the following five aids to improve learning.
(i) Interest in work.
(ii) Interest in improvement of work.
(iii) Significance.
(iv) Problem-attitude.
(v) Attentiveness.

Limitations of Thorndike's Theory of Learning

1. The theory ignores the role of understanding, experience, discrimination and insight in learning.
2. The theory over-emphasizes the role of role learning.
3. This theory is useful in the case of students of lower classes, but for students of higher classes, this theory does not provide enough guidance.

17.4 SKINNER'S THEORY OF OPERANT CONDITIONING

Meaning of Operant Theory of Conditioning

B.F. Skinner of the U.S.A. propounded his theory of Operant Conditioning in the 1930's on this basis of his experiments with rats and pigeons. Skinner called his theory as Operant Conditioning as it is based on certain 'Operations' or 'actions' which a person has to carry out. All basic principles of conditioning are found in Operant Conditioning Theory but there is a difference. In classical conditioning theory of Pavlov, the dog was harnessed on a table and was passive. The dog performed no *operations*. In the case of B.F. Skinner's learning, his subjects performed 'acts' or carried out operations—hence operant conditioning. Skinner's subjects were active. Further the nature of response is operant.

Skinner's Experiment with Rats

Skinner constructed a box which was equipped with a bar and a food tray. The bar could be pressed. Skinner placed a hungry rat in the box and the rat would wander over the bar from time to time and push the bar down. The moment it happened, a food pellet would fall into the tray. The rat learned this task of pressing the bar more frequently when the food pellet *reinforced the behaviour*. Skinner modified the procedure; food pellets would be supplied under certain conditions. When the bar was pushed down and a tone was sounded but not under other conditions. The rate generalised and pushed the bar when tone was sounded.

Skinner conducted experiments on pigeons also.

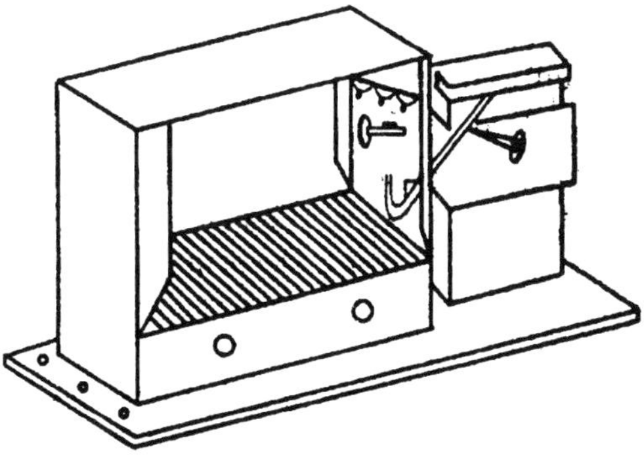

Fig. 17.2: Skinner's Box, used for the study of operant conditioning with rats.

Mechanism of Operant Conditioning

Operant conditioning is correlated with operant behaviour. An operant is a set of acts that are performed by an organism while doing something.

Steps

1. It starts with the responses as they occur naturally and not at random.
2. If they do not occur naturally, efforts should be made for *shaping* them into existence.
   Shaping implies that an organism is conditioned to perform the difficult activities through suitable rewards at the right occasion in the process of conditioning.
   An important aspect of shaping is chaining. It is a process or breaking down the main task which we want to achieve into smaller and smaller units.
3. Once a desirable response occurs, it is again reinforced through a suitable reinforcer.
4. In due course the desirable response gets conditioned by constantly reinforcing it.

As soon as a particular activity is performed in the shaped form, a more difficult activity is introduced and if the organism is able to perform it, he is again rewarded.

Skinner attaches greater importance to operant behaviour which is primarily concerned with responses rather than stimuli. It is known as R-type conditioning. Out of many responses which an organism is capable of giving, the problem with the experimenter is to evolve only the appropriate responses and fix them properly. Thus Skinner changed the usual S-R formula into an R-S formula.

According to the R-S formula, when a desired response is emitted, a reinforcing stimulus is presented. Thus a response is conditioned by constantly reinforcing it. The reinforcement must come after the response has been made and not before it. If the response is not reinforced, it results in the extinction of the response (operant).

Educational Implications of Skinner's Theory of Operant Conditioning:

Skinner's theory is very helpful in shaping the behaviour of the students in the desired direction. Important educational implications of his theory are:

1. Skinner's principles of learning focus on the individual pace of learning.
2. Learning objectives should be defined very specifically in terms of behaviour.
3. The order of arrangement of objectives should be from simple to complex.
4. According to this theory, learning and environment should be properly planned for the learner. It should provide maximum satisfaction and minimum frustration to the learner. In such an environment, the proper use of the reinforcement will lead to desired learning.
5. We should plan the learning of the child through conditioning in a systematic manner. Conditioning would lead to proper behaviour modification. As soon as the desired behaviour occurs the organism should be suitably rewarded. It should be rewarded whenever the desired behaviour occurs again.
6. The role of reward plays an important part in the development of personality. Personality is made up of consistent behaviour patterns which have been reinforced with rewards from time to time. It has been correctly said that 'We are what we have been rewarded for'.
7. The different schedules of reinforcement should be properly implemented.
8. We can say that motivation leads to a particular type of behaviour and reinforcement of that behaviour further leads to learning. Rewards or reinforcements prove good motivators to the learner.
9. This theory advocates that punishment should be avoided to the maximum. We should make a psychological approach to the problems of the child. We should accept the desirable behaviour of the child and ignore the inappropriate.
10. This theory has contributed to the growth and development of programmed learning and the use of teaching machines.

Limitations of Skinner's Theory

1. The theory considers the human being as a machine. This belief is questionable.

2. It is doubtful if the results derived from controlled experiments conducted on animals would yield the same or even similar results on human begins who live in a social environment.
3. This theory gives no place to the importance of hereditary influences.
4. This theory explains emotions, thoughts and actions solely on the basis of overt behaviour.
5. This theory does not give the consideration to the elements of curiosity, creativity and spontaneity of human beings.
6. This theory dehumanises the learning process as it emphasises the mechanisation of the mental process.
7. This theory is artificial in nature as it does not take into account the depth of mind.

17.5 GESTALT THEORY OF LEARNING OR THEORY OF INSIGHT LEARNING

Meaning of Gestalt Theory of Learning. The Gestalt Theory of Learning is the product of the work of German psychologists namely Wertheimer Kohler, Koffka and Lewin. Eventually these German psychologists settled in the U.S.A. These psychologists are known as Gestalt psychologists and their theory is known as Gestalt Theory of Learning or Theory of Insight.

'Gestalt' is a German word for which there is no English equivalent. The term was carried over to English psychological literature. The nearest English translation of Gestalt is 'configuration' or simply 'an organized whole.

The Gestalt psychologists consider the process of learning as an organized whole. According to this a thing or an idea cannot be understood by a simple study of its constituent parts but by studying it as a totality.

This theory is also known as Learning Theory of Insight.

Learning is not by trial and error, learning is not by random steps, learning is not by conditioning but by insight, introspection and understanding and the ability to see relationship among various factors involved. The learner, while learning, always perceives the situation as a whole and after seeing and evaluating the different relationships takes the appropriate decision in an intelligent manner.

Experiments of Kohler

Kohler, first of all used the term 'insight' to describe the learning of his chimpanzees. He conducted several experiments during the period 1913-17. Two of his experiments are described below.

Experiment 1: In one of his experiments Kohler shut the chimpanzee, Sultan by name, in a big cage. A banana was placed outside, at a considerable distance of the cage. Inside the cage there were two sticks—one of them a long one and the other a bit shorter. The shorter stick could be screwed into the long one. The long stick could not reach the banana but if the other one was screwed into it, the banana could be touched. Sultan tried to get at the banana. He tried the longer stick but it did not reach the fruit. The other was still smaller. He sat down and began to play with the sticks. But he was still brooding over the matter. Suddenly an idea flashed to him. He thrust the smaller stick into the hole of the longer one and thus managed to get at the banana with the help of the combined sticks.

Experiment 2: In this experiment the chimpanzee was shut up in a room with unscalable walls. A banana was hanging from the ceiling. The animal was hungry. He jumped at the fruit but it was too high. He left the efforts and sat down. There was a box lying in the corner of the room. The animal began to play with the box. He then suddenly got up and pushed the box to the centre of the room below the banana jumped from it and got the fruit.

Factors Upon Which Learning by Insight Depends

1. *Whole Situation*: The learner perceives the situation as a whole.
2. *Relationships*: The learner tries to understand the relationships among various factors involved in a situation.
3. *Experience*: Past experiences assist in the insight of the problems.
4. *Intelligence*: Basic intelligence of the learner is an important factor in insight learning.
5. *Observation*: As a common observation insight occurs when there is ample scope for observation in a learning situation.
6. *Initial Efforts*: The initial efforts in the form of trial and error open the way of insight learning.
7. *Reception and Generalization*: Learning gained in one situation helps the learner to react with insight in other identical situations.
8. *Capacity*: Learning depends upon learning capacities of the learner.
9. *Practice*: Repetitions bring to light new relationships and consolidate trace systems.
10. *Motivation*: Law of effect is recognized in motivation.
11. *Understanding*: The relationships between parts and wholes, and means and ends are emphasized.
12. *Transfer*: Generalized principles, common patterns and relationships are transferred.

Educational Implications and the Role of the Teacher in Insight learning

1. This type of learning encourages creative activity of the child.
2. This type of learning develops the reasoning, thinking and imagination of the child. He has to view the whole situation and then decide the line of action.
3. In mathematics, music, art and literature, this type of learning is specifically important.
4. This method is economical in terms of human energy. There are no useless and random trials.
5. This approach trains the child to solve his problems in later life.

The teacher should base his teaching on the following guidelines.

1. The whole problem is to be presented in the class. A piece-meal approach will not develop learning by insight.
2. The teacher should prepare children emotionally and intellectually to solve the problem.
3. The intelligence level and the maturity level of the students should be

kept in mind.

4. Insight of the child should be carefully handled by the teacher. He should know that its development is related to the physical maturation of the child. He should present the problem keeping in view the maturation of the child.
5. The teacher should organize his lessons logically. He should proceed from simple to complex. The problems presented in the class should be linked with life so that the pupils have the greatest benefit out of them.
6. He should present the subject matter of learning in the form of a problem and a problem solving approach should be followed. This will develop independent thinking and self-reliance among his pupils.
7. Role learning or memorization should be discouraged.
8. It needs a lot of patience on the part of the teacher. Insight does not develop in the student immediately. It needs persistent efforts.

Criticism of the Insight Mode of Learning

1. Insight is not needed in every situation. Slow learners need to be taught through other methods of learning.
2. Mental trial and error is involved in insight mode of learning.

17.6 COMPARISON OF THORNDIKE'S THEORY AND GESTALT THEORY

Thorndike's Theory	*Gestalt's Theory*
1. Learning depends on the efforts of the learner.	1. Learning depends on the insight of the learner.
2. Main emphasis in learning is on physiological functions.	2. Main emphasis is intellectual factors.
3. It is based on sensory-motor co-ordination.	3. It is based on perception.
4. There is relatively less work done at the sub-conscious level.	4. More work is done at sub-conscious level.
5. There is very little scope for transfer of learning.	5. There is much scope for transfer of learning.
6. It is more inapplicable to learners of less intelligence.	6. It is more applicable to person of more intelligence.
7. It is useful for younger children.	7. It is a useful for older children.

17.7 INFORMATION PROCESSING THEORY OF LEARNING BY GAGNE AND OTHERS

According to some psychologists and thinkers, there are three distinct components of the memory system. These include:

1. A sensory memory.
2. Short-term temporary memory store.
3. A long-term store—permanent store-house of information.

Following figure explains this:

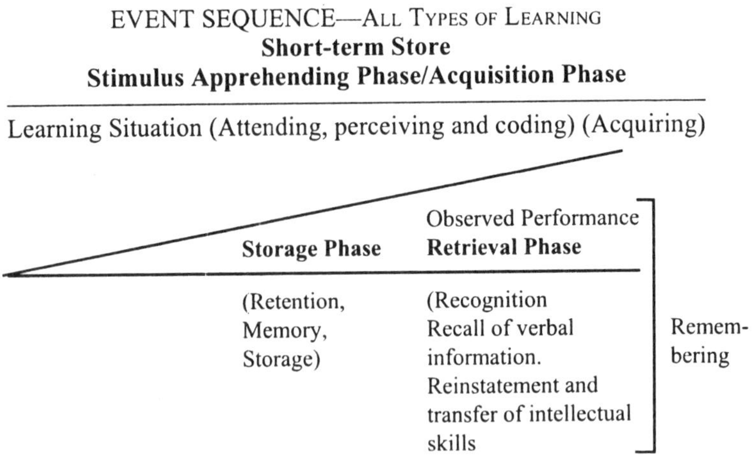

Fig. 17.3: The sequence of events in learning as suggested by Gagne.

An Overview of the Memory System

Information from the environment arrives through the senses and is held briefly in a sensory store (the sensory register) of relatively large capacity. Some of this incoming information, once it is identified and categorized, can be passed along to the short-term store and then to the long-term store.

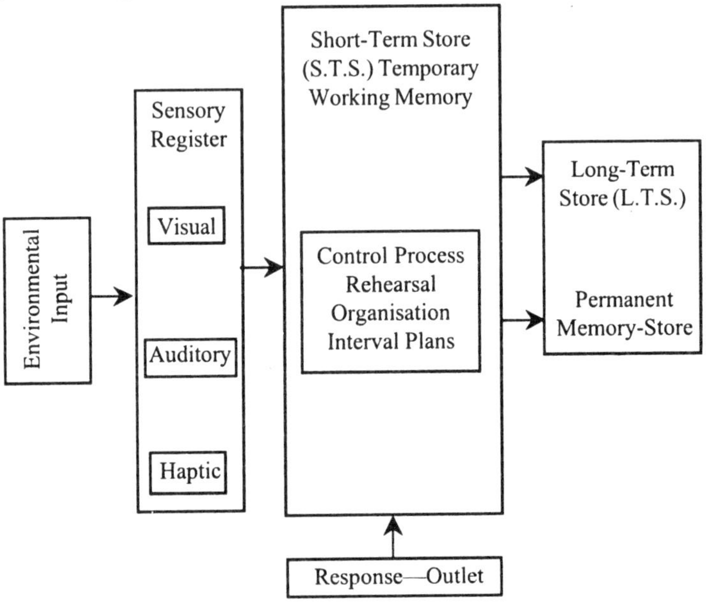

Movement of Information within memory system

Fig. 17.4: An Overview of the Memory System.

Importance of the Listener (Learner): The following diagram shows consideration to the learner.

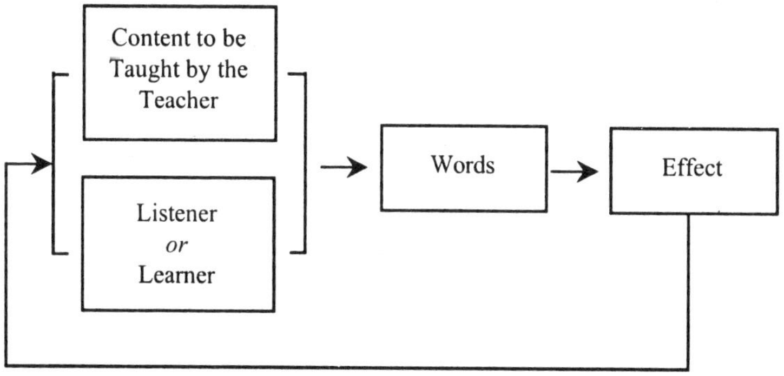

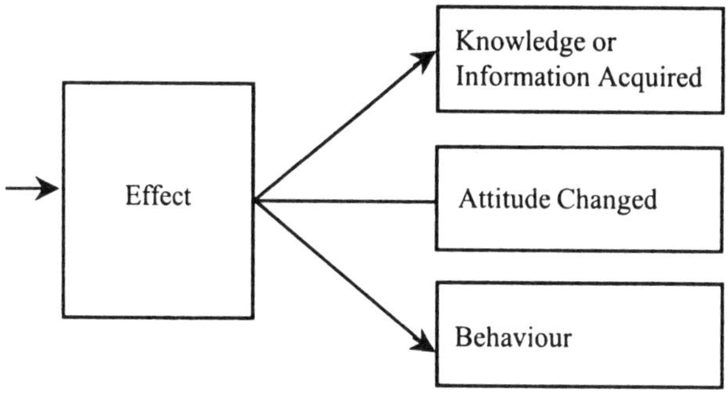

Fig. 17.5: Effect of the Information Processing Model

Short-term Store: It is assumed to be a temporary working memory with a quite limited capacity. In a sense, this is a record of the current contents of consciousness.

Long-term Store: It is conceived of as a permanent repository of information. This memory store contains essentially, our knowledge of the world, and its capacity is assumed to be very great. Once material has been transferred to long-term store, there seems to be very little—if any loss of information.

As material is acquired, it presumably passes through the sensory register and into the short-term store. Control process such as rehearsal permits the transfer of this material to long-term store , from which it may be subsequently retrieved. Actually, although not indicated in this diagram, long-term store enters the picture in a number of different ways. First, information from long-term store is necessary to permit pattern recognition and identification of raw sensory information held in the sensory register. Second, information that has been sufficiently rehearsed or organized is thought to be transferred to long-term store. Finally, the very control processes that are assumed to govern the movement of the information through the system must be represented in some way (as rules) in long-term store.

Communication and Teaching: We may quote R.E. de Kieffer and Lee W. Cochran, "Effective teaching and communications are synonymous, for good teachers are clear communicators and good communicators as effective teachers.. Our society today has a vast array of modern media of communication... These modern media are among the tools, the education profession uses to mould and shape human minds." Good teaching, in fact is intercommunication. There must be reaction and interaction with constant feedback.

The message conveyed by the teacher and or the educational media may be verbal or visual and the receiver may listen, see or examine and react in other ways. The communication channel in the classroom should ideally carry both messages and counter messages.

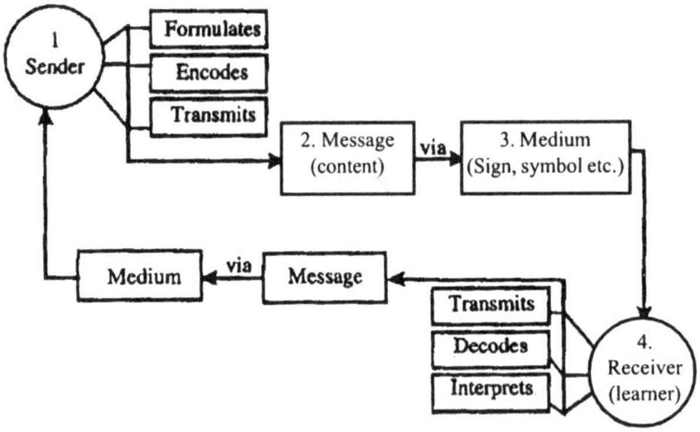

Fig. 17.6: Information Processing Model

17.8 ROGERS AND MASLOW'S HUMANISTIC THEORIES OF LEARNING

Meaning of Humanistic Learning

The word humanistic is derived from the Latin Word *'Homo'* meaning 'human being'. Thus humanistic theory gives a central place to the human being in learning. It is comparatively a new learning. It makes use of terms like belongingness, co-existence, creativity, mental health and values etc. Above all it emphasises 'self-development'. This theory is based on understanding the needs of the learners and this is the first step towards the fulfillment of learning objectives. Its watchwords are 'better learner', a 'better human being' and 'well-adjusted human being'.

Main Characteristics of Humanistic Theory of Learning

Important characteristics of humanistic theory of learning are given below:

1. Welfare of all human beings is its main concern.

2. This theory lays emphasis on learning in natural environment of co-operation equality, freedom, love and peace rather than of physical values, like money, wealth etc.
3. It believes in co-existence.
4. It stresses that learning becomes effective when it is need-based.
5. Its focus is on learning at the highest level *i.e.*, self-transcendence and self-actualisation.
6. Experience is the basis of learning.
7. It emphasises self-motivation for better learning.
8. It aims at increasing the learner's self-direction and independence.
9. It assists learners to accept more responsibility in determining what they are learning.

Educational Implications of the Humanistic Theory of Learning

Following are the main implications of the humanistic theory of learning:

1. It stresses learner-centred learning.
2. It lays emphasis on understanding individual differences, needs and interests of the learners etc.
3. It envisages active learning on the part of the learner.
4. It highlights the importance of self-discipline and self-control.
5. It considers the teacher as a friend, guide and helper to the learner.
6. It enjoins upon the teachers to involve students in the process of learning.

Limitations of the Humanistic Theory of Learning

1. It relatively ignores the significance of passive listening (a good deal of learning takes place even in passive listening) on the part of the learners.
2. It tends to develop individualistic attitudes and relatively ignores social development of the learner.

Evaluation of Various Theories of Learning

Each theory or mode of learning, in its own way has made a significant contribution to educational thought and practice. Each theory has its own way to explain the nature and process of learning. The promoters of each theory take into account only one or a few aspects of learning. Thus the totality of learning is not given its attention. The situation is like the proverbial elephant where some blind men tried to describe an elephant by touching its different parts, *i.e.*, leg, tail and trunk separately. Each person gave the description of the elephant in his own way.

An intelligent and pragmatic teacher would not remain wedded to any particular theory of learning. He would make use of all the theory of learning and their implications in the teaching-learning process. A balanced and pragmatic view of various theory of learning and their application accordingly would go a long way in making teaching-learning effective, efficient and inspirational.

Humanistic Model of C.R. Rogers (1902-1972)

In his two path—breaking books, *'On Becoming a Person' and 'Client-centred Therapy'*, Carl R. Rogers have given a lucid view of his humanistic approach. The term counselling and Rogers are also inseparable.

Carl Rogers was born in Oak Park, Illinois, U.S.A. He imbibed his scientific temper from his father. At Wisconsin University, he first studied agriculture and then religion. He went to China in 1922 for an International World Student Christian Federation Conference. His trip freed him from his fundamental religious attitudes and developed psychological independence. Thereafter he shifted from theology to psychology. He joined Teacher's College, University for courses in Philosophy of Education and Child Guidance. He studied under William Kilpatrick, a renowned educational thinker and practitioner. After this he worked as a psychologist in the Child Study Department at Rochester, New York. During the period he wrote '*The Clinical Treatment of the Problem Child,* (1939). This publication paved his way to become a professor at Ohio State University. In 1945 he joined University of Chicago and worked as the Director of a Counselling centre for about 12 years. In 1957, Rogers moved to the University of Wisconsin and then to Western Behavioural Science Institute in La Jolla California in 1963. He assisted in the setting up of the 'Centre for the Studies of the Person'.

Essence of Rogers' Humanistic Model: Bases of his Theory of Motivation

The following words of Rogers sum up his views.

1. "It is the inalienable right of every individual to be his/her real "self"".
2. "The ideal self is the self-concept which the individual would like to possess upon which he places the highest value for himself."
3. "If I keep from meddling with people they take care of themselves."
   If I keep from commanding people, they behave themselves.
   If I keep from preaching the people, they improve themselves,
   If I keep from imposing on people, they become themselves."
4. "I have found it of enormous value when I can permit myself to understand another person."
5. "It has been my experience that persons have a basically positive direction."
6. "I have found it of enormous value when I can permit myself to understand another person."
7. "I have found it enriching to open channels where by others can communicate their feelings, their private perceptual words to me."
8. "The more I am open to realities in me and in the other person, the less do I find myself wishing to rush into fixing things."

Full Functioning of Self: According to Rogers, "The full functioning person is synonymous with optimal psychological adjustment, optimum psychological maturity, complete congruence, complete openness to experience."

Self-Actualising Tendency and Motivation: Rogers explains self-actualising tendency as "The individual has within himself the capacity and tendency, latent or evident to move forward towards maturity. In a suitable psychological climate the tendency is released. He further states that urge to expand, extend become, to express in an individual enhances the development of 'self'. The tendency needs proper environment to be released and expressed. The basic actualising tendency is the only motive.

Social Relationships: Rogers believes that social interaction enables a person to discover his own 'self'. The feed back that a person gets from others provides immense scope for self-development.

Openness to Experience: Rogers explains this concept as "If a person could be fully open to his experience, however, every stimulus whether originating within the organism or in the environment; he is more able fully to like the experiences of his organism rather than shutting them out of experience."

Important Characteristics of a Self-actualised or a Fully Functioning Self

Rogers gives the following characteristics of a self-actualised person.

1. He is more able to experience all of his feelings.
2. He is his own sifter of evidence.
3. He is more open to evidence from all sources.
4. He is completely engaged in the process of being and becoming himself.
5. He is soundly and realistically social.
6. He lives more completely in this moment but learns that this is the soundest living for all time.
7. Because of the awareness of himself which flows freely in and through experience he is becoming a more fully functioning person.

Educational Implications of Roger's views on Motivation

1. The learners should be allowed to express their feelings freely.
2. Individuality of the learner should be respected.
3. The learner should be provided an environment of warmth.
4. There should be complete transparency in the environment.
5. Understanding interpersonal relationships between the learners and the teacher are very helpful in developing motivation among the learners. For this purpose, suitable teaching-learning environment must be created.
6. Suitable experiences should be provided to the learners to express themselves freely.

Publications of Rogers

1. 'Becoming Partners; Marriage and Its Alternatives'.
2. 'Carl Rogers on Encounter Groups'.
3. 'Client-Centred-Therapy'.
4. 'The Clinical Treatment of the Problem Child'.
5. 'Counselling and Psychotherapy'.
6. 'Freedom to Learn'.
7. 'On Becoming a Person'

UNIT III: Intelligence

18

Intelligence: Meaning, Nature, Characteristics and Development

18.1 MEANING AND DEFINITION OF INTELLIGENCE

Intelligence has been viewed differently by scholars. More than one hundred definitions of intelligence are found in the psychological literature. However, in general, intelligence is considered as the global capacity of an individual to think rationally, to act purposefully and to deal effectively with the environment. All the discoveries and inventions of the world are usually attributed to persons of high intelligence.

Here some of the most prominent definition of intelligence are given. These definition throw meaningful light on the meaning, nature and development of intelligence.

1. *Binet* describes intelligence as: (1) the tendency of thought to take and maintain a definite direction, (2) the capacity to make adaptations for the purpose of attaining a desired end, and (3) the power of self-criticism.

2. *Colvin* defines it as capacity to learn.

3. *Burt* calls it the power of readjustment to relatively novel situations by organising new psycho-physical co-ordination.

4. *Stern* defines intelligence as the general mental adaptability to new problems and conditions of life.

5. *William James* calls it the ability to adjust oneself successfully to a relatively novel situation.

6. *William McDougall* states "an intelligent action as one which seems to show that the creature has profited by prior experience of similar situations, that it somehow brings to bear its previous experience in the guidance of its present action; intelligence is the capacity to improve upon native tendency in the light of past experience."

7. *Thorndike* defines it as, "We may define intelligence in general as the power of good responses from the point of view of truth or fact."

8. *Terman* writes: "An individual is intelligent in proportion as he is able to carry on abstract thinking."

9. *Num* regards it as the "flexibility of the mind to meet new situations."

10. *Boynton* states, "Intelligence is an inherited capacity of the individual which is manifested through his ability to adapt to and reconstruct the factors of his environment in accordance with the most fundamental needs of himself and his group."

11. *Johnson* thinks that intelligence stands for an "ability to solve the general run of human problems to adjust to new situations and in short the ability to think."

12. *Spearman* thinks intelligence in terms of two abilities e.g. general ability or '*g*' and specific ability or '*s*'. Both kinds of abilities work in every performance. His '*g*' is the common factor which will colour every response, and his '*s*' is independent in every process. A scientist has two kinds of abilities, general as well as one specific for science. A musician has two kinds of abilities, general as well as specific, for music in this case. In the measurement of the intelligence of a person, both of these abilities should be taken into consideration.

13. *Vat Wagenen* treats intelligence as "capacity to learn and to adjust to relatively new and changing conditions."

14. *Freeman* writes, "Intelligence is represented in behaviour by the capacity of the individual to adjust himself to new situations to solve new problems to learn."

15. *Thurstone* stresses the "factorial analysis" theory which recognises intelligence as consisting of several abilities, seven of which have been identified.

(i) number facility,
(ii) word fluency,
(iii) visualizing,
(iv) memory,
(v) perceptual speech,
(vi) induction, and
(vii) verbal reasoning.

16. *Terman's* definition of Intelligence is on the following pattern

(i) Ability to carry on abstract thinking. This means, it cannot be manifested at the level of perception whereas in fact intelligence is involved in perceptual tasks.

(ii) Capacity for abstract thinking, like all other abilities, involves factors specific to itself as well as intelligence.

This definition does not state that the abstract thinking is to be directed or relevant to a question or to some end.

Definition Classification of Intelligence

Broadly speaking there are three types of definitions regarding the meaning and development of intelligence.

(i) One group of definitions emphasises that intelligence is the ability to adjust, or adapt oneself to one's total environment or to limited aspects thereof—Burt, William James, McDoughall, Goddard.

It is the capacity to organise one's behaviour pattern so as to act more effectively and more appropriately in novel situations. Thus, the more intelligent person could be one who can more easily and more extensively vary his behaviour as changing conditions demand.

(ii) The second type of definition states that intelligence is the ability to learn. Colvin is the propounder of this definition.

(iii) The third type of definition states that it is the ability to carry on abstract thinking—Binet, Terman and Freeman.

However, it would be very difficult to separate all these definitions into three clear-cut categories.

A definition of intelligence as the capacity to behave appropriately and effectively in new situations and a definition that intelligence is the ability to learn are in fact two aspects of the same process. Similarly, ability to carry on abstract thinking contributes to a person's ability to adjust or adapt to changing or new situations.

Wechsler's definition seems to combine and extend the three types of definitions. He states: "Intelligence is the aggregate global capacity of the individual to act purposefully, to think rationally and to deal effectively with his environment''.

G.D. Stoddard offers the following definition: "Intelligence is the ability to undertake activities that are characterized by:

1. Difficulty,
2. Complexity,
3. Abstractness,
4. Economy,
5. Adaptiveness to a goal,
6. Social value, and
7. The emergence of originals and to maintain such activities under conditions that demand a concentration of energy and a resistance to emotional force."

18.3 INTELLIGENCE AND SCHOLARS OF ANCIENT INDIA

Kautilya defines it as the ability to work.

According to Visnusarma, it is the power which enables human beings to control the world.

The *Brahmasutra* tells us that intelligence is the gift of God and it is fixed at birth.

The *Agnipurana* prescribes diet for infants to help the growth of their intelligence.

Types of Intelligence Accordance to Ancient View

Agadha buddhi or intelligence that cannot be measured or superior intelligence.

Mohabuddhi or great intelligence, *malin buddhi* or dull intelligence.

Sthira buddhi or calm intelligence.

Alpa buddhi or little intelligence.

In ancient India, intelligence was measured through conversation, physical features, gestures, gait, speech, changes in the eye and facial expression.

18.4 OPERATIONAL DEFINITION AND MEANING OF INTELLIGENCE

Since theoretical discussions do not lead us to some precise nature of intelligence, Vernon states: "Intelligence is what intelligence tests measure.''

Some argue, "We can measure electricity without being able to define its precise nature. But we can put electricity to use and measure it. So we can use and measure intelligence.''

Now going into the discussion of these various definitions of intelligence, it may be said that intelligence is an ability to "see the right thing at the right moment in the right way.'' It is a general capacity to understand and meet with the situations that life may present, successfully. To quote Principal R.R. Kumria: "Call it practical wisdom; call it common sense; call it genius; it is just the same in different names and grades.''

18.5 KINDS OF INTELLIGENCE AND A FEW GENERALISATIONS

Kinds of Intelligence

Thurstone has suggested three broad categories of intelligence:

1. *Abstract Intelligence*: He defined this as the "ability to understand and manage ideas and symbols, such as words, number, chemical or physical formulas, legal decisions, scientific principles and the like. ...'' In the case of students this is very close to what is called scholastic aptitude.
2. *Mechanical Intelligence*: This includes, "The ability to clean, to understand and manage things and mechanisms, such as a knife, a gun, a moving machine, an automobile, a boat, a lathe...''
3. *Social Intelligence*: "This is the ability to understand and manage men and women, boys and girls to act wisely in human relations.''

A Few Generalisations about Intelligence

Usually scholars, executives in business and Government, and scientists possess high abstract intelligence.

Mechanics, builders, expert carpenters and plumbers possess high mechanical intelligence.

High social intelligence is found in politicians, sales people and leaders in society.

A successful civil engineer presumably possesses high abstract as well as high mechanical intelligence; the successful criminal lawyer possesses abstract as well as social intelligence.

Distribution of Intelligence

The majority of the school children, say about 60%, are found in the I.Q. interval 90—110 and are referred to as 'Normal' or 'Average'.

Intelligence and Sex Differences: Generally speaking, the research studies show that the average scores of the sexes are strikingly similar.

Intelligence and Race Differences: Every racial and cultural group contains some gifted children. Franz Boas states, "If we were to select the most intelligent, imaginative, energetic and emotionally stable third of mankind, all races would be represented.''

18.6 DEVELOPMENT OF INTELLIGENCE AND MENTAL TESTING

Intelligence cannot be increased or decreased. The amount of intelligence that a person possesses is inherited and fixed. The amount though fixed does not reveal itself at the start of life. With the growth of the child, the amount inherited by a child also grows. The general belief is that the growth of intelligence stops and it reaches its limit at the age of sixteen or seventeen. It is true that a man of forty knows more than a boy of sixteen. But this does not mean that the amount of intelligence possessed by him has increased. This may be due to his experience. As regards his intelligence, his position remains the same.

The growth of intelligence of certain children may be checked on account of certain unfavourable circumstances and when these are removed, intelligence begins to grow and functions normally.

An intelligent person has the ability to adjust himself to the changing circumstances with ease, efficiency and speed. He has the capacity to assimilate ideas very quickly and clearly. He can cope with new situations very successfully. All the inventions of the world can be attributed to persons of intelligence.

The unintelligent or the dullard individuals fail to think of new situations. They are always guided by others. They lack originality.

Are all persons equally intelligent? Are all the students fit for school instruction? Are all students capable of pursuing the same course? Are all students fit for all occupations? Is it proper to educate all students in the same way?

These and various such questions have been engaging the attention of the psychologists for the past hundred years or so. Many attempts have been made to measure intelligence possessed by individuals so that necessary arrangements may be made to give them training according to their intelligence. Thanks to the ceaseless efforts of various psychologists whose standardized tests are available which can be used to measure intelligence.

Psychological Testing

Anne Anastasi observes: "Psychological testing is a relatively young branch of one of the youngest of the sciences."

One of the first problems, which stimulated the development of psychological tests, was the identification of the feeble-minded. French physician *Esqurioi* was the first person to write a two-volume work in 1938 in which over one hundred pages were devoted to feeble-mindedness.

Another French physician who made a valuable contribution was *Seguin* who in 1837 established the first school devoted to the education of mentally defective children. In 1848 he migrated to America where his ideas gained recognition.

The general aim of the early experimental psychologists of the nineteenth century was the formulation of generalized description of human behaviour and not the measurement of individual differences. Many of the early experimental psychologists received their training in a laboratory founded by *Wundt* at Leipzig in 1879.

Sir Francis Galton, an English biologist, was primarily responsible for launching the testing movement on its course. In 1882, an anthropometric laboratory was established by him in South Kensington Museum, London. In this laboratory individuals could be measured in certain physical traits by the payment of a small fee. Galton himself devised most of the simple tests. Galton also paved the way for the application of rating scale and questionnaire methods etc. One of his disciples, *Karl Pearson* carried forward his work.

James McKeen Cattell of America occupies a prominent position in the development of psychological testing. He used the term "mental test" in an article in 1890. The article related a series of tests which were being administered annually to college students in the efforts to determine their intellectual level. Cattell like Galton felt that a measure of intellectual functions could be obtained through tests of sensory discrimination and reaction time.

Among others the names of *Jastrow, Krae Pelin* and *Ferrai* may also be mentioned.

The early experiments of Wundt were all concerned with sensory discrimination and motor ability. His worthy pupil Cattell did much useful work in America. However the credit of scientific mental testing goes to Binet and Simon. The names of Terman and Cyril Burt may also be mentioned who did very useful work in mental testing.

In India, Dr. V.V. Kamat, Dr. C.H. Rice, Pt. L.S. Jha, Prof. S. Jalota and Principal R.R. Kumria have contributed a lot to psychological testing.

Landmarks in the Development of Testing

1826	Robert Owen's rating scale
1842	Seguin's form boards
1905	Binet-Simon scale
1908	Goddard translation of Binet's scale
1909	Court is practice test in arithmetic
1910	Thorndike handwriting scale
1911	Healy and Fernald performance test
1912	Hillegas composition scale
1913	Buckingham spelling scale
1915	Yerkes point scale
1916	Stanford revision of the Binet-Simon scale
1917	Army Group tests, Stenquist assembly tests
1919	Sea-shore tests of musical ability
1921	Rorschach test
1927	Strong vocational interest inventory
1933	Hildreth readiness tests
1935	Murray apperception test
1938	Thurstone primary abilities test

18.7 MEASUREMENT OF INTELLIGENCE

Intelligence is measured through a complicated process. It involves a comparison and establishment of a relationship between C.A. (Chronological Age) and M.A. (Mengal Age). This relationship is expressed by the term I.Q. (Intelligence Quotient). When the mental age is divided by the chronological age and the quotient is multiplied by 100, the result is I.Q.

$$\text{I.Q.} = \frac{\text{M.A.}}{\text{C.A.}} \times 100$$

18.8 BASIC CONCEPTS INVOLVED IN INTELLIGENCE AND INTELLIGENCE TESTING

1. *Chronological Age*: This refers to the age in years, months, hours. This is counted from the time and date of the birth of an individual. It is symbolically expressed as C.A.

2. *Mental Age* (*M.A.*): Binet was the first psychologist to introduce the concept of mental age. He gave a better footing and credibility to the intelligence test results. Alfred Binet was a French psychologist and an Education Officer. He is known as the father of Modern Psychological Testing. He was assisted by Simon and as such his intelligence test is known as Binet-Simon Test of Intelligence. The then French Government was faced with the problem of separating mentally retarded children from the normal ones. The job was assigned to Binet. It took about 15 years to complete the job. The year 1905 is a great landmark in the history of intelligence testing.

Menal age refers to *'Mental Maturity'* of a person. Corresponding to his level of performance in an intelligence test—irrespective of his C.A. If a person of C.A. 7 years old is able to score satisfactorily on a test meant for a child of C.A. 10, then the mental age (henceforth referred as M.A.) of the former is 10. Mental age can also be defined as an expression of the extent of development achieved by the individual stated in terms of the performance that can be expected at any given age.''

And when the score of a given intelligence tests are put into M.A. scores—we have with us what is known as Age Scale. Maximum mental age is 19 or 20.

3. *Basal Age*: Basal age is that age of the child with reference to his chronological age where he can solve all questions in a given test. Mental age cannot be calculated directly. It is basal age which helps in the calculation of mental age.

This concept of basal age may be explained with the help of an example. There is a child with C.A. 6. He solves all questions in a test meant for child of C.A. 7. He also does the same for a child of C.A. 8 and then his efficiency declines, *i.e.*, he solves only 2 questions out of 6 questions in a test meant for a child of C.A. 9. The basal age of a child with C.A. 6 is 8 years. His mental age will be

Mental age = Basal age + partial credit
= 8 years + 4 months
The child has an M.A. of 8-1/3 years

18.9 CLASSIFICATION OF INDIVIDUAL ON THE BASIS OF I.Q.

Terman's Classification

A. On the basis of I.Q., Terman gives the following classification on American testees:

Near genius or genius	above 140
Very superior intelligence	120—140
Superior intelligence	110—120
Normal or average intelligence	90—110

Dullness	80—90
Borderline cases	70—80
Definite feeble-mindedness which has been further classified as under:	Below 70
Morons	50—70
Imbeciles	25—50
Idiots	below 25

B. Classification of Indian Children

The Bombay-Karnataka Revision Tests: Dr. V.V. Kamat revised Binet's scale to suit Indian conditions and administered intelligence tests to 1,074 children and adolescents of all ages from 2 to 20 of both sexes. The locality selected for the experiment was the town of Dharwar in the Bombay Presidency. The children selected were fairly representative of the general population of Indian children.

Dr. V.V. Kamat classifies Indian children as under:

Class	*Range of I.Q.s*
Near genius or genius	140 and above
Extraordinary	130—139.9
Very superior	120—129.9
Superior	110—119.9
Average or normal	99—109.9
Backward	80—98.9
Very backward	70—79.9
Borderline	60—69.9
Morons	40—59.9
Imbeciles	20—39.9
Idiots	Below 20

18.10 IMPORTANT USES OF INTELLIGENCE TESTS IN EVALUATION

Intelligence tests are very useful for the following purposes:

1. *Knowing Individual Differences among Learners*: Dr. V.V. Kamat has classified Indian children as under:

Category	*Range of I.Q.*
Near genius or genius	140 and above
Extraordinary	130-139.9
Very Superior	120-129.9
Superior	110-119.9
Average or normal	99-109.9
Backward	80-98.9
Very backward	70-79.9
Borderline	60-69.9
Morons	40-59.9
Imbeciles	20-30.9
Idiots	Below 20

2. *Grouping in the Class*: Sometimes grouping in the class is done on the basis of intelligence test results.

3. *Class-room Teaching*: Intelligence tests enable the teacher to know the general mental level of the students and accordingly he adopts his teaching techniques.

4. *Identification of Slow Learners and the Gifted*: Intelligence tests help to identify learners in their capacity to learn. Accordingly enrichment programmes are provided to the gifted and compensatory/remedial education to the slow learners.

5. *Selection to Courses*: Different subjects require different degrees of intelligence. Some call for a higher order of intelligence and the others of a lower order.

A nation-wide study in the U.S.A. gave the following Median I.Q. of the high school students in different courses:

Course	*Median I.Q.*
Technical	114
Scientific	108
Academic	106
Commerce	104
Trade	92

Burt found the following correlations between:

Intelligence and arithmetic (Problems)	.65
Intelligence and the compositor	.63
Intelligence and reading	.56
Intelligence and spelling	.52
Intelligence and writing	.21
Intelligence and hard work	.18
Intelligence and drawing	.15

This implies that children of high I.Q. are superior in abstract thinking than those of low I.Q.

5. *Selection in Occupations*: Burt draws up the following provisional scheme for occupational classification according to the degree of intelligence occupations require:

S.No.	*Occupation*	*I.Q. Require*
1.	Higher professional and administrative work—Lawyer, physician, architect, teacher (University and Secondary level)	150
2.	Lower professional technical and executive work	130 to 150
3.	Clerical and highly skilled work—shorthand, typist, bank clerk, salesman, electrician, nurse.	115 to 130
4.	Skilled work—tailor, dressmaker, carpenter, cashier, printer	100 to 115
5.	Semi-skilled repetitive work—barber, welder, miner, painter, banker	85 to 100
6.	Unskilled repetitive work—manual labour	70 to 85
7.	Casual labour—simplest routine work	50 to 75

6. *Promotion*: Intelligence tests are used for the promotion of students to the next class.

7. *Selection of Students to a School*: In good schools, there is always rush for admission. All the applicants though eligible for admission cannot be admitted. It then becomes necessary to adopt some additional methods of selection. Intelligence tests help to meet out this difficulty to a considerable extent. By administering these tests, authorities pick out the innately brighter boys.

8. *The Discovery of Unusual Cases*: The lack of intelligence may be the main cause of abnormal behaviour. The intelligence tests help to find out cases of abnormal behaviour.

9. *Intelligence and Success in College*: Gates and others think that an I.Q. of at least 120 is needed to do acceptable college work in a first class college with an average expenditure of time and energy.

10. *Help in Diagnosis of Backwardness*: Ordinary scholastic examinations fail to discover 'educable abilities'. The failure of a child in the examination is no indication that he lacks intelligence. This failure may beon account of defective methods of teaching or it may be due to some temperamental or physical obstacles which might have stood in the way of the child. There may not be any fault with the intelligence of the child only it has not been allowed to work itself out.

11. *Award of Scholarship*: Various public scholarships are awarded on the basis of the results secured through intelligence tests. The Government of India selects some students for the award of scholarships for studying in Public Schools on the basis of the intelligence and achievement tests.

12. *Evaluation of Methods and Materials of Instruction*: Intelligence Tests are helpful in evaluating the results of the experiments conducted by a school in the relative importance of the different methods of instruction *i.e.*, achievement obtained with different text-books or with a certain text-book as contrasted with extensive reading material not confined to any one book.

13. *Assessment of Teacher's Work*: When the achievement of the pupils in a subject does not correspond to the scores of intelligence tests, it gives indication to the fact that the subject has not been properly taught by the teacher and properly understood by the students.

Limitations of Intelligence Tests

It would be a great mistake to think that these tests are all in all in measuring the various aspects of the learner's personality. Intelligence is one of the factors. Too much reliance cannot be made on this evaluation tool. It is to be used in conjunction with other tools. Following are the important limitations of intelligence tests:

1. Intelligence tests seek to measure intelligence which in itself is not a clear concept. Psychologists differ readically on the meaning and nature of intelligence.
2. Intelligence tests fail to measure the depth, strength, weakness and quality of an individual relating to his emotional stability.

3. Intelligence tests fail to evaluate the ethical, moral and spiritual qualities of an individual.
4. Intelligence tests fail to take into account the environmental factors. The tests may include items/material with which the children of certain socio-economic groups have more experience than those of the weaker sections.
5. Use of intelligence tests needs a good deal of care and caution on the part of the test user.

19

Classification of Intelligence Tests and Theories of Intelligence

19.1 CLASSIFICATION OF INTELLIGENCE TESTS

Intelligence tests may be classified in several ways. Some of the classifications of intelligence tests are given below:

Classification I (Based on Administration)

- (1) Individual Intelligence Tests
- (2) Group Intelligence Tests

Classification II (Based on the Form of the Test)

- (1) Verbal (Language) Intelligence Test
- (2) Non-Verbal (Non-Language) Intelligence Test
- (3) Verbal and Non-Verbal Intelligence Test

Classification III (Based on the Administration and Form of Test

- (1) Individual Verbal Intelligence Test
- (2) Individual Non Verbal Intelligence Test
- (3) Individual Verbal and Non-Verbal Intelligence Test
- (4) Group Verbal Intelligence Test
- (5) Group Non-Verbal Intelligence Test
- (6) Group Verbal and Non-Verbal Intelligence Test

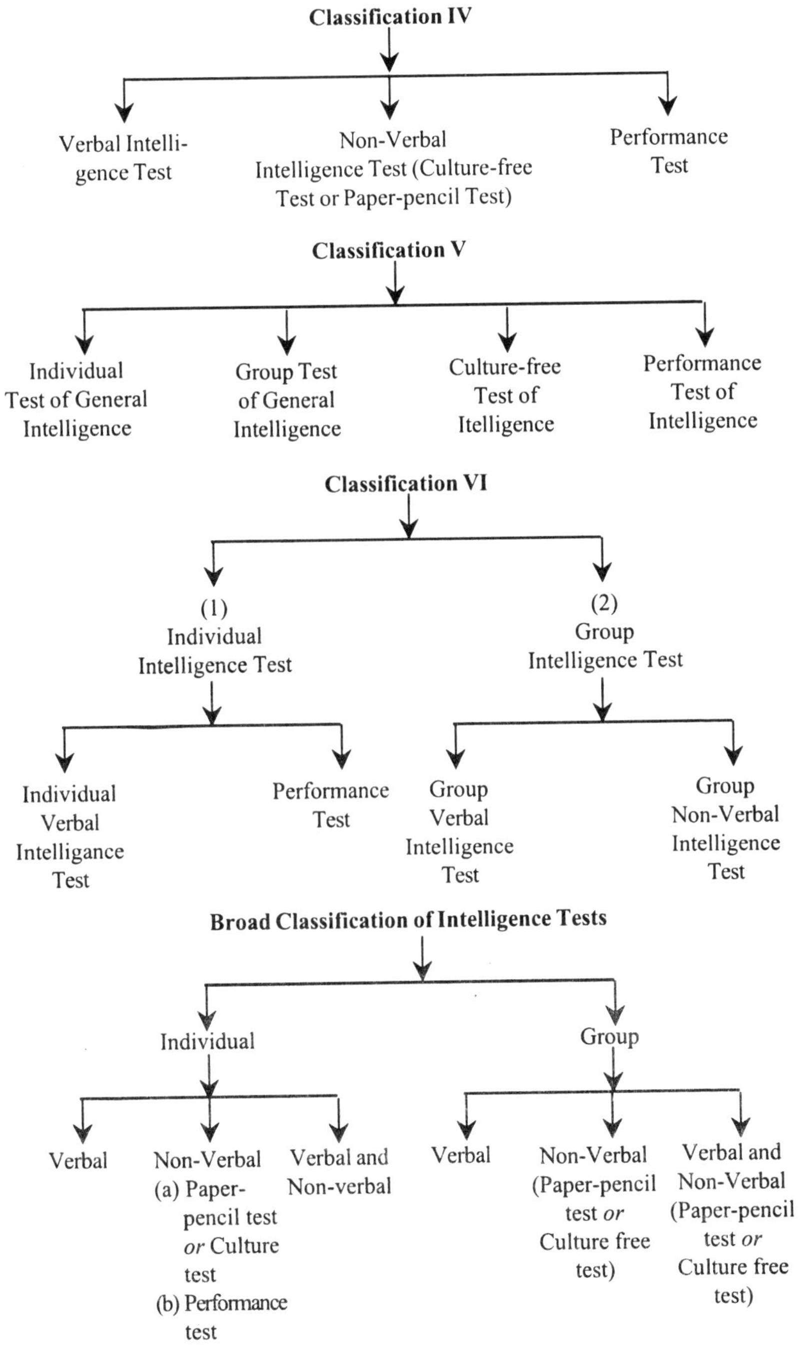

Fig. 19.1: Classification of Individual Test and Group Test of Intelligence

Advantages of Performance Tests

1. Performance tests are very useful with older children and adults who are mentally retarded.
2. Performance tests have great clinical significance.
3. Children take performance test with confidence since the test material is visually present in concrete form.
4. Performance tests enable the tester to observe the qualitative aspect of the behaviour of the individual in a variety of test situations.
5. Information obtained by the application of performance tests prove very useful when supplemented with verbal tests of intelligence.

Limitations of Performance Tests

1. The reliability of co-efficient of performance tests is low as they are more susceptible to practice-effect.
2. They fail to differentiate among above – average children.
3. They fail to test mental abilities like concept formation and abstract thinking.

Comparison between Individual Test of Intelligence and Group Test of Intelligence

Individual Test	*Group Test*
1. This test is administered to an individual at a time.	1. This test is administered to several individuals at the same time.
2. It is costly in terms of administration.	2. Group test is not costly in terms of administration.
3. It is time consuming.	3. Group test is not time consuming.
4. It needs a trained tester to administer.	4. No special training is required to administer this test.
5. Since there is face to face interaction, the tester can study the behaviour of the individual.	5. Since there is no face to face interaction, it is not possible to study the behaviour of the individual.
6. This test is more reliable as it is not affected by the reading and speed ability.	6. Group test may be influenced by the reading and speed ability of the individuals.
7. This test is most suitable for children who cannot read or write.	7. It is comparably more suitable for older children who can read and write.
8. Individual test provides qualitative performance of the individual.	8. It does not provide sufficient qualitative performance of the individual.
9. The tester can adapt to the needs of the individual child.	9. The tester cannot adapt to the individual needs of the child.
10. There is a great element of informality in the administration of the test.	10. There is greater formality in the administration.
11. Instructions can be made clear to the individual.	11. It is rather difficult to make instructions clear.
12. This test is more useful in clinical settings. A psychologist can know more about an individual.	12. A group test is not useful in clinical situation. It is more useful in educational setting.
13. Results in this test may be influenced by factors like anxiety etc. of the individual as there is close interaction between the tester and the individual.	13. Factors like anxiety and shyness are not likely to influence as there is very little interaction between the tester and the testee.

1. *Individual Tests*: These tests are administered to one individual at a time. These cover age group from 2 years to 18 years. Important individual tests are: (a) The Binet-Simon Tests, (b) Revised Tests by Terman, and (c) Mental and Scholastic Tests of Burt.

2. *Group Tests*: Group tests are administered to a group of people. Group tests had their birth in America—when the intelligence of the recruits who joined the army in the First World War was to be calculated. These are: (a) The Army Alpha and Beta Tests, (b) Terman's Group Tests, and (c) Otis Self-Administrative Tests.

3. *Performance Tests*: These tests involve manipulation of objects. The construction of certain patterns or solving problems in terms of concrete material. Some of the famous tests are: (a) Koh's Block Design Test, (b) The Cube Construction Tests, and (c) The Pass Along Tests.

19.2 INTELLIGENCE TESTING IN INDIA (A BRIEF LIST)

Verbal Individual Tests

1. *Dr. C.H. Rice's Hindustani Tests*: Dr. C.H. Rice of the Forman Christian College, Lahore, was one of the first to start this work in India. His is an adapted scale of the Binet scale, in Urdu. These tests were published by Oxford University Press in 1929.
2. *Dr. Kamat's Age Scale Revision Tests*: Dr. V.V. Kamat of Belgaum Training College followed up the Binet-Simon system with the Stanford Revision and adapted it in the age scale for Indian children knowing Kanarese and Marathi languages.
3. Stanford Hindustani Revision by Patna Training College, Patna.
4. Allahabad Intelligence Test for 11+ (in Hindi) by Dr. Sohan Lal, published by Kitabistan, Allahabad.
5. C.I.E. (Central Institute of Education) Test of Intelligence by Shri Udai Shankar, Central Institute of Education, Delhi, 1953.

Verbal Group Tests

1. The Pasrur Group Intelligence Test (Urdu) by Prof. R.R. Kumria, of Central Training College, Lahore.
2. Group Test of Intelligence (Test No. 12), Bureau of Psychology, Allahabad.
3. Samuhik Manasik Yogyata Pariksha by Prof. S. Jalota, Banaras Hindu University, 1951.
4. Buddhi-Mapak Pariksha by Shri V.G. Jhingram, Dharam Samaj College, Aligarh, 1952. The test has been prepared both in Hindi and Urdu scripts.
5. C.I.E. Group Test of Intelligence by Prof. Udai Shankar, of the Central Institute of Education, Delhi, 1953.
6. Jha's Group Tests by R.B. Pandit Lajja Shankar Jha, the late Principal of Teachers' Training College, Banaras.

Non-Verbal Group Tests

1. Hindi Adaptation of Dr. R.A.C. Oliver's Test for East Africa by E.A. Menzel, Bisrampur (M.P.)
2. Non-Verbal Group Test by T.C. Vicary and M. Draper, Union Christian Training College, Berhampore, Orissa.

19.3 DESCRIPTION OF SOME TESTS

I. SS Jalota's Group Test of Intelligence (Verbal)

1. *Year of Publication*: 1950 and modified in 1963
2. *Number of Items*: 100 taken from the following areas:
   (i) Vocabulary—Similar,
   (ii) Vocabulary—Opposite,
   (iii) Number series,
   (iv) Classification,
   (v) Best answer,
   (vi) Influence,
   (v) Analogies.
3. *Time*: Twenty minutes.
4. *User*: (1) Raw scores are used to determine mental ages and intelligence quotient (I.Q.) with the help of the manual. (2) It is widely used for the purpose of providing educational and vocational guidance. (3) It is helpful in selection, diagnosis and classification.
5. *Applicability*: It is applicable to male and female students of classes 8 to 11 and age group 12-16 years.

II. The Wechsler Scale (1939 and Revised in 1955) and Named WAIS (Wechsler Adult Intelligence Test)

It has two parts: (a) Verbal tests, (b) Non-verbal performance test.

(*a*) *Verbal Test*: It includes the following type of items—

(i) Vocabulary
(ii) Information
(iii) Arithmetic
(iv) Comprehension
(v) Similarities
(vi) Digital system.

(*b*) *Non-Verbal Test*: It includes—

(i) Block design
(ii) Picture arrangement
(iii) Object assembly
(iv) Mazes
(v) Picture completion.

Use: It is used in the age ranges from 16 to 64.

III. The Wechsler Intelligence Scale for Children

Verbal Scale	*Performance Scale*
1. *General information* A series of questions covering a wide range of information which children presumably have had an opportunity to acquire (e.g., Who discovered America) Specialized knowledge is avoided.	1. *Picture completion* Picture cards from which some part on each card (e.g. the whiskers of a cat) is missing. Child must identify the missing parts.
2. *General comprehension* Items in which the child must explain what should be done in given circumstances, why certain practices are followed, and so on. An example. Why is it better to build a house of brick than of wood.	2. *Picture arrangement* Sets of picture cards are shown to the child, who must rearrange them so as to tell a story.
3. *Arithmetic* Simple, orally presented arithmetic problems, to be solved without paper or pencil.	3. *Block design* The child is given a set of blocks, with red sides, white sides, and sides that are both red and white and must reproduce a pattern shown by the examiner.
4. *Similarities* Questions such as ``In what ways are a piano and a violin alike.	4. *Object assembly* Cardboard puzzles which the child is to assemble.
5. *Vocabulary* Increasingly difficult words are presented orally and visually; the child is asked to tell what each means.	5. *Coding* A code-substitution test in which symbols are to be paired with digits.
6. *Digit span* Orally presented lists of digits, which are to be represented (in order or back wards).	6. *Mazes* Eight printed mazes are presented; the child must trace in pencil the correct route out.

Source: Robert N. Libert, Ritu Wicks Paulos, Gloria Stratuss Mamor *Developmental Psychology*, 1979.

IV. Dr. C.M. Bhatia's Battery of Performance Tests (Dr. Bhatia was the Director of Uttar Pradesh Manovigyanshala.)

1. *Year of Publication*: 1955
2. *No. of Tests*: Within limitation, the tests are as varied as possible. The Battery includes five tests, each with its own sub-tests and time-limit: (i) Koh's Block Design Test; (ii) Alexander's Pass Along Test; (iii) Pattern Drawing Test; (iv) Immediate Memory Test; and (v) Picture Construction Test.
3. *Applicability*: The battery is applicable to the students of the age group 14-16 years.

4. *Maximum Time*: Total time for the administration of the battery to a single individual is one hour.

V. Raven's Progressive Non-Verbal Matrics Scale

Developed in U.K. by Raven, it consists of 60 matrics (designs) from each of which a part has been removed. The individual chooses the missing insert from six or eight given alternatives. The items are grouped into five services, each containing 12 designs of increasing difficulty but similar in principle. While the earlier series require discrimination accuracy, the later, more difficult series involve analogies, figure formation and alternation of pattern and other logical relations. The test is administered with no time limit.

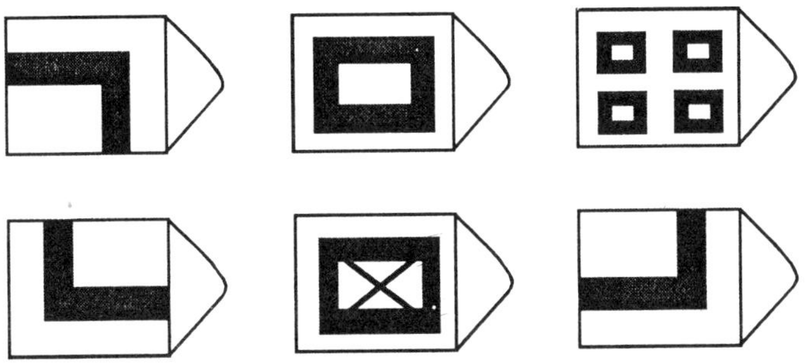

Fig. 19.2: Raven's Progressive Matrices Test (Children)

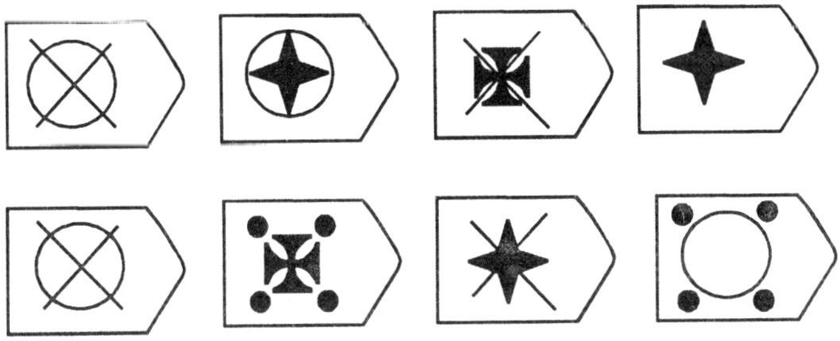

Fig. 19.3: Raven's Progressive Matrices Test (Adults)

VI. Chauhan and Tiwari's Group Verbal Test

Test: Indian Adaptation of Ottis Lennon Mental Ability Test

1. *Year of Publication*: 1918
2. Hindi Adaptation under the guidance of Prof. S.K. Bose of University of Calcutta in 1952.

3. *Test Items*: 75 as shown below:

	Category	*No. of Test Items*
1.	Best Answers	14
2.	Word meaning	06
3.	Logical Selection	13
4.	Arithmetical Reasoning	04
5.	Sentence Meaning	02
6	Analogies	13
7.	Mixed sentences	07
8.	Classification	04
9.	Number Series	06
10.	Directions	02
11.	Proverbs	04
	Total	75

4. *Time*: 20 minutes for Form B and 30 minutes for Form C.
5. *Applicability*: It is general mental ability test for adults.

19.4 THEORIES OF INTELLIGENCE

Important theories of intelligence are as under:

1. Spearman's Two-factors Theory of Intelligence.
2. Thorndike's Multifactor Theory of Intelligence.
3. Thurstone's Group-factor Theory of Intelligence.
4. Guilford's SI Theory of Structure of Intellect (SI)

19.5 SPEARMAN'S TWO-FACTOR THEORY

Chares Spearman published his book '*The Abilities of Men*' in 1927 in which he expounded his theory.

Essence of Spearman's Theory

The essence of his theory in his own words is, "That all branches of intellectual activity have in common one fundamental function (or group of functions), whereas remaining or specific elements of the activity seem in every case to be wholly different from that in all the others." We can say that on the basis of this intelligence is composed of two factors—one 'g' factor and the other 's' factor. This 'g' factor is involved in all walks of life and 's' is a special factor which is exclusive and is shared by none. The examples of 's' factor are: Artistic ability, 'Musical ability'. These 'special abilities' are independent of 'g' factor. There are 9 's' factors.

Spearman wisely refused to identify 'g' with intelligence or any other quality whose definition was controversial, he suggested that it depends upon the general mental energy with which each individual is endowed. The 's' factors he compared to a large number of mechanisms or Engines which could be activated by this energy. 'S' are largely affected by education and training whereas 'g' is innate as well as uneducable.

Main Criticism

The chief criticism that can be raised against Spearman's work is that he failed to allow sufficiently for types of abilities, which while less general than 'g' are certainly not specific. The reason was that he was unable to get at 'group factors' and his samples were small.

19.6 THORNDIKE'S MULTI FACTOR THEORY

E.L. Thorndike's Multifactor Theory stands in complete contrast to Spearman's two-factor theory. As the name of the theory indicates, intelligence is said to be a multitude of separate factors or elements, each one being a minute element of ability. Prof. N.K. Dutt in his book *'Psychological Foundations of Education'* has explained this theory as: According to this theory, any mental act involves a number of minute elements of ability, operating together. Another mental act would also involve a number of these minute elements operating together. So if these are all common elements in activity 'A' and 'B', there will be a perfect correlation between the two. The more the common elements between two mental activities, the higher the correlation. Thus really there is no such factor as 'general intelligence' or 'g'. There are highly specific elements of intelligence, their number depending upon how refined a classification we wish to make or are capable of making. While propounding this theory of intelligence, Thorndike was quite conscious of the fact that many such elements always cooperate together in any situation demanding intelligence. This is illustrated by his intelligence test known as CAVD.

CAVD consists of four parts.

1. Sentence completion (C)
2. Arithmetical reasoning (A)
3. Vocabulary (V)
4. Following directions (D)

Thorndike does not claim that these four sets of item encompass the entire range of abstract intelligence.

The theory was propounded in the beginning of the 20th century.

Types/Kinds of Intelligence

Thorndike concluded that there were three types of intelligence.

(i) *Social Intelligence* or ability to understand and deal with persons.

(ii) *Concrete intelligence* refers to dealing with things, as in skilled trades and specific appliances.

(iii) *Abstract Intelligence* or ability to understand and deal with verbal and mathematical symbols.

Abstract intelligence is the one that receives the greatest weight.

19.7 THURSTONE'S GROUP-FACTOR THEORY

Intermediate between the theories of Spearman and Thorndike is the Group-Factor Theory or the P.M.A. (Primary Mental Abilities) Theory given to us by Thurstone.

It was in the year 1938 that Thurstone gave us this theory after administering 56 types of tests to students of Chicago University. All these results were subject to factor analysis. He concluded that in all these tests, seven types of factors were working, *i.e.*, Intelligence is *composed of those seven primary mental abilities* which are working in all tests. Thurstone does not believe in 'G' and 'S' theories. Thurstone concludes that certain mental operations have a common 'primary' factor that gives them *psychological and functional unity* and also differentiates them from other mental operations. These mental operations constitute a group. A second group of mental operations has its own unifying primary factor, and so on. In all, there are seven such groups which cover the entire range of mental abilities. Each of these primary factors is independent of others.

These factors are:

N — Numerical factor (ability for mathematical operations)
V — Verbal comprehension factor (ability for verbal comprehension).
S — Space factor (ability for manipulating objects in space)
W — Word fluency factor (ability to think or to infer rules)
P — Perceptual speed factor
I — Induction factor (to infer from specific to general)
D — Deduction factor (to deduce from rules and principles to specific)
R — General Reasoning factor and
M — Rote Memory factor (ability for memorisation).

19.8 GUILFORD'S THEORY OF STRUCTURE OF INTELLECT (SOI)

Guilford and his associates, developed the theory in the psychological laboratory at the University of Southern California in 1966.

Guilford's theory of intelligence is in terms of three independent dimensions—content, operations and products. He stated that when five forms of operations of cognition, memory, divergent thinking, convergent thinking and evaluation operate upon five forms of content—visual auditory, symbolic, semantic and behavioural—and six forms of products-units, classes, relations, systems, transformations and implications—are produced. They together make up (5×5×6) 150 factors.

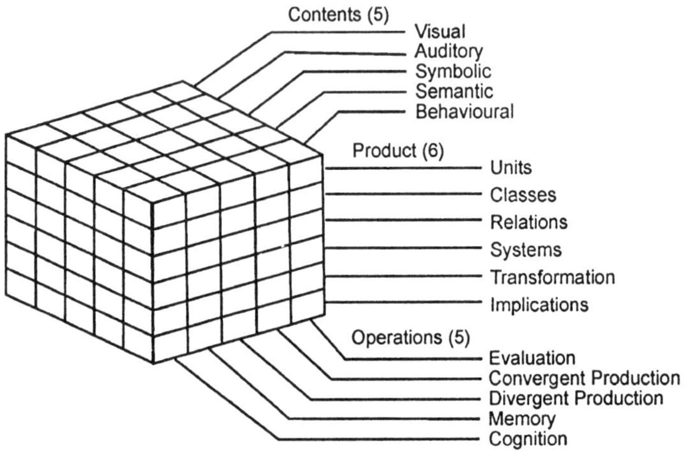

Fig. 19.3: Guilford S.I. Model

A Operation are explained as under:

1. *Cognition.* It refers to discovery, rediscovery or recognition.
2. *Memory.* It is a primary mental process. It means retention of what is recognized.
3. *Divergent Thinking.* This is thinking in different directions, seeking and searching some variety and novelty.
   Convergent Thinking. In this type of thinking what results is the right or best answer.
4. *Evaluation.* It is reaching decisions or making judgements about information.

This model of Guilford is not basic model. It can be squeezed and expanded. When squeezed intelligence consists of only 18 factors (3×2×3 = 18) *i.e.*, instead of 6 products, we have the three; 5 operations can be reduced to two (example *convergent* and *divergent* thinking are one, *memory* can be deleted, *evaluation* is based on *cognition* and as such is one. As such five operations stand reduced to two), and 4 contents to three.

When expanded by breaking, each of the products, operations and contents, intelligence is composed of 960 mental abilities, *i.e.*,

$$8 \times 12 \times 10$$

However, Guilford says that S—R bond is real thing. Eysenck also proposed squeezing in his own way. He says that intelligence comprises of nine factors, *i.e.*, 3 × 1 × 3 = 9. This means that there are three products, three contents and one process or operation. This can be safely compared to Thurstone's model which said that there were 7 primary abilities.

B. Content

A second way of classifying the intellectual factor is according to the kind of material or content involved. It involves four factors:

1. *Figural Content.* It is concrete material which is perceived through our senses, *i.e.*, size, form, colour, etc.
2. *Symbolic.* It is composed of letters, digits and other conventional signs.
3. *Semantic Content.* It is in the forms of verbal meanings or ideas which we get from others.
4. *Behavioural Contents.* It means social behaviour in society.

C. Products

When a certain operation is applied to certain kind of content as many as six kinds of products may be involved:

1. *Units.* Understanding the meaning of words, visual, auditory and symbolic units.
2. *Classes.* It means classification of words and ideas.
3. *Relations.* It implies discovering relations between various concepts and objects.
4. *Systems.* The ability to structure objects in space and to structure symbolic elements and to formulate problems.

5. *Transformations.* The ability to look into the future lines of development or to suggest changes in the existing situations.
6. *Implications.* The ability to utilise present information for future ends.

19.9 EVALUATION OF THE THEORIES OF INTELLIGENCE INCLUDING S.I. MODEL AND THEIR EDUCATIONAL IMPLICATIONS

Evaluation

The SOI model provides knowledge about the specific ability of students to guide them in the right direction. An analysis of the students abilities by the guidance worker can suggest a reliable base on which future learning could be based.

The SOI model is useful in finding out the reasons of the unsatisfactory performance of the students in spite of their adequate intelligence.

The model points out that for understanding human learning and higher mental processes of thinking, problem-solving and creativity, etc. some drastic modifications would be needed in our theory of curriculum construction and methodology of instruction.

The model has explored 120 intellectual abilities and this enables us to find out whether or not we are paying adequate attention to each of them. If not, how to improve.

The model guides us to devise enrichment programmes for the creative and the gifted children.

The model discards the ideas of transfer of learning and stresses that learning of specific skills should be our focus of attention.

Spearman's Theory is criticized on the main ground that it fails to take into account sufficiently for specific types of abilities and towards the later years of his life. Spearman himself had begun to realize the existence of group factors.

Thorndike's Theory accords undue weightage to abstract intelligence.

Guilford Theory of Intelligence seems to be the most comprehensive theory as it attempts to take into consideration all possible aspects of intellectual activity. This theory has several educational implications.

Educational Implications

The theories of intelligence have important implications for teachers. How a teacher looks upon his student's performance, in various activities of the school, depends upon the theory he believes in. For example, if he believes in uni-factor (or one factor) theory, he is likely to label his students as entirely dull or as entirely gifted or average. But if he believes in special mental abilities, he is likely to have a different estimate of his students' abilities in different areas of school activities.

The theory of intelligence, a psychologist believes in, decides the type of intelligence test he will like to construct and use.

UNIT IV: Personality

20

Personality: Meaning, Nature, Development of Integrated Personality

20.1 MEANING, DEFINITION AND NATURE OF PERSONALITY

In simple language by personality, we mean the totality of everything about an individual—his emotional, ethical, mental, physical, social and spiritual make-up. It includes an individual's appearance, emotionality, sociability, intelligence, character and moral traits.

The term 'personality' is derived from a Latin word '*Persona*' which means the mask worn by a Roman actor. In this sense personality means the individual as seen by others. Personality thus implies the cover-up of the real person. One actor plays several roles. In other words, personality is taken to refer to the outward aspect of the individual which actually does not mean anything except in theatre.

20.2 COMPLEX NATURE OF PERSONALITY AND DEFINITIONS OF PERSONALITY

As observed by Murphy (1947), "We do not believe that anyone today can seriously understand to say that he knows what personality is." Present situation also seems to be very unclear, although no topic in the field of psychology is more fascinating than personality. Volumes have been written on the topic, yet we are unable to say clearly what personality is.

Earlier in 1937, G.W. Allport, who had done a good deal of research on personality, mentioned fifty-three definitions of personality in his book "*Personality: A Psychological Interpretation*". Since then how many definitions have been added is any body's guess!

Following are some of the definitions of personality:

1. According to R.B. Cattell, "Personality is that which permits a prediction of what a person will do in a given situation."
2. In the words of L.J. Cronbach, "Character is not really a cumulation of separate habits and ideas, character is embedded in the total structure of personality."
3. J.F. Dashiell, states: "Personality is the sum total of behaviour trends manifested in social adjustments."
4. In the opinion of J.P. Guilford: 'An individual's personality is his unique pattern of traits".

5. Healy William describes personality as "an integrated system of habitual adjustment to environment particularly to social environment.
6. Kurt Lewin, considers personality as "a dynamic totality of systems."
7. Mortem Prince thinks personality as "the sum total of biological innate dispositions, impulses, tendencies, aptitudes and instincts of the individual and the dispositions and tendencies acquired by experience."
8. In the words of R.M. Ogsten, "Personality is the expression of man's inner life, character is the expression of what he does or achieves."
9. According to G.W. Allport, "Personality is the *dynamic* organisation within the individual of those *psycho-physical* systems that determine his *unique adjustment* to the environment."
10. Woodworth gives the following definition, "Personality is the '*total*' quality of an individual's behaviour as it is revealed in his characteristics habits of thought and expression, his attitudes and interests, his manner of acting and his personal philosophy of life.
11. Eysenck's definition of personality is as follows, "Personality is the more or less stable and enduring organization of a person's character, temperament, intellect and physique, which determine his unique adjustment to environment.
12. S.R. Maddi, an American psychologist in his work, '*Personality Theories—A Comparative Analysis*' (1976), one of the latest analysis has defined personality as, "Personality is the stable set of characteristics and tendencies that determine those commonalities and differences in the psychological behaviour (thoughts, feelings and action) of people that have continuity in time and that may or may not be easily understood in terms of the social and biological pressure of the immediate situation alone."

Evaluation of Definitions

A persual of the above definitions would indicate that the definition given by Eysenck (H.J.) seems to be quite functional and operational. It has the following merits.

First. It takes into consideration a balanced view of the conative behaviour or will, affective behaviour based on emotions and cognitive behaviour—intellect or intelligence. Thus this definition attempts to give a complete picture of human behaviour by involving all of its three aspects—Conative, Cognition and affective.

Second. It accords appropriate consideration to the physiological aspect of the personality of an individual.

Third. It emphasises the need to integrate the behaviourist characteristics.

Fourth. It makes personality somewhat assessable and measurable.

However, this definition has one important weakness. It may not be stable in the sense that some circumstances may bring about radical changes in the character and other aspects of an individual. The world is moving so fast that in the span of life of an individual, he may be required to change his behaviour pattern altogether to adjust himself to the changed environment.

Some scholars consider Allport's definition to be comprehensive and clear. It lays stress on these characteristics of personality: (*i*) Dynamic nature, (*ii*) Heredity and environment, (*iii*) Wholeness.

20.3 CHARACTERISTICS AND NATURE OF PERSONALITY

From the definitions given above, following characteristics of personality emerge very clearly:

1. Personality is what one is.
2. Personality of each individual is unique.
3. Personality is dynamic and not static.
4. Personality functions as a unified whole.
5. Personality is the product of both heredity and environment.
6. Personality is through and through social.
7. Personality is continually adjusting itself to environment.
8. In rare cases personality influences the environment.
9. Personality is always striving for certain ends.
10. Personality is self-consciousness. We do not attribute personality to animals.
11. Personality is influenced by the school environment.
12. It is only through the study of personality of individual students, that the relative differences among them can be known and their personality developed to the optimum level.

20.4 BEHAVIOURAL PATTERNS OF PERSONALITY

The totality of a man's personality may be described as under:

1. The attitude of an individual with which he does some work.
2. The skill of an individual with which he does a job.
3. The way he acts.
4. The way he behaves.
5. The way he dresses.
6. The way he drinks and eats.
7. The way he sits and stands.
8. The way he speaks.
9. The way he walks and so on.

20.5 MARKS OF BALANCED DEVELOPMENT OF PERSONALITY

1. Good physical appearance.
2. Emotional stability.
3. High intellectual ability.
4. High degree of social adjustment.
5. High moral character.
6. Cool temperament.
7. Good directedness.
8. High adjustability.
9. Tremendous common sense, drive and pragmatic thinking.

20.6 CLASSIFICATION OR TYPES OF PERSONALITY

Following are the important types of personality:

	Type	*Author*
1.	Active and Inactive	Heymans
2.	Active and Reflective	Jordan
3.	Extrovert and Introvert	C.G. Jung
4.	Masculine and Feminine	Apfelback
5.	Romantic and Classical	Ostwald
6.	Stable and Unstable	Trotler
7.	Subjective and Objective	Binet
8.	Tender minded and Tough minded	William James

Spranger's Six Types of Personality

1. *Aesthetic*: Lovers of beauty.
2. *Economic*: Inclined to hoard money.
3. *Political*: Interested in political affairs.
4. *Religious*: Believer in mysticism and engaged in religious activities.
5. *Social*: Interested in social affairs.
6. *Theoretical*: Theoretical in nature.

20.7 DEVELOPMENT OF PERSONALITY: BIOLOGICAL AND SOCIO-CULTURAL DETERMINANTS

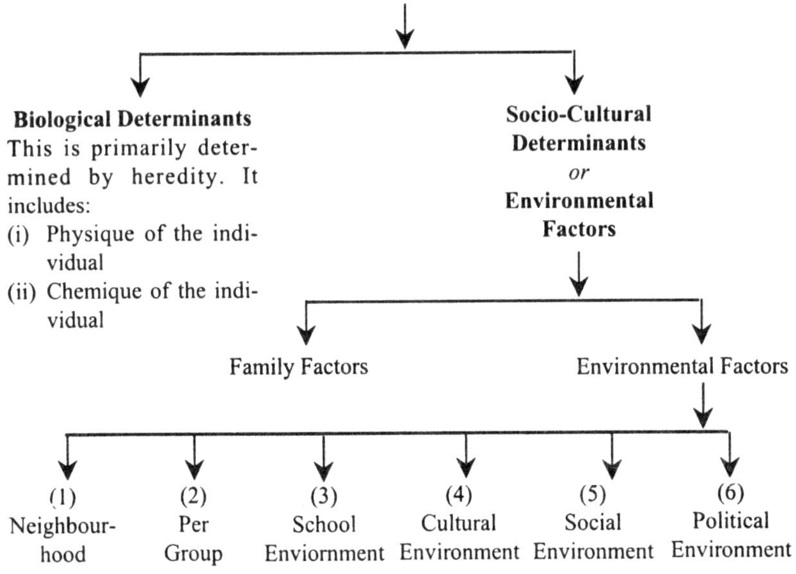

Physique: In physique are included such factors as the appearance, strength, body-build, bodily proportions, colouring and physical beauty of the individual. These factors have direct as well as indirect influence on the development of personality Deformity handicaps the child both physically and psychologically. Fewer physically handicapped develop into normal personalities. Health and vigour are significant in early years since contacts and competitions among children are often on the physical level. Even in adult years, the man with a tough constitution is at an advantage in maintaining an aggressive attitude towards life and preserving his emotional balance.

Chemique: By chemique is meant the possible effects of the *ductless glands* on the personality development. Glands are small organs which change chemical substances from one form to another in the body.

Endocrine (Ductless Glands)

Meaning: The endocrine glands bring about chemical coordination by complex organic compounds called 'hormones'. Hormones are chemical regulators or chemical messengers of body. These are secreted in response to changes in the environment inside or outside the body. Hormones are secreted by specialised glands. These lack definite ducts for the transportation of their secretion but pour them directly into the blood. Therefore, these glands are called ductless glands or endocrine glands (glands of internal secretion).

Endocrine Glands in Man

	Name of Gland	*Location*
1.	Pituitary Gland	In head (on underside of fore brain)
2.	Thyroid gland	In neck (across the front of wind pipe)
3.	Parathyroids (4)	One at each of the outer corners of thyroid
4.	Adrenals (2)	In abdominal—(across the upper end of each kidney)
5.	Thymus	
6.	Gonads or Sex Glands (Testes and ovaries)	In or below the pelvic cavity
7.	Placenta	Pregnant uterus
8.	Gastric and Intestinal mucosa	In the abdominal cavity (in the wall of stomach and intestine)
9.	Kidney	In the abdominal cavity kidney cell

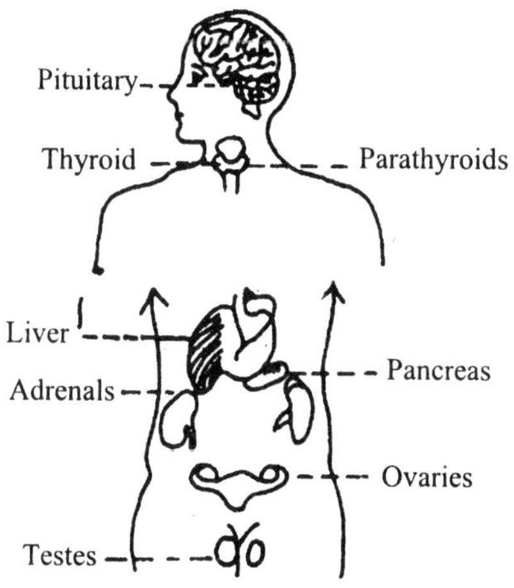

Fig. 20.1: Location of Ductless Glands

Educational Implications of Endocrine and Ductless Glands

These glands have a direct bearing on the personality of an individual. Actually, there are the hormones secreted by these glands which play an important role. These hormones are circulated throughout the body and influence all those tissues on which the functioning of body system, emotional actions and even thoughts depend. As Murphy, Gardner (1968) has observed, "these harmones, ultimately may be regarded as bathing the nervous system, including the brain, and all the organs of the body in their own appropriate chemical juices."

If the thyroid gland is overactive, it results in nervousness, dizziness and difficulty in sleeping.

Sex glands or gonads are responsible for sex drive or urge. The effects of the sex glands on emotions, particularly personality and behaviour become specially significant when adolescence is reached.

The individuals with profound imbalance of ductless glands are rarely happy or well-adjusted. They suffer from apathy, anxiety, restlessness, fatigue, irritability, etc. It is not easy for certain bearded ladies and gents to remain good-natured and mentally serene when they are continuously exposed to ridicule, jest, and social isolation. This harsh and unfair treatment makes many of them morose, hypersensitive and depressed. So like other organs of the body, the ductless glands play an important part in bodily, mental and emotional development and if defective, they may constitute an added burden contributing to abnormal behaviour.

The teacher can spot out those cases where the glands are not working properly and report those to a doctor. His duty does not finish here. He should follow up those cases and see to it that such children are getting due treatment.

The teacher must provide information to the adolscents on the functioning of sex glands as it is very essential for the mental health of the adolescent to be fully acquainted with this aspect. This will keep them on the track and they will not develop wrong notions.

There must be a periodical medical check-up in the school by a qualified doctor. Follow-up is equally important.

These glands do not function in isolation. If they are active normally, they give rise to a balanced personality. In case they are under-active or overactive, they may lead to personality problems and even abnormalities.

Family Factors: These are:

(i) Discipline: Protection and rejection etc. (ii) Number of children, (iii) Value placed on the sex of the child, (iv) Step-parents, (v) Nuclear or joint family, (vi) Accommodation in the house, (vii) Parents' ambitions and interests, (viii) Economic, political, religious and social status of the family.

School Environment: This includes:

(i) Curriculum;
(ii) Technology of teaching;
(ii) Co-curricular activities;
(iv) Discipline—constructive, creative and social;
(v) Teachers' personality and their behaviour towards students;
(vi) General tone of the school; and
(viii) Physical environment.

20.8 BARRIERS IN THE DEVELOPMENT OF INTEGRATED PERSONALITY

Family Circumstances

Personal
- Some physical defects

School
1. Unattractive school environment
2. Unsuitable curriculum or wrong choice of subjects
3. Lack of curricular activities
4. Lack of discipline

Teachers
1. Unsympathetic teachers
2. Emotinally unstable teachers

Peers
1. Undesirable interests and activities of peers
2. Non-acceptance in the group

Family Circumstances:

Economic
(i) Problem of unemployment or semi-employment
(ii) Low economic status

Psychological
(i) Over possessive parents
(ii) Unrealistic expectations from childrens
(iii) Faulty home discipline
(iv) Use of abusive language
(v) Lack of role model parents
(vi) Unequal parental treatment to siblings
(vii) Fear of insecurity

Social
(i) Loss of social status of the family
(ii) Broken homes
(iii) Fear of insecurity
(iv) Some anti-social stigma to the family

20.9 INTEGRATION OF PERSONALITY AND THE ROLE OF THE SCHOOL

Meaning of Integration of Personality

Just as a building is more than bricks, cement and wood, similarly, personality is more than basic elements or parts. Personality is formed because of the special relationship among its parts. Personality has an integrated structure. Any change in one part of the structure influences other parts.

Development of the following aspects of the personality must be fully integrated. Unbalanced development of any one of the aspects has an adverse impact on the total development of personality.

(*i*) Physical structure of the individual,
(*ii*) Emotional reactions,
(*iii*) Aspirations,
(*iv*) Aptitudes,
(*v*) Attitudes,
(*vi*) Interests,
(*vii*) Motivation,
(*viii*) Intellectual level—thinking, contemplation, reasoning, etc.

Role of the School in the Development of Integrated Personality

An individual of a well-integrated personality is aesthetically refined, culturally rich, emotionally stable, intellectually sound, physically strong, politically wide-awake, religiously pious, socially efficient, spiritually enlightened and vocationally self-sufficient.

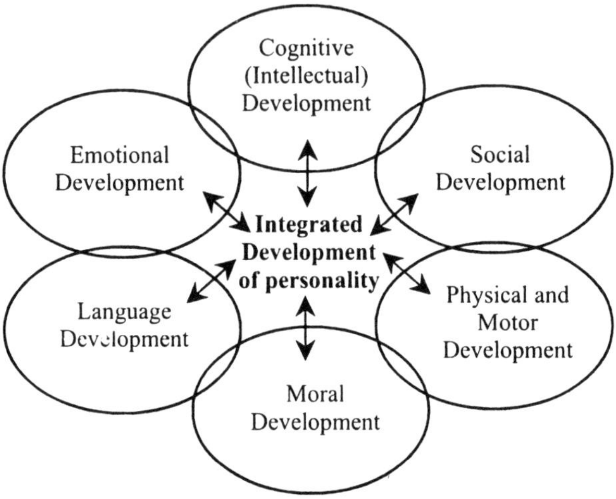

Fig. 20.2: Integrated Personality

Chart: School Programmes for the Development of an Integrated Personality of the Learner

(1) Aesthetic Development	(2) Cognitive Development	(3) Emotional Development	(4) Ethical Development	(5) Language Development	(6) Physical Development	(7) Social Development	(8) Spiritual Development
1. Provision of attractive and beautiful physical development. 2. All-round Individual	1. Psychological methods of teaching–learning 2. Provision of varied instructional material 3. Satisfaction of the individual needs	1. Balanced personality of the teacher 2. Environment of love and affection 3. Appropriate disciplinary approach	1. Personal example of the teacher 2. Social Service activities	1. Correct modes of expression by the teacher. 2. Proper check on pronunciation of the students 3. Provision of rich language material	1. Regular physical exercise 2. School health programme 3. Medical inspection 4. Provision of games and sports	1. Stress on group work 2. Equal treatment irrespective of caste etc. 3. Organisation of camps etc. 4. Social service 5. School Self-government	1. Morning Assembly and talks on spiritual matters 2. Yogic training 3. Observance of silance.

Role of the Teachers in Personality Development of the Students

1. Teacher as a 'Spiritual Preceptor' as in the Vedic Period.
2. Teacher as a 'Communicator and Provider of Knowledge'.
3. Teacher as a 'Living Facilitator'.
4. Teacher as a 'Gardener' or 'Directress' of Learning in the Naturalist Movement in Education.
5. Teacher as a 'Manager' of learning activity in the Pragmatic Philosophy of Education.
6. Teacher as an 'Ideal Person' in the Philosophy of Idealism.
7. Teacher as a 'Soldier' and 'Weapon' in Nazism and Communism.
8. Teacher as an 'Agent of Social Change' in the Democratic Philosophy.
9. Teacher as a 'Mediator' between the learner and the subject-matter.
10. Teacher as a 'Transmitter' of cultural heritage.
11. Teacher as the 'Educational Media User.'
12. Teacher as the 'Spearhead' of change in the society.
13. Teacher as the 'Harbinger' of social change.

Character and Personality of the Teacher: Character and personality of the pupils canot be developed if the teacher who is the model to be followed lacks character and personality. 'Example is better than precept' is an old saying and is absolutely true in the teaching profession. No amount of sermons from the teacher can make much headway. A teacher teaches not only by 'what he says and does' but very largely by 'what he is'.

'Man Know Thyself' is the advice of Yajnavalkya in India and Socrates, the philosopher Socrates of Greece. The teachers must undergo a spiritual inner training. They should try to find out their own shortcomings and remove them. Ryburn has observed: "Self-analysis on the part of a teacher is a necessary equipment". Montessory stresses that "every teacher worth his salt must destroy these sins: pride, anger, sloth, sensuality and envy. He should be partly a doctor, partly a scientist and completely religious. He must acquire a moral alertness, patience, love and humility". Writing about the role of the teachers, Lauri has observed: "If a teacher has not an ideal aim, he had better to take to shopkeeping at once, he will there doubtless find an ideal within his capacity."

Summing up

There is a limit to the role of the school in the integrated development of the personality of the learner. In the ultimate analysis, it must be stressed that the overall environment of the society has a great bearing on the development of the personality of the learners. In this regard, a great responsibility lies or the role of the leaders, especially political and religious.

21

Theories of Personality and Their Educational Implications

21.1 NEED FOR THEORIES OF PERSONALITY

Several Theories of personality have been developed by psychologists to explain the nature, structure and development of personality. There are numerous theories of personality and accordingly numerous ways of classifying theories. Here we shall deal with only a few theories of personality.

21.2 CLASSIFICATION OF THEORIES OF PERSONALITY

(1) Type Approach Theories by Hippocrates Kretschmer, Sheldon

(2) Trait Approach Theory by Allport

(3) Factor Approach Theory by Cattell

(4) Type-cum Trait Approach Theory by Eysenck

(5) Psycho-Analytical Theories by Freud and Adler

(6) Humanistic Approach Theory by Carl Roger and Maslow

(7) Learning Approach Theories by Dollaa and Miller, Bandura and Walter

21.3 ALLPORT'S TRAIT APPROACH THEORY

Meaning: George W. Allport (1897-1967) is the propounder of this theory. This approach theory views personality in terms of various traits. It is, therefore, essential to understand the meaning of a trait to comprehend this approach.

Allport defines a trait as, "a generalised and focalised neuropsychic system with the capacity to render many stimuli functionally equivalent and to imitate and guide equivalent (Mutually Consistent) forms of adaptive and expressive behaviour".

In the words of Michel, "Trait is a continuous dimension on which individual differences may be arranged quantitatively in terms of the amount of the characteristics, the individual has."

A trait has the following characteristics:

1. A trait is scalable *i.e.* it can be measured and scaled quantitatively.
2. A trait is manifested in a number of activities and verbal expression.
3. A trait is not static in nature. It becomes stable with the maturity of the person.
4. A trait is a higher order habit.
5. A trait is readiness to respond to a variety of situations in a consistent way.
6. A trait is an organised frame of reference.
7. A trait is learnt/acquired in the interaction with the environmental stimuli.

Allport analysed about 18,000 terms and ultimately identified 4591 traits for describing human behaviour of a personality. Accordingly he described personality as, "Personality is a dynamic organism within the individual of those phychological systems that determine the unique adjustment to his environment."

Allport suggested the following development sequence of a mature adult personality.

Classification of Traits and Development of Personality

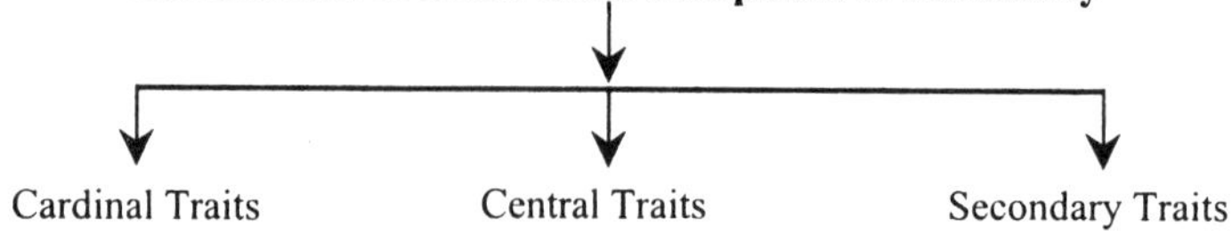

A cardinal trait is the dominant trait. Thus cardinal traits are so dominant in one's personality that they influence almost every aspect of a person's behaviour. For example, if a person has cheerfulness as a cardinal trait, he will bring a sense of cheerfulness into all situations. A persual of history makes one conclude that Mahatma Buddha was a lover of 'Ahimsa' (Non-violence). This trait was visible in nearly every aspect of his life. Gandhiji was a firm believer of truth and this trait was expressed in all his programmes. Emperor Ashoka was very pious and his pious trait was reflected in the pursuit of the welfare of his subjects and developing virtues of piety in them. Emperor Aurangzeb was very narrow minded in his religious outlook and this trait exercised the dominant influence on his personality and behaviour.

Central traits ordinarily describe a person, e.g., for instance traits like honesty, kindness, submission etc. Allport's view is that for knowing an individual's personality, we need to know only five to ten such central traits.

Secondary traits appear in only a relatively small range of situation. They are not considered strong enough to be regarded as integral parts of one's personality.

Educational Implications of the Trait Theory: Evaluation of Allport's Theory of personality

Criticism: Pervin (1964) has criticised the trait theory on the ground of division of traits into cardinal, central and secondary which he considers to be somewhat confusing. This theory, therefore, is not of much help in understanding the development of the personality of the individual.

Again when behaviour is broken down to traits, we have no way of knowing how they are actually expressed in life.

Thirdly, a change in environment may alter the expression of a trait, in a provocative environment one may demonstrate an altogether different trait.

Use of Trait Theory: The trait theory suggests appropriate methods of development of personality. It indicates the direction of the development of traits so that personality is developed in an integrated manner.

The Secondary Education Commission (1952-53) appointed by the Government of India took into consideration the various traits to be developed in the students. It laid stress on the development of seven traits and their measurement. The following 5-point scale illustrates this (see table 21.1).

21.4 RAYMOND B. CATTELL'S FACTOR ANALYSIS THEORY

Brief Life History: Born and educated in England finally he settled in the U.S.A. He started his work at the University of London where he became the Director of a Psychological Clinic. From there he moved to the USA and joined Teachers' College, Columbia University, New York. Later he became a Professor at the University of Illinois where he undertook valuable research.

Factor Analysis Theory of Personality: Cattell used a statistical technique known as 'Factor Analysis' to study the structure of personality. It makes a correlation. Starting from nearly 4,000 traits, he found out 16 factors as the building blocks of personality, *i.e.*, the characteristics in terms of which an individual's personality can be described and measured through his sixteen personality factors inventory (16F) consisting of multiple choice items (questions) out of these factors 12 are independent factors and 12 partially independent factors.

These 16 personality factors as established by Cattell are known as source factors since they are unitary and independent affecting much of the overt personality to a very great extent.

According to Cattell, "Personality is that which permits a prediction of what a person will do in a given situation."

Table 21.1: Secondary Education Commission (1952-1953) on Personality Traits and Their Assessment on a Five-Point Scale

PERSONALITY TRAITS	*A*	*B*	*C*	*D*	*E*
Initiative	Shows marked originality & independence.	Willing to take intiative.	Quite inventive, able to take initiative.	On the whole unenterprising.	Very Dependent on others, diffident.
Integrity (Moral Sense)	Completely trustworthy under all circumstances.	Of superior dependability. Honest in face of punishment.	Usually dependable.	Questionable at times.	Positively dishonest.
Persistence (State in chart in which situations)	Very Persistent.	Not easily stopped.	Works quite steadily.	Somewhat changeable, restless.	Gives up easily.
Leadership (State in chart in which situations).	Much drive, Mild, Impressive, steady, or convincing wide influence. Acceptable to group, Sought after by the group and takes the group with him.	Ready to take the lead, Works quietly for leadership, accepts responsibility.	Sometimes leads in minor affairs.	Satisfied to have others lead.	Probably unable to lead his fellows.
Self-Confidence (Poise)	Very Self-confident, Very resourceful, Willing to take reasonable risks.	Self-confident, Trusts in his own ability, well adjusted to others.	Normally confident in familiar circumstances. Does not need special assurance.	Cannot work for long without demanding attention or responds after special encouragement.	Always draws attention to self. Afraid of being overlooked or afraid to open out in presence of others, very nervous.
Emotional control	Unusual balance of responsiveness or control.	Well-balanced.	Usually well-balanced.	Tends to be over emotional.	Too easily moved to anger and fits of depression.
Social attitude	Strongly altruistic, Greater aesthetic sensibility.	Usually considerate of others, Aesthetic sensibility.	Has no positive attitude, neutral, Conscious of his rights and those of others or	Self-centred.	Anti-social

Table 21.2: Illustration of Factors

	High Scores on these Factors Indicate Tendency towards Positive Development of Personality		*Low Score on these Factors Indicate Tendency towards unbalanced Development of Personality*
Factor 1	*Cyclothymia* Emotionally expressive, frank, placid	*Vs.*	*Schizothyomia* Reserved, close-mouthed, anxious
Factor 2	*General Mental Capacity* Intelligent, smart, assertive	*Vs.*	*Mental Defect* Unintelligent, dull, submissive
Factor 3	*Emotionally Stable* Free of neurotic symptoms, realistic about life	*Vs.*	*Neurotic Emotionally* Variety of neurotic symptoms, evasive, immature
Factor 4	*Dominance* Self–assertive, confident, aggressive	*Vs.*	*Submissiveness* Submissive, unsure, complacent
Factor 5	*Surgency* Cheerful, joyous, humorous, witty	*Vs.*	*Desurgency* Depressed, pessimistic, dull
Factor 6	*Positive Character* Preserving, attentive to people	*Vs.*	*Dependent Character* Fickle, neglectful of socia
Factor 7	*Adventurous Cyclothymia* Likes meeting people, strong interest in opposite sex	*Vs.*	*Withdrawn Schizothyomia* Shy, little interest in opposite se
Factor 8	*Mature: Tough, Poised* Independent-minded, self-sufficient	*Vs.*	*Sensitive* Emotionally dependent, immature, gregarious, attention-seeking
Factor 9	*Socialised, Cultured Mind* Polished, poised, composed, introspective, sensitive	*Vs.*	*Boorishness* Awkward, socially clumsy, crude
Factor 10	*Trustful, Cyclothymic* Trustful, understanding	*Vs.*	*Parancis* Suspicious, jealous
Factor 11	*Bohemian, Unconcernedness* Unconventional, eccentric, fitful, hysterical upsets	*Vs.*	*Conventional Practically* Conventional, Unemotional
Factor 12	*Sophistication* Logical mind, cool, aloof	*Vs.*	*Simplicity* Sentimental mind

High or low a person rates on any one of these factors is determined by his answers to a Questionnaire containing several questions.

21.5 Evaluation of Cattell's Theory of Personality

Cattell's Factor Theory enables us to predict the behaviour of the individual on the basis of the factors or traits (the fundamental building blocks of individual's personality). Cattell's theory gives equal significance to the role of both heredity and environment in the development of personality. It is able to demonstrate the strong interaction between biological-genetic and the environmental influence on the predictability of human behaviour.

This theory is criticised on the ground that it puts excessive emphasis on overt behaviour of an individual.

Summing up the Educational Implications of Cattell's Theory of Personality

1. Suitable environmental conditions should be created for the development of desirable configuration of traits.
2. Curriculum should be constructed racing in view the development of suitable configuration of traits.
3. Methods of instruction should be inspirational so as to develop suitable traits.
4. The teacher should set ideal examples before the learners so that they emulate his traits.
5. The school administration and management should be developed on democratic and human basis.
6. Appropriate tools of evaluation should be used to assess the development of desirable traits. Trait inventories may be used for this purpose. (See Table 21.2)
7. Follow-up work is very essential on the basis of evaluation.

21.6 PSYCHOANALYTIC THEORY OF SIGMUND FREUD (1856-1939)

Brief Life Sketch of Freud

Sigmund Freud was born in 1856 in Czechoslovakia. He belonged to Jewish parents. On account of financial difficulties, the family moved to Vienna in Austria. Freud was very brilliant at school. Rejecting the business career to which his father belonged, he joined the Medical School at the University of Vienna in 1873. He worked as a medical practioner for some years. He took a course in Psychiatry and became interested in the relationship between physical disease and mental complexes. Thereafter he joined as a lecturer at the Vienna University. Later on, Freud went to Paris and explored the dynamics of hysteria. Then he worked on the study of Conscious and unconscious elements of mind.

In 1896, Freud first used the term 'Psychoanalysis'. In 1890 he published his book entitled "*The Interpretation of Dreams*". In the following year he brought out another book "*The Psycho-Pathology of Everyday Life*". He drew several renowned physicions like Carl Jung, Alfred Adler, Otta Rank. His disciples also made a valuable contribution to 'Psychoanalysis'.

Freud's Publications. He wrote extensively. His collective works include twenty-four volumes. It is an iron of history that in 1935, the Nazis of Germany burnt a pile of books authored by Freud. On this event, Freud commented, "What progress we are making! In the middle ages, they would have burnt me now-a-days they are content with burning my book."

His important publications are:

1. *The Interpretation of Dreams (1900).*
2. *The Psychopathology of Everyday Life. (1944).*
3. *The Three Essays on the Theory of Sexuality (1905).*
4. *Beyond the Pleasure Principle (1920)*
5. *The Future of an Illusion (1928).*
6. *Civilization and Its Discontents (1930).*

Basis of Freud's Psycho-analytic Theory

The theory of psychoanalysis is dynamic and is based on the assumption that personality and personality development are determined by conflicts and events that are largely unconscious in nature and which can be understood only by its indepth study.

Freud's assumption was that since so much of the person's personality operates at the unconscious level, the individual can bring to the surface of the consciousness only when engaged to adopt the method of *Free Association*. He also considered *dream analysis* as an important technique to explore the contents of the unconscious.

Freud's Anatomy of Personality: 'Id', 'Ego' and 'Super Ego'

Freud's anatomy of personality is built around the concept of *id, ego* and *super ego*. Each of these aspects of personality is related to the other two. Personality is a three-tier system of *Id, Ego* and *Super ego*.

'Id'. The *Id* is totally unconscious. *Ego* is partly conscious and *Super Ego* is totally conscious. The *Id* is the primary aspect of personality. Freud believed that *Id* is a mass of blind instincts. It has no logical organization. Indeed contradictory impulses may exist in it side by side. *Id* is amoral. It possesses no sense of values. It cannot distinguish between good and evil. It is dominated by the pleasure principle. The *Id* processes are unconscious *Id* is best characterised as the conative unconscious aspect of personality.

The *Id* consists of everything that is inherited psychologically. It is instinctive in nature. It is also the reservoir of psychic energy. It provides all the power for the operation of Ego and Super Ego. Id operates through the pleasure principle. It commands two processes known as *reflex action* and *primary process*. Reflex actions are inborn and automatic processes like blinking and sneezing. They reduce the tension caused on account of the non-gratification of the needs. It is a matter of common knowledge that the new born baby demands gratification or satisfaction of his needs (hunger warmth and elimination, etc.). For the satisfaction of the needs, the primary process attempts to discharge the tension. It is wish-fulfillment. The example of it is a dream. It is clear that the primary process is not able to fulfill the need. A hungry person cannot eat the image of the food or the food in the dream. Hence a secondary process starts developing. When this occurs, the Ego, second tier of personality starts taking place. The Ego fulfills the need. Ego also operates with the energy derived from the *Id* but it is part conscious. Its main work is to find ways and means for satisfaction of the needs of Ego. Since the Ego takes into consideration the pressures of reality, its actions are guided by what is called the *Principle of Reality*.

'Super Ego'. The third tier of personality development in the individual is what is called Super Ego. It is the *moral arm* of the personality. It represents the sense of *right* and *wrong, good* and *bad* for the society. It represents the *ideal* as compared with the *real* of the Ego. In a general way the Super Ego is thought to be the social development of the personality. The Ego is regarded as the psychological component of the personality while *Id* is regarded as the biological component.

Conflicts can occur between the components or the three tiers of the personality. This results in *anxiety*. For preventing the painful feeling of anxiety, the Ego adopts a number of unconscious psychological strategies which are called the defence mechanisms. Among the important defence mechanisms are: (i) Repression (ii) Suppression (iii) Reaction (iv) Rationalisation and (v) Identification.

Reflex Action

Meaning of reflex Action

A reflex action is an immediate involuntary response to a stimulus. It occurs below the level of consciousness. It occurs very fast. It takes a fraction of a second.

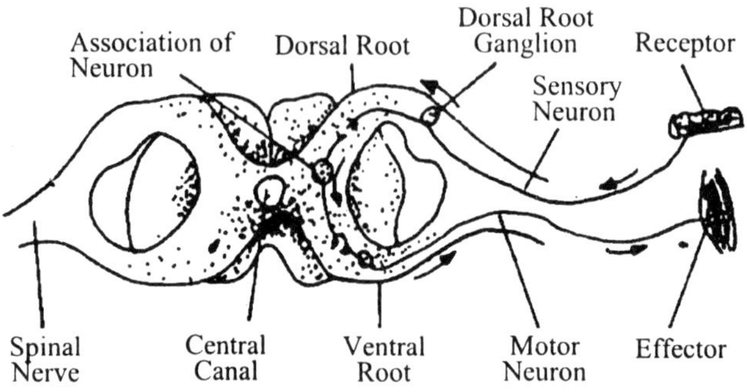

Fig. 21.1: Reflex Action

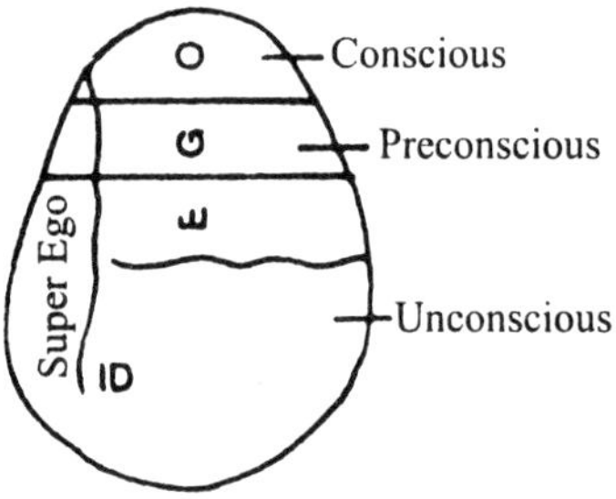

Fig. 21.2: Structure of the Mind

Explaining the relationship between Ego and *Id*, Freud once said, "Imagine that the relationship between the Ego and the *Id* is similar to the relationship between a horse (Id) and its rider (Ego). While the rider usually determines the direction of the horse, there are those times when it is the horse who leads the rider." Freud also believed that the autonomy of individual personality is built around the three unified and inter-connecting systems namely *Id*-ego and super ego. (See figures)

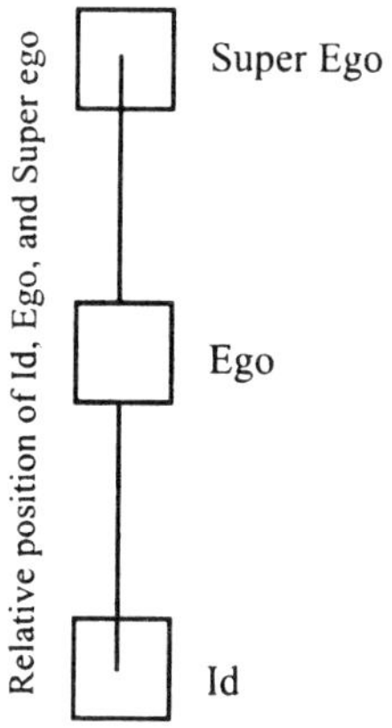

Fig. 21.3: Relative positions of *id*, *ego* and superego.

Consciousness. Consciousness gives expression to a very limited portion of human activity. It can be compared to an iceberg in which 1/10th part is visible and 9th/10th part is submerged in the water. The nature of the iceberg is to be judged more in terms of its portion under the water rather than above it. The unconscious is more powerful than the conscious. Unconscious consists of all repressed wishes and forbidden experiences. The repressed material, sometimes, appears at conscious level in a disguised form as in dreams and slips of the tongue (sex for six), etc.

Stages of Development: Infantile Sexuality and '*Libido*'

'*Libido*' is that part of the '*Id*' structure that seeks its gratification from purely sexual activity. Sexual gratification is like other gratifications and should be considered a normal need of an individual. Freud considered it as the total striving of an organism. Freud stressed that libido was always present in the orgnaism, even in the infant. Every child is born with an organically determined sexual excitability. *Libido* can be stimulated through the following zones.

Oral Zone: From birth to 2 years. At this stage, the infant gets pleasure from sucking the lips.

Anal Zone: From 2 to 3 years. The child derives much pleasure through anal expulsion or anal manipulation.

Genital Zone or Phallic Stage: From 3 to 5 years, the child derives gratification by touching his genitals.

Latency Stage: From the age of six till about thirteen, there is the latency stage where there is avoidance of sexuality on account of the pressures of society.

Fixation Stage: During this period of adolescence, homosexual and heterosexual interests develop.

Freud found that most of his patients suffered on account of sex repression, *i.e.*, non-gratification of sex. Sublimation of sexual desires helps in the development of an integrated personality.

Evaluation of Freud's Theory

Freud's theory has received mixed reaction. On the one hand, there is A. Inkeles (1963) who observes that his "theory is a tremendous factor in the growth of psychology of personality" and on the other hand, there is McDougall who writes, "that the theory of strict determination developed by Freud leaves no scope for creativity and volition on the part of human beings. The theory was taught a generation ago by men of science and philosophers with dogmatic confidence. In modern days the theory has been discredited on the basis of recent scientific investigations."

Freud's theory of personality is very helpful to understand personality and its development. According to Jacobs (1961), "to Freud goes the distinction and merit of having opened to observation dark abysses of human mind hardly suspected before him." Another psychologist Inkeles has observed, "His theory, has a scope, a unity and a coherence which is unmatched in psychology. Freud's theory of personality is a comprehensive theory and includes almost all aspects of personality and its complexities. It is a holistic approach to understand personality. It lays more stress on the functioning of the individual as a whole. It gives more freedom to the individual to respond in the form of free association. It recognises the importance of the unconscious motivation in the development of behaviour patterns. The theory emphasises the importance of early childhood experiences.

According to G. Gorer (1968), Freud's theory gives inadequate attention to the role of environment in the development of personality. Freud's experiences are based on the data collected from patients without any verification from other sources. Freud never quantified his findings. Freud's theory is based on the concept of instincts which has been discarded now. Freud's concepts of repression and libido have been used differently in different situations and thus there is a confusion regarding the precise meaning of these terms. Freud has laid undue emphasis on sex in the personality development.

Educational Implications of Freud's Theory of Personality

1. *Emphasis of Child Study*: Freud's conclusion that neurotic disturbances originate in early childhood has clearly indicated that everyone who is engaged in the care, training and education of the child must make his programmes child-centred.

2. *Need for Early Childhood Care and Education*: Freud has brought out

the need for early childhood education in the development of personality.

3. *Appropriate Learning Experiences in Early Childhood*: Psychoanalysis stresses the significance of providing early learning experiences in laying down the sound foundation of integrated personality development.

4. *Need for Positive Attitude*: Freud emphasised that among the major factors leading to the development of positive attitudes in the child towards life are affection, love and sympathy.

5. *Emphasis on Unconscious Process*: Freud emphasised the significance of the unconscious element in mental development.

6. *Freedom to Express Emotions*: Freud advocated that the children should be given opportunities to express their emotions freely in and outside the class. This he considered very conductive to the healthy development of the personality of the children.

7. *Need for Positive Outlook*: Freud observed that the teachers should display positive attitudes towards children.

8. *Knowledge of the Unconscious Mind*: The teacher should acquire sufficient knowledge to understand the characteristics of unconscious mind as it is ninth-tenth of the mind and conscious mind is only one-tenth.

9. *Sex Education*: One of the most important contribution of Freud is that he pointed out the significance of sex education.

10. *Problem-child Approach*: Freud brought to light to understand the characteristics of the problem-child and to apply corrective method.

11. *Educational and Vocational Guidance*: Freud's theory of personality has given a new direction to the process of educational and vocational guidance.

22

Exceptional Children, Their Education and Development

22.1 MEANING, DEFINITION AND CLASSIFICATION OF EXCEPTIONAL CHILDREN

Traditional Meaning of Exceptional Children: Exceptional children are those children who deviate from average/normal children to the extent they cannot receive class-room instruction in regular school or a school we perceive in general.

Modern Meaning of Exceptional Children: Exceptional children are those children who differ so much from average/normal children in their mental, physical and social characteristics that they require modification of school environment or special/supplementary educational services in order to develop to their maximum capacity. In other words, now emphasis is on 'environment' and 'special services' and not 'special schools' for all types of handicapped children. For instance, supplementary educational services in the normal school can meet the requirements of the gifted children. In some of the normal schools, blind students also receive education and special provisions are made for their special needs. For severely handicapped children special schools are needed as their special requirements cannot be met with in ordinary/normal schools. However, there is an increasing emphasis on the integration of exceptional children with normal children.

Definitions of Exceptionally Handicapped Children

In the words of W.M. Crunchshank, "An exceptional child is he who deviates, physically, intellectually, emotionally and socially so marked from normal growth and development that he cannot be benefited from a regular class-room programme and needs special treatment in school."

1. Crow and Crow have observed, "The term 'special' or exceptional is applied to a trait or to a person possessing the trait if the extent of deviation from normal possession of that trait is so great that because of it the individual warrants and receives special attention from his fellows and his behaviour responses and activities are thereby affected."

2. J.E. William depicts the pen picture of exceptional children as, "In a typical group of elementary school children from environments of inferior, medium and superior economic and social status about 500 children will present problems calling for special educational, psychological, social, physical adjustments because of exceptional scholastic, intellectual, emotional, social pecularity or physical conditions."

3. K.C. Panda defines exceptional children as, "Exceptional children are those who differ from the average to such a degree in physical and psychological characteristics that the traditional school programme does not allow all – round development and progress for them. They need special education or special ancillary services to grow according to their ability."

4. According to Kirk, "An exceptional child is one who deviates from normal or average child in mental, physical and social characteristics to such an extent that he requires a modification of school practices or special educational services or supplementary instruction in order to develop to his maximum capacity."

5. Telford and Sawrey observe as, "The term exceptional children refer to those children who deviate from the normal in physical, mental, emotional or social characteristics in such a degree that they require special social and educational services to develop their maximum capacity."

Chief Characteristics of Exceptional Children

1. Exceptional children are quite distinct and different from the average/normal children.
2. Exceptional children can be easily recognised as their deviation from the average/normal children is quite marked.
3. The deviation of exceptional children in terms of their development or acquired traits may fall in any behavioural or developmental dimension—emotional, intellectual, physical or social etc.
4. The exceptional children need special environment for the full development and nurturing of their talents.

22.2 BROAD CLASSIFICATION OF EXCEPTIONAL CHILDREN

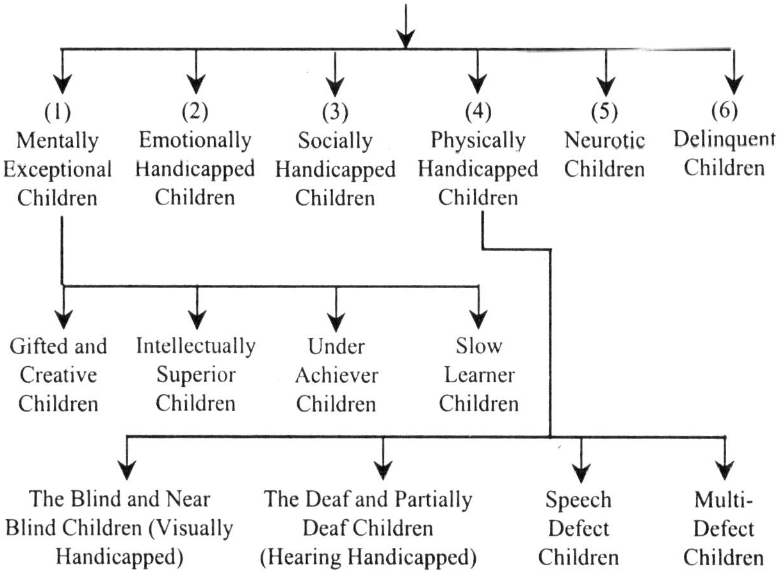

The Working Group on the Education of the Disabled Children (1981), set up by the Government of India recommended that the following categories of handicapped children should be served:

1. The blind or the virtually handicapped.
2. The deaf or the hearing handicapped.
3. The orthopaedically handicapped.
4. The educable and trainable mentally retarded.
5. The cerebral palsied.
6. The neurologically handicapped, including epileptic.
7. Children with speech and language disorders.

Classification of Children Including Exceptional on the Basis of I.Q.

Categorisation of Children on Intelligence Quotient (IQ) on Stanford Revision (USA)

IQ	*Percent*	*Classification*
160-169	0.3	
150-159	0.2	Very Superior/Gifted/Creative
140-149	1.1	
130-139	3.1	
120-129	8.2	Superior/High Average
110-119	18.1	
100-109	23.5	Average
90- 99	23.0	
80- 89	14.0	Low Average
70- 79	5.6	Borderline Defective
60- 69	2.0	
50- 59	0.04	Mentally Defective
40- 49	0.02	
30- 39	0.03	

Source: Terman and Merril

Dr. V.V. Kamath's Classification of Indian Children

I.Q.	*Category*
140 and above	Near genius or Genius
130-139.9	Extraordinary
120-129.9	Very superior
110-119.9	Superior
99-109.9	Average or Normal
80-98.9	Backward
70-79.9	Very Backward
60-69.9	Borderline
40-59.9	Moron
20-39.9	Imbecile
Below 20	Idiot

22.3 NEED FOR THE EDUCATION OF CHILDREN WITH SPECIAL NEEDS OR EXCEPTIONAL CHILDREN

Why Education for the Exceptional Children!

Following are the important considerations for making provision for the education of the gifted children:

1. The Constitution lays down that the State will endeavour to provide Compulsory Primary Education for all children.
2. In 1959 the United Nations in its Declaration of the Rights of the Child laid down, "The child who is physically, mentally or socially handicapped shall be given the special treatment in education and care required by his particular condition."
3. India's National Policy for Children (1974) envisages that "socially handicapped children who have become delinquent..., shall be provided facilities for education, training and rehabilitation..." It further states, special programmes shall be formulated to spot, encourage and assist gifted children, particularly those belonging to the weaker sections of society.
4. The National Policy on Education 1986 as amended in 1992 provides for special provision for education of the handicapped.
5. Regular classes for normal children do not meet the needs of exceptional children. Hence they need separate classes.
6. Under normal conditions, exceptional children may develop behaviour problems.
7. The principle of equalisation of educational opportunities highlights that exceptional children should have opportunities to develop themselves to the maximum.
8. Proper opportunities will make them economically self-sufficient.
9. Special categories of children like deaf, dumb, blind, etc. require special school's learning.

The World Conference of Education for All held in Jomitan (Thailand) in 1990, which was participated by 150 countries and over 150 non-governmental organisations observed, "The learning needs of the disabled demand special education. Steps need to be taken to provide equal access to education to every category of disabled persons as an integral part of the education system."

The Salamance Statement (1994) adopted by 98 countries and 25 international organisations, *'inter-alia'* observed, "Those with special educational needs must have access to regular schools which should accommodate them within a child-centred pedagogy capable of meeting these needs." It further stated, "Regular schools with this inclusive orientation are the most effective means of combating discriminatory attitudes."

22.4 SPECIAL EDUCATION

Generally speaking the term special education is applied to education of exceptional children.

Education Services for the Exceptional Children

Prof. K.C. Panda (2000) mentions the following types of education services to be provided to the exceptional children depending upon the nature and intensity of the handicap.

1. Regular class-room with minor in-class support.
2. Regular class-room with weekly 'itinerant' teacher.
3. Regular class-room with daily resource room supplemental programming.
4. Resource room with several hours of daily regular class-room instruction and non-instructional activities.
5. Regular room with limited hours of weekly non-instructional activities with regular classmates.
6. Self-contained special class-room.
7. Special day school.
8. Homebound or hospitalization.
9. Residential.

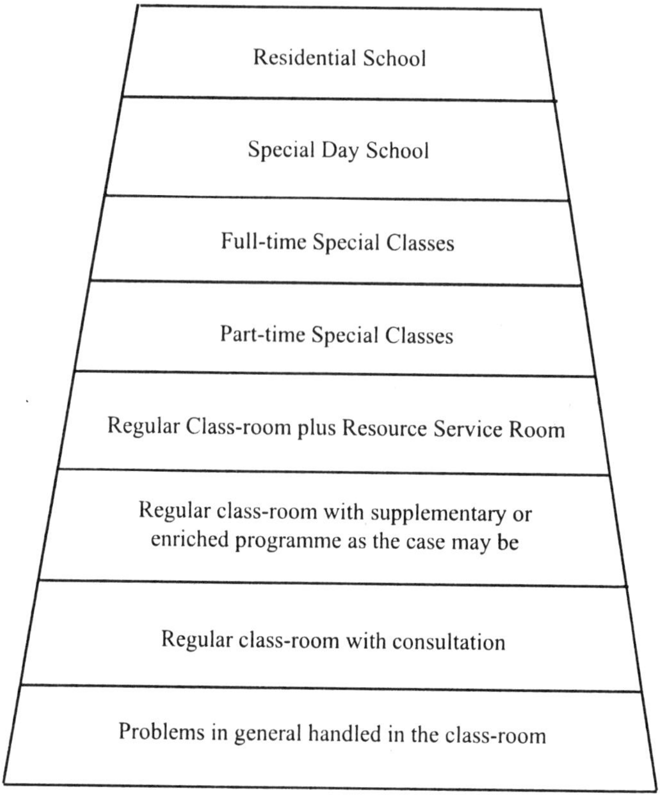

Fig. 22.1: Hierarchy of Services for Special Education Programme

22.5 INTEGRATION OR MAINSTREAMING APPROACH TO THE EDUCATION OF THE EXCEPTIONAL CHILDREN

Integration implies the existence of following elements:

1. Sharing the same class-room, resources and opportunities by the handicapped as well as the regular students.
2. Providing special services needed for the exceptional (handicapped) students in the regular schools.
3. Having handicapped (disabled) students follow the same schedule as normal (non-disabled) students.
4. Involving disabled students in several academic courses and co-curricular activities including art, field trips, music and exercises etc.
5. Enabling disabled students to use library, playground and other facilities at the same time as normal students use.
6. Encouraging friendly relation between disabled and normal students.
7. Arranging for disabled students to receive their education in the regular environment of the community when feasible.
8. Advising all students to understand the limitations of the disabled students and accept human differences.
9. Enrolling children with disabilities in the same schools they would have attended if they were not disabled.
10. Attending to parents' concern about their disabled children seriously.
11. Providing an appropriate individualised programme.

To sum up; integration approach is a particular orientation towards providing education to the majority of the handicapped children.

It is estimated that nearly 10 per cent of handicapped students receive most of their education in regular schools. An additional 20 to 25 per cent students are enrolled in special classes located in the same building.

22.6 ROLE OF THE REGULAR TEACHER WHEN INTEGRATED SYSTEM COMES INTO OPERATION

1. He should learn about the students' handicapping conditions.
2. He should understand the common characteristics of the handicapped children.
3. He should appreciate the common difficulties that the handicapped children experience.
4. He should learn about the special materials the handicapped children use, e.g., pushing a wheel chair up or down stairs etc.
5. He should meet the special education teacher to chalk out appropriate strategies to meet the special needs of the handicapped children.
6. He should accept appropriate behaviour in order to stimulate continuous effort.
7. He should seek the co-operation of normal students to improve the psychological climate of the class so that the disabled students are encouraged to put in their best.

Role of the Special Education Teacher

1. He should identify the academic or physical adaptations needed in the class-room for the disabled students.
2. He should develop programmes to prepare disabled students for entry into regular classes.
3. He should involve parents in setting appropriate goals for their students.
4. He should prepare a variety of activities that will involve the entire class in grouping patterns that are flexible.
5. He should design a variety of altenative teaching stratgegies.
6. He should prepare a flexible time schedule for learning as well as physical and social needs of each student.
7. He should fully co-operate with the regular teacher.

22.7 NECESSARY EQUIPMENT NEEDED FOR THE RESOURCE ROOM

1. Braille writer for the teacher.
2. Braille books.
3. Braille slates and stylus for students.
4. Abacus for the teaching of mathematics.
5. Braille sheets of paper.
6. Low vision aids.
7. Large print books.
8. Braille bulletin boards.
9. Equipment for teaching industrial and other arts.
10. Tape-recorders and cassettes.
11. Braille type duplicating machines.
12. Teaching aids.
13. Class-room furnitute.

22.8 COMPARATIVE STUDY OF TWO TYPES OF PROGRAMMES: SPECIAL AND INTEGRATED FOR THE EDUCATION OF THE HANDICAPPED

In the special programmes, the handicapped children are isolated from the normal ones and placed in special institutions. In the educationally advanced countries, however, a great deal of stress is now being laid on the integration of handicapped children into the regular school programmes. This arrangement has two important advantages: reduction of costs and promoting mutual understanding between handicapped and the non-handicappd children. This has also its disadvantages. For instance, many handicapped children find it psychologically disturbing to be placed in an ordinary school.

To develop integrated programmes adequately, attention will have to be paid to the following matters:

1. The preparation of teacher will need emphasis and special attention. This will necessitate a considerable increase in the capacity of existing training institutions and the establishment of new ones.
2. It is necessary to co-ordinate the efforts of different agencies working in the field.

3. It is also necessary to develop adequate research in the problems of integrated programme.

22.9 PROJECTS OF INTEGRATED EDUCATION FOR DISABLED/ PHYSICALLY HANDICAPPED CHILDREN

1. *Statutory Provisions*: With the coming into force of the 'Persons with Disabilities Act, 1955', there is now a statutory responsibility of the Central, State and Local Governments in India, to provide free education in an appropriate environment to all disabled children upto the age of 18 years.
2. *Centrally Sponsored Scheme for the Disabled Students* : The Department of Education, Ministry of Human Resource Development, Government of India has been implementing the Scheme for Integrated Education of Disabled Children (IEDC) since 1974.

Main Features

Following are the important features of the scheme:

1. The scheme includes pre-school training for disabled children and counselling for their parents.
2. Cent per cent financial assistance is provided as per prescribed norms for facilities for disabled children. This covers costs of books and stationery, uniforms, transport and escort allowance for severely handicapped children, reader allowance for blind children and equipment which includes educational aids and assistive services.
3. The scheme also provides assistance to non-governmental Organisations (NGOs), engaged in the field of integrated education. *Coverage*: The IEDC scheme is being operated in 26 States/UTs through nearly 15,000 schools and over 55,000 children are being benefited under this scheme.
4. *Polytechnics:* Two polytechnics for disabled students have been set up at Mysore and Kanpur.
5. *Curriculum for Teacher Training:* The NCTE (National Council for Teacher Education) has developed curriculum for teacher training and orientation so that both general teachers as well as resource teachers are trained to handle disabled children.
6. *NCERT Programmes:* The NCERT has also taken up several programmes in this area:
7. *India-Australia Training and Capacity Building Project* (IACBP): The programme includes:
   (i) Intensive training of 10 teacher educators in Australia to turn them into Master Trainers.
   (ii) Further training by the Master Trainers along with three Australian experts in various places in India.
   (iii) A study-tour of 6-10 Officers of the Government of India and State Governments as well as educational institution to have first hand experience in Australia in the field of IEDC.
   (iv) Technological exchange programme in this field.

Summing up

NCERT's *'The National Curriculum Framework for School Education, 2000'* considered various aspects of special education/education of the handicapped children and made the following recommendation, "Segregation or isolation is good neither for learners with impairments nor for general learners without treatment. Societal requirement is that learners with special needs should be educated along with other learners in inclusive schools; which are cost effective and have sound pedagogic practices."

22.10 (See also chapter 25 for detailed characteristics of each type of handicapped children and their education)

23

Children with Learning Disability (Dyslexia) and Other Problems

23.1 CHILDREN WITH LEARNING DISABILITY

Meaning and Definition of Children with Learning Disability: Those children who suffer from serious learning disabilities are known as learning disabled children or children with learning disability. In this regards, following definitions should help us to know about such children in more detail and thus the concept would be more explicit:

1. Kavale and Forness (1964) define learning disabilities as, "People with learning disabilities do not learn in the same way or as efficiently as their non-disabled peers. Although most possess normal intelligence, their academic performance is significantly behind their classmates. Some have great difficulty in learning mathematics, but most find the mastery of reading and writing to be their most difficult challenge."

2. The Association of Children with Learning Disabilities, USA (1967) regarded learning disabilities as, "Children who have central nervous system dysfunctions which is expressed primarily in impaired learning efficiency."

3. The National Advisory Committee of the USA for the handicapped (1969) gave this definition of learning disabilities, "Specific learning disability means a disorder in one or more of the basic psychological processes involved in understanding or in using language spoken or written, that may manifest itself in an imperfect ability to listen, think, speak, read, write, spell or to do mathematical calculations. The term includes such conditions as perceptual disabilities, brain injury, minimal brain dysfunction, dyslexia and developmental aphasia. The term does not apply to children who have learning problems that are primarily the result of visual, hearing, or motor disabilities, of mental retardation, of emotional disturbance, or of environmental, cultural or economic disadvantages".

4. In the words of S.A. Kirk, "The term learning disability is not meant to be used for children with minor or temporary difficulties in learning but with a severe discrepancy between abilities and achievements in educational performance and such several discrepancies described as learning difficulties with significant learning problems that cannot be explained by mental retardation, sensory impairment, emotional disturbance or lack of opportunity to learn".

5. The World Federation of Neurology gives the following definition, "A disorder manifested by difficulty in learning to read despite conventional instructional, adequate intelligence and socio-cultural opportunity. It is dependent upon fundamental cognitive disabilities which are frequently of constitutional origin."

An analysis of these definitions would reveal the following elements relating to the meaning and concept of the term 'learning disability':

1. Learning disability refers to certain kind of disorder in the basic psychological process of the learner.
2. The disorder is mainly caused by some intrinsic element lying within the individual. This element may be central nervous system dysfunction—Some brain or neurological damage obstructing learner's learning ability, specific deficiencies in information processing or in the ability to learn.
3. Learning disability in general is not the direct result of extrinsic elements like mental retardation, sensory impairment, emotional disturbance, cultural differences, lack of educational opportunities, poverty, etc., though any of these elements may exercise some influence on learning disability.
4. Learning disability is usually manifested in one or two cognitive areas like inability to grasp or understand things. Disorder may be manifested in language related areas like communication, written or reading language. It may also occur in acquiring mathematical or social skills.
5. On account of learning disability, a learner always lags behind in terms of his educational progress in comparison to the peers of his class and age.
6. Learning disability may lead to a distinct gap between a learner's potential and actual educational performance. Thus the learner may need special educational service, care and attention for his adjustment.

Characteristics of the Children with Learning Disability

1. A learner with learning disability suffers from serious learning disorders or problems on account of several reasons.
2. A learner faces significant difficulty in acquiring and using language—listening, speaking, reading, writing, reasoning or mathematical ability or social skills.
3. A learner may exhibit symptoms of hyperactivity and impulsivity.
4. A learner may suffer from emotional problems.
5. A learner may demonstrate signs of anxiety.
6. A learner may become moody.
7. A learner suffers from severely impaired learning hand or inefficiency which is just as real as crippled hand.
8. A learner displays a significant gap between his learning potential and actual educational achievement.

9. A learner with learning disability may exhibit disorders of attention, thinking, memory, perception, etc.
10. Such a learner lacks motivation.
11. A learner with learning disability may have normal intelligence.
12. A learner with learning disability may have a good vision, sound ears and above all robust body.
13. Such a learner requires special educational services.

Causes of Learning Disabilities

(1) Hereditary or genetic factors

(2) Physiological or Organic

(3) Environmental

Educational Implications

1. *Methods of Identification of Learning Disabled Children*

(*a*) Standardised diagnostic tests:
(*b*) Ability tests; and
(*c*) Achievement test.

2. *Educational Provisions for the Learning Disabled*

(*a*) Making provision for special classes;
(*b*) Making provision for special schools;
(*c*) Making provision for remedial educational services; and
(*d*) Improving the existing environmental set-up.

Learning Disabilities in Specific Areas

A. Languages

1. Problems in reading—accuracy, speed and comprehension.
2. Repeated spelling errors.
3. Using reversal letters when read or written, e.g., was-saw; quiet-quite
4. Delayed spoken language.
5. Error in letter naming.
6. Difficulty in learning and remembering printed words.
7. Cramped or illegible handwriting.
8. Lack of awareness of sound in words.
9. Difficulty in finding the correct word when speaking.

B. Disabilities in Mathematics

(*i*) Difficulty in calculations
(*ii*) Difficulty in sequencing of steps.

Remedial Measures for Some Specific Learning Deficiencies

1. *Remedial Measures for Developing Reading Skills*

(*i*) Phonetic guidance and drill should be used in the case of learners who cannot pronounce a word, letter or sound correctly.

(*ii*) Model reading should be demonstrated to learners who are handicapped with inadequacy or wrong type of reading.

(*iii*) Multi-sensory techniques should be used with learners who feel difficulty in comprehension. Stories, discussions and personal experiences may be used.

(*iv*) Meaning of difficult words should be explained through concrete materials.

2. *Remedial Measures for Removing Handwriting Disabilities*

(*i*) Using manipulative exercises for strengthening muscles. The learners should be provided opportunities in writing letters by manipulative exercises like writing on sands, clay modelling games and doing chalk-board practice etc.

(*ii*) Assisting learners to learn proper position and form of writing, i.e., holding writing instrument—pen or pencil between thumb and middle finger with index finger applying pressure.

(*iii*) Helping learners taping alphabet forms to the floor and asking them to reproduce forms with coloured chalk.

(*iv*) Helping learners in building appropriate associations for the shape of letter.

(*v*) Giving sufficient practice to learners to write in straight lines. Lined paper may be used for this purpose. Graphs can also be used.

(*vi*) Advising and providing where needed ink, paper and pencil of good quality.

(*vii*) Helping learners to write legibly from the very beginning.

(*viii*) Helping learners to maintain proper links and gaps between the lines and curves of the letter.

(*xi*) Asking learners to avoid cutting and overlapping in their written work.

3. *Remedial Measures for Improving Thinking and Reasoning Ability of Children with Such Disabilities*

(*i*) Initially asking the learners to collect data by listening, doing observing and reading.

(*ii*) Asking them simple questions on this data and helping them to analyse the same, to find the similarities and dissimilarities.

(*iii*) Asking them to classify data in groups. Some examples from the data may be given.

(*iv*) Asking them to find some other ways of classifying data.

(*v*) Giving examples for learning how to discriminate.

(*vi*) Assisting them to integrate this new information and new experience with their existing knowledge and experience.

Standardised Material for Use with Learners Having Learning Disabilities

1. Diagnostic Test in Decimal Systems and Percentages by V.P. Sharma and Shukla.
2. Durrell Analysis of Reading Difficulty by Durrell.
3. Gates McKillop Reading Diagnostic Test.
4. Spache Diagnostic Reading Scales by Space.
5. Stanford Diagnostic Arithmetic Test by Betty, Madden and Gardener.
6. Marianne Frosting Developmental Test of Visual Perception by Frosting, Lefever and Whittlesey.
7. *'Listening to Children Reading'*, a book by Helen Arnold.
8. Margaret Peters' *'Look, Cover, Write Check Method'*.

Teaching Strategies to be used in the case of Learners with Learning Disabilities

1. Promote the idea that all learners can learn.
2. Use appropriate assessment techniques including cumulative records.
3. Provide educational services to learners as early as any disability is detected.
4. Use adaptive approach. The term adaptive approach refers to the modification of school learning environments to respond to learner's differences and to enhance the individual's ability to succeed in learning in such environments.
5. Use concrete examples and materials.
6. Develop and use multisensory approaches to learning.
7. Model what learners are to do rather 'just telling' them 'what to do'.
8. Let children practise or perform a certain behaviour.
9. Create a dependable class-room schedule.
10. Identify appropriate tasks which learners can accomplish on their own.
11. Adopt the technique of co-teaching. Co-teaching is the process by which a regular class-room professional and a special educator or a person trained in disabled learner education team teach.
12. Encourage parents to volunteer at school and to read to their children at home.
13. Individualise Education Programme (IEP) where possible, integrate learners with learning disabilities into those without learning disabilities.

23.2 EDUCATION OF THE UNDERACHIEVER CHILDREN

Meaning and Characteristics of the Underachievers

Usually we hear parents making such remarks such as "Mohan is bright and intelligent. We do not understand why he gets so poor marks," or "Lata could do much better if she really tried and took an interest in her studies. She has the ability." Such remarks indicate that most of us are aware of the fact that many school children work far below of their expected level of intellectual development. If such situations are not corrected, students gradually lose interest in academic work and may generally drop-out from school. They become a liability not only to themselves and their parents but also to the society. It is, therefore, very necessary to identify under-achievers early. We must help them to progress in their work.

Meaning and Characteristics of the Under-achiever Children: There is no set definition of the under-achiever children. Several writers and experts do not refer to under-achiever children as a special category of children. They club this category with the slow learning children. Some authors and experts use terms like mentally retarded children and backward children. Hence there is a lot of confusion regarding the use of terms. An under-achiever child generally speaking, is one whose achievement falls below the level of his natural abilities.

Some experts regard an under-achiever child as one who compared with other children of the same chronological age shows marked educational deficiency. The generally accepted meaning of under-achievement implies that a student's academic achievement is below on certain norm or standard which is expected of him on the basis of his potential ability. This means that we consider a student an under-achiever when his achievement is not at par with his intelligence.

From a broader point of view, an under-achiever child is one who has high potential in fields other than intellectual also but he is not using his potential adequately.

According to John Holt, an under-achiever child fails to develop more than a tiny part of the tremendous capacity for learning, understanding and creating with which he was born.

Categories of Under-achiever or Under-functioning Students

(*i*) An under-achiever with superior intelligence but having average performance in school subjects.

(*ii*) An under-achiever with average intelligence but whose achievements are significantly below a reasonable level of age and who does not appear to be making much progress.

(*iii*) The dull and the slow learner who is not working up to his capacity and is capable of improvement.

(*iv*) One who is highly creative and talented in fields other than intellectual but has not been able to develop his creative powers and talents to the full.

(*v*) An under-achiever who has lived under deprived, restricted and unstimulating conditions for prolonged periods during early childhood and therefore, shows low scores on an intelligence test. His achievement is usually unsatisfactory in the school situation.

Factors Responsible for Under-achievement

(1) *Physical Factors*	(2) *Intellectual Factors*	(3) *Emotional Factors*	(4) *Factors Relating to Home*	(5) *Factors Relating to the Community*	(6) *Factors in School*
1. Poor physique of the child. 2. General disability of the child. 3. Chronic illness 4. Lack of stamina etc. These prevent a child from doing his best in the academic field.	1. Weakness in some specific area of cognitive functioning. 2. Poor power of attention and concentration. 3. Lack of aptitude for a particular subject. 4. Lack of curiosity. 5. Lack of eagerness to learn.	1. Emotional insecurity. 2. Emotional immaturity.	1. Unfavourable physical conditions. 2. Unfavourable parental relations leading to tension and worries. 3. Inconsistent disciplinary methods. 4. Siblings relations and personal fondness for some children and indifference to others. 5. Lack of encouragement by parents to child's school work. 6. Frequent transfer of parents.	1. Neighbourhood Social group norms. Poor influence.	Discussed separately.

Unhealthy School and Class-room Environment: This refers to the following:

1. Absence of social security.
2. Absence of emotional security.
3. Faulty curriculum.
4. Ineffective and uninspiring methods of teaching.
5. Authoritative and unsympathetic attitude of the teacher.
6. Faulty class-room organisation.
7. Lack of co-curricular activities.
8. Lack of equipment.
9. Overcrowded classes.
10. Lack of effective guidance and counselling.

Identification of the Under-achiever

1. Use of intelligence tests.
2. Achievement tests.
3. Observation
4. Parents' view.
5. Sociometric techniques.
6. Participation in co-curricular activities.

Curriculum Provision, Methods of Teaching and Learning. Role of the Teachers in the Education of the Under – achiever

Curriculum may be the same for the under-achiever and the normal child. In the case of the under-achiever, the role of the teacher assumes special significance. He is expected to take the following measures to bring about achievement in the under-achiever:

1. All possible efforts should be made by the teacher not only in detecting the element of under-achievement but also in trying to understand the nature of the problem in each individual case. A child may be carefully observed in different situations. Relevant information about his development may be found out. Parents may also be contacted and consulted. The school counsellor, if any, may be approached to study the under-achiever. Thereafter a remedial programme suitable to child's needs may be prepared and implemented.
2. At the early stages, attempts should be made to lay the foundations of good work habits and attitudes in children.
3. Emotional support by teachers should be provided to children. This will help them in meeting the developmental tasks which are a part of their normal growth.
4. Tensions in child's environment should not be allowed to build up. Sympathy and patience should be the watch words.
5. Genuine interest in the welfare of the students should be taken.
6. A few periods per week should be set apart for a small group of under-achievers for solving their problems.
7. One or two periods per week may be devoted for individual counselling to such students.

8. The under-achiever should be encouraged at his performance and thus helped in building his self confidence.
9. Outlets for children's tensions through provision of play in the form of dramatics, games, sports and a variety of other self-expressive and creative activities should be provided.
10. Assignment should be adapted to the needs of students.
11. Special care should be taken to accept the under-achiever child as a unique individual. His particular needs should be immediately attended to.
12. Efforts may be made to re-establish child's confidence in himself.
13. Remedial work for the under-achievers should be undertaken.
14. Class teacher should seek the cooperation of other teachers and the parents of the under-achievers.
15. In case of deep-rooted emotional problems which lie at the root of under-achievement, referral may be made to a child guidance clinic after taking the parents into confidence.

Education of Slow Learners

Meaning of Slow Learning Child: In the words of Prof. T.N. Birkett, "A slow learning child is one whose capacity for learning the kind of material which is taught in the ordinary school is limited by some deficit in intellectual capacity. Limited intelligence, however, is the chief characteristic of the slow learning child.

Categories of Slow Learners/Classification of Slow Learners

Following are the main categories of slow learners.

1. Children, whose capacity for education or training is limited by low intelligence, cover a fairly wide I.Q. range from approximately 40 to 80 or 90. However students whose I.Q. ranges between 50/55 and 85/90 are capable of benefiting from the kind of education which is offered within the normal school system. These may be subdivided into two groups:

(a) The Educable Mentally Retarded (I.Q. range 50 to 70).
(b) The Dull Normal (I.Q. range 70 to 85).

2. Students whose I.Q. range is between 35/40 and 50 are usually termed as Trainable Mentally Retarded. Provision for education of such children may be made outside the normal school system.

Characteristics of Slow Learners

Sullivan summarises the characteristics of these children as follows:

1. Short attention and concentration span.
2. Slow reaction time.
3. Limited ability to evaluate materials for relevancy.
4. Limited powers of self-direction.
5. Limited ability to work with abstractions and to generalize.
6. Slowness to form association between words and phrases.
7. Failure to recognise familiar elements in new information.
8. Habits of learning very slowly and forgetting very quickly.

9. Very local point of view.
10. Inability to set up and realize standard of workmanship.
11. Lack of originality and creativeness.
12. Lack of ability to analyse, to do problem solving or think critically.
13. Lack of ability to use higher mental processes.

Identification of Slow Learners

Following methods are usually employed to identify the slow learners.

1. Achievement Tests.
2. Intelligence Tests (Individual)
3. Intelligence Tests (Group)
4. Observation by teachers and others including the school counsellor.
5. Diagnostic Tests.

Measures for the Education of the Slow Learners

Educational Provisions in Terms of Curriculum, Teaching Methodologies and Evaluation

1. *Diagnostic Tests:* Diagnostic tests should be employed in working with slow-learning children.
2. *Curricula According to Interests:* Courses and curricula should be selected by the students with the help of their counsellors on the basis of aptitude, interest and need.
3. *Vocational Programmes:* Vocational programmes should not be forced upon slow-learners. Such children do not always have the necessary aptitude to acquire vocational skill.
4. *Special Classes:* Special classes for slow-learning children should be organised. However, partial segregation is preferable to total segregation.
5. *Partial Segregation*: It has been stated, "These children should be included in the total school set-up, regularly participating in assembly programmes, organised play, and other activities enjoyed by all children." The problems should be clearly explained. Prof. Udai Shankar has emphasised the need of segregation in these words, "If they are kept with normals, they will be pushed back and the backward will become more backward with children of their own level. But they will be less conscious of their drawbacks and they will feel more secure in a group of their own type where there will be more encouragement and appreciation and less competition."
6. *Short Assignments:* Assignments given to the students should be broken up into short and simple units. The problems should be clearly explained.
7. *Drill Work*: Sufficient drill work should be done.
8. *Summaries:* Frequent summaries of the important points of discussion should be used.
9. *Praise:* Slow-learners should be praised occasionally when they have done their assignments properly.

10. *Proper Evaluation:* Good set of tools should be used.
11. *Close Supervision:* Supervision should be very close.
12. *Use of Audio-visual Aids:* Auditory and visual aids facilitate their learning.
13. *Opportunities for Creative Expression:* Opportunities for expression of creativeness with their hands for slow-learning children should be provided.
14. *Equality of Opportunity in Recreational Programmes:* The whole programme of recreational activities, athletics, music, art, dramatics, etc., should be opened to all on an equal basis. Mones summarizes the advantages which the slow-learners will get as, "When these pupils are accepted in secondary schools, the school clubs, the bands, the patrols, the clean-up squads, the down and ground squads, the cafeteria patrols, athletics teams—are all possible instrumentalities of their education. If they can find educational outcome as a means of developing traits, attitudes, purposes, and satisfactions, that will give them a sense of integrated personality.
15. *Remedial Teaching.* Remedial teachers who meet such students twice a week should be appointed.
16. *Regular Medical Check-up and Follow-up.* Such arrangements must exist in every institution.

23.3 EDUCATION OF THE BACKWARD CHILDREN

Meaning and Definition of the Term Backward Child

Scholars have defined the term 'Backward Children' in several ways:

In the words of *Bartan Hall* (1947), "Backwardness in general is applied to cases where their educational attainment falls below the level of their abilities."

According to *Schonell* (1948), "Backward pupil is one who, compared with other pupils of the same chronological age, shows marked educational deficiency."

Burt gives the definition of a backward child as, "A backward child is one who in his midschool career is unable to do the work of the class next below that which is normal for his age."

From the above definitions of a backward child or backwardness, following characteristics of a backward child emerge:

1. A backward child is unable to keep pace with the normal school work.
2. The attainment of a backward child falls below his natural abilities.
3. In studies, a backward child falls far behind other children of his age.
4. Usually a backward child remains in the same class for more than one year.
5. A backward child is not able to learn at the same level as other children of the same age.
6. A backward child may also find it difficult to keep pace with children in the lower class.
7. A backward child may not possess a lower I.Q. In other words a lower

I.Q. alone necessarily does not make a child backward.

8. A backward child may be weak in one school subjects or more than one.

Need for the Education of the Backward Children

We cannot ignore the care and education of the backward children who are found in varying degrees in every school. Such children behave like other children with the exception that they take longer time and effort to learn. Slow-learners are sometimes referred to as "backward children". Schonell called a backward pupil as "one who compared with other pupils of the same chronological age shows marked educational deficiency." With proper guidance, backward children can become useful members of the society.

Causes of Backwardness

There is no denying the fact that backwardness of the child is on account of a number of causes which operate upon simultaneously to contribute to the backwardness of a child. Each child has to be studied individually. The causes of backwardness may be groupd conveniently on the basis of their origin.

1. *Home Conditions*: Lack of accommodation, overcrowding, uneducated parents; emotional and moral conditions of the home also influence the attainment of the child in school.
2. *General Health*: Defects of general health such as poor general health; malnutrition, diseases, etc., contribute towards backwardness.
3. *Intellectual Deficiency*: (a) *General*—Intellectual deficiency or inborn dullness is the most common and important cause of backwardness. (b) *Special*—Apart from general intelligence, there may be other special intellectual disabilities like perceptual and associative disabilities.
4. *Physical Conditions*: Physical and mental growth are closely related. Physical defects give rise to backwardness.
5. *School Conditions*: Inefficient teaching, ill-organised school organisation, unsympathetic behaviour of the teachers, lack of individual and group counselling, absence of the child from the school are the important factors which are responsible for backwardness.
6. *Sensory Defects*: Weak sight, poor hearing, bad control of the hands also hamper the work of the class-room more directly than physical defects. Sensory defects prove to be a great barrier to the acquisition of knowledge thereby causing backwardness.
7. *Social unhealthy Environment*: A number of surveys have been conducted in various countries by eminent psychologists to find out the backwardness in relation to the social environment of the child. A survey conducted by Burt during 1925-35 covering the entire area of London reported that backwardness and poverty go hand in hand.
8. *Temperamental Defects*: Emotional instability, excitability, depression, apathy, lack of industry and lack of honesty are some of the numerous temperamental disorders which can be equally responsible for backwardness.

Problems of a Backward Child

1. A backward child remains behind his classmates. He, therefore, becomes bitter and hostile towards himself and others.
2. A backward child is flooded with anxiety.
3. A backward child lacks motivation to learn.
4. Repeated failures deprive him of his confidence.
5. A backward child may become a problem child.

Identification of Backwardness

In this regard it may be borne in mind that backwardness may be specific, affecting only one subject or part of a subject area, or general appearing over a range of school subjects. In carrying out the procedures we should endeavour to be as objective and scientific in our appraisal as circumstances permit and remain alive to the dangers of intuitive assessment.

1. *Assessment.* As a general rule, it is advisable that more than one assessment of mental ability should be made using different tests, and at least one of these should be of the individual type.
2. *Attainment Tests.* The normal method of getting this information is through the administration of standardized tests of achievement in the various subject areas. Such tests usually yield scores in terms of Subject Ages which can be compared to the child's chronological age level and thus provide an index of backwardness where this exists.
3. *Teacher's Observation.* Teachers are the best judges of identifying backward children on the basis of their observation in and outside the class.
4. *Personality Inventory and Case History.* For supplementing information gathered from other sources, tools of personal inventory and case history may also be used.

Planning Educational Programmes for the Backward Children

Following programmes are suggested for improving the educational attainment of the backward children.

1. Regular check-up and follow-up treatment.
2. Provision of special coaches, special classes.
3. Provision of special schools in special cases.
4. Provision of a separate curriculum. The curriculum should cover less ground than the curriculum meant for the normal children.
5. Use of simple methods of instruction based on concrete and living experiences.
6. Use of a variety of audio-visual aids.
7. Checking non-attendance and truancy.
8. Making available a variety of co-curricular activities.
9. Maintaining proper progress record.
10. Providing guidance services.
11. Providing positive environment based on patience and sympathetic understanding of the needs of the children.
12. Taking the help of experienced educational psychologists.

(*Note*: It is very difficult to make a clearcut distinction between slow learners, under-achievers and backward children. Educational psychologists have used these terms usually simultaneously.)

23.4 COGNITIVE DIFFERENCES AND COGNITIVE DEVELOPMENT

Dimensions of Individual Differences in the Cognitive Domain

Various dimensions of the cognitive behaviour of the students are as under:

1. Thinking
2. Remembering
3. Analysing
4. Interpreting
5. Reasoning
6. Problem solving

Identification of Cognitive Differences

Following are the important methods adopted for identifying cognitive differences of students:

1. Intelligence Tests
2. Aptitude Tests
3. Creativity Tests
4. Academic Achievement Tests

Educational Implications

1. Small classes may be organised.
2. Much responsibility may be given to the students for organising their programmes.
3. School marks should not be accepted as the sole evidence of successful student development.
4. Undue reliance should not be placed on tests and measurements.
5. Case histories of each child from kindergarten through higher secondary school must be made available to concerned persons and kept up-to-date.
6. A good system of accessible cumulative records must be developed.
7. Time table should be arranged in a way that the teachers may compile cumulative records and use them.
8. Opportunity to secure advice from specialists in diagnosis of difficulties should be provided.
9. Time for home visits or conferences with parents should be provided.
10. School personnel and parents should accept the statement that honest labour performed to the best of one's ability is worthy of commendation, whether the work be in the shops or offices, factories or farms.
11. Professional service to aid teachers in developing the attitudes, skills and techniques necessary for successful counselling should be provided.

12. Necessary material for testing and recording data needed to understand the individual child's needs, aptitudes and interests be provided.

Using Existing Cognitive level as Base: Here several maxims of reaching like linking present knowledge with the past and future, direct to indirect or whole to parts may be adopted.

Use of Mnemonics (Aiding the Memory) for Strengthening Memory: For instance for remembering, reading, writing, arithmetic, rights, responsibilities and relationships, the term 7 R's may be used. Likewise 4 H's for head, hand, health and heart may be used.

24

Individual Differences and Accommodating them in the Classroom

24.1 SIGNIFICANCE OF INDIVIDUAL DIFFERENCES IN TEACHING-LEARNING

Teaching-learning process to be effective and inspirational must take into consideration the individual differences of the learners. The focus should be on the ability of the learners. There cannot be child-centred education without realising the differences and similarities among learners. At the same time, it must be appreciated that there cannot be, in general, individualised instruction in normal schools of the formal system of education. In Chapters 22 and 25, we have discussed teaching-learning strategies relating to learner centred techniques of exceptional children. In this chapter we are primarily concerned with individual differences in general and their classroom implications.

The following description of individual differences has been very beautifully given by Rita Malhotra, Director of a Guidance Centre in New Delhi in *'Journal of Indian Education'* (Volume XXII, February 2002, No. 4).

Millions and millions of persons have been born and have died.

But no two persons were identical.

Billions and billions of persons will be born and will die.

But no two persons will be identical.

Trillions and trillions of leaves grow and fade away.

But no two leaves are identical.

Nature is perfectly imperfect.

Universe is designed to coexist with imperfections and individual differences.

This description equally applies to individual differences of learners.

Individual differences play the most dominating role in the development of the individuality of the child. It is of utmost importence to study the significances of individual differences.

H.C. Mckown has given a very vivid description of individual differences, "In the whole world there are probably no two things alike—no two trees, no two leaves, flowers, blades of grass, rocks, drops, clouds, animals, houses, pianos, books, baseballs or photographs, even though at first glance they appear to be identical. Similarly no two human beings are alike, they differ physically in size, weight, height, colour of eyes and hair, texture of skin—

and in a thousand other details as well as in thousands of details of mental, social and spiritual life". Not only this, an individual reacts to the same situation in different manners at different times. Mass procedures, no matter, how well-intentioned, fail to accomplish the desired results in educational programmes, unless they are supplemented by adequate attention to the individual needs of the learner. In the words of Charles E. Skinner, "Today we think of individual differences as including any measurable aspect of the total personality." Differences in children may be slight, moderate or extreme.

24.2 TYPES OF INDIVIDUAL DIFFERENCES

Following are the important types of individual differences:

1. *Differences in Physique*: This means tall or short, thin or fat, fair or black, normal or handicapped, etc.
2. *Differences in Health:* It means healthy or ill, weak or strong.
3. *Differences in Intelligence*: Here the range is very wide—from almost nil intelligence to 140 or above. On the basis of one's I.Q., one can be classified to fall in any of the idiot to genius categories.
4. *Differences with Reference to Achievements:* Pupils differ in achievements in school subjects and their efficiency in vocation.
5. *Differences in Affective Factors:* There are differences in attitude towards ideas, subjects, things and people, etc. Likewise differences in interests.
6. *Differences in Motor Ability:* This means control over muscles. The performance of some in some mechanical task is superior and the performance of others is inferior.
7. *Sex Differences:* Sex differences operate in different ways.
8. *Differences with Reference to Learning Ability and Speed of Learning:* This is evident from daily example. Take a class-room. Some boys learn things quickly—other take days to learn it and some do not learn at all.
9. *Differences with Reference to Race and Nationality:* Many studies lead us to conclude that people belonging to different races and nationalities differ in respect of nature, physical and mental traits, interests and personality, etc. It can be intelligence also.
10. *Personality Differences:* Many classifications of personality differences are made. According to Hipprocrates, people are of four types: (a) sanguine, (b) choleric, (c) melancholic, (d) phlegmatic.
    According to Jung, people can be classified into three types: (a) Introverts, (b) Extroverts, (c) Ambiverts.
    Terman has classified people on the basis of intelligence into nine categories—from genius to idiot.
11. *Differences with Respect to Development:* It includes social development, emotional development which includes emotional maturity, emotional stability, etc.

24.3 INDIVIDUAL DIFFERENCES: READINESS

On account of differences in ability and in previous experiences all children are not at the same readiness (preparation for action) for learning when they enter school or when they learn a new topic or unit in the same subject or when they are promoted to the next class. This makes difference in the new situation because of differences in basic concept formation and the level of knowledge required as foundation on which to build a new lesson.

Thorndike has propounded the Law of Readiness. The law states, "When any conduction unit is not in readiness to conduct, for it to conduct is annoying. When any conduction unit is in readiness to conduct, for it not to do so is annoying."

The law is indicative of learner's state to participate in the learning process. According to Thorndike, readiness is preparation for action. Readiness does not come automatically with maturation. It is a law of preparatory adjustment, not a law about growth. Thorndike termed the neurons and synapses involved in the establishment of a specific bond or connection, a conduction unit. According to this law, for a conduction unit ready to conduct, to do, is satisfying and for it not to do so is annoying.

Educational Implications of Readiness. The teacher sould prepare the minds of the students to be ready to accept their knowledge, skill and aptitudes. For this, he should provide suitable opportunities for those experiences in which students can spontaneously participate. In other words, he should arouse their capacity to link the experiences with their everyday life. 'Simple to complex' is the important maxim. Aptitude tests may be given to the students to find out their readiness to learn.

24.4 EDUCATIONAL IMPLICATIONS OF INDIVIDUAL DIFFERENCES

Some students go faster than others and such students may be given double promotion or separate streams formed or some additional work given to them so that their progress is not retarded due to slow learners. Similarly, steps will have to be taken to ensure that the slow learners also make satisfactory progress commensurate with their capacity and ability to work.

A deaf, dumb, blind, undersized, oversized, too fat or too lean learner needs guidance in the selection of such a vocation where his physical defect may not be a handicap and he may be able to earn his living in an honourable manner. Such students need special educational courses. Ordinary schools fail to do justice to them.

There are some students whose parents are very dominating with the result that their children develop inferiority complex. Too lenient parents allow their children to be freelancers and such children suffer from other complexes and develop bad habits. Children of the rich and the poor have altogether different situations to be faced with.

The problems are as numerous as the learners.

The programme of guidance is not confined to the selection of subjects, schools, vocations, etc. All children need guidance in every aspect of their harmonious development. They need guidance in fields, such as, recreation, moral and religious, social adjustments, cultural pursuits, physical development, etc.

Democratically, all individuals are equal but phsyically and psychologically all individuals are unequal and in other words each individual is different from the other. All the same, all are agreed that equal opportunity or equality of opportunity must be provided to every individual for drawing out the best that an individual has so that an individual achieves optimum development. It has been aptly stated by Benjamin S. Bloom, an American educator, "A society which places such great value on education and schooling that it requires the individual to attend school for a long period of time must find the means to make education attractive and meaningful to the individual learner." This implies that education should be *individual-centred.* But in spite of the loud talk on *child-centred or individual-centred* education, it is observed that there is very little practical action in this regard.

Undoubtedly, all the students need guidance in one or the other aspect, some need more guidance and others less. Without proper guidance the superior child may go astray, the average one may become backward and the backward may be lost to the society altogether.

24.5 MEETING NEEDS OF INDIVIDUAL DIFFERENCES: TEACHING STRATEGIES AND CLASS-ROOM MEASURES

In view of the individual differences, it is quite clear that the same curriculum, same methods of teaching and same discipline and in some cases even the same educational institution will not serve the individual needs of children. Ideally speaking each student needs a particular setting and individual instruction with a lot of group interaction. This, however, is not feasible in normal classroom routine. At the same time individual differences of children must be catered to. There are nine broad areas, in which a lot of work could be done to take into consideration individual differences. These are:

1. Streaming of students, *i.e.,* making ability groups.
2. Curriculum planning, *i.e.*, providing advanced and ordinary curriculum in different disciplines.
3. Disciplinary treatment.
4. Guidance and counselling.
5. Special schools for the handicapped children.
6. Combining individualised, group and class instruction.
7. Using maxims of teaching and mnemonics.
8. Using team teaching.
9. Taking up projects where possible.

24.6 GENERAL GUIDELINES FOR MEETING INDIVIDUAL DIFFERENCES

1. Courses should be selective to meet the needs of individual students.
2. Opportunities for acquiring manual and mechanical skills should be provided.
3. A wide range of pupil experiences may be provided in the school.
4. Remedial instruction should be made available to such students who need it.
5. Courses should be organised in such a way as bright pupils can learn at their own speed and slow pupils follow their own speed.

6. Guidance regarding co-curricular activities should be provided.
7 Counselling should be given to students.
8. Assignments should be adapted to the needs of students.
9. Special care should be taken to accept the under-achieving child as a unique individual. His particular needs should be immediately attended to.
10. Efforts may be made to re-establish child's confidence in himself.
11. The teacher should seek the co-operation of other teachers and the parents of the under-achievers.
12. In case of deep-rooted emotional problems which lie at the root of under-achievement, referral may be made to a child guidance clinic after taking the parents into confidence.
13. Students should be taught to recognise their handicaps, and counselled in methods to overcome or compensate for them.
14. Some programme of parents' education may be taken up as many problems of the students result from unsatisfactory home conditions.
15. School programme should take into account the needs of those students who are not likely to go to college and those who would join college.
16. The school programme, administration and management should be made flexible enough to allow for adjustment to individual differences.

24.7 INTEGRATING HANDICAPPED CHILDREN, BACKWARD CHILDREN AND CHILDREN WITH OTHER DIFFERENCES WITH THE MAINSTREAM (REGULAR TEACHING)

(See Chapter 23.5)

Summing up

In the end it must be stressed that there is a limit to which individual differences of students can be accommodated in the normal class-room teaching. This is possible to some extent when the number of students in a particular class or section is small. In larger classes, it is not feasible to meet with all the individual differences. There must be some sort of flexible environment like the Dalton Plan. Additional time, *i.e.*, other than the normal class time schedule is needed to cater to the specific individual learning needs of the students.

25

Learner Centred Techniques for Exceptional Children

25.1 INTRODUCTION

In this chapter, the meaning, characteristics, identification, problems and remedial measures for the following types of exceptional children are taken up:

1. The Gifted Children
2. Physically Handicapped Children
3. Blind Children
4. Children with Visual Impairments or Disabilities (other than Blind Children)
5. Children with Speech and Hearing Impairment or Disability
6. Children with Orthopaedic and Locomotive Impairment or Disability
7. Mentally Retarded Children

25.2 THE GIFTED CHILDREN

Meaning of the Gifted and the Creative: In simple language a gifted child is one who can make outstanding contribution in any area of national life. Giftedness generally speaking includes actual or potential qualities of creativity, emotional stability and social adaptability. Following are the important definitions of gifted children:

1. *Fleigher and Bush* write about gifted children as, "The term gifted enecompasses those children who possess a superior intellectual potentiality and functional ability to achieve academically in the top 15 to 20 per cent of the school population, and/or talent of a high order in which special areas as mathematics, mechanics, science, expressive arts, creative writing, music and social leadership; and a unique creative ability to deal with their environment."

2. *Guilford* gives the picture of a gifted child as, "The gifted are those students whose potential intellectual powers are at such a high ideational level in which both productive and evaluative thinking that it can be reasonably assumed, they could be the future problem solvers, innovators and evaluators of the culture of adequate educational experiences are provided."

3. In the words of *Hillingworth*, "By a gifted child we mean one who is far more educable than the generality of children are. The greater educability may lie along the lines of one of the arts, as in music or drawing, it may lie in

the sphere of mechanical aptitude, or it may consist in surpassing power to achieve literacy and abstract knowledge."

4. *James Drever* is of the view that "Children possessing high intellectual ability, generally or in a particular field are gifted children."

5. In the views of Marland Report, "The gifted are those who possess outstanding abilities or potential in the area of general intellectual capacity, specific academic attitude, creative or productive thinking, leadership ability, visual or performing arts and psycho-motor activity."

6. *Paul Witty* states, "Those whose performance in a worthwhile human endeavour is constantly remarkable as well as those who are academically superior."

7. *Prem Pasricha*, an Indian psychologist describes a gifted child as, "The gifted child is the one who exhibits superiority in general intelligence or the one who is in possession of special abilities of a high order in the fields which are not necessarily associated with a high intelligent quotient.

8. *R.J. Havighurst* observes, "Gifted children are those individuals from kindergarten to high school age who show unusual promise in some socially useful area and whose talent might be stimulated."

9. *Tannenbaum* states about gifted children, "The term giftedness denotes their potential for becoming critically acclaimed performers or exemplary producers of ideas in spheres of activity that enhance the moral, physical, emotional, social, intellectual, or aesthetic life of humanity."

10. According to *Telford and Sawrey*, "The intellectually gifted can be defined in terms of test scores or demonstrated performance or as the upper 1 or 2 per cent of the general population as measured by some designated intelligence test."

11. Terman and Oden state, "Gifted children are far above the average in physique, social adjustment, personality traits, school achievement, play, information and versatility of interests."

12. The U.S. Commisioner of Education in 1972 defined gifted children in these words, "Gifted and talented children are those identified by professionally qualified persons who by virtue of outstanding abilities are capable of high performance. These are children who require differentiated educational programmes and services beyond those normally provided by regular programme in order to realise their contribution to self and society."

13. The USA Federal Register in 1981 gave this definition, "Gifted and talented are those who give evidence of high performance capability, in areas, such as, intellectual, creative, artistic, leadership capability, or specific academic fields, and who require services or activities not ordinarily provided by the school in order to fully develop such capabilities."

Broadly speaking 'gifted children' should include all those children who give promise of creativity of a high order in any worthwhile line of human endeavour. They have superior ability that can make them contribute to the quality of living in society. Therefore, we include not only the intellectually gifted but also those who show promise in music, the graphic arts, creative writing, dramatics, mechanical skills and social leadership. Nevertheless, here we are dealing with children having gifted intellectual ability.

While discussing education of the gifted, the creative and the intellectually superior, it may be observed, that in essence, all these three types of children may be placed in the same category. In practice, it is very difficult to formulate separate policies. These categories differ in degrees only and not in kind.

Wide Variety of Gifted Children: In the words of Hollingworth, "By a gifted child we mean one who is far more educable than the generality of children. The greater educability may lie along the lines of one of the arts, as in music or drawing, it may lie in the sphere of mechanical aptitude, or it may consist in surpassing power to achieve literacy and abstract knowledge." Paul Witty, Ruth Strang, Havighurst and many others think that the term gifted children should include all those children who give promise of creativity of a high order in any worthwhile line of human endeavour. They have superior ability that can make them contribute to the quality of living in society. Therefore, we include not only the intellectually gifted but also those who show promise in music, the graphic arts, creative writing, dramatics, mechanical skills and social leadership.

Main Characteristics of the Gifted

1. Very high I.Q.
2. Ability to apply knowledge to unfamiliar situations.
3. Ability for abstract and symbolic thinking.
4. Annoyance with details.
5. Attention span long for age.
6. Curiosity indicated by asking serious questions.
7. Dislike of rigid time schedule.
8. Energy level (physical and intellectual) very high.
9. Exposure needed limited and fewer repetitions to learn.
10. Intense interest in one area.
11. Knowing a lot about things of which other students are unaware.
12. Learning commensurate with that expected of older students, often start of reading at an earlier than average age.
13. Memory very extraordinary.
14. Often thinking faster than they write (can result in sloppy work).
15. Spontaneous and diverse interests.
16. Standards and goals unusually high.
17. Vocabulary very high and mature expressive ability enormous.

Those students who show some or several of the characteristics mentioned above are referred to by many adjectives such as 'genius', 'gifted' and 'talented' etc.

Types or Categories of Gifted Children: Usually following are considered as the categories of the gifted on the basis of Intelligence Quotient (I.Q.). (Stanford Revision—USA).

I.Q.	*Per cent of Population*
160-169	0.3%
150-159	0.2%
140-149	1.1%
130-139	3.1%
120-129	8.2%

On the basis of Dr. V.V. Kamat's classification, 120 I.Q. may be considered as the lower limit of giftedness.

Usually it is said that nearly 2 to 3 per cent of the population may be placed under the category of the gifted children.

Growing Interest in the Education of the Gifted Children

The following memorable stanza of Thomas Gray in his memorable poem 'enjoins upon us, to appreciate the talents of the gifted children.

"Full many a gem of purest ray serene,
The dark unfathom of caves of ocean bear;
Full many a flower is born to blush unseen,
And waste its sweetness on the desert air."

It is of great importance to bring out the hidden *'gem like'* potentialities in pupils.

We are interested in the gifted on account of the following considerations:

1. There is a limited pool of ability and special talent in every country. This must be identified and developed to save it from loss.
2. The gifted individuals have played an important role in the preservation and advancement of civilization.
3. Values of democracy will be realized in the fullest sense when we recognize the full range of ability within our total population.
4. Many gifted children languish in educational institutions simply because they are not aware of their 'gifts' and the school programmes do not provide them enough motivation and challenge.
5. We need leaders for our business, education research and government etc. These leaders are provided by this class of gifted children.

Adjustment Problems of Gifted Children: A gifted child may become a problem for the parents and the teacher if he is not handled properly. Following problems may arise:

1. When he is not properly guided, he utilises his superior intelligence in mischief, indiscipline, gang-formation and revolts against his elders. He becomes a nuisance.
2. Because of lack of opportunities and lack of recognition, he sometimes develops inferiority complex.
3. Too much of recognition or applause by the parent or teacher also develop in him boastful conceit.
4. There is lack of stimulation for him in the subjects of his interests when he does not get opportunities of progressing according to his own pace.

5. He revolts against the parents and teachers when they do not recognise him, and sometimes creates mischief in order to catch their attention or to show his superiority.

Identification of the Gifted Children: For identifying the gifted children, following techniques are employed:

1. Intelligence Tests (Individual)
2. Intelligence Tests (Group)
3. Achievements Tests and Batteries.
4. Observations by Teachers and others.

It may be observed that reliance should not be made only on one technique.

Educational Provisions in Terms of Curriculum, Teaching Methodologies and Evaluation for the Gifted Children

1. *Enrichment Programmes:* Enrichment consists in giving the gifted child the opportunity to go deeper or to read more intensively than the average child in his intellectual, social and artistic experience. Such a programme may be characterized by (1) Emphasis upon the creative or the experimental pursuit; (2) Emphasis on developing the skill of investigation and learning; (3) Independent work, stressing initiative and originality; (4) High standard of accomplishment; (5) Co-operative planning and activity that provides opportunity for leadership training and experiences in social adjustment; (6) Individual attention to be given by the teacher to the student; (7) Providing first-hand experiences; (8) Flexibility of organization and procedure; (9) Extensive reading; and (10) Concern with community responsibility.

2. *The Triple Track Plan:* In this type of learning plan, there are three tracks or courses:

(*a*) The first is for the dull child who may cover it in a longer duration of time.

(*b*) The second one is for the average child who covers it in an average period of time.

(*c*) The third is for the child of superior intelligence. He covers the entire work in a shorter period of time due to his intelligence, efforts and initiative.

Such a system has been adopted in many schools in the United States.

3. *Rapid Promotion:* Gifted children should be promoted to the next higher grade as soon as they achieve the target of a particular grade.

4. *Special Schools:* In some countries special schools are organised for gifted children. Some educationists have pointed out some limitations in organising such schools.

5. *Acceleration:* Acceleration offers opportunity for a gifted pupil to move at a pace appropriate to his ability and maturity and to complete an educational programme in less than the ordinary amount of time. It involves advancing the gifted child rapidly from grade to grade in school.

6. *Segregation or Ability Grouping:* The gifted pupils may be placed in special groups for the entire or part of the school day. The purpose of ability grouping is usually to provide for enrichment of children's experiences in both depth and breadth, and to permit the children to stimulate one another.

7. *Summer programmes:* Special cultural and educational programmes may be organised for gifted children during the summer season. This approach is being tried in U.S.A. and in a limited measure in our country as well.

8. *Scholarships*: Gifted children should be given special scholarships for pursuing their studies. This will lead the gifted child in the right direction.

9. *Special visits:* Groups of gifted children may formally visit places of historical, industrial, geographical and economic interest. This would enable them to understand and appreciate important places of social value also.

10. *Contact with Eminent Persons:* Gifted children may show interest in any special field of activities. Their meetings may be fixed up with persons of eminence of that particular field.

11. *Proper Educational and Vocational and Personal Guidance and Counselling:* The gifted children should receive proper guidance in all areas of life so that their total development is of an optimum level.

The role of the counsellor in the promotion of talent can be very important. The counsellor with his detailed knowledge of each talented student is in a unique position to formulate a programme of enrichment for him and to suggest the necessary modifications in the curricular and co-curricular requirements. Where trained counsellors are not available, this task will fall on the teachers. It will, therefore, be necessary to train teachers for this responsibility through in-service seminars and special courses. It should be impressed on them that the class-room atmosphere and the attitudes of teachers is of considerable importance. In a social and educational set-up like ours where the relationship between the teachers and the taught is still largely authoritarian, the general tendency is to suppress any urges and interests that deviate from the class norm. The first requirement for the promotion of talent, therefore, is for the teachers to create an atmosphere of free expression in the class-room and to provide opportunities for creative work.

We may remember the words of wisdom said by A.N. Whitehead, "Any race which does not value trained intelligence is doomed."

25.3 PHYSICALLY HANDICAPPED CHILDREN

Meaning of a Physically Handicapped Child: A physically handicapped child is one who is affected with a physical impairment that in any way limits or inhibits his participation in normal activities. Impairment implies abnormalities of body structure and appearance. It represents disturbance at the organ level. The impairment may be of a serious type or it may be slight in degree. For instance, a person hit by polio may be having only 15 per cent impairment on a certain part of the body or may have a total loss of mobility. Similarly, the visual defect may be total and it may not be restored. Other visual impairments may not pose serious problems and may be overcome with some aids.

Types of Physically Handicapped Children

Generally speaking, the physically handicapped may be classified as:

1. The cripple.
2. The blind or near blind or partially blind.
3. The deaf or hard of hearing.
4. The language handicapped.
5. Cerebral palsied.
6. Orthopaedically handicapped.

In addition, the chronically ill children who may have health problems like heart defects or cardiac problems, epilepsy, allergies, diabetes, rheumatism, muscular and tuberculosis etc. also fall in the category of physically handicapped children.

Objectives of Education of the Physically Handicpped Children: Following are the chief objectives of the education of the physically handicapped children:

1. To pursue those curricular matters and other activities that strategically determine effecive living for specific type of handicapped school children.
2. To take note of the mental as well as the physical hygiene of handicapped school children and to take suitable measures.
3. To develop rational patterns in the handicapped that will produce achievement in school and out of school.
4. To produce in the handicapped a desire to participate in the activities of non-handicapped persons.
5. To develop a realistic self-concept in handicapped children.
6. To reach the maximum level of effectiveness in school subjects.

Why Education of the Physically Handicapped Children?

The education of handicapped children has to be organized not merely on humanitarian grounds, but also on grounds of utility. Education should enable a handicapped child to overcome largely his (or her) handicap, and make him a useful citizen. Social justice also demands this. It has to be remembered that the Constitutional Directive on compulsory education includes handicapped children as well. However very little has been done in this field so far on account of several difficulties. There is much in this field which we could learn from the educationally advanced countries which in recent years has developed new methods and techniques, based on advances in science and medicine.

The primary task of education for a handicapped child is to prepare him for adjustment to a socio-cultural environment designed to meet the needs of the normal. It is essential, therefore, that the education of handicapped children should be an inseparable part of the general educational system. The differences lie in the methods employed to teach the child and the means the child uses to acquire information. These differences in methodology do not influence the goals of education. This form of education is, therefore, referred to as 'special'.

Characteristerics and Problems of Physically Handicapped Children

A physical handicap may directly or indirectly create the following types of problems for the children and their parents:

1. *Academic Performance*: (i) Physically handicapped children generally work below their capacity in several areas, (ii) Some of the physically handicapped children find it difficult to deal with abstract concepts.

2. *Emotional Reactions or Social Relationships:* (i) Quite a large number of physically handicapped children suffer from feelings of inferiority. (ii) They also suffer from feelings of failures. (iii) Normal children are at times not only indifferent to the handicapped but also make fun of them. Thus the handicapped children are withdrawn. (iv) Aggressive feelings and tensions get accumulated in the handicapped as they have fewer opportunities for expressing their feelings. (v) Sometimes parents', teachers' and students' attitudes may make a physically handicapped child feel 'unwanted' or 'rejected'. (vi) Handicapped children are more prone to accident and injury. Thus, they are not in a position to participate in several co-curricular activities. This also creates a feeling of disgust and inferiority in them.

Fundamental Principles for the Education of the Physically Handicapped Children

1. Recognition of the handicap of the child by the teacher as early as possible.
2. Taking all available correctional measures.
3. Development of favourable attitude towards the child.
4. Diagnostic and remedial work by the guidance counsellor.

Pattern of Education of the Physically Handicapped Children: Following are the usual patterns of education of the handicapped:

1. *Integration:* Integration implies that the education of the handicapped should be so organised that they freely mix up with normal children. This can be achieved in various ways:

(a) Having regular classes for all children.

(b) Deliberate architectural planning to allot space for regular classes and special classes separately but in the same building.

2. *Partial Integration.* The brightest and the handicapped children join with regular groups for carefully selected experiences, games and play.

3. *Total Segregation.* Under this system, the handicapped children are completely separated from other children. They are taught in special schools.

Curriculum Provisions and Methods of Teaching of the Physically Handicapped Children

Following points may be considered while taking measures for the education of the physically handicapped children:

1. *Normal Curriculum.* Quite a large number of the physically handicapped children are quite normal except for their physical handicap. Such children may be provided all those educational facilities and activities which are meant for the normal children, keeping in mind, of course, their physical disability.

2. *Special Classes*. For the partially sighted students, special classes may be organised.

3. *Special Equipment and Methods of Teaching*. Blind children need special equipment and medium for their education. They also need special teaching methods like the following:

(*i*) Use of embossed diagrams in geometry.
(*ii*) Use of relief maps and globes.
(*iii*) More stress on mental work.

4. *Special Subjects*. (*i*) Modelling may be substituted for drawing and painting. Blind children take pleasure in working with clay and plasticine.

(*ii*) Dramatic art may be cultivated.
(*iii*) Music may be given adequate encouragement.

5. *Physical Education*: Corrective posture work, gymnastics, running, wrestling and sports etc. should form part of the physical education programme.

6. *Vocational Education and Handicrafts*: A variety of handicafts may be taught to the physically handicapped.

7. *Therapeutic Assistance*: Special programmes in the form of speech-therapy, physiotherapy, play therapy should be undertaken to help physically handicapped children make the correct and maximum use of whatever abilities and capacities they possess.

8. *Education for Living in Society with Handicap*: Handicapped children have to live in a world of normal people. They, therefore, should be provided all types of education, training and guidance which enable them to face their disability realistically and make suitable adjustments accordingly and live without bitterness and meet unpleasant situations boldly.

25.4 EDUCATION OF THE BLIND

Children whose vision is so impaired that they can see objects at a distance of 20 ft. which a normal eye can see at a distance of 200 ft. are legally blind. The totally blind children read Braille. Blindness affects the life of the individual in the physical, mental, social, educational and vocational aspects.

Usually for blind children, going to school implies admission to a residential school for the blind (Braille classes). Of late some attempts have been made to integrate them with the normal children by admitting them to normal schools but the coverage of blind population of the students in this respect is not significant. A blind school aims at assisting the blind child, through the use of special methods and aids, in his adjustment to the world in which he has to live as an adult.

Schools for the blind usually provide for activities such as dancing, scouting, and dramatics.

Special equipment and methods of teaching are employed for the education of the blind.

Particular attention is given to practice on type writer because it permits written communication with the seeing.

Methods of Teaching the Blind

(*i*) As many as concrete experiences as possible, either by letting them observe the object as such or by providing replicas to the blind students.

(*ii*) Blind children at least during the primary classes, should be taught by a unit plan of instruction.

(*iii*) Topics of the units may consist of everyday experiences, such as, provision shops, post offices, etc.

(*iv*) Self-activity should be made an integral part of the education of the blind.

(See also Chapter 23)

25.5 CHILDREN WITH VISUAL IMPAIRMENTS OR DISABILITY (OTHER THAN BLINDNESS)

Meaning

Several children do not have sufficient vision. They find it difficult to read the writing on the blackboard clearly. There are partially sighted children also. Some can read only large print. Visual impairment results in several learning problems. Children with visual impairments may have enormous capacity to work. However, this depends upon the nature of the impairment.

Characteristics and Identification of Children with Visual Impairments

It is very necessary to identify each category of children with visual impairments. Medical treatment may become necessary in some cases. Parents also need to be informed.

Children with visual impairment may be identified from the following:

1. Having watery eyes.
2. Rubbing eyes frequently.
3. Reddening of eyes frequently.
4. Covering one eye and tining the head forward.
5. Holding objects and books close to the eyes.
6. Asking help from others when taking notes from the blackboard.
7. Blinking frequently—squinting eyelids together.
8. Complaining about headache following close eye work.
9. Bumping into people or objects.
10. Skipping words or lines while reading.
11. Having poor eye-hand coordination.
12. Moving head forward and backward while looking at distant objects.

Meaning and Characteristics of Visual Acuity

Visual handicap is defined in terms of visual acuity, field of vision and visual efficiency. Snellen chart, developed by Herbart Snellen, a Dutch doctor, is used to assess the visual ability. The chart starts with a big 'E' which a normal eye can see at a distance of 200 ft.

Visual acuity is not the only criteria for measuring acquisition of basic sk 'ls. Following tests are used for measuring intellectual abilities.

1. The Blind Learning Aptitude Test.
2. The Haptic Intelligence Test for the Adult Blind.

Role of the School and the Teacher in the Education of Students with Visual Impairment or Disability

1. Children with visual impairment may be seated in the front rows so that they can read the writing on the blackboard without any difficulty or pressure.
2. Such children may be given training in listening with comprehension.
3. Books with bold letters may be provided to such children.
4. Radio and T.V. broadcasts may be arranged for such children.
5. Efforts may be made to procure cassettes in different curricular areas. State Institutes of Education or State Councils of Educational Research and Training or District Institutes of Education and Training or Centres or Institutes of Educational Technology may be approached for this purpose.
6. Blind children need Braille script books.
7. School doctor may be consulted from time to time.
8. Co-operation of the parents be sought in the follow-up work.

25.6 CHILDREN WITH HEARING AND SPEECH IMPAIRMENT

Listening plays an important role in academic learning. Hearing problems interfere with the achievement of the students. It is, therefore, desirable to identify such children and take steps to meet their educational needs. Such children may be identified as under:

—Some observable deformity of the ear or ears.
—Frequent complaints of pain in ears.
—Frequent scratching of ears.
—Frequent discharge from ears.
—Turning head on one side to hear better.
—Frequent requests to teachers to repeat questions and directions etc.
—Making errors in taking dictation or notes.
—Displaying speech difficulty.

Education of Children with Hearing and Speech Impairment or Disability: Guidelines

1. Children with hearing problems may be given front seats.
2. While speaking, the teacher may use a reasonable level of pitch.
3. The teacher should avoid mumbling.
4. The teacher should avoid speaking too fast.
5. Students should be encouraged to speak gradually and steadily.
6. Other students of the class may be asked to give due consideration to such students.
7. A lot of visual aids may be used in the class-room.
8. Some of the hearing problems can be corrected through drill and practice.

9. Medical help may be needed if speech disorder is due to an organic defect in speech mechanism.

25.7 CHILDREN WITH ORTHOPAEDIC AND LOCOMOTOR IMPAIRMENT/DISABILITY

Identification: Such children can be easily identified as their impairment is usually observable.

1. Deformity may be observable in fingers, hands, legs, neck or waist, etc.
2. Showing difficulty in sitting, standing and walking.
3. Showing difficulty in picking up and holding objects and putting them on the ground.
4. Frequently complaining of pains in the joints.
5. Experiencing difficulty in holding the pen to write.
6. Walking with jerks.
7. Experiencing difficulty in the movement of limbs.
8. Amputated limbs.

Children with Orthopaedic and Locomotor Impairment Disability

1. The teacher should accept such children as he accepts other children.
2. The teacher should avoid sarcasm for the disability of the child.
3. Other children should be advised to appreciate the disability and show due regard to such children. They should be made to understand the disability.
4. Seating arrangement in the class may be adjusted to the specific needs of such students.
5. Reasonable opportunities for participation in recreational activities, sports and games should be provided to these children.
6. Remedial teaching may also be arranged for them.

25.8 THE MENTALLY RETARDED CHILDREN AND THEIR EDUCATION

Meaning of Mentally Retarted Children

1. In the words of Fox and Gregory, "Mental retardation refers to a chronic condition present from birth or early childhood which is characterised by both impaired intellectual functioning as measured by standardized tests and impaired adaptation to the daily demands of the individual's social environment."
2. Page (1976) is of this opinion, "Mental deficiency is a condition of sub-normal mental development, present at birth or early childhood and characterised mainly by limited intelligence and social inadequacy.
3. According to British Mental Deficiency Act 1981, "Mental deficiency is a condition of arrested or incomplete development of mind existing before the age of 18 years whether arising from inherent causes or induced by disuse or injury.

4. The American Association of Mental Deficiency (1983) has given the following definition, "Mental retardation refers to significantly sub-average intellectual functioning existing concurrently with defect in adaptive behaviour, and manifested during the development period.

Nomenclature of Mental Deficiency: Terms like mentally deficient children, mentally retarded children, feeble-minded children, mentally handicapped children, mentally sub-normal children and mentally sub-average children are used simultaneously.

Characteristics of Mentally Retarded Children

1. Mental retardation is a condition of mind.
2. Mental retardation is the sub-normal development of the mind or brain.
3. Mental deficiency may be observed at birth or it may manifest later during the course of development.
4. Mental deficiency is generally manifested before the end of the years of adolescence.

Identification of Mental Deficiency: It can be identified in the following ways:

1. Very low scores on intelligence tests.
2. Observation of the behaviour.
3. Inadequacy of adaptive behaviour.

Level of Retardation and I.Q.

Level of Retardation	*I.Q. on Standard-Binet*
Profound	under 10
Severe	20-35
Moderate	36-51
Mild	52-69

Educational Implications of the Mentally Retarded Children

Clarification: Following are the broad categories of mentally retarded children from educational points of view:

1. Educable mentally retarded (EMR) mentally mild children.
2. Trainable—mentally moderate children.
3. Custodial—mentally severe and profound child.

Following measures may be adopted:

1. They should be properly grouped.
2. They need special education.
3. The institution of boarding school would best serve the needs of mentally retarded children.
4. The retarded children need 3A's—Personal Adequacy, Social Adequacy and Occupational Adequacy instead of the traditional 3R's.
5. Special instructional material is needed for the mentally retarded children.

26

Mental Hygiene and Delinquency

26.1 MEANING OF MENTAL HYGIENE

While discussing mental hygiene, two points may be kept in mind. One. Mental hygiene has an important place in educational practices. With the working knowledge of the meaning and principles of mental hygiene, teachers have several opportunities to develop among students social attitudes, training social skills and thus enabling them to develop better personal and social adjustment. Two. Some psychologists consider mental hygiene and mental health as synonymous.

The following definitions are very helpful in understanding the meaning of mental hygiene.

1. In the words of Klein, D.B., "Mental hygiene as its name suggests, is concerned with the realization and maintenance of the mind's health and efficiency."
2. Wallace-Wallin has defined mental hygiene as "the application of a body of hygienic information and techniques culled from science of psychology, child study, education, sociology, psychiatry, medicine and biology for the purpose of observation and improvement of mental health of the individuals and of the community for the prevention and care of minor and major mental diseases and defects and of mental, educational and social maladjustments."
3. Drever, James considers mental hygiene as "investigation of the laws of mental health and the taking or advocacy of measures for its preservation."
4. Hadfield considers mental hygiene as "concerned with the maintenance of mental health and the prevention of mental disorder."
5. American Psychiatric Association observes, "Mental hygiene consists of measures to reduce the incidence of mental illness through prevention and early treatment and to promote mental health."
6. Crow and Crow conceive mental hygiene "as a science that deals with human welfare and pervades all fields of human relationship."
7. *The Dictionary of Education* by Carter W. Good defines mental hygiene as "Establishment of environmental conditions, emotional attitudes and habits of thinking that will resist an onset of personality maladjustments. It is the study of principles and practices in the promotion of mental health and prevention of mental disorders."

8. According to Boring, E.G., the aim of mental hygiene is to "aid people to achieve more satisfying and more productive lives through the prevention of anxieties and maladjustments."

The movement of mental hygiene began in the first decade of 20th century with the publication of '*A Mind That Found Itself*' (1908) authored by Clifford Beers). His book revolutioned the concept of mental health. Beers, a graduate of Yale University, had become so much mentally disturbed on account of unnecessary strain and stress, that he attempted to commit suicide. He, however was saved and treated of his mental illness. After recovery, he described his experiences and treatment the received, in his book which created awareness in the general public for mental hygiene as a movement.

26.2 PRINCIPLES OF MENTAL HYGIENE/MENTAL HEALTH: CLASSIFICATION

(1) Principles of Seeking Adjustment with Oneself

(2) Principles of Seeking Adjustment with One's Environment

I. The Principles of Seeking Adjustment with Oneself

Following principles come under this category:

1. Principle of knowing the self
2. Principle of accepting one's self
3. Principle of balancing one's development
4. Principle of self drive and shaping
5. Principle of self control.

II. The Principles of Seeking Adjustment with Environment

Following principles may be included under this category:

1. Principle of understanding others
2. Principle of accepting and understanding others
3. Principle of socialising oneself
4. Principle of satisfying needs adequately
5. Principle of training emotions.
6. Principle of adjusting with the world of work
7. Principle of developing positive attitude towards life.
8. Principle of bearing the stresses and strains of life
9. Principle of good physical health
10. Principle of faith in God

26.3 PRINCIPLES OF MENTAL HYGIENE/MENTAL HEALTH

1. Principle of prevention
2. Principle of preservation
3. Principle of cure

1. *Principle of prevention of mental disorders through an understanding*

of the relationship that exists between wholesome personality development and life experiences: This implies:

(*i*) Listing various causes of maladjustment—personal as well as social.
(*ii*) Furnishing the knowledge of drives, needs, motives, conflicts of motives, frustrations and tensions etc.
(*iii*) Suggesting ways and means of achieving emotional and social adjustment, and
(*iv*) Suggesting the solution for the inner conflicts and frustrations and thus relieving from the tensions, anxieties and emotional disturbances.

2. *Principles of preservation of the mental health of the individual and of the group*. This means:

(*i*) Developing total potentialities of an individual.
(*ii*) Attaining emotional maturity and stability.
(*iii*) Achieving personal and social security as well as adequacy.
(*iv*) Developing healthy human relationships and group-interaction.
(*v*) Helping an individual in acquiring sound body and normal mental health.

3. *Principle of cure of mental health*. This is related to:

1. Suggesting various forms of therapy for treatment and curing specific mental illness and disorders.
2. Suggesting means for the rehabilitation and readjustment of the mentally ill persons.

26.4 MEANING OF MENTAL HEALTH

In the words of N.E. Cutts and N. Mosely, "Mental health has various strains of the environment we meet in life and mental hygiene as the means we take to assure the adjustment."

26.5 ROLE OF THE PARENTS (HOME) IN PROMOTING MENTAL HEALTH OF THEIR CHILDREN

1. Providing proper affection and love to children
2. Providing conducive environment in the home
3. Developing proper attitudes to life
4. Critising the children when absolutely essential
5. Discarding the tendency to compare their children with other children
6. Accepting the limitation of their children
7. Avoiding over protection to their children
8. Becoming democratic in their behaviour with children
9. Setting proper examples of cooperation between husband and wife and with other members
10. Meeting the legitimate needs of children
11. Building confidence in children
12. Providing guidance where necessary
13. Avoiding frequent change of address
14. Encouraging sibling cooperation
15. Paying equal attention to sibling

26.6 MENTAL HEALTH HAZARDS IN THE SCHOOL

We may briefly mention the following factors which adversely affect the mental health of the child

1. Lack of friendliness on the part of teachers.
2. Undue stress on scholastic and other competitions.
3. Defective system of evaluation—element of subjectiviyy and unreliability—loss of confidence in the teacher's marking.
4. Fear of failure resulting in tension.
5. Excess of home work.
6. Heavy curriculum and failure of the child to cope with it.

26.7 SYMPTOMS OF A MENTALLY ILL CHILD

Symptoms can be divided into the following three categories:

(a) *Physical Symptoms*: Drumming with fingers, facial twitching, nail biting, restlessness, rocketing feet, scratching head, stammering, and vomiting.

(b) *Behavioural Deviations*: Aggression, bullying hyperactivity, lying, negativism, poor school achievement and sex disturbances.

(c) *Emotional Symptoms*: Persistent anxiety, intense conflicts and tensions, fear, hatred, inferiority complex, extreme timidity, tempertantrum and excessive worry.

26.8 ROLE OF THE SCHOOL IN PROMOTING MENTAL HEALTH OF THE CHILDREN

The school has a great responsibility in the promotion of mental health of the children. It must provide a suitable emotional, intellectual and physical environment in which a child should develop the 'feeling of security' and the 'feeling of belongingness'. He should feel that his personality is given its due recognition.

Following measures can be very helpful in securing mental health of the students.

1. *Relationship Between Mental Health and Physical Health*: Mental health is tied up with the physical health of an individual. A sound mind in a sound body is a popular saying which truly reflects the vital connection between the mind and the body. Apart from a well organized programme of games and sports in a school, there should be a regular programme of yogic exercises. The yogic exercises help to maintain a sort of psycho-physical balance. They tone up the endocrine glands, nervous system and the muscular system. When the yogic exercises are combined with *pranayam*, the individual enjoys a good physical and mental health.

2. *Emotional stability of the teacher*: A teacher's personality has a great bearing on the personality development of the students. It is stated, "While books can teach, only personality can educate". It is observed in a UNESCO publication entitled *The Education and Training of Teachers*: "Various researches show clearly that the emotional stability of teachers affects that of pupils. Unhappy, frustrated, dissatisfied teachers cannot help their pupils to

become happy, well-adjusted young people". The teachers should be mentally alert and stable to develop alertness and stability in the students. They should undergo self introspection, find out their limitations and shortcomings in their behaviour and temperament and try to remove them so that the students are saved from the adverse influence of their maladjusted personalities. They should purge themselves of all kinds of prejudices affecting the emotional behaviour of the students. They should, as far as possible, have high ideals before them.

3. *Love for Children*: A teacher must have abundance of love for children. "One who does not like children should not stay in the teaching profession".

4. *Missionary zeal*: Dr. E.A. Pires opines that the great teacher has the zeal of the missionary. There is a certain aptness in the analogy between a missionary and a teacher, for every true missionary is first and last a teacher.

S. Balakrishna Joshi feels, "Without a band of devoted teachers who are inspired by a holy zeal, an institution with the paraphernalia of modern convenience will be like a beautiful corpse without spark of life, a carcass without soul." According to the same author teaching is a divinely ordained mission.

5. *Meditation and Moral Education*: On the face of it, it looks strange to suggest meditation for students in the school. Here it is clarified that meditation need not be done in an elaborate manner accompanied by several rituals. Meditation is just observance of silence for a few minutes either in the morning assembly or in a regular period. Meditation is likely to provide peace of mind and calmness, if practised regularly.

6. *According respect for the individuality of the child*: A child should not be treated just like a dumb driven cattle. He has his own individuality. He thinks and feels. He sense of respect should not be injured. Emerson has rightly remarked, "The secret of education lies in respecting the pupil." A child wants to be heard. His opinion should not be brushed aside merely because he is a child.

7. *Establishing close pupil-teacher contacts*: The teacher is expected to observe the child carefully in and outside the class and also to know his home environment. This will enable him to understand the child in a better way.

8. *Regular medical examination*: There should be a regular medical check up of the students and follow up action taken to safeguard the health of the students. Cases requiring special treatment should be sent to child guidance clinics.

9. *Patience*: A teacher has to deal with a large number of students having low and high power of understanding. He may have to repeat his lessons many a time for the sake of the less intelligent and he should not be irritated in doing so. Some students, by nature, pick up lessons very slowly and a teacher should possess the required patience to make them understand gradually. Good habits are not formed overnight. It requires time and patience to inculcate virtues in the students.

10. *Consistent behaviour of the teacher and the head*: The inconsistent behaviour of the teacher and the head disturbs the mental attitude of the child. The teacher should not be moody and whimsical.

11. *Democratic attitude of the Teacher and the Head*: A teacher cannot afford to be an autocrat. Present day education lays much stress on the inculcation of democratic ideals in the students. A teacher who is to show the way of democracy to the students must develop in himself a democratic attitude. His role is that of a friend, philosopher and guide and not of a policeman.

12. *True to his commands*: Less commands should be given to the students and when given, they must be stuck to, otherwise they lose their effectiveness and are like to create conflict.

13. *Just and impartial*: The teacher and the head should not show undue favour to any student. All should be equal in their eyes. Undue favour to some students will lead to frustration among others.

14. *Provision of educational, vocational and personal guidance*: It is not essential that a psychologist must be appointed in every school. Trained teachers may be provided opportunities to undergo short term courses in guidance. For difficult cases, area counselors may provide necessary guidance.

15. *Balanced curriculum*: Curriculum should be in accordance with 3 A's i.e. age, ability and aptitude of the students. A rigid curriculum does not suit all categories of students.

16. *Imparting sex education*: It is now increasing being realized that there should be a well-drawn up programme of sex education in schools so that the students develop positive attitudes towards sex.

17. *Motivating intellectual environment of the school*: Sound methods of teaching-learning suited to the individual needs of the students should be adopted. Activity methods e.g., Play-way, Project Method, Dalton Method etc. should be encouraged. Special attention may be paid to the weak students.

18. *Provision of co-curricular activities*: Properly planned co-curricular activities are very helpful in providing suitable opportunities to the students to sublimate their instincts.

19. *Balanced Approach to freedom and self-discipline*: A child who breathes in an environment of freedom develops courage and initiative. Unregulated punishment results in mental retardation. Let us be wise and remember the words of advice of Hobbes, "The fool cannot be mended by flogging, and he who flogs is the greatest fool". A.S. Neill has observed, "We could abolish caning by an act of Parliament, but no act of Parliament can abolish the fear of teacher or a system." Discipline should be through doing and through a constructive approach.

20. *Proper level of aspiration*: Goals set before the students should be achievable by them. Too high goals may lead to frustration. While expecting achievement level from the students, their aptitudes and interests along with their limitations and strengths should be taken into consideration.

21. *Healthy competitions*: Students should not be made to engage themselves in the blind race of excelling others. This disturbs their mental equilibrium. For winning, they may resort to unethical ways which may lead to conflicts.

26.9 COMMON CHARACTERISTICS OF A MENTALLY HEALTHY PERSON

The common characteristics of psychologically healthy individual as given by several psychologists are listed below:

1. Adaptable and resilient
2. Calm
3. Cheerful
4. Conscious control of life
5. Emotionally balanced
6. Definite philosophy of life
7. Enthusiastic and reasonable
8. Independent in thinking
9. Insight into one's own conduct
10. Instincts and habits well regulated
11. Free from prejudice
12. Good tempered
13. Normal sex-consciousness
14. Realistic imagination
15. Satisfied with the work or occupation
16. Socially adaptable.

26.10 DELINQUENCY

Meaning. According to Had field, " Delinquency may be defined as anti-social behaviour. It is primarily a term of social application. It is a failure in social adaptation."

In the words of H.C. Bart, "A child is to be regarded as technically delinquent when his anti-social tendencies appear so grave that he becomes or ought to become the subject of official action."

However, considers delinquency as 'moral deficiency'. Valentine has observed, "Broadly speaking the term delinquency refers to the breaking of some law."

Chief Characteristics of Delinquency

1. Delinquency is deviation from the accepted standards of the culture of a society.
2. Delinquency is the deviation from the laws of the land.
3. The delinquency is deviation detected.
4. Delinquency may result in punishment.

Types of Delinquent Acts

1. Acquisitive tendency resulting in stealing etc.
2. Attitudinal marked by defiance, hostility, etc.
3. Aggressiveness marked by damaging school property, bullying and torturing etc.
4. Forgery leading to forged signatures of the parents on cheques, etc.
5. Sex delinquency.

Causes

(1) Home Environment | (2) Social Environment | (3) School Environment

Home Environment. This includes:

(i) Broken homes and marital misadjustment.
(ii) Crowded families.
(iii) Defective discipline.
(iv) Disability of parents.
(v) Extreme poverty and extreme wealth also.
(vi) Lack of affection.
(vii) Lack of recreation.
(viii) Lack of Moral code.
(ix) Partiality of parents.
(x) Servant's company.
(xi) Sudden accidents or deaths in the family.

School Environment. This includes:

1. Unhealthy physical environment of the school.
2. Unhealthy school surroundings.
3. Defective school organisation.
4. Unsuitable curriculum.
5. Uninspiring methods of instruction.
6. Casual and indifference attitude of the teachers.
7. Unhealthy influence of the peers in the school.

Social Environment. This includes.

1. Social inequalities.
2. Class conflict.
3. Natural calamaties.
4. Corruption at various levels.

Role of the School and the Teacher in Preventing Delinquency

1. The teacher's attitude must be sympathetic. He should appreciated difficulties and help the delinquent to overcome those. He should develop wholesome human relationship.
2. Guided group activities must be started, like group play, group games, scouting, social service, group therapy, etc. This will strengthen their ego and super ego.
3. Special classes must be started for the low achievers.
4. Crafts or skills have been found useful in engaging the less developed mind to proper action.
5. The impulses and emotions of children must be sublimated. Instead of advising them, they should be engaged in activities.

6. Punishments, corporal or otherwise, should not be taken recourse to, as these only create reaction and revolt in the mind of delinquents.
7. Moral and religious teaching in the schools can go a long way in strengthening the super ego of the children. Noble sentiments should be developed.
8. Proper supervision should be done regarding the gangs and their activities in the school and community. Gang-formation leads to unsocial behaviour. On the other hand, self-government should be started in the schools so that their energies are redirected to proper course.
9. The change in the environment also helps certain cases. Children can be removed from bad homes and put in foster homes, from bad schools and admitted into reputed schools.
10. The parents should be educated and they should be appraised of the activities of the child. The parent's attitude must be changes and if the father is made to understand the nature and the cause of the boy's trouble; further dangers can be averted.
11. The teachers should take the help of clinical services in understanding the specific problems.

27

Memory and Forgetting

27.1 SIGNIFICANCE OF MEMORY

There is no doubt that memory is one of the best friends, guides and philosophers of an individual. Memory enables a person to be efficient, both individually and socially. Memory enables us to remember and recall important facts, ideas, names etc. One of the important functions of school instruction is, therefore, to encourage the students develop good and sharp memory to use in school life for the purpose of examination and evaluation etc. and also to meet out-of-school life problems successfully.

27.2 MEANING OF MEMORY

Memory may be defined as the function of the mind by virtue of which it records, retains, and processes ideas gained by its activity.

According to Woodworth, four main elements of memory are: learning (acquisition), retention, recall and recognition.

Learning: It is the process of establishing association of the ideas in mind.

Retention: It is the process of relegation of the past experience in the sub-conscious mind of the individual in the from of a mental experience.

Recall. It is bringing again to mind the past experience on the basis of *association of ideas*.

Recall is of two types: (1) Spontancous and (2) Deliberate. In spontaneous recall we make no effort to recall but the experience or ideas just flow. In deliberate recall, we make an effort to recall something.

Recall is dependent on association of ideas. This association of ideas is dependent on these laws: (*i*) Law of Similarity, (*ii*) Law of Contrast, (*iii*) Law of Contiguity, (*iv*) Law of Regency, (*v*) Law of Frequency, (*v*) Law of Primacy, and (*vii*) Law of Vividness.

Recognition: It is the capacity to recognize or express knowledge of all—seeing a thing that has been seen earlier.

27.3 DEFINITIONS OF MEMORY

Some of the important definitions of memory are given below. These illustrate the various elements involved in memory.

1. James Drever in *Dictionary of Psychology* has defined memory as "The characteristic of living organisms by virtue of what they experience? leaves behind effects which modify future experience and behaviour."

2. Woodworth and Marquis says, "Memory consists in recalling what has been previously learnt."

3. Stout defines memory as the "ideal revival", i.e., to revive the things, objects or experiences in the same order and form.

4. Ross defines memory as "a new experience determined by the disposition laid down by previous experiences and the relation between the two being clearly apprehended."

5. J.A. Adams—Memory is the "learning capacity for responding, and its persistence over time is measured by the retention test. Memory is the state of a subject that gives the capability for correct occurrence of a criterion response. There is an initial acquisition session in which the subject makes a discriminative response to a stimulus, followed by a period of time called the retentional interval when the criterion response does not occur."

27.4 MEMORY SYSTEM

Information from the environment arrives through the senses and is held briefly in a sensory store (the sensory register) of relatively large capacity. Some of this incoming information, once it is identified and categorized, can be passed along to the short-term store and then to the long-term store.

Short-term Store: It is assumed to be a temporary working memory with a quite limited capacity. In a sense, this is a record of the current contents of consciousness.

Long-term Store: It is conceived of as a permanent repository of information. This memory store essentially contains, our knowledge of the world, and its capacity is assumed to be very great. Once material has been transferred to long-term store, there seems to be very little—if any loss of information.

As material is acquired, it presumably passes through the sensory register and into the short-term store. Control process such as rehearsal permits the transfer of this material to long-term store, from which it may be subsequently retrieved. Actually, although not indicated in this diagram, long-term store enters the picture in a number of different ways. First, information from long-term store is necessary to permit pattern recognition and identification of raw sensory information held in the sensory register. Second, information that has been sufficiently rehearsed or organized is thought to be transferred to long-term store. Finally, the very control processes that are assumed to govern the movement of the information through the system must be represented in some way (as rules) in long-term store.

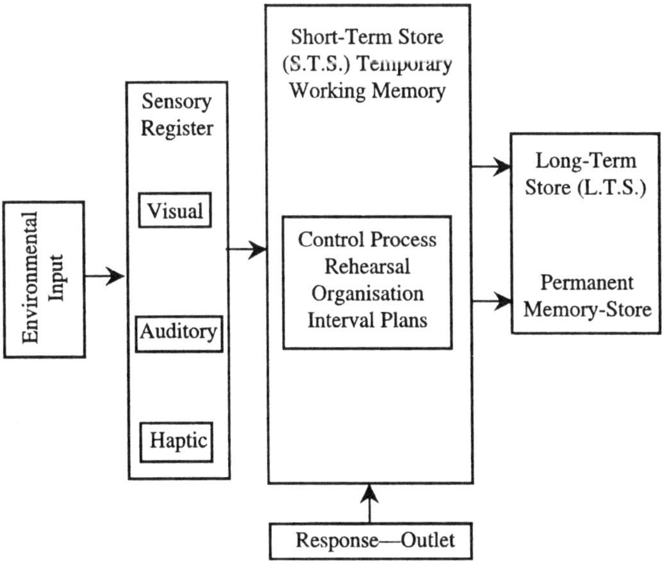

Movement of Information within

Memory System

Fig. 27.1: An Overview of Memory System

27.5 KINDS AND TYPES OF MEMORY

Kinds and Types of Memory: Classification I

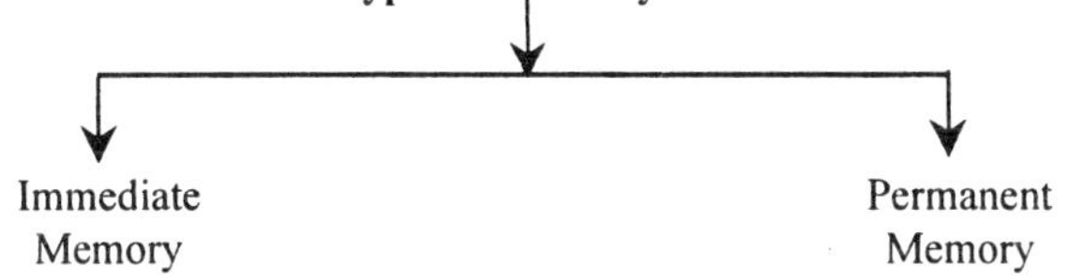

Kinds and Types of Memory: Classification II

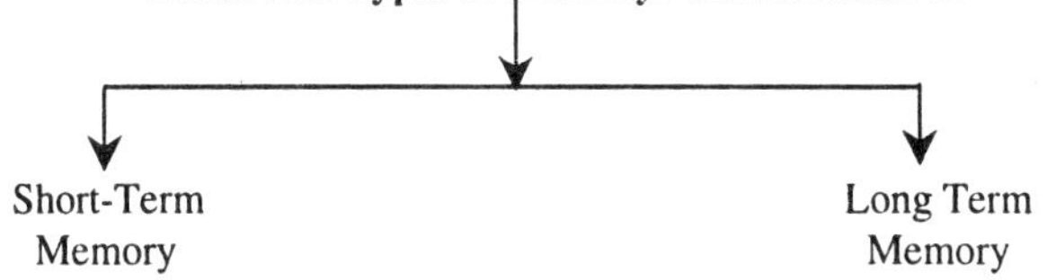

Kinds andTypes of Memory: Classification III

- Personal Memory
- Impersonal Memory

Kinds and Types of Memory: Classification IV

- Active Memory
- Positive Memory

Kinds and Types of Memory: Classification V

- Rote Memory
- Logical Memory

Immediate and Permanent Memory: The span of immediate memory is very wide. An example of immediate memory is memory near the examination. When things or ideas etc. are recalled after sometime, it is called long-term memory or permanent memory. Immediate memory is also called short-term memory (STM) and permanent memory as long- term memory (LTM).

(*ii*) *Personal and Impersonal Memory*: When personal experiences are recalled, it is called personal memory and when dry facts are recalled, it is called impersonal memory.

(*iii*) *Active and Passive Memory*: When effort is made to remember things, it is active memory, and when things come to mind automatically, it is passive memory.

(*iv*) *Rote Memory/Logical Memory*: In rote memory, there is no understanding of things, and when things are learnt by insight, it is logical memory.

27.6 FACTORS CONTRIBUTING TO GOOD MEMORY

Factors Contributing to Good Memory: Classification I

- (1) Factors Relating to the Learner
- (2) Factors Relating to Different Types of Material
- (3) Factors Relating to Retention or Retention as Affected by Original learning

General Factors Contributing to Good Memory: Classification II

(1)	(2)	(3)	(4)
Health of the Learner	Attentiveness of the Learner	Distinct and Vivid Impressions	Repetition Insight

1. Factors in the Learner. These are as under:

(*i*) Age of the learner.
(*ii*) Intelligence of the learner.
(*iii*) Mental state of the learner.
(*iv*) Physical state of the learner.
(*v*) Health of the learner.
(*vi*) Attitude of the learner.

2. Factors Relating to the Subject Matter or Types of Materials to be Learnt

(*i*) Meaningfulness of the material
(*ii*) Pleasantness of the material

3. Factors in Retention or Retention as Affected by Original Learning

(*a*) *Will to remember*—the mental set with which the material is learnt enhances retention. When one is motivated to learn, this leads to better attention and better retention.
(*b*) *Recitation increases* the amount retained.
(*c*) Materials learnt by *distributed practice* are better retained than those learnt by massed practice.
(*d*) *Associations* also help retain better. Most of us remember while learning arithmetic problems of simple fraction. We associate the technique with the word 'BODMAS' and this leads to better retention of the procedure of simplification.
(*e*) Material learnt by the *whole method* is better retained than that learnt by the part method. But relative efficiency of the whole method also depends upon the nature of the material learnt.
(*f*) *Over-learnt* material is better retained. Over-learning is the term applied to learning beyond the stage where the material can be said to have been learnt.

27.7 SIGNS OF GOOD MEMORY

Psychologists identify five signs of good memory.

1. ***Rapidity***: The first sign of good memory is rapidity, *i.e.*, how quickly

the learner recalls his experiences. How little time the learner takes in recalling his experience is denoted by rapidity.

2. *Accuracy*: This implies the exactness with which a past experience is recalled. There may be rapidity in memory but accuracy may be missing. A good memory must possess these elements simultaneously.

3. *Length of Time:* This element denotes the time for which one can retain the past experiences and recalls them accurately. One individual may be able to retain and recall only a small quantity of the experience while another is able to retain and recall a large quantity of the experience. The latter has relatively a good memory.

4. *Quantity of Experience:* Some persons are able to recall whatever they learn while others can recall only a little.

5. *Promptness*: It implies the ease and spontaneity with which experience is recalled.

6. *Serviceableness*: It refers to the recall of right experience at the right time at the right place and in the right manner.

27.8 METHODS OF MEASUREMENT OF RETENTION

Recall Method or Reproduction Method

For instance, the learner may learn a list of 40 words and after 8 hours he is able to recall or reproduce only 20 words. Thus his recall store is 20 out of 40 words or 50 per cent.

Methods of Measurement of Retention

- (1) Recall or Reproduction Method
- (2) Relearning Method
- (3) Recognition Method
- (4) Reconstruction Method

Relearning or Saving Method: In this method we first calculate the number of trials taken to learn the material in the beginning and then note down the saving of trials on relearning it after some lapse of time. For example, if the subject takes 10 trials to recite a whole poem correctly, and only takes 6 trials to master the same after 2 days, his saving score would be:

$$\frac{10-6}{10}=\frac{4}{10} \text{ or } 40\%$$

Recognition Method: In a typical recognition test, the learner's ability to recognize items he has just studied is tested by showing him the study items together with new items and asking the learner to identify the study items.

Method of Reconstruction: In this method, the learner first learns material in a serial order and then the items of the learning material are mixed up and shuffled. Then the learner is required to rearrange the items in their proper sequence.

27.9 GENERAL CHARACTERISTICS OF CHILDREN'S MEMORY AND ADULT'S MEMORY

Children's Memory	*Adult's Memory*
1. Children commit to memory without any logic.	1. Adults have a logical memory. They observe facts intelligently and organize them logically in their mental make up. This makes assimilation of facts possible.
2. Children have a mechanical memory. It is by mechanical repetition that they remember facts.	2. Adults have an understanding memory.
3. Children learn more quickly and retain their impressions in a better way about concrete things.	3. Adults have a better memory of concrete things as well as abstract ideas.
4. Memory of children is short-lived. They are not able to retain it for long.	4. Adults have relatively a long-lived memory.
5. Children's memory is passive.	5. Adults have an active memory.
6. Children recall facts spontaneously. Past experiences are recalled without any effort.	6. They have to make a conscious and deliberate effort to recall facts.

27.10 ECONOMICAL METHODS OF MEMORIZING

Following are the important economical methods of memorizing:

1. *Principle of Association:* The law of association is very helpful in memorization.
2. *Law of Exercise and Intelligent Repetition*: Repetition and its quality affects memorizing. Several psychological experiments have shown that the items repeated more often are remembered longer than those repeated less. However, repetition should be with understanding.
3. *Spaced Repetition*: The material to be committed to memory should be repeated at intervals with periods of rest. This will save the learner from fatigue. Effort-rest-Effort will lead to better memorization.

4. *Use of Progressive Methods of Teaching-Learning*: The project method and the problem method are very helpfu! in making the matter interesting. Students assimilate easily and retain for a longer period.
5. *Use of Modern Technology*: A variety of aids should be used in the teaching-learning process to make the students motivated in the lesson. They help in enhancing the concentration of the students.
6. *Whole or Part Method:* There are two methods of memorizing any content of learning which are known as the *whole method* and the *part method.* We may give an example of a poem which the child wants to memorize.

According to the *whole method* the child may read the whole poem again and again from the beginning to the end and thus memorize it.

According to the *part method*, the poem may be divided into smaller units and the child may try to memorize each part intelligently until the skill related to that learning has been fully acquired.

THE WHOLE METHOD AND PART METHOD

The Whole Method: Advantages

1. The parts are combined into one and give a meaning to the child.
2. If the child has learnt some content material by heart, this method works.

Limitations: This method does not operate if the subject matter for memorization is too long and difficult.

The Part Method: Advantages

1. It works well when the subject matter of learning is short.
2. It gives better results if the learner is young and the subject matter is difficult.

Limitations

1. The structure of the entire poem is not clear to the child till the end of the learning.
2. The child finds it difficult to link the parts of the poem into the whole poem.
3. It is psychologically unsound.

Latest Researches

1. Aveling came to the conclusion that nearly one-fifth of the time of learning can be economized with the wise use of the whole method.
2. Pyne and Syner came to the conclusion that the whole method is more effective when the poem has about 240 lines.

The Part Progressive Method or Mediating Method

A modification of the whole method is suggested which is known as Part Progressive or Mediating Method. The outlines are as follows:

1. The difficult words or phrases may be mastered or understood before hand and then the whole method may be employed.
2. The learner should make a cautious approach while making use of the whole method.
3. The poem may be sub-divided into three units. The child may combine 1 and 2 and later on combine 2 and 3 and finally 1, 2 and 3.

The Recitation Method

Features

1. In this method the learner first reads the matter once or twice and then recites and recalls that matter without looking at the matter.
2. The learner evaluates himself from time to time and notes down those points which he has not been able to recall.
3. Small children really recite their lessons in a sing-song manner with a rhythm.

Advantages of the Method

1. The learner is able to constantly evaluate himself and find out his limitations.
2. This leads to concentrated attention as the weak links in his learning are strengthened.
3. The child is able to find out his own mistakes and thus explores new avenues of further improvement.
4. The learner comes to have a sense of achievement leading to further effort.
5. It saves the efforts of the teacher in the learning process.
6. In case of small children the rhyme and rhythm help to fix up words in the mind and enable the child to enjoy the music. This enjoyment leads to retention and memorization.
7. The subject matter is learnt as is to be used. Little transfer is necessary in the later reproduction.

Spaced and Unspaced Methods of Learning

Spaced or Distributed Method of Learning

In this type of learning the child is not required to memorize the entire subject-matter in one continuous sitting. After learning for some time some rest is given to the child. The principle of '*work and rest*' is followed.

If the child has to memorize a poem, he at the initial stage is advised to go on repeating it for many times. After repetition, he takes rest for some time. After rest the child again repeats the poem and takes rest. In this way with repeated intervals of work and rest he will be able to have mastery over the poem or any other assigned work.

Unspaced or Spaced Method

The child has to memorize the assigned work in one sitting without any interval or rest. The learning goes on continuously without any interruption till it is mastered.

Suggestions: Many experimental studies have been conducted to assess the relative values of these two methods. It has been found that:

1. In short lessons unspaced method of learning may be followed.
2. In giving lessons spaced method of learning should be followed. One suggested modification is that it is better to distribute the hours of work in the sittings of the child and also introduce the periods of rest in between these sittings. This helps in removing the monotony caused by long periods of study. Rest keeps away the fatigue element and the attention also does not flag. The child feels fresh after a period of rest and his interest is kept alive.

Improvement of Development of Memory: suggestion

Memory may be improved by following the techniques as give below:

1. *Law of Exercise and Intelligent Repetition:* Repetition and its quality affects memorizing. Several psychological experiments have shown that the items repeated more often are remembered longer then those repeated less. However, repetition should be with understanding.
2. *Spaced Repetition:* The material to be committed to memory should be repeated at intervals with periods of rest. This will save the learner from fatigue. Effort-rest-effort-will lead to better memorization.
3. *Use of Modern Technology:* A variety of aids should be used in the teaching-learning process to make the students motivated in the lesson. They help in enhancing the concentration of the students.
4. *Use of Progressive Methods of Teaching-Learning:* The project method and the problem method are very helpful in making the matter interesting. Students assimilate easily and retain for a longer period.
5. *Interest:* For proper memorizing, interest in the topic or subject is essential. There is a popular saying 'you can take the horse to water for drinking but you cannot make him drink unless he is interested

in drinking.' Similar is the case with the children.

6. *Motivation in Learning:* Motivation creates interest and produces the right condition for memorization.
7. *Will:* Will to learn a topic or subject enhances interest and motivation, and thereby it leads to better retention.
8. *Association:* The law of association is very helpful in memorization.
9. *Over-learning:* Over-learning implies practice that continues after a perfect recall has been established. Over-learning leads to better retention. However, over-learning should be moderate. Excessive over-learning will lead to boredom. Under-learning hinders retention.
10. *Use of Mnemonics*: Mnemonic devices are useful in retaining several types of material. Through this device, information in the brain is deliberately transformed into meaningful system to improve memory. For instance, aims of education may be memorized with the aid of 7 R's. 7 R's denote Reading, Writing, Arithmetic, Rights, Responsibilities and Recreation.

    Three A's may represent Age, Ability and Aptitude of students while referring to individual differences.

    Four H's may denote four aims of education: Development of Head, Hand, Heart and Health.
11. *Meaningful Organization of the Subject-Matter*: One of the most effective methods to improve memory or retention which teachers can use is the meaningful organization of the subject-matter. Approach should be logical-cum-psychological.
12. *Formation of Clear Concept*: Efforts should be made to improve memory with the help of illustrations, and various types of audio-visual aids.
13. *Principle of Learning by Doing*: Learning experiences acquired through doing are remembered for a longer period.
14. *Overall Classroom Environment*: It includes proper physical conditions and the attitude of the teacher.

Conclusion

1. It is difficult to specify which method is the best one. It may be pointed out that a single method cannot work on all occasions.
2. The abilities of the child also determine the success of the method.
3. The quantum of work also determines the methods to be adopted.
4. Environment also plays an important role in learning.
5. The will of the child determines the efficiency and effectiveness of learning.

Latest Research: Gates conducted an experiment with sixteen non-sense syllables and five short biographical materials accounting for about 170 words. He used two methods: (*a*) Reading and re-reading of the subject-matter by one group of students. (*b*) Another group was asked to follow the recitation method. Gates came to the conclusion that recitation method proved to be better than the reading and re-reading method.

Suggestion: It may be pointed out that the child should devote three-fifths of the period of study to recitation. This method will help both in the immediate and delayed recall.

27.11 FORGETTING

27.12 MEANING OF FORGETTING

Following are a few definitions of forgetting which throw light on the concept of forgetting.

Adams—"True learning is judicious forgetting."

James Drever—"Forgetting means failure at any time to recall an experience when attempting to do so, or to perform an action previously learned."

Nunn—"Forgetting is failing to retain or able to recall what has been acquired."

Munn.—"Forgetting is the loss, permanent or temporary of the ability to recall or recognize something learned earlier."

27.13 NATURE AND CHARACTERISTICS OF FORGETTING

1. Forgetting is a process of fading with the passage of time.
2. Forgetting occurs when memories of the same type interfere with each other.
3. Forgetting is attributed to change in traces in the brain.
4. Forgetting is not losing something but rather is more like being unable to find it.
5. Forgetting is influenced by motivation.
6. Forgetting is caused by lack of proper organization and systematization of the learned material.
7. Forgetting takes place on account of change of stimulating conditions.

Summing up: Forgetting's nature requires more than one explanation.

27.14 CURVES OF FORGETTING

Following two curves based on Ebbinghaus illustrate the amount of forgetting with time to lapse. (Nonsense syllabus—meaningless words like Nof, bdf and cem etc.)

Table 27.1: Time lapsed and percentage of amount forgotten

Time Lapsed	*Percentage of Amount Forgotten*
20 minutes	47%
One day	66%
Two days	72%
Six days	75%
Thirtyone days	79%

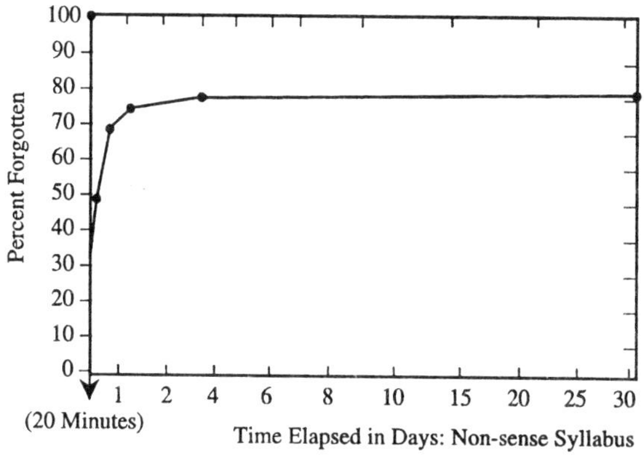

Fig. 27.2: Time Elapsed in Forgetting

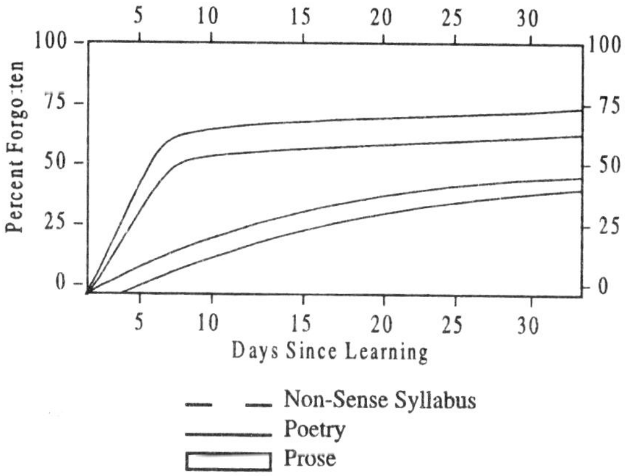

Fig. 27.3: Different Types of Forgetting

27.15 TYPES OF FORGETTING

Types of Forgetting: Classification I

- Natural Forgetting or Passive Forgetting
- Unnatural or Morbid Forgetting or Active Forgetting

Types of Forgetting: Classification II

- General Forgetting
- Specific Forgetting

Types of Forgetting: Classification III

- Physical or Organic Forgetting
- Psychological Forgetting

27.16 CAUSES AND MINIMISING FORGETFULNESS

Causes of Forgetting

1. Lack of interest in work.
2. Disuse of activity.
3. Lapse of time.
4. Lack of integration and synthesis. This may be due to:
   (*i*) Interference of another activity.
   (*ii*) Continued experience of various kinds, all serious in nature.
   (*iii*) No time for rest after serious activity for integration and synthesis.
5. Emotional disturbance.
6. Fatigue.
7. Morbid forgetfulness on account of unpleasant and painful experiences.

Minimising Forgetfulness

1. *Vividness*: Vivid impressions backed by illustrations and aids are better retained.

2. *Organization of the Learning Material*: Material which is properly related and organized is easily retained than the material which is unrelated and disconnected.
3. *Recapitulation and Review*: The lesson or experience needs to be recapitulated or reviewed.
4. *Nature of Learning Material*: Meaningful material is better retained than material which is confusing.
5. *Distributed Learning:* Retention is definitely better if the learning material is spread over suitable sittings.
6. *Over-learning*: Studies have shown that an over-learned lesson is better retained than one barely learned. Of course, *extreme* is always bad.

28

Assessment of Personality

28.1 METHODS OF ASSESSMENT OF PERSONALITY

The methods of assessing personality may be categorized into the following heads:

1. Objective methods or Standarised tests
2. Subjective methods or Non-standerised tests
3. Projective techniques

28.2 OBJECTIVE OR STANDERISED TESTS OR METHODS

These include the following:

1. Achievement Tests
2. Aptitude Tests
3. Intelligence Tests
4. Interest Tests
5. Inventories

28.3 SUBJECTIVE METHODS OR NON-STANDERISED TESTS

These include methods as under:

1. Anecdotal
2. Autobiography
3. Case conference
4. Comulative Records Card
5. Interview
6. Observation
7. Personal Data Blank
8. Questionnaire
9. Rating Scale
10. Schedule
11. Score Card
12. Sociometry

28.4 PROJECTIVE TECHNIQUES

These are as stated below:

1. BG Test
2. Black Picture Test
3. Children Apperception Test (CAT)
4. Clay Modelling
5. Cloud Picture Test
6. Draw-a-man Test
7. Graphology
8. Mosaic Test
9. Psychodrama
10. Rorschach Ink Blot Test
11. Sentence Completion Test
12. Socio-drama
13. Thematic Apperception Test (TAT)
14. Toy and Doll Playing Test
15. Word Association Test

28.5 PROJECTIVE METHODS

1. Meaning

The projective methods are those methods which are designed to penetrate somewhat below the peripherial personality of the subject who unconsciously projects himself and reveals his attitudes and feelings etc. Examples of materials presented to the subject are: making a story, inkblots, drawing a picture, etc. The test material of the projective techniques serves as a sort of screen upon which the subject projects himself.

In the words of Ruth strange, "Projective metchniques are a method of understanding the inner world of the individual."

According to Murray the "purpose of this procedure is to stimulate literacy creativity and thereby evoke factasies that reveal covert and unconscious complexes. The test is based on the well-recognised fact that when a person interprets an ambiguous social situation, he is apt to expose his own personality as much as the phenomenon to which he is attending."

The term 'Projective Technique' was first of all used by L.K. Frank in 1939, although such methods had been in use for many years.

Some examples of projective techniques are given below:

Incomplete Sentence Technique

In this method some incomplete sentences are presented to the child which he completes in anyway he likes. By reading the individual's responses, the counselor records observations which indicate unhealthy or conflicting, positive or healthy attitudes, etc. Stimulus in the form of the following words may be presented to the child.

(i) My best friend............
(ii) Money............
(iii) My father............
(iv) My home............
(v) The world............
(vi) A baby............

The child may complete these sentences in this manner:

(i) My best friend is very poor.
(ii) Money is everything in life.
(iii) My father is very cruel.
(iv) My home is not a good place to live in.
(v) The world is full of cruel people.
(vi) A baby is very lovely.

2. Original Drawing and Paintings

Original drawing and paintings of the children provide an idea of the personality of the child. The theme or subject he chooses, the colour he uses, the masses and the open spaces that the paintings contain, the length, direction, curvature of the lines—all these give an indication of the various traits of the personality of the child.

3. Play Situation

Several dolls are given to the child to play with. These dolls represent a father, a mother, a boy and a girl and provide the medium through which the child might act out or reveal his thoughts, impulses and feelings about himself and others. Situation should be such as to give a free play to his ideas at the unconscious level. Controlled play techniques are also used.

In a free play a boy who happens to be jealous of his sister might assign the role of the sister to the baby doll and cause it punished by the father doll or mother doll, or shut the baby doll to a far corner of the room. This will indicate that the girl is preferred to him in the family.

A great variety of material may be used in play situations.

4. Rorschach Ink Blot Test

Rorschach was a Swiss psychologist who experimented with the use of ink blots as a means of diagnosing mental disorders. He experienced for years together with thousands of inkblots and ultimately selected ten ink blots which proved to have the maximum diagnostic value. These are ten ink blots, five in black and white, two with splashes of red and three in colours. They are printed on 7×9½ inch cards, is asked to tell what he sees in the ink blots, what that means to him and what that might be. The counselor notes whatever the subject says. Then the counselor shows the cards a second time and elicits answers through well-worded questions. Special techniques have been designed for recording the responses of the subject.

Important uses of this technique are:

(1) This is helpful to distinguish between 'normal' persons and persons in need of psychiatric treatment.
(2) This is helpful to show the potential intelligence of an individual.
(3) This helpful to predict and plan for academic success and adjustment in college.
(4) This is helpful in indicating personality tendencies significant for vocational success.

5. Thematic Apperception Test (TAT)

The test designed by Morgan and Murray in 1935 involves a systematic use of pictures representing a number of dramatic events. The pictures are shown to the child who identifies himself with some picture. The picture presents a stimulus to the child to talk freely. The child makes interpretations in accordance with his own past experiences and present interpretations in accordance with his own past experience and present needs and attitudes. In the words of Ruth Strang, "To some extent, he reads into the pictures his own experiencesμthe responses made in the test situation also reveal the person's attitudes and ways of thinking in life situations."

The pictures selected have the following characteristics:

1. No detail is provided in the background so that this may not limit the picture to a certain time or place.
2. The theme of these pictures is vague.

3. The action and expression of the characters in the pictures are not very clear and are rather vague and ambiguous.
4. The contents of the pictures do not give the whole story. They are incomplete.
5. Nome and social situations relate to the ordinary situations of life.
6. Characters in the pictures are such as the child can very easily identify himself.

The test can be employed suitably to persons over four years of age whose intelligence quotient is not lower than 80. The counselor shows one or more of the pictures and puts questions like these. What does the picture mean to you? What can be the factors that have led to that situation? What will be the outcome?

In interpreting pictures, it is important to note only turn of the thoughts the child injects into the situation, but also his mood.

Story-telling and Story Completion. An incomplete story may be told to the child and he may be asked to complete it. While completing the story, the child may reveal something about his feelings and desires. He may be asked to let his imagination go to show how imaginative he is. The situation selected should be such as touches the emotional life of the child whose personality traits we wish to assess. For instance, the child is asked to relate a story about an innocent child who was beaten by his father. The child is likely to depict his innermost feelings, wishes and thoughts while he narrates the story. Take another case when a child is told about the beginning of a story. Father is ready to take the children to the Exhibition. All of a sudden a guest comes. The child may be asked to complete the story. As the child finishes the story, the psychologist comes to know the personality traits of the child.

This method is usually employed in the case of delinquent children.

Merits of Projective Methods

1. The child reveals himself in various situations and sometimes he is not aware of this fact. Thus we get reliable information.
2. These encourage spontaneous responses.
3. It is not possible for the individual to give readymade, habitual or conventional responses as the tasks presented are novel and unstructured.
4. The connection between diagnosis and the situation is very close.
5. It is possible to have a total view of the personality of an individual, rather than in piece-meal.

Limitations

From the point of view of the school counselor, the projective techniques have certain limitations.

One. They are very subjective.

Two. They require a lot of training in their administration. Only trained psychologists can administer them.

Three. They are time-consuming.

Four. They are very difficult to interpret.

Five. There are very few such techniques standardised.

(See also chapter 2)

29

Statistics: Meaning and Uses
Tabulation of Data Central Concepts

29.1 NEED AND IMPORTANCE OF STATISTICS IN EDUCATION

In the modern world, our work culture in different fields, to a great extent, has become a 'statistical culture'. Even on the elementary level, it is very difficult to understand several disciplines including education without some general idea of statistics. A knowledge of elementary statistics, thus, is an essential part of the training of teachers at various levels.

The current research on education and allied disciplines needs for its understanding, a sound statistical base. At the advanced level of education, the student is required to design research investigations and any design of research is inseparable from statistical treatment of data.

Statistical methods are extensively used in the field of education and psychological testing. There is a varied and wide application of it, to the measures of ability, personality, attitudes, interests, and any other aspects of the human behaviours in modern education.

Talking in numbers always carries conviction. Telling the child's mental age (MA) or calculating his IQ is a modern device and with the help of this figure we measure and denote the child's mental ability. The main business of statistics is to provide us with the greatest possible information about everyday facts in the briefest possible manner. Standardized tests would not have been possible without the tool of statistics for finding out the relationship between scores in the test with some other previously known scores of judgements. Standardization of the test materials and its results would not have been possible without the help of statistics. Validity and reliability of test could be fixed only with the help of different statistical formulae. Statistical method of factor-analysis of intelligence is a very well-known device.

The chief concern of the teacher is with the general ability of the class, and the special abilities of the individuals, as well as the inter-relationships of these abilities. The teacher is sometimes interested in comparing one group with another. Thus a teacher is called upon to deal with the masses of quantative data collected from the scores in standardized tests and ordinary examinations and from other school records. All these data need *organisation, condensation and analysis,* otherwise, they would yield nothing specific. It is thus clear that mental test is of little significance to the teacher unless it employs statistical devices. *Statistical methods* are especially adopted to the evaluation of quantitative data affected by a multiplicity of causes. *Statistics gives us a technique to obtain, condense, analyse and relate numerical data.* Statistical methods are of a supreme value in education and psychology.

Educational statistics and especially standardized tests help the educator/teacher in the following ways:

(i) to know individual differences of students.
(ii) to compare the results of one system of evaluation with the other.
(iii) to provide guidance to the students.
(iv) to compare the working of educational institutions.
(v) to group students in different grades.
(vi) to compare the suitability of one method or technique with the other.
(vii) to make prediction regarding the future progress of the students.
(viii) to make selection, classification and promotion of the students.
(ix) to prepare educational plans at various levels.
(x) to coordinate education policy with the manpower planning.

29.2 GENERAL STATISTICAL TERMS USED IN EDUCATION

Population and Sample: Here population refers to an aggregate or group of people in particular setting. For example, we are studying the 'Study Habits of Tenth Grade Students in Delhi'. Now for this investigation we are not likely to take all the students studying in the tenth grade in all the schools of Delhi for our study, instead we would take only a limited number of cases representative of the total group and base our findings on that group (limited) for drawing inferences about the total group. All the students in the tenth grade studying in all the schools of Delhi, in this case would comprise the population, whereas a limited representative section of the total lot would constitute the sample.

Measurement: We can define measurement as assigning numbers according to some rule. There are two main purposes of all measurement. Firstly to know the magnitude or quantity of the trait or thing possessed and secondly to compare the quantities possessed. To measure the things we need a scale that is, the rule according to which we assign numbers. All the things cannot be measured on the same type of scale. We have, therefore, been following four types of scales of measurement.

Score: Score or other numbers in a continuous series are considered as distances along a continuum or a line rather than as separate points. A centimetre is the distance between two divisions on a metric rod. Similarly a score on a mental test is a unit distance between two limits. A score of 100 on an achievement test represents an interval from 99.5 to 100.5. The following illustration will clarify the point:

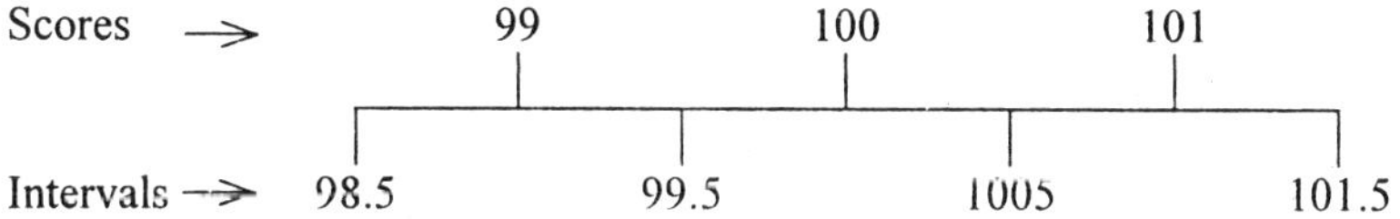

In the above example 99, 100, and 101 are the scores. Half the distance on either side is the lower and upper limit of the score. In other words from 98.5 to

99.5 or from 99.5 to 100.5 is the distance and the mid-point of this distance is the score. Other scores are also interpreted in the same way. A score of 17 includes all values from 16.5 to 17.5 and a score of 160 includes all values from 159.5 to 160.5. The usual mathematical meaning of a score is, therefore, an interval which extends from 0.5 units below and above the face value of the score. These 0.5 lower and 0.5 upper values of the score are called lower and upper limits of the score. The lower and upper limits of 25 are 24.5 and 25.5 respectively.

Scale and Series: When *scores* are expressed in equal units, they constitute a scale. Scores are usually obtained in terms of time taken to complete a task, or amount done in a given time. "Scale tests in psychology and education have equal units or steps but do not possess an absolute zero point." When measures of a similar type are compiled, it is known as a *series,* and when compilations are arranged in order of size, they are termed as *ordered* or a *rank series.* When a ranked series presents measures which increase or decrease by steps of even amounts, it is known as a scale; *viz.,* 2, 4, 6, 8, etc.

Continuous and Discrete Series: Quantitative data are expressed in two kinds of series: (i) the *continuous* series, and (ii) *The discontinuous or discrete* series. The series which exhibits real gaps are called discrete or discontinuous, such as 12, 14 are not represented as 12.3, 14.6, etc. Physical measures, such as height, weight, score from mental tests, etc. fall into continuous series. In psycho'ogy and education we usually deal with continuous series as 5′-3′′ to 5′-4′′ etc.

Mid-Point: In statistics practically all test scores are treated by measures falling at the *mid-point.* Thus the score of 28 in a test is the mid-point of the *interval* 27.5 to 28.8 or 27.5-28.5. Recording of ages is also followed by a method. If a child has passed his eighth birthday, in real statistical terms he is considered 8 1/2 years old or halfway between 8 and 9. A child would be called 8 years old whose age is now nearer to 8 than to either 7 or 9, the age being taken to the nearest birthday.

Group Interval or Class Interval: A *group interval* or *class-interval* is one in which two or more adjacent measures are placed together. The ages of pupils of 5(4.5-5.4), 6(5.5-6.4), and 7(6.5-7.4) may be grouped into one interval or class 4.5-7.4 having a value at the mid-point, or 6, and pupils falling in this group are thought of as being roughly 6 years of age. This assumption is no doubt not true, but when there is a large number of cases such errors tend to neutralize one another, and the resulting compilation may be said to be fairly accurate. But the point about fixing the class interval or the class-limits seems to be a matter of a great controversy. Class-interval can be as 0 to 10; 10 to 20, 20 to 30; and so on. As stated above, the class interval is denoted by the mid-point of the interval instead of the whole range. Thus the class interval is stated as 24, 35, 45 instead of 20 to 30, 30 to 40, etc. We can put each score in this interval or class. A still better method is of selecting the class-intervals as 10 and onwards but less than 20; 20 onwards but less than 30, etc.; and they are written as 10-; 20-; 30-; etc. A better method than this is to designate the class-interval as 09.9′; 10-19.9′; 20-20.9′; 30-39.9′; etc. Here by 9.9′ we mean

9.9999... *i.e.*, a number almost equal to 10 but not exactly equal to 10. We shall follow all these methods in computing the scores in the course of our description. The size of the class or interval may vary. In the above case it is 10 and in the earlier case above it was 8. Any convenient size may be selected by the computator.

Frequency Table: The *frequency table* is a table indicating the distribution of measures in a body of data. It shows how many times each of the measures occurs. The measures are arranged in a scale and they may be in terms either of *unit intervals* or *group intervals*. This is also called tabulation of data.

Meaning of Statistical Analysis in Education

Analysis is the process of considering something carefully and in details in order to understand or explain it. In simple words, statistical analysis in education is the process of considering numbers carefully in details to understand their occurrence, their behaviour, their impact and their significance. Statistical analysis occupies an important place in the sphere of social sciences including education. It has become an important tool in educational planning. In the age of computers and information technology (IT), quantitative analysis has acquired such a great significance that on several occasions it becomes extremely difficult to take educational decisions without its help.

Presentation and Tabulation of Data

Presentation of data implies the process by which classified data are presented in some understandable form. Presentation of data is done primarily for the purpose of a quick grasp of data. It helps in further statistical treatment and analysis. The act of presenting a statistical table is called tabulation. Tabulation gives the desired shape and structure to data. A table can be defined as the systematic arrangement of statistical data in columns and rows. Columns are vertical arrangements, while rows are horizontal arrangements of the statistical data.

Tabulation serves the following purposes:

1. It simplifies data by eliminating unnecessary data.
2. It gives a definite shape to data by arranging it in neat rows and columns.
3. It helps in illustrating relationships. Comparisons can be made with great ease. Totals and sub-totals of various groups and sub-group help in making quick comparisons.
4. It helps in understanding the characteristics of data at a glance.
5. Tabulation gives identity to the data and it can be used as a source of reference at a glance.

29.3 FREQUENCY DISTRIBUTION AND GRAPHIC PRESENTATION OF DATA

Meaning of Graphic Representation: A table condenses a mass of data into an understandable form but it may still fail to convey the result of the enquiry or research fully. Thus to aid presentation of data, graphics are used. A graph can be broadly defined as the depiction of inter-related data on a graph paper. Graphic representation of data, thus can be described as a pictorial representation of statistical data. Graphic representation conveys facts in pictures and highlights the most important features of the data.

Advantages of Graphic Representation: Graphic representation often facilitates understanding of a set of data. If the graph is well drawn, it is usually easier to read and interpret than the table. Graphs are useful in visualizing the important properties of frequency distributions and are of great help in enabling us to comprehend the features of frequency distributions and in comparing one frequency distribution with another.

Methods of Graphic Representation: (i) Histograms; (ii) Frequency polygons; (iii) Cumulative frequency polygon or Ogive; and (iv) Cumulative percentage or polygon.

Histogram

A histogram is a graph in which class intervals are represented along horizontal axis called X-axis and their corresponding frequencies are represented by areas in the form of rectangular bars drawn on the intervals.

To prepare a histogram, we proceed as follows:

Step 1: Draw a horizontal line at the bottom of graph paper along which mark off units to represent the class intervals. It is usual to start with the class interval of lowest value.

Step 2: Draw a vertical line through the extreme end of the horizontal axis along which mark off units to represent the frequencies of the class intervals.

Step 3: Draw rectangles with class interval's units as base, such that the areas of the rectangles are proportional to the frequencies of the corresponding class intervals. If all class intervals are of the same size, the heights of the rectangles will be proportional to respective frequencies.

Preparation of Histogram from the data given below.

Class Interval	Frequency (f)
95-99	1
90-94	2
85-89	4
80-84	5
75-79	8
70-74	10
65-69	6
60-64	4
55-59	4
50-54	2
45-49	3
40-44	1

The histogram of the given data is shown in Fig. 29.1

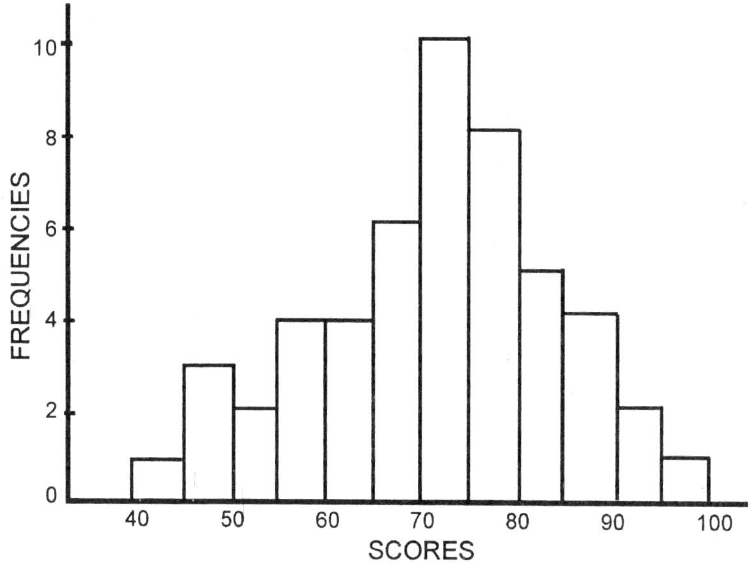

Fig. 29.1: Histogram

Frequency Polygon

Another method of representing a frequency distribution graphically is what is known as the frequency polygon. This is the most common form of representing a frequency distribution. The steps to draw a frequency polygon are as follows:

Step 1: Same as for histogram.

Step 2: Same as for histogram.

Step 3: Directly above the point on the horizontal axis representing the mid-point of each class interval of each individual score, plot a point at a height proportional to the frequencies. Join three points by straight lincs. The frequency polygon for the given distribution is shown in Fig. 29.2

If the points plotted for the frequency polygon are joined free hand, we get a curve, which is known as frequency curve.

Cumulative Frequency Polygon

Cumulative Frequency Polygon differs from frequency polygon in two respects.

First, instead of plotting points corresponding to frequencies, we plot points corresponding to cumulative frequencies. Second, instead of plotting points above the mid-points of each class interval, we plot points above the exact upper limit of the interval. This is done because in this graph we wish to represent the number of cases falling above or below particular values. For understanding the methods of drawing this graph, let us consider the distribution given above.

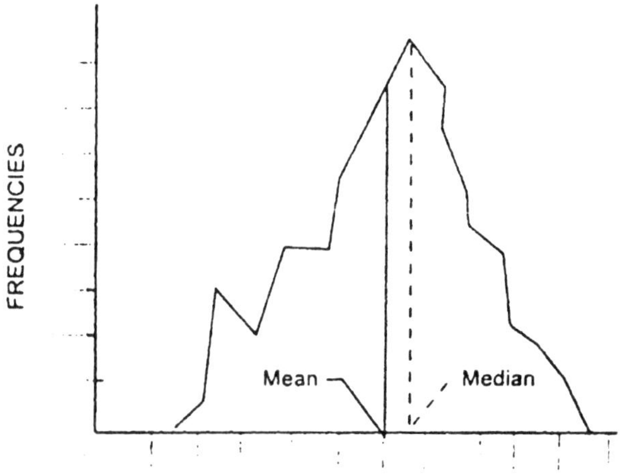

Fig. 29.2: Frequency Polygon

As illustrated in the column 5 of the Table, the first cumulative frequency from the low end of the distribution (of interval 40-44) is 1, the next cumulative frequency (of interval 45-49) is 4 and so on. The last cumulative frequency is equal to 50, or N, the total frequency.

In the above frequency distribution we had recorded our observations in discrete form. In interval 40-44 we graphed all measurements taking the values 40,41,42,43 and 44. The limits of the lower value *i.e.,* of 40 are 39.5 and 40.5 while those of the upper value are 43.5 and 44.5. The total range or exact limits which the interval is presumed to cover is clearly 39.5 and 44.5. Similarly exact limits of the interval 45-49 are 44.5 and 49.5, of 50-54 are 49.5 and 54.5....so on.

For drawing cumulative frequency polygon each cumulative frequency is plotted corresponding to the exact upper limit of the interval. For the distribution first value of F (cumulative frequency) corresponding to 44.5 is 1: the second value of F corresponding to 49.2 is 4; the third value of F corresponding to 54.5 is 6 and so on to the last point for which value of F corresponding to 99.5 is 50.

Now if we join the plotted points by straight lines we get cumulative frequency polygon and if we join the plotted points by free hand curve we get cumulative frequency curve.

In order to have the curve begin on the x-axis it is started at the exact lower limit of the lowest class (39.5 in the above case) the cumulative frequency of which is 0.

The cumulative frequency curve of the above mentioned distribution is drawn in Fig. 29.3

Cumulative Percentage Polygon or Ogive

If the frequencies in the cumulative frequencies table are expressed as percentages of the total frequency N, (as in col. 6 of the table above), the table is somewhat easier to interpret.

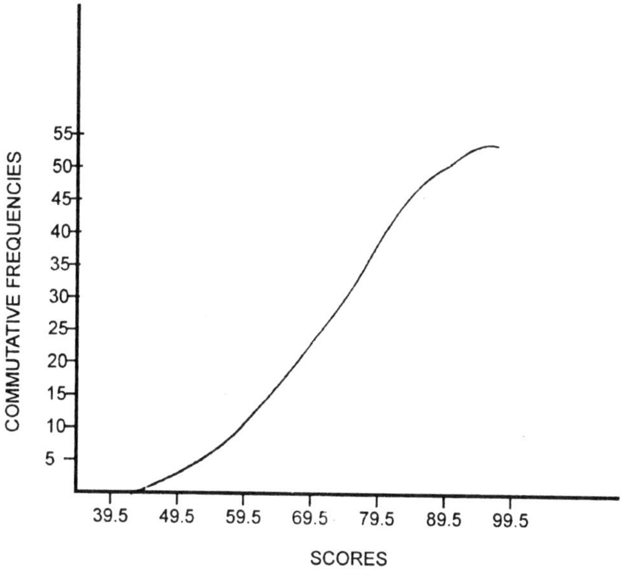

Fig. 29.3: Cumulative Frequency Curve

After finding cumulative percentage frequencies we may then plot these frequencies corresponding to upper exact limits of class intervals. A curve joining the points, thus obtained is called cumulative percentage polygon or Ogive. The advantage of Ogive is that from it, we can read off directly the percentage of observation less than or greater than any specified value. It is particularly useful in determining the norms.

Difference between Histogram and Frequency Polygon

Histogram	*Frequency Polygon*
1. Histogram is essentially the bar graph of the given frequency distribution.	1. The frequency distribution is shown by a line graph.
2. Histogram provides an accurate and clear picture of the relationship of frequency from interval to interval.	2. Frequency simply points out the graphical relationship between mid-points and frequencies. It does not show the distribution of frequencies within each class interval.
3. Relatively it does not give a better conception of the contour of distribution.	3. Relatively polygon gives a much better conception of the contour of the distribution.

30

Central Tendency: Mean, Median and Modes. Uses

Averages: Measures of Central Tendency

Meaning of Average: When a large number of scores are given, we cannot make anything out of them or reach any conclusion. Suppose we have thirty scores in respect of 30 students in one section and also thirty scores in respect of 30 students in the other section of the class. We want to compare in a general way the achievement level of two sections of the class. Data can be condensed into one single value which may have the characteristics of the whole data. Such a single value is known as 'average' or the central tendency. The term average means the most typical or the most representative value for a group of numbers. It means a value that lies somewhere between the two extremes—the highest and the lowest, the greatest and the smallest, the tallest and the shortest and so on. That is why an average is also called a measure of central tendency.

Nature of an Average: Average is a value which may be repeated the greatest number of times in a distribution, or it may lie exactly in the middle of a distribution, or it may be some other value based on more sophisticated methods of calculator. Whatever be an average, it stands for a 'representative' value possessing the characteristics of distribution.

Objects of an Average: (i) To get one 'single value' which represents the characteristics of the entire data.

(ii) To facilitate 'comparison' for analysis.

Characteristics of Good Average (i) It must be 'simple' to understand.

(ii) It must be 'easy to calculate'.

(iii) It must be 'well-defined'.

(iv) It must not be 'influenced by extreme values'.

(v) It must be 'based on all the items of the distribution.'

(vi) It must have the 'sampling stability'.

(vii) It must be capable of further algebraic treatment.

Different Types of Averages

(1) *Average Mean*
(a) Simple
(b) Weighted mean

(2) *Median*

(3) *Mode*

(4) *Geometric Mean*

(5) *Harmonic Mean*

Deviation

Items within a group differ in size from one another. There is a lack of uniformity in their magnitudes. This scatter or spread is known as dispersion. Various scores scatter below and above the averages. If the difference between scores are slight, we say that dispersion is not much. The case may also be just otherwise. The mean of two groups in some attribute may be the same, but their dispersion may be different. For example, the scores of two groups of students may be as follows:

Group A	*Group B*
38, 32, 40, 52, 42	36, 32, 36, 44, 36
24, 32, 36, 22, 100	20, 30, 40, 50, 38
12, 4, 10, 80, 16	54, 32, 34, 28, 30

In both these groups, the number of students is 15 and total number of scores is 540 for each group. Thus the average for each group is 36, But in the first group, the difference in the score between the highest and the lowest group is 100 – 4 = 96, while in the second group it is 54 – 20 = 34 only. The variability of the two groups is obviously different.

The variation can be determined by one of the four procedures:

1. The Range
2. The Quartile Deviation (Q)
3. The Mean Deviation (M.O.)
4. The Standard Deviation (SD or σ)

30.1 MEAN AND ITS USES

Definition and Meaning of Mean: The mean may be defined as the sum of the values in a series divided by the number or items of the series. Using $X1$, $X2$, $X3$,. ... XN to represent N items the definition may be written as:

$$M = \frac{X1 + X2 + X3 + \ldots XN}{N}$$

In brief it can be written as

$M = \Sigma X/N$ where Σ stands for sum of the values of the items and N for the number of items.

Calculation of Mean from an Ungrouped Data: It is easy to calculate mean for short series of an ungrouped data, For example 8 students scored 10, 16, 17, 22, 26, 24, 26 and 11 marks, in an arithmetic test. Here N is 8 and ΣX is equal to 10+16+17+22+26+24+26+11 = 152

Now applying Formula $M = \frac{\Sigma X}{N}$

$$= \frac{152}{8}$$

$$= 19$$

Calculation of Mean from Grouped Data: There are two methods for computing mean from the grouped data:

(1) Long Method (2) Short Method

Long Method

Class Interval	*f*	*x*	*fx*
60-64	2	62	124
55-59	4	57	228
50-54	7	52	364
45-49	5	47	235
40-44	9	42	378
35-39	7	37	254
30-34	6	32	192
	$N = 40$		$\Sigma fx = 1780$

$$\text{Mean} = \frac{\Sigma fx}{N}$$

$$= \frac{1780}{40}$$

$$= 44.5$$

Short-Cut Method for Calculating Mean: The above method of calculating the mean involves considerable work of addition when the series is large and each number has several digits. For saving time and labour the short-cut method is used. To use this method, midpoint of any class interval is taken as assumed mean and deviations in terms of class intervals are found from this interval of assumed mean. Proper algebraic signs are put down with the deviation. Algebraic sum multiplied by class interval is divided by the number of cases. When this is added to assumed mean, it gives the required mean.

Symbolically $M = AM + \dfrac{\Sigma fd}{N} \times i$

where AM = assumed mean.

Σ stands for sum of.

d is the deviation in terms of class intervals from the interval in which the AM lies.

i = size of class interval.

$N = \Sigma f$ = Total number of cases.

Calculation of Mean by this method from the above data is as follows:

Score (Class Interval)	*f*	*d*	*fd*	
60-64	2	3	6	
55-59	4	2	8	
50-54	7	1	7	= 21
45-49	5	0	0	
40-44	9	–1	–9	
35-39	7	–2	–14	
30-34	6	–3	–18	= –41

Now according to formula $M = AM + \frac{\Sigma fd}{N} \times i$

$$M = 47 + \frac{-20}{40} \times 5$$

$$- 47 + (-2.5)$$

$$= 44.5$$

Uses/Advantages of Mean

1. Its meaning is easily understood.
2. It is easy to calculate.
3. It uses the entire data in the group.
4. It is amenable to algebraic manipulation.
5. It can be located definitely.
6. It best conveys the idea of mean or average values.
7. It is derived by the exact scores of values in the series.
8. It gives weight to all scores, whether extreme or not.
9. Combined mean can be obtained if the mean of constituent units is known.

Disadvantages/Limitations

1. It cannot be used with advantage in the extreme scores.
2. It can hardly be located by inspection while the median and mode can be located.
3. It can mislead in the absence of actual data.
4. Abnormal differences between the highest and the lowest values would lead to fallacious conclusions.

30.2 MODE AND ITS USES

Meaning of Mode: Mode may be defined as the value which occurs most frequently in a series. In other words, it is a value which has the greatest frequency in a distribution. For example, the marks of 10 students in a subject are: 20, 21, 21, 23, 23, 23, 23, 25, 26, 26. Here mode or modal value is 23. Thus it can be determined by mere inspection of frequencies.

Calculation of Mode

(a) When Mean and Median of the distribution are known, it can be calculated as:

Mode = 3 Median – 2 Mean

In a particular distribution if Mdn = 25.5 and Mean = 26; then

Mode = 3 × 25.5 – 2 × 26

or 76.5 – 52

or 24.5

In an ideal distribution (Normal distribution), Mean, Median and Mode, all the three have same value.

(b) Mode can also be calculated by the formula:

$$\text{Mode} = l + \left(\frac{fx}{fx + fx'}\right) \times s$$

In which l = lower limit of the class interval having the highest frequency.
fx = frequencies of the class interval above it.
fx' = frequencies of the class interval below it.
s = size of the class interval.
Example:

Scores & Class interval	*f*
45-49	2
40-44	3
35-39	5
30-34	9
25-29	6
20-24	4
15-19	1

$$\text{Mode} = l + \left(\frac{fx}{fx + fx'}\right) \times s$$

$$= 29.5 + \frac{5}{5+6} \times 5$$

$$= 29.5 + \frac{5}{11} \times 5$$

$$= 29.5 + \frac{25}{11} = 29.5 + 2.27$$

$$= 31.77$$

Merits of Mode

1. It can easily be located by mere inspection.
2. It eliminates extreme variations.
3. It can be determined even when the distribution is open-ended as knowledge of extreme items is not necessary.
4. For the determination of mode, it is not necessary to know the values of all the items of a series.
5. It is very easily understood.
6. To the ordinary mind, it appears the best means to represent the group.

Limitations/Shortcomings

1. It is not reliable in small samples . For example, if model marks of 40 students is 80, but 35 out of them get different marks, the mode is very unreal and gives a false picture.
2. It is not amenable to algebraic treatment.
3. In several cases, no single well-defined mode exists.
4. It is not based on all the observations of a series.

30.3 MEDIAN AND ITS USES

Meaning of Median: Median is the item in the series above and below which lie 50 per cent cases or it is the mid-point of an arranged series of scores, above and below which lie the 50% scores.

Calculation of Median in an Ungrouped Data: If the number of scores are arranged in ascending or descending order, the middle score will be the median of the series. When the number of scores is even, then the median is calculated by the following formula.

$$\left(\frac{N+1}{2}\right)\text{th item}$$

For example, the median of 17, 18, 21, 24, 26 and 29 will be

$$= \left(\frac{6+1}{2}\right)\text{th item}$$

$$= \frac{7}{2}$$

$$= 3.5\text{th item (mid point of 21 and 24)}$$

i.e. $$= \frac{21+24}{2}$$

$$= \frac{45}{2}$$

Median $= 22.5$

Calculation of Median in Grouped Data: In the case of grouped data the median has to be interpolated in the class interval having the median. It is done on the assumption that the magnitude or the median class interval is uniformly spread over its frequency.

Example:

Scores	*f*	*cf*
91-100	9	368
81-90	44	359
71-80	83	315
61-70	88	232
51-60	72	144
41-50	49	72
31-40	18	23
21-30	4	5
11-20	1	1

$$\text{Mdn} = \text{size of } \frac{N}{2}\text{th item}$$

$$N = 368$$

$$\frac{N}{2} = \frac{368}{2} = 184\text{th item}$$

Item 184th is located in the class-interval 61-70 scores. This is called median class. Since we do not know the value of each item in the class, we have to interpolate the median in the class 61-70. The frequency for this group is 88 and magnitude is 10. It is assumed that 10 marks are evenly distributed over 88 students. 144 students get marks upto 60.5. Therefore 184th student should get 10/88 (184–144) or 10/88 × 40 = 50/11 = 4.55 or 4.6 marks more than the 144th student. Hence the size of the 184th item in the series, that is median, is 60.5+4.6 = 65.1.

The above can symbolically be written as

$$\text{Mdn} = l_1 + \left(\frac{l_2 - l_1}{f_1}\right)\left(\frac{N}{2} - C\right) \text{ where}$$

Mdn stands for median; l_1 for the lower unit of same class interval in which median stands; l_2 is the upper limit of the same class interval; f_1 the frequency of median class; C the cumulative frequency of the group lower than the one in which median lies.

Applying the formula we have

$$\text{Mdn} = 60.5 = \left(\frac{70.5 - 60.5}{88}\right)(184 - 144)$$

$$= 60.5 + \frac{10}{88} \times 40$$

$$= 60.5 + \frac{50}{11}$$

$$= 60.5 + 4.6 = 65.1$$

If all the class intervals of the frequency distribution are equal the formula is further simplified as

$$\text{Mdn} = l + \frac{\left(\frac{N}{2} - C\right)}{f_1} \times i$$

Where l is the lower limit of the interval in which median lies, f_1 is the frequency of the median class, N = total number of cases in the distribution, C is the cumulative frequency upto median class and i is the size of the class interval, thus in the above case

$$\text{Mdn} = 60.5 \frac{\left(\frac{368}{2} - 144\right)}{88} \times 10$$

$$= 60.5 = \frac{40}{88} \times 10$$

$$= 60.5 + 4.6$$

$$= 65.1$$

Advantages of Median

1. It is rigidly defined. Therefore, it is an ideal average.
2. It is not influenced by extreme variation.
3. It is very useful when the series contain some extreme cases. In that case, it is the most representative measure of central tendency.
4. It is easily understood and determined. It can be located with great exactness than mode.
5. It can be determined without the knowledge of the magnitude of the extreme item provided the number of items is known.

Limitations/Shortcomings

1. The arrangement of items in the ascending or descending order is sometimes very tedious.
2. We cannot get the total of scores by multiplying the median by N.
3. It is non-algebraic measure.
4. It is not useful in those situations where it is desirable to give large weights to extreme cases.
5. It is not determined by the simple arithmetic process as the mean. It is, therefore, less dependable and cannot be used in higher statistical calculations or inferences such as S.D. or co-efficient of correlation.
6. When there are wide variation between the values of different items, median may not be the representative of the series.

30.4 RELATIVE USE OF MEAN, MEDIAN AND MODE: WHEN TO USE THE MEAN, MEDIAN AND MODE

When to use the Mean

1. Mean is computed for the given data when a reliable and accurate measure of central tendency is needed.
2. Mean is used for the computation of various statistics like Standard Deviation and Co-efficient of Correlation etc.
3. Mean is calculated when the series has no extreme items and each score carries equal weight in determining the central tendency.

When to use the Median

1. We use median when the exact mid-point of the distribution is desired.
2. Mean is computed when a series contains extreme scores.
3. Median is the most reliable measure in case of an open end distribution (incomplete distribution 80 and above or 20 and below etc.)
4. Median is computed when we have suitable graphs like frequency curve, polygon etc.

When to use the Mode

1. Mode is computed where quick and approximate measure of central tendency is desired.
2. Mode is calculated when we need to know the most often recurring score or value of the item in a series.
3. Mode is computed when we have a graphical representation of the distribution.

30.5 SOLVED EXAMPLES OF MEAN, MEDIAN AND MODE

Examples 1: Calculate the Mean, Median and Mode of the following distribution:

Class Interval	*Frequency*
95-99	1
90-94	6
85-89	8
80-84	33
75-79	40
70-74	50
65-69	26
60-64	14
55-59	10
50-54	6
45-49	4
40-44	2

Ans. *Calculation of Mean, Median and Mode.*

Class Interval	*f*	*d*	*fd*	
95-99	1	5	5	
90-94	6	4	24	
85-89	8	3	24	
80-84	33	2	66	
75-79	40	1	40	= +159
70-74	50	0		
65-69	26	−1	−26	
60-64	14	−2	−28	
55-59	10	−3	−30	
50-54	6	−4	−24	
45-49	4	−5	−20	
40-44	2	−6	−12	= −140
	200		Σfd	= 19

Let the assumed mean (*A.M.*) be 72 i.e. midpoint of class interval 70-74

$$M = A.M. + \frac{\Sigma fd}{N} \times i$$

$$= 72 + \frac{19 \times 5}{200} = 72 = 0.475$$

$$= 72.475 \text{ or } 72.5$$

Mean = 72.5

(Note: we can take the A.M. in any class interval.)

Calculation for Median

We have already worked out the cumulative frequencies for this purpose.

$$\text{Median} = l - \frac{\left(\frac{N}{2} - C\right)}{f_1} \times i$$

Where l is lower limit of C.I. where median lies, f_1 is the frequency of median class; N is the total number of cases and C is the cumulative frequency upto the median class.

In this case median *i.e.* $N/2$ or 100th case will lie in the class interval 70-74, which becomes our median class.

Therefore,

$$\text{Median} = 69.5 + \frac{\left(\frac{200}{2} - 62\right)}{50} \times 5$$

$$= 69.5 + \frac{100 - 62}{50} \times 5$$

$$= 69.5 + \frac{38 \times 5}{50}$$

or $\quad 69.5 + 3.8$ or 73.3

Median $= 73.3$

Mode:

Mode $= 3$ median 2 mean

Mode $= 3 \times 73.3 - 2 \times 72.5$

$= 219.9 - 145.0 = 74.9$

Ans.: Mean $= 72.5$

Median $= 73.3$

Mode $= 74.9$

Example 2: The following table gives a description of the marks obtained by 41 students of a class. Find out the median of the marks obtained.

Marks obtained	20	15	17	30	22	23
Frequencies	10	2		4	12	8

Ans. Arranging in ascending order and preparing the cumulative frequency table, we have:

Marks Obtained	*Frequency*	*Cumulative Frequency*
15	2	2
17	5	7
20	10	17
22	12	29
25	8	37
30	30	41

Total number of terms is $n = 41$

So, median = marks obtained by the (41+1/2)th, i.e. 21st student

But 21 comes under the cumulative frequency 29

And the term against cumulative frequency 29 is 22

Hence the median is 22

Example 3: Weighted Arithmetic mean

If $w_1, w_2, \dots w_n$ are the weights assigned to $x_1, x_2, \dots x_n$ respectively, then we define:

$$\text{Weighted arithmetic mean} = \frac{w_1x_1 + w_2x_2 + \dots w_nx_n}{w_1 + w_2 + \dots + w_n} = \frac{\Sigma w_i x_i}{\Sigma w_i}$$

A candidate obtained the following percentage of marks in an examination:

Hindi	*English*	*Mathematics*	*Sanskrit*	*General Science*
72%	43%	58%	84%	51%

It is agreed to give double weightage to marks in English and mathematics as compared to other subjects. Find the weighted mean.

Ans. We may prepare the following table:

Subject	*% of marks obtained* x_i,	*Weightage* w_i,	$w_i x_i$
Hindi	72	1	72
English	43	2	86
Maths	58	2	116
Sanskrit	84	1	84
Gen. Science	51	1	51
		$Sw_i = 7$	$Sw_i x_i = 409$

$$\therefore \text{ weighted mean} = \frac{\Sigma w_i x_i}{\Sigma w_i} = \frac{409}{7} = 58.43$$

If in a certain class the highest scores scored by a student in English are 70 and the lowest score 54, here the range would be 70 – 54 = 16.

The range is the most general measure of variability. It is calculated only when we want to make a rough estimate of two or more groups or variability.

31

Measurement of Variability: Standard and Mean Deviation

31.1 COMPUTATION OF VARIABILIGY (VARIANCE, STANDARD DEVIATION, RANGE AND QUARTILE DEVIATION)

Computation or Measuring Variability

Measures of central tendency, i.e., mean, median and mode provide central value or typical representative of a set of scores as a whole. But the central value or an average alone cannot describe the distribution adequately. We can compare the achievement of two groups by comparing typical representative of the different sets of scores. The representative measures do not show how the individual scores are spread out. For example, let us consider

Scores of first group: 20, 80, 60, 45, 60, 40, 55

Scores of second group: 50, 45, 45, 40, 55, 65

Here both groups have the same mean score of 60. But a close examination reveals that the two sets of scores differ widely from each other. The scores in the first group range from 20 to 80 while in the second group, they range from 40 to 65. The difference in range shows that the students in the second group are more homogeneous in scoring from those in the first. The scores fall around the same point on the scale, and *variability=, dispersion= scatteredness=* of scores is relatively less. This measures of *Variability=* or *dispersion=* help us in studying the extent to which observations are scattered about the average or the central value.

Following are the measures used for computing the variability or dispersion.

1. Standard Deviation
2. Range
3. Quartile Deviation
4. Percentile

31.2 MEAN DEVIATION

Meaning of Mean Deviation (Average Deviation): Mean deviation may be defined as the average of the deviation of the group measured from an average (Mean, Median or Mode), taking all the deviation as positive. In actual calculation, we find some of the deviations positive and some negative. Deviations, thus, are taken in their absolute values, without regard to sign (+ or –)

Uses of AD: (i) Quartile deviation is based on quartiles and affords a general idea of the variability of a group without taking account of each and every item. When we want to take account of all items, we use average deviation.

(ii) It is used when it is desired to weigh all deviations from the mean according to their size.

(iii) It is used when extreme deviations would influence Standard Deviation (SD) unduly.

Calculation of Average Deviation from Ungrouped Data

$$\text{Average Deviation or AD} = \frac{\Sigma|x|}{N}$$

Where Σ stands for sum and | *x* | for deviation from Mean, Median or mode, ignoring the sign.

Calculation of Average Deviation for Ungrouped Data

Score X	| *x* |
72	3.5
70	1.5
70	1.5
69	0.5
69	0.5
68	0.5
67	1.5
67	1.5
67	1.5
66	2.5
Σ = 685	Σ = 15.0

$$\text{Mean} = \frac{15}{10} = 68.5$$

Substituting the values in the formula we have:

$$\text{AD} = \frac{15}{10} = 68.5$$

Calculation of AD for Grouped Data

Scores	*Md. val*	*f*	| *x* |	*f* | *x* |
91-100	95.5	3	23.00	69.00
81-90	85.5	5	13.00	65.00
71-80	75.5	15	3.00	45.00
61-70	65.5	18	7.00	126.00
51-60	55.3	3	17.00	51.00
	Mean = 72.5	44		356.00

Here we apply the formula for $AD = \frac{\Sigma f\,|x|}{N}$

Substituting the values, we have $AD = \frac{356}{44} = 8.1$

Merits of Average or Mean Deviation

1. It is a simple measure of variability.
2. It is easily understood.
3. It is very meaningful even to persons not trained in statistical procedures.
4. It takes into account the fluctuations of all the items or values in a given series. It is not based on extreme values alone.
5. It is a very reliable measure even in small samples and where it is desirable to give due consideration to all the deviations.

Limitations or Shortcomings of Mean Deviation

1. Since signs are disregarded and only absolute values are taken, it is not an algebraic measure. So it cannot be reliably used in mathematical operations.
2. It may be inflated or depressed by a single extreme value, which is very high or very low.

31.3 STANDARD DEVIATION (SD)

Meaning of Standard Deviation: Standard deviation may be defined as the square root of the sum of the squares of the deviations calculated from each item.

While calculating the Average Deviation we ignore the signs. An alternative method for eliminating the signs is to square up each deviation. We employ this method for the calculation of standard deviation. For the calculation of SD one thing is certain that it is calculated from mean alone. Conventional symbols used for SD is Greek letter sigma (σ).

Formula used for the calculation of SD for ungrouped data is $\sqrt{\frac{\Sigma d^2}{n}}$ and for grouped data $\sqrt{\frac{\Sigma d^2}{n} - \left(\frac{fd}{n}\right)^2} \times i$

where d is the deviation from the mean.

Use of the SD

1. We use SD when the statistics having the greatest stability is sought.
2. We use SD when the extreme deviations should exercise a proportionally greater effect upon the variability.
3. We use SD when coefficient of correlation and other statistics are subsequently to be computed.

Calculation of Standard Deviation for Ungrouped Data

Scores	*d*	*d²*
72	3.5	12.25
70	1.5	2.25
70	1.5	2.25
69	0.5	0.25
69	0.5	0.25
68	–0.5	0.25
67	–1.5	2.25
67	–1.5	2.25
67	–1.5	2.25
66	–2.5	6.25
	0	30.50
M = 68.5		

Substituting the values in the formula $\sqrt{\frac{\Sigma d^2}{2}}$ we get

SD or $\sigma = \sqrt{\frac{30.5}{10}} = \sqrt{3.05} = 1.75$

Calculation of Standard Deviation for Grouped Data

Scores	*f*	*d*	*fd*	*fd²*
91-100	3	2	6	+12
81-90	5	1	5	+5
71-80	15	0	0	0
61-70	10	–1	–18	+18
51-60	3	–2	–6	+12
	44		–13	47

Substituting the values in the formula $\sqrt{\frac{\Sigma fd^3}{n} - \left(\frac{\Sigma fd}{n}\right)^2} \times 10$

$$\sigma = \sqrt{\frac{47}{44} - \left(-\frac{13}{44}\right)^2} \times 10$$

$$= \sqrt{1.07 - (-0.3)^2} \times 10$$

$$= \sqrt{1.07 - 0.09} \times 10$$

$$= \sqrt{0.98} \times 10$$

$$= 9.9$$

Example for Practice

Calculate Mean and Standard Deviation for the following distribution:

Scores	*Frequencies*
48-52	2
53-57	3
58-62	5
63-67	9
68-72	10
73-77	12
78-82	7
83-87	2
88-92	3
93-97	1

Ans. Calculation of Mean and Standard Deviation

Scores	f	X_1	fx_1	fx_2
93-97	1	5	5	25
88-92	3	4	12	48
83-87	2	3	6	18
78-82	7	2	14	28
73-77	12	1	12	12
68-72	10	0	0	0
63-67	9	–1	–9	9
58-62	5	–2	–10	20
53-57	3	–3	–9	27
48-52	2	–4	–8	32
	$N = 54$		$Sfx_1 = 13$	$Sfx_2 = 219$

(a) (Mean) $M = A.M. + \frac{\Sigma fx_1}{N} \times i$

A.M. = Assumed mean = 70

$$\therefore \quad M = 70 + \frac{13}{54} \times 5 \;.$$

$$= 70 + \frac{65}{54}$$

$$= 70 + 1.2 = 71.2$$

Ans. $= 71.2$

(b) (S.D.) Standard Deviation

$$\sigma = i\sqrt{\frac{\Sigma fx'^2}{N} - \left(\frac{\Sigma f'}{N}\right)^2}$$

$$= 5\sqrt{\frac{219}{54} - \left(\frac{13}{54}\right)^2}$$

$$= 5\sqrt{\frac{219}{54} - \frac{169}{54\times 54}}$$

$$= 5\sqrt{\frac{219\times 54 - 169}{54\times 54}}$$

$$= \frac{5}{54}\sqrt{11826 - 169}$$

$$= \frac{5}{54}\sqrt{11657}$$

$$= \frac{5}{54}\times 107.96$$

$$= \frac{5\times 107.96}{54}$$

$$= \frac{539.80}{54} = 9.998$$

Ans. $= 9.998$

Uses/Merits of Standard Deviation

1. SD is the most reliable measure of variability and it is useful in further statistical operations and in making inferences.
2. It is very useful in those cases where mean has been taken as a measure of central tendency.
3. The greater the value of SD, the more would score scatter from the mean.
4. It is an algebraic measure and does not suffer from the mathematical fallacy of the M.D. in which signs are disregarded.
5. SD can be reliably used in those cases when extreme deviations exercise greater influence than other deviations.

Limitations and Shortcomings of SD

1. SD is not easily understood.
2. Persons not trained in statistical procedures find it difficult to interpret.
3. It is sensitive to extreme values.

31.4 RANGE

Range is the difference between the highest value and the lowest value in a distribution. It is not related to frequency symbolically.

Range = $L - S$

Where, L = Largest value or the highest value.

S = Smallest value.

If in a certain class the highest scores scored by a student in English are 70 and the lowest score 54, here the range would be 70 – 54 = 16.

The range is the most general measure of variability. It is calculated only when we want to make a rough estimate of two or more groups or variability.

31.5 WHEN TO USE THE VARIOUS MEASURES OF VARIABILITY

Use the range: (i) When the data are too scant or too scattered to justify the computation of a more precise measure of variability, and (ii) when a knowledge of extreme scores of or total speed is all that is wanted.

Use the Q: (i) When the median is the measure of central tendency, (ii) when there are scattered or extreme scores which would influence the S.D. disproportionately, and (iii) when the concentration around the median the middle 50% cases is of primary interest.

Use the AD or MD: (i) When it is desired to weigh all deviations from the mean according to their size, and (ii) when extreme deviations would influence SD unduly.

Use the SD: (i) When the statistics having the greatest stability is sought, (ii) when extreme deviations should exercise a proportionally greater effect upon the variability, and (iii) when coefficient of correlation and other statistics are subsequently to be computed.

31.6 QUARTILE DEVIATION AND PERCENTILES

Meaning of Quartile Deviation or Q: The quartile deviation or Q is one half of the distance between the 75th and 25th percentiles in a frequency distribution. The 25th percentile, termed Q_1, is the *first quartile* on the scale of scores, the point below which lie 25% of the scores. The 75th percentile or Q_3 is the third quarter or quartile on the score-scale, the point below which lie 75% of the score. The *second quartile* or (Q_2) is the median. The median value is the second quartile or (Q_2) and the median value of half the group is the first quartile (Q_1), and the median value for the second half of the group is third quartile (Q_3). The figure for one-half of the difference in the values of the first quartile and the third quartile individuals, gives the *semi-inter-quartile range* (S.I.Q.R or Q) and is expressed thus:

$$Q = \frac{Q_3 - Q_1}{2}$$

Calculation of Q: The calculation of Q from the Data Grouped into a Frequency Distribution.

Scores Intervals	*f*	*cf*
91-100	3	44
81-90	5	41
71-80	**15**	**36** Q_3
61-70	**18**	**21** Q_1
51-60	3	3
	$N = 44$	

$$Q_1 = \frac{44}{4} = 11\text{th term}$$

$$Q_1 = 60.5 + \frac{11-3}{18} \times 10$$

or $$60.5 + \frac{8 \times 10}{18}$$

or $$60.5 + \frac{80}{18}$$

or $$60.5 + 4.44$$

or $$64.94$$

$$Q_3 = \frac{44 \times 3}{4} = 33\text{ rd term}$$

$$= 70.5 + \frac{36-21}{15} 10$$

or $$70.5 + \frac{15 \times 10}{15}$$

or $$70.5 + 10$$

or $$80.5$$

Now apply the formula

$$Q = \frac{Q_3 - Q_1}{2}$$

to find out the value of Q or quartile deviation. Substituting the values in the formula we get

$$Q = \frac{80.5 - 64.94}{4}$$

$$= \frac{15.56}{2} = 7.78 \text{ or } 7.80$$

Uses: It should be used as under:

(i) When the median is the measure of central tendency.

(ii) When there are scattered or extreme scores which would influence the SD disproportionately.

(iii) When the concentration around the mean the mid. 50% of the cases is of primary interest.

Percentiles and Percentile Ranks. Robert L. Ebel and David A. Frisbie explain the term percentile rank as under:

The percentile rank of a particular test score can be defined in three similar but significantly different ways. It is the percentage of scores in a distribution of scores that:

1. is below the given score, or
2. is the same as or below the given score, or
3. is below the midpoint of the score interval of the given score.

Table 31.1 shows the effect of using each of these different definitions to compute the percentile ranks of 5 hypothetical scores. The highest score gets a percentile rank of only 80 under definition 1. The lowest score gets a percentile rank of 20 under definition 2. The median score gets a percentile rank of 40 under definition 1 and of 60 under definition 2. But under definition 3 the median score gets a percentile rank of 50, as it should in a symmetric distribution of scores. In addition, the highest and lowest scores are both the same distance from the extremes of the percentile rank scale, as they also should be. For these definition 3 is preferred and we will use it here.

There are seven steps in the process of computing the percentile rank of a given score in a particular distribution using definition 3.

Table 31.1: Implications of Different Definitions of Percentile Ranks

Score	*1*	*2*	*3*
5	80	100	90
4	60	80	70
3	40	60	50
2	20	40	30
1	0	20	10

1. Prepare a frequency distribution.
2. Beginning with the lowest score, add successive frequency values to obtain a column of cumulative frequencies.
3. For the given score, identify the cumulative frequency up to but not including, the score.
4. For the same given score, divide its frequency by 2.
5. Add the values from steps 3 and 4.
6. Divide the sum from step 5 by the total number of scores.
7. Multiply the result by 100 to obtain a percentile rank (rounded to the nearest whole number).

Table 31.1 illustrates the computation of percentile ranks for the spelling scores from the table of spellings. Notice that the score scale extends from one score below the lowest score obtained to the highest score obtained. And the scale always includes all possible scores between the extremes, even when no student may have actually obtained some of those scores. The number of students who received each of the scores is shown in the second column of the table.

The third column gives a cumulative frequency for each score. It is calculated by counting the number of scores lower than the given score and adding the frequency at that score point. Consider the score 19, for example. There are 11 scores lower than 19 and four scores of 19. So we get a cumulative frequency of 15.

Scores of 30 Students on a 25 items Spelling Test and Computation of Percentile Ranks

Aruna	16	Deepa	20	Jagdish	20
Sita	19	Gary	17	Pant	17
Ram	20	Kishan	18	Vedi	23
Sohan	17	Sarita	21	Biala	23
Sham	21	Suman	14	Biswas	19
Carmille	24	Shruti	19	Surindra	22
Donald	15	Smridhi	22	Ravindra	21
Satish	18	Sanjay	18	Kiran	19
Aslam	20	Aarti	21	Nidhi	21
Singh	16	Pramila	20	Rajat	15

(Adopted from Robert L. Ebel and David A. Frisbie)

To obtain the percentile rank for a score of 19, the value in the fourth column, we proceed as follows. Take the cumulative frequency of scores below 19 (which is 11) and add to it half of the frequencies at a score of 19 (one-half of 4 is 2). The sum, 13, is divided by 30 (the number of scores) to yield 0.433. That quotient is multiplied by 100 (43.3) and then rounded to obtain 43. In summary, we take half the scores at the given score value plus all the scores below, we divide that sun by the total number of scores, and we change the result to a rounded percentage value.

Table 31.2: Computation of Percentile Ranks

Score	*Frequency*	*Cumulative Frequency*	*Percentile Ranks*
24	1	30	98
23	2	29	93
22	2	27	87
21	5	25	75
20	5	20	58
19	4	15	43
18	3	11	32
17	3	8	22
16	2	5	13
15	2	3	7
14	1	1	2
13	0	0	—

32

Correlation: Rank Difference, Normal Curve

32.1 CORRELATION

Sir Francis Galton and Karl Peason developed the theory and statistical basis of what is now called 'correlation'. Galton studied the relationship between variables weight and height and found that both go together. Taller persons weigh heavier than shorter persons. There are several examples to indicate that many variables go together. There, generally speaking, exists a positive relationship between intelligence of father and sons.

Croxton and Cowden state about correlation, "When the relationship is of a quantitative nature, the appropriate statistical tool for discovering and measuring the relationship and expressing it in a brief formula is known as correlation." The statistical measures used for such an analysis is called coefficient of correlation.

A. M. Tuttle describes correlation in these words, "An analysis of co-variation of two or more variables is called correlation."

The terms correlations, co-variation and concomitant are used interchangeably.

Significance of Measuring Correlation: The correlations between different variables is measured on account of the following reasons:

(i) to find out the cause and effect relationship.
(ii) to determine whether a relationship exists or not.
(iii) to find out whether it is significant.
(iv) to find out the direction of relationship.
(v) to derive or analyse usefulness of data.

Positive and Negative Correlation: Positive correlation is a relationship in which a change in the value of one variable is accompanied by a change in the value of the other variable in the same direction. The rate of change may be less, equal or more than that of the other variable and vice versa.

Negative correlation signifies a situation in which the movement of values of variables are in the opposite directions. In other words, increase in the value of one variable is accompanied by a decrease in the value of another variable and vice versa.

The following examples illustrate these relationship in marks of x and y students.

Positive Correlation		*Negative Correlation*	
x	y	x	y
6	10	20	12
8	15	30	8
10	18	40	7
12	20	50	6
14	21	60	

Simple Correlation: In simple correlation, only two variables are studied.

Multiple Correlation: In multiple correlation, more than two variables are studied.

Partial Correlation: In partial correlation we recognise the existence of only two variables influencing each other.

Linear Correlation: In the linear correlation, change in the value of one variable is accompanied by a change in the value of the other variable in the same proportion. Consider the following illustration:

x	6	8	10	12	14	16
y	60	80	100	120	140	160

Thus if the points are plotted on a graph, they would be in a straight line.

Non-linear Correlation: The non-linear relationship is one in which the change in the value of one variable is not accompanied by a proportionate change in the value of the other variable. Thus, the rates of change for the two variants are different.

Zero Correlation: There is yet another, possibility that half of the cases may show perfect positive correlation and the remaining half a perfect negative correlation. In such a case the correlation will come to be zero. Zero correlation means no correlation.

Coefficient of Correlation: The relationship between the two variables is expressed in statistics on a quantitative scale called coefficient of correlation.

For a perfect positive correlation the coefficient of correlation is +1 and for perfect negative it will be –1. Perfect positive or negative correlation is possible in physical sciences. In social sciences like education, psychology, economics etc., the correlation will lie within the limits of +1 and –1. Hence the perfect positive and perfect negative correlation can be treated as limiting cases.

Methods of Measuring Correlation: Following are the methods of measuring correlation between two variables:

1. Scatter Diagram Method.
2. Graphic Method.
3. Karl Pearson's Coefficient of Correlation.
4. Rank Method.
5. Concurrent Deviation Method.
6. Least Squares Method.

32.2 RANK DIFFERENCE

In this method we rank the individual scores both the scores. In both the variables we give 1 to the students who gets the highest scores. Then we find the difference for the ranks.

$$P = 1 - \frac{\Sigma D^2}{N(N-1)}$$

Where S stands for the sum and D^2 is the square of each rank difference. N is the number of items. Let us consider the following example.

Students	*Scores in Maths*	*Rank*	*Scores in Music*	*Rank*	*Rank Dif. D*	*Square Dif. D^2*
A	5	6	21	4	2	4
B	15	4	14	5	1	1
C	10	5	28	3	2	4
D	20	3	7	6	3	9
E	25	2	35	2		0
F	30	1	42	1	0	0
						18

Substitutiing the values in the formula

$$= 1 - \frac{\Sigma D^2}{N(N-1)}$$

we have $= p - \frac{18}{6(6-1)}$

$$= 1 - \frac{18}{6 \times 5}$$

$$= 1 - \frac{18}{30}$$

$$= 1 - \frac{3}{5}$$

$$= 1 = 0.6 = 0.4$$

32.3 NORMAL DISTRIBUTION AND PROBABILITY CURVE

Meaning: If we observe the frequency distribution of student's marks in any examination, we will observe that the maximum frequencies are in the middle while towards the end the frequencies are low. The same thing happens in other variables also, for example, in an examination result of say Hindi we will find that a few students will get marks very high or very low, while a great majority will have their marks in the middle of the range. If we examine a very large number of students we will find that the distribution of their scores will be very similar to imaginary mathematical normal curve. This is why we say that the achievement in Hindi is normally distributed. For example, height, weight, intelligence, speed of work, even errors in measurement are all normally distributed in the population. Thus the properties of normal distribution are of great use in statistics.

The following figure shows the Normal Probability Curve.

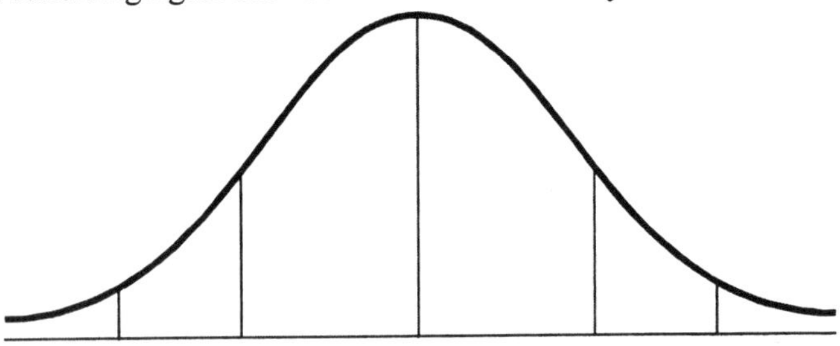

Fig. 32.1: The Normal Probability Curve

A normal curve is a bell-shaped symmetrical curve. It has the highest frequency in the middle. The frequencies keep on reducing as we move towards left or right of the middle point. The fall in frequencies on either side is equal.

Properties of Normal Distribution

1. If the total area under the normal curve is represented by N, the number of cases, we can find out the area between any two points with the help of the mathematical formulae. For the convenience of users, tables have been prepared which give fractional part of the area of the curve between the mean (M) and a certain distance from it.

2. In a normal distribution 34.13% cases are included between M and σ distance from M as is shown in Fig. 22.2 below. Thus 68.26% cases are included between C1 σ and + 1 σ. 99.73% or almost all the cases are included between C3 σ and + 3 σ.

What does a Normal Curve Indicate?

A normal curve indicates the following:

1. The trait which is measured is normally distributed in the universe. (Statistical term and not in the literal sense).
2. Most of the cases are average in the measured trait.
3. The percentage of the average cases is 34.13 + 34.13 = 68.26.
4. Approximately 15.87% of [50 (mean)-34.13] cases are low in the trait measured.
5. Similarly 15.87% of [50 (Mean)-34.13] cases are high in the trait measured.
6. The test used for measuring the trait is good.
7. The test differentiates between high, average and poor ability group individuals. Hence it has good discriminating power.
8. The items contained in the test used are fairly distributed in terms of difficulty level.

Significance of Normal Distribution Curve

Significance of the normal curve is as under:

1. Normal curve is very helpful in educational evaluation and measurement as it provides relative position of the individual in a group.
2. Normal curve can be used as a scale of measurement in behavioural sciences.
3. Normal distribution is an important tool in the hands of the classroom teacher as it enables him to decide the nature of the distribution of the scores obtained on the basis of measured variable. It gives him an indication to the difficulty level of the test items in the question paper. He comes to know about the class whether it is homogeneous to the ability measured or it is heterogeneous one.

Areas Under the Normal Probability Curve

The distance, always in units of SD, is measured on the base line of the normal curve from the mean as origin.

The number of cases in the normal distribution between the mean and the ordinate erected at the distances of $\pm 1\sigma$, $\pm 2\sigma$ and $\pm 3\sigma$ is shown below:

(i)	Between mean and 1σ	:	34.13%	i.e.
(ii)	Between mean and -1σ	:	34.13%	i.e.
(iii)	Between 1σ and 2σ	:	13.59%	*i.e.*, 1359 cases in 10,000
(iv)	Between -1σ and -2σ	:	13.59%	*i.e.*, 1359 cases in 10,000
(v)	Between 2σ and 3σ	:	2.15%	*i.e.*, 215 cases in 10,000
(vi)	Between -2σ and -3σ	:	2.15%	*i.e.*, 215 cases in 10,000
(vii)	Beyond 3σ	:	B13%	*i.e.*, 13 cases in 10,000
(viii)	Beyond -3σ	:	B13%	*i.e.*, 13 cases in 10,000
			100.00%	10,000

The total area under the normal curve is 1, but for the sake of convenience, the total area under the normal curve is taken to be 10,000 because of the greater ease with which fractional parts of the total area may be calculated.

Applications and Uses of Normal Curve

(i) Normal curve is used to determine the percentage of cases (in a normal distribution) within given limits or scores.

(ii) Normal curve is used to determine the percentage of cases that are above or below a given score or reference point.

(iii) Normal curve is used to determine the percentile rank of a student in his own group.

(iv) Normal curve is used to compare the two distributions in terms of overlapping.

(v) Normal curve is used to determine the levels of scores which include a given percentage of cases.

(vi) Normal curve is used to determine the relative difficulty of test items.

(vii) Normal curve is used to divide a group into sub-groups according to certain ability and assigning the grades.

(viii) Normal curve is used to compare the two distributions in terms of overlapping.

Index